CONTENTS

PART 1   CONSUMER DECISION MAKING
Richard Teare

PART 2   SEGMENTING TRAVEL MARKETS
Josef A. Mazanec

PART 3   NEW PRODUCT RESEARCH AND DEVELOPMENT
Simon Crawford-Welch

PART 4   STRATEGIC MARKETING COMMUNICATION
Stephen Calver

ABOUT THE AUTHORS

Richard Teare (author of Part 1) is Professor and Associate Head of the Department of Service Industries at Bournemouth University and a non-executive director of the National Society for Quality through Teamwork, UK. He received his PhD in Business Administration from the City University Business School, London. He is a Fellow of the Hotel, Catering and Institutional Management Association, and previously worked for both national and international hotel companies. He is editor of the *International Journal of Contemporary Hospitality Management*, associate editor of *International Marketing Review* and a member of the Editorial Advisory Boards of the *Journal of Foodservice and Restaurant Marketing*, and *The Journal of Travel and Tourism Marketing* and *Strategic Insights into Quality*. His publications include six books on aspects of strategic management and marketing in service industries.

Josef A. Mazanec (author of Part 2) is Professor and Director of the Institute for Tourism and Leisure Studies at Vienna University of Economics and Business Administration (VUEBA) Austria. He received his PhD from VUEBA, became *venia docendi* for business administration in 1979 and a full professor in 1981. He was the Austrian delegate to the European Association of Advertising Agencies (1971–81), and in 1992, a visiting scholar at the Alfred P. Sloan School of Management, Massachusetts Institute of Technology, USA. He is resource editor for *Annals of Tourism Research*, a member of the American Marketing Association, American Marketing Academy, European Marketing Academy, Travel and Tourism Research Association, and Tourist Research Centre, a committee member of the International Association of Scientific Experts in Tourism and a founding member of the International Academy for the Study of Tourism.

Simon Crawford-Welch (author of Part 3) is President of SERVICE Associates, a consulting organization with clients throughout the world. Recent clients have included the Russian Ministries of Aerospace and Tourism Development, Snowbird Ski Resort, Utah, Holiday Corporation, IBM, General Motors and International Resort Group Inc. He received his PhD in Hospitality Management from Virginia

Polytechnic Institute and State University and he is a former graduate faculty member of the William F. Harrah College of Hotel Administration at the University of Nevada, Las Vegas. Specializing in marketing and research, he has held senior management positions in leisure and tourism organizations in the UK and USA, including Director of Marketing and Research for a major US resort development and marketing corporation. He is editor of the *Journal of Restaurant and Foodservice Marketing* and co-author of a forthcoming book entitled *Theory S: Total Customer Service.*

Stephen Calver (author of Part 4) is Head of the School of Hospitality Management in the Department of Service Industries, Bournemouth University, UK, where he is responsible for the co-ordination of marketing teaching for hospitality programmes. He received his Master of Business Administration degree with a specialism in marketing for the City University Business School, London, and he is a member of the Chartered Institute of Marketing and its Hotel Sector Group. Prior to his current position he worked for several international hotel firms, tourist boards and international consultancy companies. He had undertaken a number of surveys for commercial and public sector organizations, including consumer, destination and tourism impact studies. He has published several articles and made book contributions in the fields of consumer and market reseach, leisure and hospitality management.

PREFACE

To succeed in the hospitality and tourism markets of the 1990s, firms must be able to interpret the needs of their customers, identify apropriate ways of segmenting the markets in which they wish to compete, develop and launch products with the right product–market fit and communicate effectively with potential consumers of the product. These issues are closely interrelated as they form the basis of the marketing interface between the organization and the outside world. If these issues are fully researched, understood and disseminated by marketing professionals, the organization as a whole stands to benefit from an appropriate consumer focus.

This book aims to integrate the theory and practice of hospitality and tourism marketing from the perspective of understanding, interpreting and meeting the needs of consumers. The approach throughout is to review and apply empirical evidence and address the methodological implications of undertaking consumer research, with reference to examples and case study illustrations drawn from national and international hospitality/tourism organizations.

Specifically, the book is divided into four parts, each of which provides a comprehensive analysis and review of the four key areas of marketing which are of growing interest and importance to practitioners, industrialists and hospitality and tourism educators. These are consumer decision making, market segmentation, product development and marketing communication. Collectively, they provide a framework upon which organizations seeking to sustain a consumer focus must build.

Part 1: Consumer Decision Making
Provides an overview of research on consumer decision making and identifies the theoretical, methodological and practical implications of designing consumer research for hospitality and tourism services. Part 1 also addresses the gap between the 'ideal' service experience and the 'actual' service that customers receive, and the implications for a strategy of continuous improvement in hospitality/tourism organizations.

Part 2: Segmenting Travel Markets
Focuses on the use of 'a priori' and 'a posteriori' explanatory models for predicting consumer behaviour and segmenting travel markets using criterion (a priori) and multivariate profiling (a posteriori) methods. Examples are drawn from the latest Austrian National Guest Survey, one of the world's largest on-going tourism surveys, and the concept of EUROSTYLES (lifestyle profiling) used throughout Europe.

Part 3: New Product Research and Development
Reports on the sophisticated consumer research and multivariate modelling techniques (e.g. conjoint and trade-off analysis and econometric modelling) which are now being used by North American lodging (or hotel) corporations such as Marriott and food service chains like Burger King, Kentucky Fried Chicken and McDonald's to research and develop new products and services.

Part 4: Strategic Marketing Communication
Establishes a framework for devising and directing marketing communications at the various target markets for hospitality and tourism products and services. This includes a review of the way in which attitudes can influence the consumer's interpretation of marketing messages and the wide-ranging implications for formulating an effective marketing communications strategy.

These areas of study are traditionally addressed by books on consumer behaviour and marketing research, few of which contain hospitality or tourism examples. Further, the interrelationships between marketing and the wider organizational environment are seldom fully addressed. It is our hope that this book will help to encourage a broader view of the leading role that marketing can and should assume in establishing a consumer focus in hospitality/tourism organizations. In so doing, the marketing function plays a pro-active part in the creation of a realistic customer service vision to which every part of the organization can contribute.

Finally, our thanks to Chris Bessant and to Steve Cook, Judith Entwisle-Baker and Peter Harrison at Cassell.

Richard Teare, Josef Mazanec,
Simon Crawford-Welch, Stephen Calver
September 1994

PART 1

CONSUMER DECISION MAKING

Richard Teare

INTRODUCTION

Although commercial hospitality services make an important contribution to the service sector of the economy, empirically based understanding of the interactions between the customer and the organization are limited. Therefore the aim of Chapter 1 is to provide an overview of the factors affecting consumer decision making, explained with the aid of a descriptive model of the consumer decision process. The purpose of this is to identify potential focal points for theory development which might draw upon the actual experiences of customers.

Chapter 2 seeks to establish the value of the contributions made principally during the 1970s and 1980s to our current understanding of the consumer decision process for goods and services. It begins with a review of progress in consumer decision modelling and continues with a broad-based review of the implications arising from key empirical studies. The main purpose is to identify the influences and relationships applicable to the design of consumer research for hospitality and tourism services, and in order to focus the review as precisely as possible, research findings for each decision process stage are grouped in relation to emerging research themes.

Empirical evidence suggests that our knowledge of consumer decision making for hospitality services would benefit from sustained and systematic investigation, and further, that progress might best be achieved by using theory-generating rather than theory-testing research methods. Chapter 3 begins by assessing the requirements of consumer theory development, including the selection of appropriate research methods. Following this, the Glaser and Strauss grounded theory method of theory generation is introduced and described. The account refers to procedures for sampling, data collection and categorization, and integration of field data. The chapter concludes with a case study illustration which uses grounded theorizing to uncover patterns of consumer decision making in the UK hotel leisure break market.

The hotel service environment is characterized by many different kinds of interaction between consumers and the staff, facilities and amenities which are needed to provide services. It follows, therefore, that hospitality firms wishing to close the gap between the 'ideal' service experience and the actual service that consumers receive, must seek to involve all of their employees in a process of continual improvement. Accordingly, Chapter 4 focuses on the interface between the consumer and the provider of hospitality services during the consumption stage of the decision process. The chapter opens with a review of several techniques for cognitive mapping and modelling. They facilitate reconstructions of service events by drawing on the expectations, perceptions and experiences of consumers. The chapter concludes by tracing the steps taken by Scott's Hotels Limited in its quest to build and sustain a total quality culture throughout its UK hotel operations.

ACKNOWLEDGEMENTS

The case study contained in Chapter 4 draws extensively on the total quality management experiences of Scott's Hotels Limited. The help, support and encouragement provided by Jan Hubrecht, Managing Director, and Paula Simmons, formerly Quality Support Manager, Scott's Hotels Limited, during the preparation of the case study is gratefully acknowledged.

ONE

An overview of consumer and producer perspectives on hospitality services

INTRODUCTION

Although commercial hospitality services make an important contribution to the service sector of the economy, empirically based understanding of the interactions between the customer (or consumer) and the provider (or producer) is limited. In this context, it is helpful to establish an overview of the dynamics of decison making by examining the characteristics of hospitality services and the differing perspectives of the consumer and the producer. After this, a hypothetical model of the consumer decision process is presented so as to identify focal points for theory development and, specifically, theory generation which is derived from the actual experience of consumers. This is termed 'grounded' theory development as it originates from consumer experiences of, and reflections on, decison-making issues and events.

THE CONCEPT AND CHARACTERISTICS OF HOSPITALITY SERVICES

The origin of the word 'hospitality' can be traced to the Latin noun *hospice* meaning 'place of entertainment or of shelter'. Usage of the generic term 'hospitality industry' describes what is more traditionally known as the 'hotel and catering industry'.[1]

Hospitality services are associated with the commercial provision of catering, accommodation and leisure facilities, and can be classified as profit-centred (e.g. hotels and restaurants) or cost-centred (e.g. employee and institutional catering). The service offering consists of both tangible and intangible components which are designed and managed by the producer with the aim of satisfying the needs of the consumer.

Figure 1.1 suggests that consumers formulate a hierarchy of expectations and needs,

5

and that these relate to perceptions of 'standardized' products such as a fast-food meal experience and 'personalized' products like a mid- to upper-market-price short break (or leisure break) taken in a hotel. In the 'personalized' domain, promotional activities such as advertising and brochure distribution may stimulate a telephone or written enquiry, but in both cases the main consumer–producer interaction occurs at the point of consumption where the effectiveness of service delivery, especially the behaviour of service staff, is a critical determinant of consumer satisfaction.

Referring to the environment in which hospitality managers work, Nailon[2,3] observed that many operational problems occur because the consequences of service interactions are not fully understood. As the period of consumption can range from a few minutes for a fast-food meal to several days and nights for a leisure break, consumer–producer interactions are necessarily varied and complex. Inevitably, consumer needs and expectations differ according to the situation, circumstances, expenditure and other personal factors affecting the purchase decision. From the producer standpoint, it is easier to legislate and control 'standardized' products, especially if the technological input can be designed to limit the amount of discretion used by operatives during the production process. These and the many other variables which influence consumer satisfaction highlight the need for empirical research focusing on the behaviour of consumers and producers of hospitality services in different contexts.

Hospitality services and the consumer perspective

As Figure 1.1 shows, hospitality services have both functional and expressive roles to fulfil. The consumer is primarily concerned with the desire to satisfy basic functional (or physiological) needs, such as hunger and thirst. These are accompanied by more complex expressive (or psychological) needs, such as identity, status and security. Psychological needs may be determined by expectations derived from the consumer's lifestyle and prior experience. They may also be motivated by aspirations to experience surroundings beyond current lifestyle expectations.

Consumer needs require an immediate response from the producer. If they are not satisfied, complaint behaviour may be triggered by physiological discomfort or psychological ego-defensive mechanisms. The consistency and quality of service delivery are important because the consumer has little or no control over the environment in which consumption takes place. Service efficiency is often vulnerable because of the long operational service periods and demand fluctuations which occur throughout the day, week, month and year.

Hospitality service interactions are typically short and variable in nature, with the degree of formality influenced by the situation and personalities of the participants. Every consumer has a unique set of expectations about the role of staff during service delivery. If these expectations are not met, the consumer may feel dissatisfied, although the feeling may be internalized if it is not strong enough to cause complaint behaviour. For example, non-verbal communication by staff relating to the expected payment of gratuities may cause the consumer to feel irritated or embarrassed. This source of dissatisfaction is unlikely to be reported to management.

Consumer satisfaction is derived from different kinds of service experience and interaction which are unique to the occasion and situation. As noted above, the time period for using hospitality services can vary from several minutes to a week or more. Consumption over a longer time period requires a more sophisticated form of

F·1.

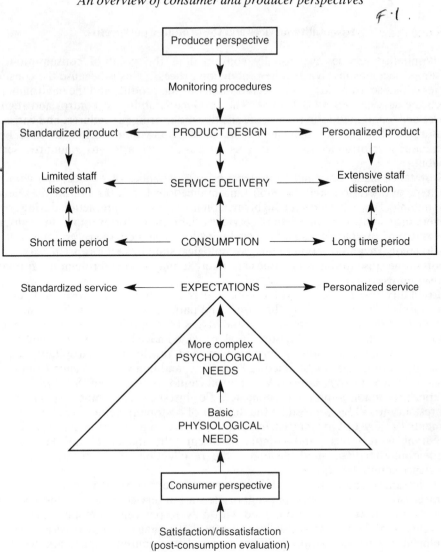

Figure 1.1   The interdependency of hospitality services

Source: Adapted from Teare, R., Moutinho, L., and Morgan, N. (eds), *Managing and Marketing Services in the 1990s*, Cassell, London, 1990, p. 236.

consumer evaluation. This is because satisfaction with service delivery is linked to the accumulation of many impressions from successive and usually transient experiences and interactions. The evaluative procedure must be able to cope with this complexity, and provide the consumer with an overall post-consumption measure of satisfaction.

Hospitality services and the producer perspective

As hospitality services are usually consumed at the point of consumption, the consumer becomes involved in the production process. This is because the consumer arrives with a set of needs and expectations about the product and the environment in which the service will be delivered. The producer's ability to control and regulate service delivery depends on the use of sensitive monitoring procedures, and corrective measures. When service delivery occurs over a long time period, as in a hotel, continuous performance monitoring is necessary in order to minimize service variability.

Hospitality managers need to understand the dynamics of service interaction for their type of operation, and the important implications for staff recruitment, selection and training. This is because the highly personalized form of interaction during service delivery exacerbates the problem of service variability. If, for example, the consumer arrives feeling tired and tense after travelling a long distance, the receptionist must be able to recognize and respond to this psychological state in an appropriate way. This is important because initial interactions are likely to play a critical role in the formation of first impressions.

Hospitality operations are often characterized by high fixed costs and sensitive profit ratios. This is especially the case if the pattern of business is irregular, which may contribute to short-term sales instability.[4,5] To minimize these effects, reduced cost options such as the hotel leisure break provided have been used to penetrate new market segments and improve productivity and profitability. Hospitality services cannot be stored, as can manufactured products, and hence the revenue from unsold meals or bedrooms over a given time period cannot be recouped. Similarly, product experiences cannot be precisely replicated. For instance, the atmosphere and service in a restaurant will be affected by the number of customers being served at any given moment. Too few or too many customers may create an undesirable impression. If the restaurant is too busy and complaints occur, the manager can only offer to compensate the dissatisfied customer; the recollection of an unsatisfactory meal experience cannot be erased.

Service and manufacturing industries have different consumer–producer interface characteristics. As many as 90 per cent of the staff in service organizations have direct contact with the consumer, compared with only 10 per cent in manufacturing.[6] The different orientation of service delivery means that management theories and methods developed in manufacturing industries may have limited application to service management problems. The logical focus for consumer research in hospitality services therefore lies at the point of simultaneous production and consumption where consumer–producer interactions are concentrated.

DEFINING THE HOSPITALITY PRODUCT

Baker[7] suggests that the distinction between products and services is often based on the traditional view that 'goods are produced, services are performed'.[8] This boundary is rather rigid and unhelpful compared with Levitt's[9] view which recognizes that products and services both have tangible and intangible characteristics. Levitt recognizes a common objective (to satisfy the consumer) and a distinction based solely on how satisfaction is derived from differing combinations of tangible (physical) and intangible (emotional) properties.

Buttle[10, 11] applies Levitt's definition to hospitality services, arguing that consumers seek intangible benefits in the form of satisfaction, regardless of whether the product is tangible or intangible. He illustrates this with the example of a restaurant meal occasion characterized by consumer–producer interactions which are both tangible (such as the experience of food and personal service) and intangible (such as the emotional reaction to the décor and quality of furnishings). Buttle calls the sum of these experiences the 'catering product'.

Nightingale[12, 13] describes the 'hotel experience' as a composite of many activities and interactions, each with physical and emotional content. This view implies that the consumer continually assesses the product, combining individual assessments to evaluate overall product satisfaction at the end of the stay.

Doswell and Gamble[14] define the hotel product as a composite of physical products (such as food, beverages and accommodation) and their associated service elements. Their definition also recognizes the importance of product intangibles such as image and atmosphere, which have an emotional impact on the customer.

Medlik[15] identified five factors which may affect the level of consumer satisfaction with the hotel product. These are:

- Location – geographical convenience, accessibility, attractiveness of surroundings, freedom from distractions (such as traffic noise).
- Facilities – including bedrooms, restaurants, bars, function and meeting rooms, and leisure and recreational facilities for customer use, differentiated in various ways, including by type and size.
- Service – the availability and extent of hotel services in conjunction with facilities, and the style and quality of these facilities in terms of formality/informality, degree of personal attention, speed and efficiency.
- Image – defined in terms of the way in which the hotel is perceived by an individual or group. This is partly a function of location, facilities and service, and is also influenced by the name, reputation, appearance, atmosphere and other associations.
- Price – value for money expressions about the hotel made by consideration of location, facilities, service, image and the satisfaction derived by its users from these and other components of the hotel product.

Although this list of product-specific factors affecting consumer satisfaction provides a helpful overview, it requires empirical verification.

A HYPOTHETICAL MODEL OF THE CONSUMER DECISION PROCESS

The purpose of this section is to introduce a hypothetical model of the consumer decision process for hospitality services, developed from the observations made above. The explanation that follows relates to a complex decision process with high personal involvement of the type which is associated with consumer decision making for a hotel leisure break.

As the leisure break is primarily a social activity, the decision process is likely to be characterized by joint or family decision making and greater caution than might be

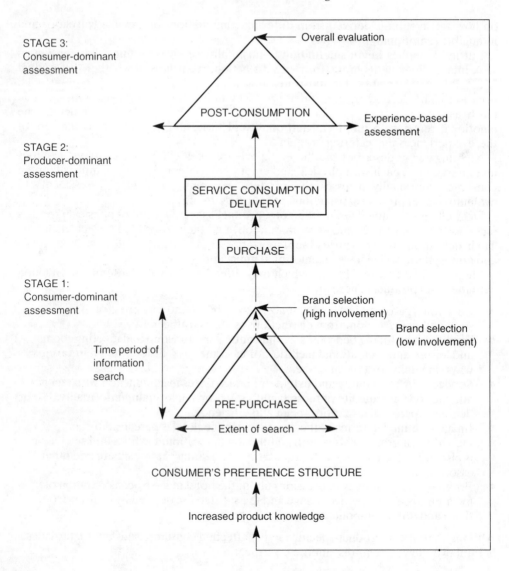

STAGE 3:
Consumer-dominant
assessment

STAGE 2:
Producer-dominant
assessment

STAGE 1:
Consumer-dominant
assessment

Overall evaluation

POST-CONSUMPTION

Experience-based
assessment

SERVICE CONSUMPTION
DELIVERY

PURCHASE

Brand selection
(high involvement)

Brand selection
(low involvement)

Time period of
information
search

PRE-PURCHASE

Extent of search

CONSUMER'S PREFERENCE STRUCTURE

Increased product knowledge

Figure 1.2   The consumer decision process for hospitality services

Source: Adapted from Teare, R., Moutinho, L., and Morgan, N. (eds), *Managing and
Marketing Services in the 1990s*, Cassell, London, 1990, p. 239.

expected for non-leisure hotel use or non-residential hospitality services. This is
because of the comparatively high financial investment with no tangible return, and
the perceived need to assess the associated costs and benefits. Figure 1.2 shows the
hypothesized change in emphasis between consumer- and producer-dominant
assessment during the consumer decision process for hospitality services.[16, 17]

The changes correspond to the three main stages of the decision process: pre-
purchase, consumption and post-consumption evaluation, which are described below.

1. At the pre-purchase stage, consumer-related factors are likely to be more influential than product-related factors in reaching a purchase decision.

When joint or family decision making occurs during the course of reaching agreement on a purchase decision, role specialization is commonplace.[18] Role adoption will be determined by personal, consumer-related factors such as self-confidence and assertiveness, and the product-related factor of prior experience. Stage 1 assumes that consumer-related factors are the dominant influence on the purchase decision because the subjective interpretation of product information and recommendations feature prominently in pre-purchase activity.

If family members have limited prior experience, the perceived risk is likely to be higher, requiring greater personal involvement in order to resolve sources of anxiety. Conversely, consumers with extensive prior experience will be able to make a purchase decision more easily and with greater confidence. In this situation, consumer-related factors are less dominant because product knowledge provides a stabilizing influence. Therefore, the relationship between prior experience and product involvement is important because it is likely to determine the amount of time, the extent of information search and the level of involvement required to assess the purchase options and reach a decision.

2. During consumption, product-related factors are likely to be more influential than consumer-related factors in determining product satisfaction.

A leisure break provides the consumer with personalized service over a time period of between two and four days. As the needs of consumers cannot be fully anticipated during consumption, hotel staff must be able to exercise discretion during service delivery in order to respond effectively. Stage 2 therefore assumes that product-related factors such as service interactions and subjective impressions of product experience will have a greater impact on satisfaction than internalized consumer-related factors such as prior expectations. This is because the consumer becomes co-producer during consumption,[19] helping to create atmosphere in restaurants and bars and simultaneously assessing the many tangible and intangible impressions and interactions which occur. The consumer must integrate all of these individual assessments in order to evaluate post-consumption feelings of satisfaction or dissatisfaction.

3. During post-consumption evaluation, consumer-related factors are likely to be more influential than product-related factors in determining overall satisfaction.

The overall feeling of satisfaction formulated during post-consumption is an enduring, cumulative measure derived from the many assessments made during consumption. Although the consumer may need to recall sensory product-related impressions, such as visually appealing guest room design features, the final evaluation is more likely to be influenced by consumer-related factors. These are principally end-state feelings of a psychological nature, such as feeling relaxed and refreshed. If the outcome of stage 2 is a negative psychological state, such as increased tension, then the consumer is likely to experience an overall feeling of dissatisfaction during post-consumption evaluation, and this in turn will influence brand attitudes and future purchase behaviour.

EMERGING IMPLICATIONS

The characteristics of hospitality services and the structure of the hypothetical model have two implications:

- The model provides guidance and direction for the review of prior research in Chapter 2. Of particular importance is the need to investigate the extent to which prior product experience affects pre-purchase decision making and consumption stage assessment procedures.
- A theory-generating emphasis on the consumption stage of the decision process is shown to be desirable. This is because the consumption stage is longer and more complex for residential hospitality services, and because of the need for research designed to investigate how consumers react to and assess the consumption environment. These issues are addressed in Chapter 3, which contains a discussion of theory-generating research methodology and a hotel leisure break case study.

NOTES

1. Burgess, J., 'Perspectives on gift exchange and hospitable behaviour', *International Journal of Hospitality Management*, vol. 1, no. 1, 1982, pp. 49–57.
2. Nailon, P. W., 'Theory and art in hospitality management', Inaugural lecture, University of Surrey, Guildford, 1981.
3. Nailon, P. W., 'Theory in hospitality management', *International Journal of Hospitality Management*, vol. 1, no. 3, 1982, pp. 135–43.
4. Kotas, R., *Marketing Orientation in the Hotel and Catering Industry*, Surrey University Press, Guildford, 1975.
5. Kotas, R., *Management Accounting for Hotels and Restaurants*, Surrey University Press, Guildford, 1977.
6. Irons, K., 'How to manage services', *Management Today*, November 1983, pp. 90–168.
7. Baker, M. J., 'Services: salvation or servitude?', *Quarterly Review of Marketing*, vol. 6, no. 3, 1981, pp. 7–18.
8. Rathmell, J. M., *Marketing in the Services Sector*, Winthrop, Cambridge, MA, 1974.
9. Levitt, T., 'Marketing intangible products and product intangibles', *Harvard Business Review*, May–June 1981, pp. 94–102.
10. Buttle, F. A., 'Unserviceable concepts in service marketing', *Quarterly Review of Marketing*, vol. 11, no. 3, 1986, pp. 8–14.
11. Buttle, F. A., *Hotel and Food Service Marketing*, Holt, Rinehart & Winston, Eastbourne, 1986.
12. Nightingale, M., 'Determination and control of quality standards in hospitality services', M. Phil. thesis, University of Surrey, Department of Management Studies for Tourism and Hotel Industries, 1983.
13. Nightingale, M., 'The hospitality industry: defining quality for a quality assurance programme – a study of perceptions', *Service Industries Journal*, vol. 5, no. 1, 1985, pp. 9–22.

14. Doswell, R., and Gamble, P. R., *Marketing and Planning Hotels and Tourism Projects*, Hutchinson, London, 1979, pp. 19–20.
15. Medlik, S., *The Business of Hotels*, Heinemann, London, 1980, pp. 115–16.
16. Teare, R., 'The consumer decision process for hospitality services', *Conference Proceedings, Current Issues in Services Research Conference*, Dorset Institute, November 1988.
17. Teare, R., 'An exploration of the consumer decision process for hospitality services', in Teare, R., Moutinho, L., and Morgan, N. (eds), *Managing and Marketing Services in the 1990s*, Cassell, London, 1990, pp. 233–48.
18. Davis, H. L., and Rigaux, B. P., 'Perception of marital roles in decision processes', *Journal of Consumer Research*, vol. 1 (June), 1974, pp. 51–61.
19. Teare, R, and Gummesson, E., 'Integrated marketing organization for hospitality firms', in Teare, R., and Boer, A. (eds), *Strategic Hospitality Management: Theory and Practice for the 1990s*, Cassell, London, 1991, pp. 144–57.

TWO

The consumer decision process:
a paradigm in transition

INTRODUCTION

The consumer decision process introduced in Chapter 1 broadly describes the tasks relating to product assessment and evaluation across the three decision stages of pre-purchase, consumption and post-consumption. There are, however, differences of opinion concerning the sources of influence operating at each stage, and the relationships between the stages.

Chapter 2 begins by reviewing progress in consumer decision modelling with particular reference to Moutinho's descriptive model of vacation tourist behaviour.[1,2,3] As the model was designed to depict international long holiday behaviour, it is not wholly applicable to the study of decision making across the range of hospitality services. Nonetheless, there are areas of commonality, and the model provides some insights which guide theory construction. Following this is a broad-based review of key research contributions to the study of consumer decision making. The review aims to identify the main influences and relationships applicable to the design of consumer research for hospitality and tourism services. To focus the review as precisely as possible, research findings for each decision process stage are grouped in relation to emerging research themes.

GENERAL DECISION MODELS AND THE COGNITIVE PARADIGM

Anderson[4] and Peter and Olsen[5] identify the need for a theoretical framework or 'paradigm'[6] when making empirical observations. This viewpoint is strengthened by the findings of Bagozzi,[7] Foxall[8,9] and Jacoby,[10] who have reviewed and commented on the limited success of attempts to construct and test theory in isolation from existing theory. Others have argued that any given theory only has meaning and significance within the paradigm from which it is derived.[10,11]

The dominant tradition in consumer research is the cognitive paradigm, which assumes that consumers have considerable capacity for receiving and handling quantities of information and for understanding pre-purchase search and evaluation. The consumer is also assumed to process information in a rational way, and by so doing to become progressively convinced of the need to purchase the focal brand. The central component of these models is an extended consumer decision sequence in which information is received and classified by the individual. It is subsequently transformed by cognitive processing into attitudes and intentions, which determine purchase behaviour and brand choice.[12]

A decision process model is typically represented by a set of propositions, or a series of related statements and ideas, which attempt to predict how consumers and markets will react. Created by defining the variables and specifying the relationships between them, it also facilitates the prediction of outcomes under specified conditions, and provides a framework for analysis.

There have been many attempts to develop general consumer decision process models, and those devised by Nicosia,[13] Howard and Sheth[14] and Engel Kollat and Blackwell[15,16] have been especially influential. These models, in particular, were instrumental in identifying and defining components of the decision process and the nature of relationships which may occur, such as the widely accepted pre-purchase sequence of problem recognition, search and choice. However, attempts to validate the models have met with only limited success, and the utility and value of general models remains questionable. There are several reasons for this, notably the complexity of model relationships and their unreliability as a means of predicting consumer behaviour or guiding communication strategy.[17] These reasons also account for the limited appeal of decision model research to practitioners, who might usefully employ empirical approaches to solve marketing problems if the model relationships were relevant and easier to understand. Emerging from the criticisms directed at the general consumer decision process models is the need to enhance theoretical and practical understanding of consumer decision making in specific product fields and situations.

Moutinho's model of vacation tourist behaviour

In service industries, the consumer decision process is likely to be directly influenced by the nature of the service activity. For example, Moutinho suggests that the tourist product purchase is rarely spontaneous, being preceded by planning and saving over a long time period, with no tangible return on investment. The similarities with hospitality services are evident from the review of consumer and producer perspectives in Chapter 1.

The basic framework of Moutinho's model[1,2,3] is derived from general decision model assumptions and published research relating to vacation tourist behaviour. The model construction is underpinned by three behavioural concepts: motivation, cognition and learning. The assumption is that purchase motives initiate the sequence of behavioural events, cognition activates mental processing, and learning causes subsequent changes in behaviour. Behaviour is defined as a function of intention to act, which may in turn be influenced by situational factors that intervene between intended and actual behaviour. The model consists of three parts: pre-decision and decision processes, purchase evaluation and repeat-buying probabilities.

The decision process stages in the model are problem recognition, search, alternatives evaluation, choice and outcomes. The assumption is that, as the consumer proceeds through these stages, progressive focusing occurs, giving rise to three options at the alternatives evaluation stage:

- Destinations may be rejected by the travel decision-maker because they have no potential to satisfy travel objectives.
- Destinations which are considered to be neutral alternatives may require further information, and discussion inputs from other family members.
- Destinations considered after preliminary judgement to be viable alternatives may require more detailed evaluation.

The model implicitly recognizes that, during the evaluation of alternatives, the evoked set of brands is unlikely to contain more than seven options for most tourist destination decisions.[18] The model also recognizes that family influences are an important factor in vacation decision making. For example, it is conceivable that different family members may assume specialist roles to identify holiday needs, search for information and make the purchase decision.

Part I of the model is concerned with pre-decision and decision processes, beginning with need arousal and the receipt of travel stimuli, and culminating in product purchase. The pre-decision field of preference structure has subfields of stimulus filtration, attention and learning processes and choice criteria. The two decision fields are labelled 'decision' and 'purchase'.

The assumption is made that the consumer's preference structure for a tourist destination is influenced by internalized environmental factors derived from many sources. These include cultural norms and values, family and reference groups, financial status and social class. It is also assumed that affective judgements are influenced by factors such as the consumer's own personality, lifestyle, perceived role set, and purchase motives. The consumer's preference structure may also be influenced by exposure to travel stimuli, portraying product attributes such as quality, price, distinctiveness, prestige, service and availability. The act of filtering these stimuli enables the consumer to organize information in a meaningful way. If, however, the stimuli contain ambiguity, the consumer may feel the need to search for additional information.

When a consumer feels uncertain about the merits of alternative brands and or destinations, it is assumed that the extent of external information search activity will be proportional to the degree of perceived risk. In contrast, the consumer with extensive product knowledge derived from prior experience may engage in little or no external information search. It is assumed that attention to media and other information sources will lead to active comparison of new information with that stored in memory. Learning occurs as new information and experiences are integrated into the consumer's organized system of beliefs and knowledge, referred to in the model as the 'cognitive structure'. When potential sources of conflict or ambiguity have been resolved by assimilating new information, the consumer may begin to feel more confident about the purchase decision.

The model assumes that the criteria used to assess the suitability of tourist services are derived from the components of the holiday (such as travel, hotel and resort facilities) and performance expectations for each component. If, however, the consumer has relevant prior experience, then individual assessment of each separate component of the holiday package may not be necessary. Instead the consumer may

PART I PRE-DECISION AND DECISION PROCESSES

Personality
|
Internalized   Confidence
environmental   Lifestyle   Attitude   generation
influences | | |
                 Perceived   Family   Inhibitors
                 role set   influence
                    |
                 Motives

F | Preference structure | ————————— Intention ————

Travel   **S** Stimulus
stimuli ——— filtration ——— Search ——— Evoked set ——— **S** ——— Choice criteria
display   (stimulus |
               ambiguity)   Comprehension   Perceived risk
                                 |
Sensitivity   Perceptual bias   **F** | Decision |
to information |
                             Cognitive structure   **F** | Purchase |
                Attention
        S and learning

PART II POST-PURCHASE EVALUATION

Post-purchase   ┌ Expectations ┐
information   Confirmation   Disconfirmation   Latitude of ╱ ╱   High
                     └ Reality ┘   acceptance   positive
                                                           (+)
                                                                            Medium
S Adequacy ——— **F** | Satisfaction | Reinforcement   Non-commitment
evaluation | Dissatisfaction | cognitive
                                            dissonance   Medium
Cost–benefit   Levels of   Latitude of
analysis   reward   rejection   High
                                                           (–) ╲ ╲   negative
Product
consistency

PART III FUTURE DECISION MAKING

F | Repeat-buying |
      | probability | Subsequent behaviour:

Repeat-buying   ● Straight rebuy
(high positive) ————————————   ● Future rebuy
                                       subsequent
Repeat-buying   short term
(medium positive) ——————————   medium term
                                       long term
Hesitation ◁————————   ● Modified rebuy

Refusal to buy ———————————— Go to competition

F = Field   **S** = Subfield

Figure 2.1   Moutinho's vacation tourist behaviour model

Source: Moutinho, L., 'Consumer behaviour in tourism', *Management Bibliographies and Reviews*, vol. 12, no. 3 (1986), MCB University Press, Bradford.

be able to use a decision rule to select the holiday option with the highest perceived overall rating. The consumer does this by recalling overall evaluations of different brands and destinations which are stored in long-term memory.

When the consumer has selected the preferred brand or holiday option, a purchase intention is formed. In addition to prior experience and family influences, the purchase intention may be mediated by situational factors such as tourism promotions and advice received from travel intermediaries. If, for example, price reductions are displayed at the point of sale, they may influence the purchase intention, and the consumer may buy a lower-cost holiday solely because it is perceived to be better value for money.

Part II of the model is concerned with purchase evaluation, which is the mechanism by which the consumer's frame of reference for future purchase intentions is developed. The post-purchase evaluation field is labelled 'satisfaction/dissatisfaction' and the subfield is referred to as 'adequacy evaluation'.

The model proposes that, during adequacy evaluation, the consumer will evaluate brand attributes against a notional ideal for each attribute. This ranking procedure represents a form of mental cost–benefit analysis. Aggregated scores brand performance assessments are then used to determine the overall level of satisfaction or dissatisfaction with the brand.

Part III of the model is concerned with future decision making, and the implications arising from a particular vacation destination or tourist service for repeat buying. The repeat-buying probabilities field assumes that the consumer will consider a number of purchase options, which may involve straight repurchasing or modified repurchasing behaviour.

Summary

The vacation tourist behaviour model has a number of similarities with hospitality services: in particular, the high investment requirement with no tangible return on investment. It is also assumed that satisfaction is derived from many transient impressions and experiences that occur during consumption, which affect the consumer's state of mind at the end of the consumption period. These factors are likely to affect the way in which the consumer approaches the decision process for hospitality services, and the sources and methods used to overcome feelings of perceived risk associated with the purchase decision.

THE PRE-PURCHASE STAGE OF THE CONSUMER DECISION PROCESS

The hypothetical model presented in Chapter 1 implicitly recognizes that pre-purchase behaviour may be influenced by many different factors. Consequently, the following review of research on pre-purchase behaviour aims to identify key findings and their implications for the pre-purchase stage of the decision process for hospitality and tourism services. The principal pre-purchase concepts are depicted in Figure 2.2.

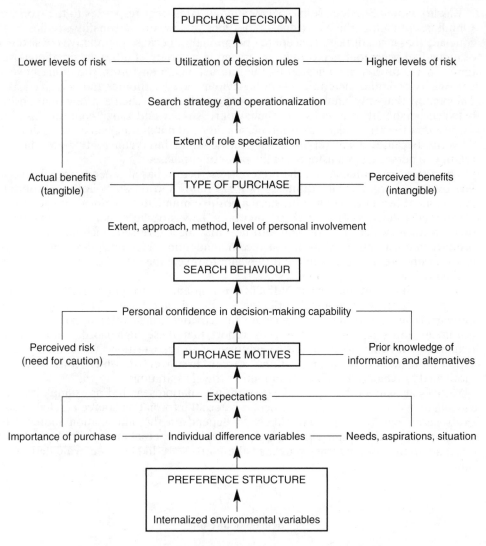

Figure 2.2   Interrelationships and influences on pre-purchase behaviour

Preference structure

As noted by Moutinho,[1,2,3] consumer preferences are influenced by internalized environmental factors such as cultural norms and values, family and reference groups, financial status and social class, and by individual differences. In an investigation of households undergoing life status changes such as retirement or unemployment, Andreasen[19] found that spontaneous changes in brand preferences were also occurring. Consumers were generally more open to persuasion because of this.

The individual differences that influence the consumer's preference structure include personality, beliefs, attitudes and purchase motives.

Kassarjian and Sheffet[20] define personality as 'consistent responses to the world of stimuli surrounding the individual'. In their review of personality studies they conclude that it is a difficult concept to operationalize because the relative consistency of individual behaviour needs to be measured in a variety of different situations over time. This is further complicated by the interactions in any given situation between personality and other determinants of behaviour such as attitudes and perceived risk. They report that only a few studies have successfully established a strong relationship between personality and consumer behaviour. Kakkar and Lutz[21] confirm this, and suggest that the relationship between personality and purchasing behaviour is difficult to verify because of the reported high incidence of intervening situational factors relating to personal circumstances at the point of purchase.

The attitudinal influence on the preference structure has also been inconclusive so far. Fishbein[22] argues that attitudes towards brands and products are inappropriate predictors of consumer behaviour, since a positive brand attitude does not necessarily lead to the formation of a purchase intention. This is because there are a variety of other ways in which a favourable attitude may be expressed, including increased product interest and word-of-mouth recommendations. He concludes that research observations are more meaningful if they aim to reveal the set of beliefs that underlie a given attitude.

Motives have an important influence on intention to purchase, since much consumer behaviour is goal orientated. Beard and Ragheb[23,24] suggest that individuals are motivated to participate in activities which offer opportunities for fulfilment and self-actualization. They report that these higher-order motives are revealed by measurements of leisure motivation and satisfaction. Their findings also support the notion of 'a motivational career' in travel[25] in which consumers are motivated by a hierarchy of needs and future travel aspirations.

Motives also affect the type and extent of information search. For example, where consumers feel confident that a particular external information source is reliable and easily accessible, they are more likely to depend on this information source.[26] In situations where the optimal choice is desirable, both internal and external sources of information are used because purchase alternatives are likely to be evaluated more carefully.[27,28]

Search behaviour

The extent of search behaviour, especially in connection with external information gathering, has been debated extensively in the literature. Some studies have found that pre-purchase external search is either absent or restricted to specialized or first-time purchases.[29,30] Large individual differences in the extent of search have also been observed.

Duncan and Olshavsky[31] have classified the factors which may explain these differences as follows:

- Environmental factors – in particular, the availability of information and the number of purchase alternatives present.
- Consumer factors – including perceived benefits, risk and household roles, brand preferences and differences between alternatives, knowledge, experience, time and financial pressures, personality and socioeconomic demographic factors.

Duncan and Olshavsky cite Newman[32] to support their view that search activity only increases when the consumer believes that the purchase is important, that there is a need to learn more, or that information is easy to obtain and utilize.

Information search strategies

In a study of search behaviour relating to long-holiday purchase decisions, Schul and Crompton[33] found that consumers may seek information from a variety of sources before making a decision about the destination and the holiday package. They point out that, unlike in most shopping decisions, when buying long holidays consumers cannot observe what they are buying, and because they must rely on secondary and tertiary sources of information the search is longer and involves more informational sources.

Furse, Punj and Stewart[34,35] support the view that systematic search strategies are common among consumers. They suggest that search activity is likely to be a function of product knowledge and experience, individual differences such as ability, situational variables such as time pressure, and product importance. Differences in the type of information search have also been reported,[36] where brand-loyal behaviour was closely associated with stored information about the properties of a particular brand.

Individual differences and search behaviour

Some studies have found significant, but not always consistent relationships between information search and age,[37,38,39] and between information search and educational attainment.[27] Newman and Staelin[29] reported a drop in external search among respondents who had undergone higher education. They suggest that this may be explained by greater information-processing efficiency. The relationship between income level and external search remains unclear, with both positive[27] and negative[34,38] relationships reported. It is possible that, as income level increases, the cost–benefit relationship changes. For instance, the cost of time required for external search may begin to outweigh the perceived benefits of engaging in extensive information search.

The role of prior product experience in search behaviour

Alba and Hutchinson[40] suggest that product knowledge has two major components: familiarity and expertise. They define 'familiarity' as the number of product-related experiences that have been accumulated by the consumer, and 'expertise' as the ability to perform product-related tasks successfully. They conclude that increased product familarity generally leads to increased consumer expertise.

The extent of pre-purchase search is likely to depend on the consumer's familarity with the product category.[14,41,42] Search behaviour generally begins with the recollection of information held in memory, as the consumer tries to determine whether choice can be based on prior experience. Insufficient information or experience is likely to activate external information search.

Consumers who have limited prior experience are inclined to rely more heavily on currently available information than on their own product knowledge.[43] However, as the decision process continues beyond information search, use of internal and external sources of information is more likely to occur.[41]

The role of product involvement in search behaviour

Involvement is considered to be a causal, individual difference variable which affects purchase behaviour. It has been defined as 'an unobservable state reflecting the amount of interest, arousal or emotional attachment evoked by the product in a particular individual'.[44]

The degree of consumer involvement in a product category is recognized as an important variable in the context of advertising strategy, since it may lead to different patterns of consumer decision making.[45] Characteristic differences include the number of attributes used to compare brands, and the duration of the search and selection process. Product involvement is also likely to affect information-processing activity, since variables include the extent of information search, receptivity to advertising, and the type of cognitive responses generated during exposure to information sources.[46]

In a study of decision-making involvement, Slama and Tashchian[47] found that some consumers tend to be more involved in the decision-making process, regardless of the product class. They conclude that involvement is a useful marketing variable because product and situational involvement can be combined to provide a more insightful explanation of decision-making behaviour.

Involvement is difficult to operationalize as it cannot be measured directly. However, a number of studies have overcome this problem by clustering respondents by involvement type. For example, Lastovicka and Gardner[48] measured the relative strength of product importance, commitment and emotional reaction to a group of fourteen products. Their analysis revealed a typology of low, high and special interest involvement in the product group.

The degree of product involvement in pre-purchase decision making may also be linked to antecedents such as perceptions of product importance, risk, symbolic or sign value and hedonic or emotional value.[49]

Block and Richins[50] argue that product importance has been inadequately defined and understood. In their view product importance has three dimensions:

- Perceived product importance – the extent to which a consumer links a product to salient, enduring or situation-specific goals.
- Instrumental or situational importance – a temporary perception of product importance based on the consumer's desire to obtain particular extrinsic goals that may derive from the purchase and/or usage of the product.
- Enduring importance – a long-term perception of product importance based on the strength of the product's relationship to central needs and values.

Moreover, they argue that perceived product importance as well as beliefs about situational and enduring importance may change at different stages in the decision process. It appears to operate through high involvement, and is associated with products that have a symbolic meaning closely related to self-image and expression ideals.

Most empirical work on product symbolism has paid relatively little attention to how products are used by consumers in social situations. Solomon[51] suggests that the subjective experience of product usage contributes to the consumers' structuring of social reality, self-concept and behaviour. He concludes that the symbolism embedded in many products may in fact be the primary reason for purchase and use.

Perceived risk

Perceived risk has been defined as an outcome of uncertainty about the product.[52] The sense of risk is commonly associated with the place and mode of purchase, and the financial and psychosocial consequences of product purchase.[53] Ahtola[54] concludes that perceived risk is related to the degree of uncertainty experienced during decision making.

A study of perceived risk associated with leisure activities[55] found that levels of risk varied substantially from one activity to another. They also found that perceived risk related to leisure activity is different from that associated with manufactured goods, and that its effect diminishes as individuals become more familar with, or interested in, a particular leisure activity.

Role specialization in information search and brand selection

Role specialization has been found to be closely related to information search in family decision making, especially in terms of time allocation and the use of specialist skills.[56,57]

In a review of research on family decision making, Jenkins[58] highlighted the need to investigate the various dimensions of power associated with decision-making roles. The most influential factors affecting the family role structure were found to be income, education, time availability, prior experience and role specialization.

Davis and Rigaux[59] examined the patterns of influence exerted by husbands and wives at different stages in the decision process. They found that marital roles are likely to be differentiated by stage and consumption category. While no significant differences were apparent in the relative influence of marital partners, information search was characterized by considerably more role specialization than other pre-purchase activities. The most likely explanation for this is that differences in the degree of role specialization relate to the nature of the task and the allocation of role responsibilities.

Burns and Granbois[60] found that family decision-making roles are often related to the perceived influence of husbands and wives as portrayed by their recollection of decision process events. But the reasons why decision-making roles vary from one family to another can only be identified by investigating the situational factors which influence information search and other pre-purchase behaviour.[61]

Reviewing the literature on household decision making, Davis[62] identified two key implications for research:

- The need to consider in more detail the extent to which prior experience influences family decision-making responsibilities for evaluating the consumption experience, storing information for future use and utilizing the stored information when the need arises.
- The need to explore how families make decisions rather than simply who is involved. This is important because the nature of family relationships and the financial and time constraints faced by the family constitute a unique decision-making environment.

The evoked set

The range of purchase alternatives available to the consumer can be described as the 'universal set'. As the consumer becomes familiar with some of these alternatives through search, incidental learning and experience, brand categorization occurs.[63] The group of acceptable brands is termed the 'evoked set' and represents the small number of alternatives which the individual is familiar with, remembers, and finds acceptable for further consideration.[14]

Further to the brand-based definition, Moutinho[3] found that consumers sometimes use situation-specific criteria to assess tourist destination options. This provides the customer with an alternative approach to brand selection derived from comparative assessment against specific decision criteria.

The role of decision rules in choice behaviour

Reviewing psychological theories of consumer choice, Hansen[64] concludes that choice processes vary on a continuum ranging from very simple or routinized to more complex behaviour. For example, when an alternative that has performed well in the past is selected, a simple choice process has been used. Such a process, repeated many times, may become established as an integral part of a behavioural sequence. This acts as a guiding principle or decision rule which can be applied to subsequent choice decisions.

Product familiarity can lead to increased confidence during subsequent consumer decision making.[65] This enables the experienced consumer to be more selective in searching information, and to use established decision rules instead of repeating preliminary explorations of external information on subsequent purchase occasions.

The latitude of product acceptance is also likely to narrow as new experiences are assimilated, and preferences become more focused.

The influence of product knowledge on choice behaviour can be summarized as follows:

* Brand-based information processing is more likely to occur among consumers who are familiar with the product category, and attribute-based processing among consumers who are unfamiliar with the product category.[43,66,67,68,69].
* Consumers tend to start with attribute-based comparative assessments, turning to brand-based processing in the later stages of information search and selection. This suggests that attribute-based comparisons are more easily undertaken. Experienced consumers also tend to make comparisons against an established reference standard in order to evaluate alternatives and make trade-off decisions.[43,67]

These findings suggest that experienced consumers are able to construct a prototype for the product class within an internal knowledge structure, and process information schematically. This enables the consumer to make the fullest use of similarity and difference information.

Non-compensatory decision rules

More complex choice processes occur when non-compensatory choice principles are invoked. Typically this happens when a weakness in one product attribute is not compensated for by the strengths of another. Alternative approaches include:

- Lexicographic – which involves the ranking of product attributes from most important to least important, usually in situations where the number of brand alternatives is fixed.
- Conjunctive – which determines the *minimum* acceptable performance level or standard for each product attribute.
- Disjunctive – which determines *acceptable* performance standards for each attribute.

As non-compensatory choices become more complex, the consumer may try to rank choice criteria using a weighting, or subjective probability procedure. The composition and individual importance of the evaluative criteria have been found to vary at different stages of the decision process:[63,70] 'Consumers will recall with greatest ease how they made the choice from amongst alternatives in the choice set, and if not prompted may ignore how this choice set was created'.[70]

Bettman[71] considered the use of evaluative criteria during choice, and concluded that an overall evaluation is more likely to occur in high-involvement situations characterized by brand-organized information, and when there are factors present which prevent the use of a simple choice process.

The role of price information in product choice

During the evaluation of choice alternatives, consumers often use price information as a criterion against which product attributes can be ranked and evaluated.[72] Price information also provides an indicator of product quality, especially if product information is limited.

In making price comparisons, the consumer considers alternatives which lie within an acceptable price range. Alternatives outside the range may be rejected because they are perceived to be either too expensive or too cheap. A brand may also be rejected if the price is considered to be incompatible with the purchase occasion.[73]

Family role influences in choice behaviour

Focusing on the different influence strategies used by marital partners in resolving disagreements about purchase decisions, Spiro[74] found that people who are more traditional in their lifestyles and attitudes are more likely to use persuasive influence. However, husband and wife perceptions of each other's influence attempts differ, especially for decisions involving other family members.[75] Choice behaviour is also influenced by the wider circle of family and friends. One explanation for this is that the consumer has more empathy with those whose patterns of consumption are more like his or her own.[76]

Midgely and Christopher[77] found that the problem-solving approach adopted by the consumer is related to his or her perception and classification of the decision-making situation. In this context, they cite differences between the approaches required for joint and individual decision making. For example, when joint decision making occurs, it often involves discussion and negotiation relating to different or even opposing viewpoints. As a consequence of this interaction, they found that less information may be used and retained than during individual decision making.

THE PURCHASE DECISION

Concluding a review of research on pre-purchase behaviour, Olshavsky and Granbois[30] make two observations about the relationship between pre-purchase activities and the purchase decision:

- Many purchases are likely to occur out of necessity, because of deeply rooted preferences, conformity to group norms or imitation of others based on recommendations from personal or non-personal sources.
- Even when the purchase decision is preceded by a choice process, it is typically limited to the evaluation of a few alternatives, little external search, few evaluative criteria and simple evaluation processes.

They believe that a stronger emphasis on the study of situational factors is necessary in order to develop a broader understanding of consumer decision making. To achieve this objective, they add that observational research methods will need to be used more widely, thereby reducing the dependence on model-based predictions of consumer choice.

Belk[78] defines the situational context in which decision making occurs as 'a point in time and space'. He also describes five situational factors which commonly influence decision making. These are physical surroundings, social surroundings, antecedent states, task definition and the temporal perspective of the decision process. He defines task definition as 'an intent or requirement to select, shop for, or obtain information about a general or specific purchase'.

Situational factors are also known to affect consumer satisfaction. For example, the results of a study carried out by Granzin and Schjelderup[79] showed that situational factors affected the level of anticipated satisfaction with car repair decisions. They conclude that situational factors may also affect levels of self-confidence, and perceived risk associated with the decision process.

As noted in Chapter 1, hospitality services are delivered in a wide variety of situations and physical environments. Therefore the relationship between self-confidence and consumer satisfaction may be important, especially if the consumption environment is an unfamiliar one. The concept of situational self-image provides a link between personal and situational influences on consumer behaviour. For example, Schenk and Holman[80] believe that the consumer develops a repertoire of self-images which may vary as the situation requires. Interpreting this view, the consumer who is selecting a hotel might be expected to seek confirmation that he or she will feel comfortable with the physical environment and the services provided.

Factors influencing the purchase decision are depicted in Figure 2.3.

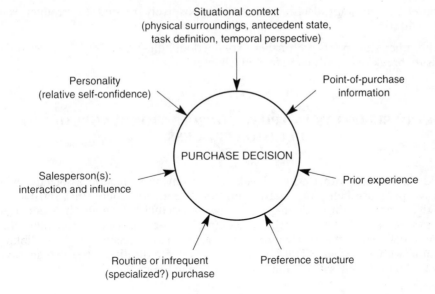

Figure 2.3 Factors influencing the purchase decision

Implications arising from the review of pre-purchase and purchase studies

In order to identify different patterns of consumer decision making, it is necessary to establish a framework for comparative analysis. The review of pre-purchase studies has shown that there are problems associated with isolating preference structure variables, and that prior attitudinal and search behaviour studies have resulted in inconclusive or inconsistent findings. However, the review has also indicated that there are several promising variables, notably prior experience with the product category, and product involvement. These two variables are interrelated, and may also influence the way in which assessment and evaluation are undertaken during the consumption and post-consumption stages of the decision process. Their potential explanatory value is summarized in the following research statements:

1. The propensity of consumers with extensive prior experience to engage in high-involvement decision making is related to the perceived importance of the product.
2. The propensity of consumers with extensive prior experience to engage in low-involvement decision making is related to product familiarity and personal confidence in product class decision-making ability.
3. The propensity of consumers with limited prior experience to engage in high-involvement decision making is related to perceived risk, and limited personal confidence in product class decision-making ability.
4. The propensity of consumers with limited prior experience to engage in low-involvement decision making is related to pre-knowledge of product suitability and low perceptions of risk.
5. The use of pre-purchase decision rules, and their relative effectiveness during the assessment of choice criteria, are positively related to the consumer's prior product experience.

6. Confidence in joint decision making is positively related to product role specialization.

These and other statements are further explained and illustrated by reference to the hotel leisure break case study contained in Chapter 3.

THE CONSUMPTION AND POST-CONSUMPTION STAGES OF THE DECISION PROCESS

In a study concerned with tracking levels of consumer satisfaction associated with consecutive purchase behaviour, LaBarbera and Mazursky[81] found that satisfaction plays a significant role in mediating intentions and actual behaviour. It is apparent that consumers do not always recall evaluations, but there is a high probability that they will recall past satisfaction prior to a repurchase decision, thereby linking expectations with experience. This is shown together with the alternative explanations linking expectations with satisfaction/dissatisfaction in Figure 2.4.

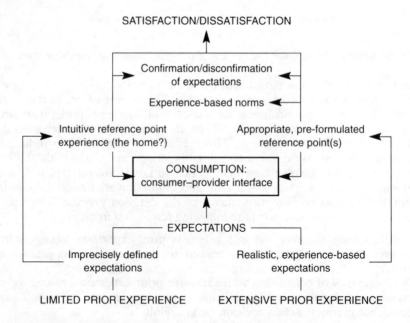

Figure 2.4 Interrelationships between prior experience, expectations and satisfaction/dissatisfaction

Consumer expectations and experience

In the context of consumer behaviour, Olson and Dover[82] define expectation as 'the perceived likelihood that a product possesses a certain characteristic or attribute, or will lead to a particular event or outcome'.

Nightingale[83,84] investigated the different expectations and perceptions of quality and service held by consumers, managers and staff in the hospitality industry. His findings suggest that efforts to improve consumer satisfaction may be seriously impeded by perceptual differences. Managers and staff tend to focus on tangible elements of the product in their role as service providers, whereas consumers often have a wider set of expectations which are not always easy to anticipate. To some extent, as Burnkrant and Cousineau have argued,[85] this may be explained by the influence of word-of-mouth communications on the formation of expectations. They found that recommendations from people who are known to be familiar with a particular product category have an influence on the way in which products are perceived by others.

A reference standard may be used by consumers for making attribute-based product comparisons. This is usually described in terms of experiences which fall above or below a reference point experience. For example, LaTour and Peat[86,87] found that prior experience and product satisfaction are linked by product attribute comparisons.

Swan and Jones Combs[88] and Howes and Arndt[89] found that product attributes are likely to be assessed according to their perceived product importance, suggesting that consumer satisfaction consists of many differently weighted individual satisfactions. Howes and Arndt argue that consumers often seek 'bundles or clusters of satisfactions', especially from service products where the consumer actively participates in the service provision. Further evidence is provided by Westbrook,[90] who concludes that consumers add together their experiences so that high levels of satisfaction from some sources compensate for lower levels from others.

The concept of satisfaction

In a review of the research literature on consumer satisfaction, McNeal[91] discovered that numerous definitions have been supported by empirically based studies. He concludes that the term 'consumer satisfaction' is most frequently used to refer to the fulfilment of a motivating state or the meeting of an expectation, through the purchase of a product or service.

In a study concerned with the measurement of tourist satisfaction with a destination area,[92] satisfaction is defined as 'the result of the interaction between a tourist's experience at the destination area and the expectations he had about that destination'. In this instance, satisfaction was derived from the evaluation of tourist product components such as accommodation, eating and drinking experiences, destination accessibility, attractions, cost and services. The outcome, satisfaction (or dissatisfaction), was derived from the weighted sum total of comparative assessment ratings, guided by expectations and reference standards.

Lounsbury and Hoopes[93] found that an important dimension of tourist satisfaction is relaxation and leisure. This is related to the way personal plans work out in practice; emotional and physical well-being; the 'pace of life' experienced; opportunities for familiar and new leisure activity participation; and the feeling of enjoyment associated with each experience.

The majority of studies concerned with consumer satisfaction subscribe to one of two alternative viewpoints: first, that satisfaction results from the confirmation of expectations and dissatisfaction from disconfirmation; or second, that satisfaction/dissatisfaction is derived from measurements made against experience-based norms.

Confirmation/disconfirmation of expectations

Confirmation/disconfirmation begins prior to brand purchase and use, when the consumer formulates expectations about brand performance in a given situation. After using the brand, the consumer compares perceived actual performance with expected performance. Confirmation of expectations, leading to a feeling of satisfaction, occurs when the two perspectives coincide or if perceived brand performance exceeds expectations. Disconfirmation occurs if perceived brand performance falls below expectations, thereby leading to a feeling of dissatisfaction.

Oliver[94] concludes that expectations provide a standard against which product performance can be measured, thereby influencing subsequent product preferences and behavioural intention. Westbrook and Cote[95] support this view, suggesting that the consumer compares actual experience with prior expectations, noting any performance disparity. This information provides the basis for assessing relative satisfaction or dissatisfaction with the overall experience.

Experience-based norms

Woodruff, Cadotte and Jenkins[96] propose a model for conceptualizing consumer satisfaction which replaces expectations with experience-based norms as the standard for comparing brand performance. They suggest that, after using a brand the consumer will note how it performed. When there are many attributes to consider, overall brand performance may be determined by a combination of beliefs about the brand's various performance dimensions.[90] In this way, beliefs are either strengthened or weakened according to how closely actual brand performance matches expected brand performance.[87]

Experience-based norms provide a frame of reference for evaluating performance. There is also some evidence to suggest that they are better predictors of satisfaction than evaluations based solely on brand expectations.[97] As experience will vary for different product categories, two types of experience-based norm are hypothesized:

- A brand-based norm in situations when one brand dominates the consumer's set of brand experiences.
- a product-based norm in situations when the consumer has had experience with several brands within a product class, but does not have a specific reference brand.

Experience-based norms are utilized in different ways during the decision process, ranging from single norms for familiar low-involvement products, to multiple norms associated with important events such as the purchase of a car or holiday. When actual brand performance is close to the norm, it is described as being within an acceptable latitude of performance. If, however, brand performance is considered to be outside the latitude of acceptance, dissatifaction occurs. Comparing the two explanations, Woodruff, Cadotte and Jenkins regard the experience-based norms viewpoint as more realistic because norms provide an integrated frame of reference derived from evaluations of prior experience.

Implications arising from the review of consumption and evaluation studies

Research evidence indicates that prior experience is likely to be an important factor during the consumption of hospitality and tourism services, influencing the formation of expectations, assessment criteria and the way in which experiences are integrated into the consumer's personal rating system. The system is derived from experience-based norms, and enables the consumer to assess and evaluate the extent of satisfaction with the consumption experience. These points are summarized in the following research statements:

7. The correlation between product expectations and experience is positively related to product familiarity.
8. The degree of sophistication inherent in the operation of the consumer's personal rating system is positively related to the extent of prior product experience.
9. Satisfaction during product consumption is a function of many differently weighted impressions and experiences that are cumulative, and which are continually being integrated into the consumer's personal rating system.
10. Satisfaction during post-consumption evaluation represents the sum total of individual assessments made during consumption. This evaluation reinforces or modifies the consumer's preference structure and influences future decision making.

As noted above, the significance of the research statements is explained at the end of Chapter 3.

NOTES

1. Moutinho, L., 'An investigation of vacation tourist behaviour', PhD thesis, University of Sheffield, 1982.
2. Moutinho, L., 'Vacation tourist decision process', *Quarterly Review of Marketing*, vol. 9, no. 3, 1984, pp. 8–17.
3. Moutinho, L., 'Consumer behaviour in tourism', *Management Bibliographies and Reviews*, vol. 12, no. 3, 1986, pp. 3–42.
4. Anderson, P. F., 'Marketing, scientific progress, and scientific method', *Journal of Marketing*, vol. 47 (Fall), 1983, pp. 18–31.
5. Peter, J. P., and Olson, J. C., 'Is science marketing?', *Journal of Marketing*, vol. 47 (Fall), 1983, pp. 111–25.
6. Kuhn, T. S., *The Structure of Scientific Revolutions*, University of Chicago Press, Chicago, IL, 1970.
7. Bagozzi, R. P., 'A prospectus for theory construction in marketing', *Journal of Marketing*, vol. 48 (Summer), 1984, pp. 11–29.
8. Foxall, G. R., 'Academic consumer research: problems and potential,' *European Research*, vol. 8, no. 5, 1980, pp. 20–3.
9. Foxall, G. R., 'Marketing models of buyer behaviour: a critical review', *European Research*, vol. 8, no. 5, 1980, pp. 195–206.
10. Jacoby, J., 'Consumer research: a state-of-the-art review', *Journal of Marketing*, vol. 42 (January), 1978, pp. 87–96.

11. Hunt, S. D., 'General theories and the fundamental explananda of marketing', *Journal of Marketing*, vol. 47 (Fall), 1983, pp. 9–17.
12. McGuire, W. J., 'Some internal psychological factors influencing consumer choice', *Journal of Consumer Research*, vol. 2 (March), 1976, pp. 302–19.
13. Nicosia, F. M., *Consumer Decision Processes*, Prentice-Hall, Englewood Cliffs, NJ, 1966.
14. Howard, J. A., and Sheth, J. N., *The Theory of Buyer Behavior*, John Wiley, New York, 1969.
15. Engel, J. F., Kollat, D. T., and Blackwell, R. D., *Consumer Behavior*, Holt, Rinehart & Winston, New York, 1968.
16. Engel, J. F., and Blackwell, R. D. *Consumer Behavior*, Dryden Press, New York, 1982.
17. Tuck, M., *How Do We Choose?*, Methuen, London, 1976.
18. Woodside, A. G., Ronkainen, I., and Reid, D. M., 'Measurement and utilization of the evoked set as a travel marketing variable', in *The '80s: Its Impact on Travel and Tourism Marketing*, Travel Research Association, Proceedings of the 8th Annual Conference, Salt Lake City, Utah, 1977, pp. 123–30.
19. Andreasen, A. R., 'Life status changes and changes in consumer preferences and satisfaction', *Journal of Consumer Research*, vol. 11 (December), 1984, pp. 784–94.
20. Kassarjian, H. H., and Sheffet, M. J., 'Personality and consumer behavior: an update', in Kassarjian, H. H., and T. S. Robertson, T. S. (eds), *Perspectives in Consumer Behavior*, Scott Foresman, Glenview, IL, 1981.
21. Kakkar, P., and Lutz, R. J., 'Situational influence on consumer behavior: a review', in Kassarjian, H. H., and Robertson, T. S. (eds), *Perspectives in Consumer Behavior*, Scott Foresman, Glenview, IL, 1981.
22. Fishbein, M., 'An overview of the attitude construct', in Hafer, G. B. (ed.), *A Look Back, A Look Ahead*, American Marketing Association, Proceedings of the 10th Attitude Research Conference, Chicago, IL, 1980, pp. 1–19.
23. Beard, J. G., and Ragheb, M. G., 'Measuring leisure satisfaction', *Journal of Leisure Research*, vol. 12, no. 1, 1980, pp. 20–33.
24. Beard, J. G., and Ragheb, M. G., 'Measuring leisure motivation', *Journal of Leisure Research*, vol. 15, no. 3, 1983, pp. 219–28.
25. Pearce, P. L., and Caltabiano, M. L., 'Inferring travel motivation from travelers' experiences', *Journal of Travel Research*, vol. 22, no. 2, 1983, pp. 167–20.
26. Capon, N., and Burke, M., 'Individual product class and task-related factors in consumer information processing', *Journal of Consumer Research*, vol. 7, no. 3, 1980, pp. 314–26.
27. Claxton, J. D., Fry, J. N., and Portis, B., 'A taxonomy of pre-purchase information gathering patterns', *Journal of Consumer Research*, vol. 1, no. 3, 1974, pp. 35–42.
28. Jacoby, J., Chestnut, J. W., and Fisher, W. A., 'A behavioral process approach to information acquisition in nondurable purchasing', *Journal of Marketing Research*, vol. 15 (November), 1978, pp. 532–44.
29. Newman, J. W., and Staelin, R., 'Prepurchase information seeking for new cars and major household appliances', *Journal of Marketing Research*, vol. 9 (August), 1972, pp. 249–57.
30. Olshavsky, R. W., and Granbois, D. H., 'Consumer decision making – fact or fiction?', *Journal of Consumer Research*, vol. 6 (September), 1979, pp. 93–100.

31. Duncan, C. P., and Olshavsky, R. W., 'External search: the role of consumer beliefs', *Journal of Marketing Research*, vol. 19 (February), 1982, pp. 32–43.
32. Newman, J. W., 'Consumer external search: amount and determinants', in Woodside A. G., Sheth, J. N., and Bennett, P. D. (eds), *Consumer and Industrial Buying Behavior*, Elsevier North-Holland, New York, 1977, pp. 79–94.
33. Schul, P., and Crompton, J. L., 'Search behavior of international vacationers: travel specific lifestyle and sociodemographic variables', *Journal of Travel Research*, vol. 22, no. 2, 1983, pp. 25–30.
34. Furse, D. H., Punj, G. N., and Stewart, D. W., 'Individual search strategies in new automobile purchases', in Mitchell, A. (ed.), *Advances in Consumer Research*, vol. 9, Association for Consumer Research, Ann Abor, MI, 1981, pp. 379–84.
35. Furse, D. H., Punj, G. N., and Stewart, D. W., 'A typology of individual search strategies among purchases of new automobiles', *Journal of Consumer Research*, vol. 10 (March), 1984, pp. 417–31.
36. Jacoby, J., Chestnut, R. W., Weighl, K. C., and Fisher, W., 'Pre-purchase information acquisition: description of a process methodology, research paradigm and pilot investigation', in Anderson, R. E. (ed.), *Advances in Consumer Research*, vol. 3, Association for Consumer Research, Ann Arbor, MI, 1976, pp. 306–14.
37. Phillips, L. W., and Sternthal, B., 'Age differences in information processing: a perspective on the aged consumer', *Journal of Marketing Research*, vol. 14 (November), 1977, pp. 444–57.
38. Kiel, G. C., and Layton, R. A., 'Dimensions of consumer information seeking', *Journal of Marketing Research*, vol. 18 (May), 1981, pp. 233–9.
39. Biehal, G. J., 'Consumers' prior experiences and perceptions in auto repair choice', *Journal of Marketing*, vol. 47 (Summer), 1983, pp. 82–91.
40. Alba, J. W. and Hutchinson, J. W., 'Dimensions of consumer expertise', *Journal of Consumer Research*, vol. 13 (March), 1987, pp. 411–54.
41. Bettman, J. R., *An Information Processing Theory of Consumer Choice*, Addison-Wesley, Reading, MA, 1979.
42. Punj, G. N., and Staelin, R., 'A model of consumer information search behavior for new automobiles', *Journal of Consumer Research*, vol. 9 (March), 1983, pp. 366–80.
43. Bettman, J. R., and Park, C. W., 'Effects of prior knowledge and experience and phase of the choice process on consumer decision processes: a protocol analysis', *Journal of Consumer Research*, vol. 7 (December), 1980, pp. 234–48.
44. Bloch, P. H., 'Involvement beyond the purchase process: conceptual issues and empirical investigation', in Mitchell, A. (ed.), *Advances in Consumer Research*, vol. 9, Association for Consumer Research, Ann Arbor, MI, 1981, pp. 413–17.
45. Vaughn, R., 'How advertising works: a planning model', *Journal of Advertising Research*, vol. 20 (October), 1980, pp. 27–33.
46. Krugman, H. E., 'The impact of television advertising: learning without involvement', *Public Opinion Quarterly*, vol. 29 (Fall), 1965, pp. 349–56.
47. Slama, M. E., and Tashchian, A., 'Selected socio-economic and demographic characteristics associated with purchasing involvement', *Journal of Marketing*, vol. 49 (Winter), 1985, pp. 72–82.
48. Lastovicka, J. L., and Gardner, D. M., 'Components of involvement' in Maloney, J. C., and Silverman, B. (eds), *Attitude Research Plays for High Stakes*, American Marketing Association, Chicago, IL, 1979, 53–73.

49. Laurent, G., and Kapferer, J. N., 'Measuring consumer involvement profiles', *Journal of Marketing Research*, vol. 22 (February), 1985, pp. 41–53.

50. Bloch, P. H. and Richins, M. L., 'A theoretical model for the study of product importance perceptions', *Journal of Marketing*, vol. 47 (Summer), 1983, pp. 69–81.

51. Solomon, M. R., 'The role of products as social stimuli: a symbolic interactionism perspective', *Journal of Consumer Research*, vol. 10 (December), 1983, pp. 319–29.

52. Bauer, R. A., 'Consumer behaviour as risk taking', in Hancock, R. S. (ed.), *Dynamic Marketing for a Changing World*, American Marketing Association, Chicago, IL, 1960, pp. 389–98.

53. Stem, D. E., Lamb, C. W., and Maclachlan, D. L., 'Perceived risk: a synthesis', *European Journal of Marketing*, vol. 11, no. 4, 1977, pp. 312–19.

54. Athola, O. T., 'An empirical investigation of the evaluative aspect of certainty/uncertainty' in Olson, J. C. (ed.), *Advances in Consumer Research*, vol. 7, Association for Consumer Research, Ann Arbor, MI, 1979, pp. 345–9.

55. Cheron, E. J., and Brent Richie, J. R., 'Leisure activities and perceived risk', *Journal of Leisure Research*, vol. 14, no. 2, 1982, pp. 139–54.

56. Grashof, J. F., and Dixon, D. F., 'The household: the "proper" model for research into purchasing and consumption behavior', in Olson, J. C. (ed.), *Advances in Consumer Research*, vol. 7, Association for Consumer Research, Ann Arbor, MI, 1979, pp. 486–91.

57. Heffring, M. P., 'Measuring family decision making: problems and prospects', in Olson, J. C. (ed.), *Advances in Consumer Research*, vol. 7, Association for Consumer Research, Ann Arbor, MI, 1979, pp. 492–8.

58. Jenkins, R. L., 'Contributions of theory to the story of family decision-making', in Olson, J. C. (ed.), *Advances in Consumer Research*, vol. 7, Association for Consumer Research, Ann Arbor, MI, 1979, pp. 207–11.

59. Davis, H. L., and Rigaux, B. P., 'Perception of marital roles in decision processes', *Journal of Consumer Research*, vol. 1 (June), 1974, pp. 51–61.

60. Burns, A. L., and Granbois, D. H., 'Advancing the study of family purchase decision making', in Olson, J. C. (ed.), *Advances in Consumer Research*, vol. 7, Association for Consumer Research, Ann Arbor, MI, 1979, pp. 221–6.

61. Holman, T. B., and Epperson, A., 'Family and leisure: a review of the literature with research recommendations', *Journal of Leisure Research*, vol. 16, no. 4, 1984, pp. 277–94.

62. Davis, H. L., 'Decision making within the household', *Journal of Consumer Research*, vol. 3 (March), 1976, pp. 241–60.

63. Fletcher, K., 'Search behaviour: an analysis of information collection and usage during the decision process', PhD thesis, Department of Marketing, University of Strathclyde, 1986.

64. Hansen, F., 'Psychological theories of consumer choice', *Journal of Consumer Research*, vol. 3 (December), 1976, pp. 117–42.

65. Johnson, E. J., and Russo, J. E., 'Product familiarity and learning new information', in Monroe, K. (ed.), *Advances in Consumer Research*, vol. 8, Association for Consumer Research, Ann Arbor, MI, 1980, pp. 151–5.

66. Russo, J. E., and Johnson, E. J., 'What do consumers know about familiar products?', in Olson, J. C. (ed.), *Advances in Consumer Research*, vol. 7, Association for Consumer Research, Ann Arbor, MI, 1979, pp. 417–23.

67. Beattie, A. E., 'Effects of product knowledge on comparison, memory, evaluation, and choice: a model of expertise in consumer decision-making', in Mitchell, A. (ed.), *Advances in Consumer Research*, vol. 9, Association for Consumer Research, Ann Arbor, MI, 1981, pp. 336–40.

68. Biehal, G., and Chakravarti, D., 'Exploring memory processes in consumer choice', in Mitchell, A. (ed.), *Advances in Consumer Research*, vol. 9, Association for Consumer Research, Ann Arbor, MI, 1981, pp. 65–73.

69. Biehal, G., and Chakravarti, D., 'Information accessibility as a moderator of consumer choice', *Journal of Consumer Research*, vol. 10 (June), 1983, pp. 1–14.

70. Fletcher, K., 'Evaluation and choice as a satisficing process', *Journal of Marketing Management*, vol. 3, no. 1, 1987, pp. 13–23.

71. Bettman, J. R., 'A functional analysis of the role of overall evaluation of alternatives in choice processes', in Mitchell, A. (ed.), *Advances in Consumer Research*, vol. 9, Association for Consumer Research, Ann Arbor, MI, 1981, pp. 87–93.

72. Park, C. W., Lessig, V. P., and Merrill, J. R., 'The elusive role of price in brand choice behavior', in Mitchell, A. (ed.), *Advances in Consumer Research*, vol. 9, Association for Consumer Research, Ann Arbor, MI, 1981, pp. 201–4.

73. Monroe, K. B., and Petroshius, S. M., 'Buyers' perceptions of price: an update of the evidence', in Kassarjian, H. H., and Robertson, T. S. (eds), *Perspectives in Consumer Behavior*, Scott Foresman, Glenview, IL, 1981.

74. Spiro, R. L., 'Persuasion in family decision-making', *Journal of Consumer Research*, vol. 9 (March), 1983, pp. 393–402.

75. Belch, M. A., Belch, G. E., and Sciglimpaglia, D., 'Conflict in family decision making: an exploratory investigation', in Olson, J. C. (ed.), *Advances in Consumer Research*, vol. 7, Association for Consumer Research, Ann Arbor, MI, 1979, pp. 475–9.

76. Belk, R. W., 'Effects of consistency of visible consumption patterns on impression formation', in Olson, J. C. (ed.), *Advances in Consumer Research*, vol. 7, Association for Consumer Research, Ann Arbor, MI, 1979, pp. 365–71.

77. Midgely, D., and Christopher, M., 'Household decision-making', in *Customers in Action*, MCB University Press, Bradford, 1975, pp. 33–73.

78. Belk, R. W., 'Situational variables and consumer behavior', *Journal of Consumer Research*, vol. 2 (December), 1975, pp. 157–64.

79. Granzin, K. L., and Schjelderup, K. H., 'Situation as an influence on anticipated satisfaction', in Mitchell, A. (ed.), *Advances in Consumer Research*, vol. 9, Association for Consumer Research, Ann Arbor, MI, 1981, pp. 234–8.

80. Schenk, C. T., and Holman, R. H., 'A sociological approach to brand choice: the concept of situational self image', in Olson, J. C. (ed.), *Advances in Consumer Research*, vol. 7, Association for Consumer Research, Ann Arbor, MI, 1979, pp. 610–14.

81. LaBarbera, P. A., and Mazursky, A., 'A longitudinal assessment of consumer satisfaction/dissatisfaction: the dynamic aspect of the cognitive process', *Journal of Marketing Research*, vol. 20 (November), 1983, pp. 393–404.

82. Olson, J. C., and Dover, P., 'Effects of expectation creation and disconfirmation on belief elements of cognitive structure', in Anderson, R. E. (ed.), *Advances in Consumer Research*, vol. 3, Association for Consumer Research, Ann Arbor, MI, 1976, pp. 306–14.

83. Nightingale, M., 'Determination and control of quality standards in hospitality services', M.Phil. thesis, Department of Management Studies for Tourism and Hotel Industries, University of Surrey, 1983.

84. Nightingale, M., 'The hospitality industry: defining quality for a quality assurance programme – a study of perceptions', *Service Industries Journal*, vol. 5, no. 1, 1985, pp. 9–22.

85. Burnkrant, R. E., and Cousineau, A., 'Informational and normative social influence in buyer behavior', *Journal of Consumer Research*, vol. 2 (December), 1975, pp. 206–15.
86. LaTour, S. A., and Peat, N. C., 'Conceptual and methodological issues in consumer satisfaction research', in Wilkie, W. (ed.), *Advances in Consumer Research*, vol. 6, Association for Consumer Research, Ann Arbor, MI, 1978, pp. 431–40.
87. LaTour, S. A., and Peat, N. C., 'The role of situationally produced expectations, others' experiences and prior experiences in determining consumer satisfaction', in Olson, J. C. (ed.), *Advances in Consumer Research*, vol. 7, Association for Consumer Research, Ann Arbor, MI, 1979, pp. 588–92.
88. Swan, J. E., and Jones Combs, L., 'Product performance and consumer satisfaction: a new concept', *Journal of Marketing*, vol. 40 (April), 1976, pp. 25–33.
89. Howes, D., and Arndt, J., 'Determining consumer satisfaction through benefit profiling', *European Journal of Marketing*, vol. 13, no. 8, 1979, pp. 284–98.
90. Westbrook, R. A., 'Sources of consumer satisfaction with retail outlets', *Journal of Retailing*, vol. 57, no. 3, 1981, pp. 68–85.
91. McNeal, J. U., 'The concept of consumer satisfaction', *Management Bibliographies and Reviews*, vol. 3, 1977, pp. 231–40.
92. Pizam, A., Neumann, Y., and Reichel, A., 'Dimensions of tourist satisfaction with a destination area', *Annals of Tourism Research*, July/September 1978, pp. 314–22.
93. Lounsbury, J. W., and Hoopes, L. L., 'An investigation of factors associated with vacation satisfaction', *Journal of Leisure Research*, vol. 17, no. 1, 1985, pp. 1–13.
94. Oliver, R. L., 'Effect of satisfaction and its antecedents on consumer preference and intention', in Monroe, K. (ed.), *Advances in Consumer Research*, vol. 8, Association for Consumer Research, Ann Arbor, MI, 1980, pp. 88–93.
95. Westbrook, R. A., and Cote, J. A., 'An exploratory study of non-product related influences upon consumer satisfaction', in Olson, J. C. (ed.), *Advances in Consumer Research*, vol. 7, Association for Consumer Research, Ann Arbor, MI, 1979, pp. 577–81.
96. Woodruff, R. B., Cadotte, E. R., and Jenkins, R. L., 'Modeling consumer satisfaction processes using experience-based norms', *Journal of Market Research*, vol. 20, no. 3, 1983, pp. 296–304.
97. Swan, J. E., and Martin, W. S., 'Testing comparison level and predictive expectations models of satisfaction', in Monroe, K. (ed.), *Advances in Consumer Research*, vol. 8, Association for Consumer Research, Ann Arbor, MI, 1980, pp. 77–82.

THREE

Generating consumer theory

INTRODUCTION

The discussion of hospitality concepts and research evidence in the previous chapters has shown that consumer decision making for hospitality services require further, systematic investigation. In this sense, progress might best be achieved by using theory-generating rather than theory-testing research methods.

This chapter begins by assessing the requirements of consumer theory development, including the selection of appropriate research methods. Following this, the Glaser and Strauss grounded theory method of theory generation is introduced and described. The account refers to procedures for sampling, data collection and categorization, and integration of field data. The chapter concludes with a case study illustration which uses grounded theorizing to uncover patterns of consumer decision making in the UK hotel leisure break market.

SCIENTIFIC PROGRESS AND METHOD IN MARKETING

The potential value of theory development in marketing is frequently underestimated. Foxall[1] asserts that this is because practitioners and applied researchers try to avoid academic speculation. They tend to make unadorned descriptions of marketing phenomena through direct observation and empirical generalizations built up from multiple observations. He believes that, whereas theory and metatheory are widely held to be irrelevant or even obstructive, they are inextricably linked with observation and practice. Baker[2] agrees and notes four essential functions of theory which share concepts familiar to practitioners and academics:

- The means of classifying, organizing and integrating information relevant to the factual world of business.
- A technique of thinking about marketing problems, and a perspective for practical action.
- An analytical tool-kit to be drawn on as appropriate in the solution of marketing problems.
- The possibility to derive, in time, a number of principles, or even laws, of marketing behaviour.

These common areas of interest provide a basis for developing theory which has practical value. Kelly[3] states that theory should possess several qualities: 'A theory may be considered as a way of binding together a multitude of facts so that one may comprehend them at all once. When the theory enables us to make reasonably precise predictions, one may call it scientific.'

In unifying facts into theory, an explicit framework is created within which deductions can be made and future events anticipated. Supported by the work of Kuhn[4] and Popper,[5] Kelly asserts that theory generation should:

- Facilitate the integration of new ideas, and the production of testable hypotheses.
- Provide a better understanding of the phenomena represented by systemizing facts, and facilitate modification in the light of subsequent observations.

The review of general decision models and the cognitive paradigm in Chapter 2 identified a number of shortcomings. Principally, these were the difficulties of operationalizing model concepts and establishing consistent relationships between variables. Foxall[1] summarizes the sustained criticisms as follows:

- Comprehensive models of consumer decision making are often too complex and/or too generalized to test empirically,[6,7] indicating that an alternative approach, located much closer to observable consumer behaviour, is needed.
- Empirical research has often revealed low correlational consistency between decision process components.[8,9,10]
- Consumers are thought to use less information than the cognitive paradigm generally assumes,[11,12] and too much information may actually impede rational decision making.[13,14]
- Sequences other than cognition–affect–conation have been shown to describe more accurately the consumer choice process. For example, the low-involvement hierarchy and alternative views of the learning of brand preferences in response to advertising have been proposed.[15,16]

Foxall argues that the success of the cognitive paradigm has actually impeded various forms of theoretical progress which run contrary to the fundamental assumptions of the paradigm. He suggests that this is because there are so many 'ready-made' explanations which can be inferred for any observed behaviour.

Hunt[17] reviews the marketing literature in order to establish the expectations of theory. He concludes that a formal theory, operating across product classes or fields, would explain all the phenomena within one of the following categories:

- The behaviours of consumers or producers in the context of the exchange.
- The framework within which the exchange occurs.
- The consequences on society of the behaviours of consumers or producers.

According to Arndt[18] the methodological tradition in marketing has hindered the development of consumer theory. He asserts that fragmentation in the subject matter can be explained by the fact that the great majority of studies are non-cumulative, and tend to use reduced-form models or selected constructs which are isolated from consumer behaviour as a whole. He believes that data sources are often selected because they are easily available, and that convenient research and mathematical techniques have been used to analyse 'appealing' behavioural constructs. He concludes:

> Such opportunism and reductionism have subordinated conceptualisation and theory–building to measurement and manipulation of data by high powered statistical tools. This has resulted in a large number of isolated facts, which lack consistency and which are difficult to integrate into formal comprehensive theories . . . there is little doubt that the fragmentation of the subject matter is a symptom of the absence of adequate theoretical underpinnings in the area, which could give direction and meaning to empirical research.

Arndt's analysis of consumer theory development is supported by other critics. Kassarjian[19] agrees that the field of consumer behaviour is more realistically described as 'fragmented' than 'interdisciplinary'. Anderson[20] adds that it is often difficult to determine what problem the research is attempting to solve, or if the solution has any real significance for the advancement of knowledge. He emphasizes three points:

- Too often the focus of theory development is 'relationship studies', where an attempt is made to determine whether an independent and a dependent variable are related.
- There is little serious effort to link the result to an established body of theory.
- Follow-up studies to explore and develop the area are rare.

Anderson concludes that the quantitative approach appears to follow an empiricist model of science, which assumes that if enough scattered facts or relationships are gathered, they will somehow assemble themselves into a coherent body of theory. He advocates a greater commitment to theory-driven research capable of solving both theoretically and commercially significant problems.

Deshpande[21] believes that a broadening of the theoretical tradition is necessary. This is due to the methodological bias evident in new theoretical contributions which use methods more appropriate to theory testing than to theory generation. He suggests that this could be achieved by making greater use of qualitative methods when attempting to generate new theory. This approach may also be more relevant to practitioners who need to understand the social realities of the marketplace in which they operate.

Qualitative approaches to consumer research

Qualitative methods were originally used in market research to uncover subconscious consumer motivations. This work still continues, but of wider interest today is the link between the decision-maker in marketing and advertising and the consumer. The Market Research Society[22] has identified a number of applications which have commercial and theoretical significance in this context:

- The gathering of information about the characteristics of a changing, new or unfamiliar consumer market. The nature of this information requires exploration and discovery using personal interview methods.
- The gathering of information which is too subtle and too complex to be tailored to the structured, standardized techniques and criteria of quantitative research. Typically this might be consumer information about needs and emotions with varied conscious and unconscious motives and influences.
- The gathering of information for advertising purposes which provides a more complex picture than could be achieved using quantitative research. For example, consumer language use and non-verbal behaviour can provide insights about the consumer–media and consumer–product relationship, and about behavioural, emotional and lifestyle patterns associated with product usage.

To summarize, the use of a qualitative methodology offers several distinct advantages. It provides the means of exploring the consumer decision process holistically, and thereby enables the construction of a theoretical framework on which subsequent relationship studies can be based. It also makes the integration of data easier, and is therefore more likely to meet the expectations of marketing theory. The use of qualitative methodology in grounded theory generation is explained in the following section.

Theory generation using qualitative methods

The limited application of qualitative methods in consumer theory generation can be traced to the 1960s. Case studies were not generally considered to be as scientific as statistical methods of investigation because they require subjective interpretation.[23, 24] More recently, the debate has centred on the quality and applicability of the theory generated. These criteria provide a more objective basis for research design than the intrinsic merits of quantitative and qualitative methods.[25]

Theory generated using quantitative methodology requires a deliberate, predetermined focus on specific variables and their assumed relationships. This formula may preclude important variables from the research design if they cannot be accommodated within the analytical framework. In contrast, qualitative data collection techniques are less rigid and more responsive to changes in research direction, although the non-standardized approach can inhibit definition and clarification of research variables and their relationships.[26] Hawker[27] argues that this difficulty can be overcome by carefully documenting the way in which analytical procedures are developed and used during data collection.

The main advantage of qualitative theory generation is that it facilitates closer and more detailed observation within the defined area of research. This is an important consideration in generating consumer theory. Diesing[28] emphasizes this, suggesting that theoretical concepts are more realistic if they are derived from observation rather than abstraction.

There are numerous texts which describe qualitative research techniques and methods, and the recommendations concerning data collection and analysis vary. Most authors describe the use of analytical methods during or after data collection.[29,30,31,32] The approach introduced by Glaser and Strauss[33] involves constant comparision of new data with existing data so that they can be integrated into categories as they are collected. They call this a 'constant comparative method'. It has

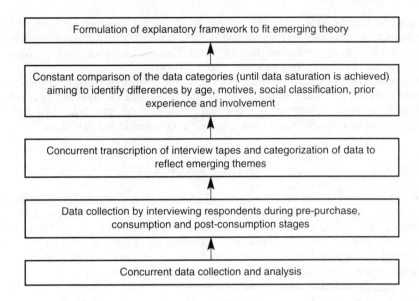

Figure 3.1   An overview of the grounded-theorizing process

the advantage of bringing consistency to the field work through the systematic cross-comparison of data, and ensuring that the emerging theory is centred or 'grounded' in the research observations.

THE DISCOVERY OF GROUNDED THEORY

The term 'grounded theory', meaning the discovery of theory from field data, is derived from the work of Glaser and Strauss,[33] later refined by Glaser.[34] They argue that research potential has been restricted by two much concern for the testing and verification of theories. Their approach to handling quantitative data enables the generation of theoretical explanations as the investigation progresses, although subjective judgement at each stage of theory development is necessary. The purpose of this is to verify the fit between emerging research themes and the situation or events that they represent. An overview of the grounded-theorizing process is shown in Figure 3.1

Sims[35] suggests that the need to make subjective judgement is common to all forms of social enquiry. However, the discipline of the constant comparative method provides effective guidance because of the interrelatedness of the data: 'an observer always has several different kinds of evidence available to him, and can form some impression of the validity of any one of these in the context of the others'.

The credibility of grounded theory is derived from its objective basis which is, wherever possible, free from a priori assumptions and hypotheses which may otherwise 'mask important features of social reality'.[36] The objective of grounded theory, according to Silverman, is to 'seek to mobilise, as an explanatory tool, the categories which the participants themselves use to order their experience'.

To achieve this objective, various methods of data collection may be necessary. These include participant observation, semi-structured or unstructured interviews and the use of case study material. Brown[37] and Trend[38] conclude that each of these methods is well suited to grounded theory generation.

The grounded theory method has been used in a variety of contexts. These include problem construction in organizations[35] and the interaction between hospital nurses and patients' relatives.[27] Other applications of grounded theory[39,40] and methodological developments[41,42] have also been reported in the literature.

Theoretical sampling

Glaser and Strauss use the term 'theoretical sampling' to describe the process of data collection for theory generation. This involves the joint collection, coding and categorizing of data. As the theoretical concepts begin to emerge from the categories, they determine the direction and emphasis of subsequent field work. The purpose is to discover and explore the emerging themes or categories until they become 'saturated'. This occurs when no new category properties or characteristics are evident in the data.

Glaser and Strauss state that initial decisions about data collection should be based on nothing more than a general understanding of the subject or problem area, to avoid imposing a preconceived framework on the research. Glaser later modified this view, conceding that some researchers necessarily begin field work with pre-understanding of the concepts involved. He comments that this is less than completely open, but may be unavoidable. He adds that, in this situation, the researcher should be aware of the possibility of introducing subjective bias during the interpretation of data.

The inductive process of grounded theorizing requires that data are collected and categorized until the theory crystallizes. At this point it can be substantiated from the subject literature, although Glaser believes that insights from the literature may be necessary to guide the early stages of theory development:

> It is vital to read, but in a substantive field different from the research. This maximizes the avoidance of pre-empting, preconceived concepts which may easily detract from the input . . . It is hard enough to generate one's own ideas without the 'rich' derailment provided by the literature in the same field.

Once the field work has commenced, the constant comparative method yields insights which direct theoretical sampling. However, the direction may be complicated by multiple options. If this occurs, Glaser suggests that different approaches should be tried until categories have been identified which reflect the complete data set.

Differences between consumers can be identified by comparing subgroup data. This procedure also enables the progressive focusing of interviews. Glaser and Strauss suggest that data collection should continue until the differences and similarities within and between comparison groups have been established. This process begins with open-ended interviews which gradually become more structured as the researcher becomes aware of the subgroup differences and similarities that exist.

Summarizing the central aspects of theoretical sampling:

- Grounded theory is shaped by emerging categories. These also control the subsequent research direction. This includes the subject matter focus and the selection of respondents.

- Preconceptions about the field of enquiry should be minimized, although theoretical contributions from subject areas other than the one under investigation, provide initial guidance.
- The requirement to saturate the categories by a process of continual data comparison determines the sample size and the duration of field work.
- The emergent theory should possess relevance and 'goodness of fit' in describing the total data set.

Data collection and categorization

In order to investigate patterns of behaviour, Jones[42] asserts that it is necessary to interpret the meaning and significance that consumers attribute to their actions. Drawing from Kelly's work,[3,43] she believes that individuals use a complex personal framework of beliefs and values to categorize, explain and predict events. The ability to make predictions about product suitability corresponds with the function of a decision rule as described in Chapter 2. If the prediction proves to be inaccurate, the framework of beliefs may, as a consequence, need to be modified.

Depth interviewing is an effective way of investigating the consumer's personal construct system. This provides 'the opportunity for the researcher to probe deeply, to uncover new clues, to open up new dimensions of a problem and to secure vivid, accurate, inclusive accounts that are based on personal experience'.[44] The purpose of depth interviewing is to understand the respondent's constructions of reality by seeking explanations and consequences of his or her behaviour. It is important to hear the respondent's interpretation of events rather than make assumptions based on behavioural observations. The Market Research Society supports this approach in situations requiring a 'highly detailed understanding of complicated behaviour or decision-making patterns'.[22] They cite as an example the planning process for a family holiday.

As personal interviews provide an effective way of identifying decision-making activities and consumer reactions to the hotel experience, this method of data collection is an appropriate way of exploring thinking and actions.

The volume and complexity of data generated by using the grounded theory method necessitates the use of an effective coding and categorization procedure. As the data are collected, they need to be compared and coded into as many categories as are applicable. The theory begins to take shape as the categories are gradually defined. Glaser advises of the need for sensitivity during the early stages of categorization because the established framework provides the factual basis of the theory. Ultimately each component category becomes saturated, and can be explained by its properties or characteristics. The theory finally becomes integrated when the relationships between categories are understood.

Turner[39,41] emphasizes the importance of being well organized during the period of data collection. This involves ensuring that field notes are chronologically ordered and easily retrievable. He discusses three aspects of data recording, involving the continual processes of note writing, category discovery and definition. He uses notes to comment on the content and context of interview data, recording events, impressions and interactions with respondents. He refers to category discovery as the process of moving from data to a category. This requires a variety of data giving nominal definition, theoretical meaning and substantive content to the category. He suggests that this information about categories can be held on separate cards for ease of use.

According to Bailyn[45] the way in which the researcher organizes and responds to emerging themes in the data is critical. As data collection, comparison and categorization are concurrent activities, the researcher can easily be overwhelmed by the data. The objective should be to balance these activities in such a way that they stimulate rather than impede conceptualization. This has two implications:

- The period of data collection should permit the research to proceed sequentially, and allow sufficient time for preliminary analysis and conceptualization.
- As the analytical process is slow, it may be necessary to re-examine data gathered at different stages of the field work. The need for backward reflection is most likely to arise when categories are close to saturation, and during the formulation of theoretical propositions.

Bulmer[46] argues that theory generation requires the discipline of observing patterns in the data and making them intelligible.

Turner[39] suggests that this involves converting 'concepts which are built covertly into any descriptive account of the world' into theoretical categories which can be rigorously examined and defined. However, the categories by themselves do not explain the differences in the consumer's cognitive structure which influence decision-making behaviour. In order to elaborate the grounded theory categories, further analysis is often desirable. This can be undertaken using a cognitive modelling procedure derived from Kelly's personal construct theory. An explanation and brief illustration of this technique is given in Chapter 4.

CASE STUDY: CONSUMER DECISION MAKING IN THE UK HOTEL LEISURE BREAK MARKET

A prominent feature of product development in the hospitality industry during the 1980s was the integration of a wider range and type of consumer services. The hotel short break product (or leisure break) exemplifies this trend, with catering and leisure activity components packaged with two or three nights' accommodation at an inclusive price. As there are many choice options available, and the investment cost is higher than for non-residential hospitality services, the consumer decision process might be expected to vary according to factors such as the level of perceived risk and the extent of prior experience with the product category. The case study aims to illustrate the discovery of theory from data collected using the grounded-theorizing approach. After an explanation of the method, explanations given by consumers are used to elaborate the key dynamics and interactions of decision making in this market.

Method

The case study material is extracted from a longitudinal study conducted over a three-year period, utilizing participant observation and personal interviewing techniques. Interviews were conducted with leisure break consumers in their homes, at their places of work and at hotels throughout the UK. The interviews were semi-structured in format with direction provided by themes emerging from the constant comparison of field data.

As noted above, theoretical sampling requires the constant comparison of data during field work in order to develop and substantiate data categories. The purpose of this is to identify similarities and differences between respondents and to facilitate integrated theory development. In order to undertake constant comparison, it is necessary to identify appropriate measures or groups which can be used to differentiate the data.

The need to identify the expectations of consumer subgroups is a common requirement in most product fields. The conventional response is to segment the marketplace by defining specific target groups of consumers, and positioning products and services accordingly. A key objective is to find the most effective way of differentiating the target groups.

Wind[47] observes that two methods are commonly used in commercial segmentation practice to estimate segment size and consumer demographic, socioeconomic and psychographic characteristics:

- A priori segmentation design – in which managers predetermine the basis for segmentation. Examples include product purchase, brand loyalty and customer type.
- A clustering-based segmentation design – in which segments are determined in relation to particular variables such as perceived benefits, needs and attitudes.

Wind believes that theoretical and commercial approaches to segmentation can be integrated by 'narrowing the gap between the academically oriented research on segmentation and the real-world application of segmentation research'. This view emphasizes the importance of consumer classification based on actual market behaviour and personal characteristics, as suggested by Lunn,[48,49] whereby:

- Market or direct classification is concerned with ownership, purchase and usage behaviour or product-related behaviour.
- Personal or indirect classification is concerned with consumer demographics, geographical differences and psychosociological characteristics which embrace traits such as personality, life-cycle stage and product-oriented consumer values.

Lunn argues that consumer research data may be misleading if they are presented in aggregate form, since the 'universal product' and the 'average consumer' are atypical. The method of classification should therefore facilitate explanation of the market structure, consumer subgroups and market gaps that exist. He concludes that a specific, market-related basis for classification may be more useful and relevant than an indirect method because of the growing concern for precise and sensitive measures of consumer behaviour. In this context, qualitative research has an important role in generating explanatory theory.

Indirect measures: age and estimated socioeconomic group

The study used both direct and indirect comparison group measures to categorize the field data. The indirect measures were predetermined in order to assess the representativeness of the sample, but the direct measures were not defined until the early stages of data collection. At this point they were adopted because it was apparent that they had the potential to provide effective comparison group measures.

The theoretical sampling procedure was guided throughout by the indirect comparison groups of age and estimated socioeconomic group membership. Published statistics for the hotel leisure break market had indicated the predominance of consumers in the age range 35–54, with a socioeconomic profile of A, B or C1,[50] and these statistics were reflected in the sample. It must be noted, however, that there is increasing dissatisfaction with the accuracy of socioeconomic measures in the research literature. The main criticism is that classification is often interpreted in a subjective way, and can be misleading because of this. For instance, socioeconomic grade is defined by occupation, but could also be interpreted as measuring income, social values or lifestyle.

Direct measures: motives, prior product experience and involvement

Evidence that leisure activities are often goal oriented[51,52,53] indicates that motives are likely to play an important role in the consumer decision process for hospitality and tourism services. If, for example, a consumer is unable to take a summer holiday, the leisure break may assume more importance. However, in other circumstances, such as using a break in conjunction with business travel, the consumer may not attribute the same significance to hotel selection because the purpose of the break is more routine.

The importance of two related variables, prior product experience and involvement, was noted in the research literature. Fifty-eight per cent of the respondents were experienced hotel users, and the remaining 42 per cent has little or no prior experience of the type and standard of hotel accommodation featured in the collaborating company's leisure break programme. The degree of commitment to, and involvement in, the product category is also thought to play an important role during the decision process. High involvement is characterized by extensive pre-purchase activity, and may be linked to antecedents such as perceptions of product importance, risk, symbolic or sign value and hedonic or emotional considerations.[54]

Study findings

The study findings are presented in the form of an overview of the consumer decision process, which illustrates the key themes emerging from the data categorization using the constant comparative method. The case study is summarized by referring back to the hypothetical decision process model presented in Chapter 1, and by reporting on the empirical support emerging from the data categories for the research statements contained in Chapter 2.

Pre-purchase decision making

The role of motives

A six-part classification of primary motives was derived from the field data. All of the respondents identified at least one of the following as their primary reason for taking a leisure break:

1.   To coincide with attending a pre-arranged event.
2.   In response to the need for a break from family/domestic commitments/routine problems/employment-related pressures.

3. In response to a desire to relax/recover in different/comfortable/surroundings.
4. In response to a desire to visit a particular town/region/hotel/somewhere new.
5. To compensate for a missed summer (main) holiday opportunity.
6. For the specific benefits derived from taking short breaks on a regular/seasonal basis.

The findings indicate that motives exert a strong influence on pre-purchase behaviour, but that other factors may intervene and mediate behaviour.[55] For instance, the link between motives and perceived risk may be influenced by the extent of prior experience with the product category. If a family has for some reason had to forgo their summer holiday, they may be expected to undertake a detailed investigation of the leisure break alternatives because of the compensatory role which may be attributed to the break. If, however, a member of the family is an experienced hotel user, hotel selection may be made quickly and confidently despite the perceived importance of the purchase occasion.

In Chapter 1, the characteristics of hospitality services were identified from the different perspectives of the consumer and the producer. The needs and expectations of the consumer were subdivided according to whether they were of a physical or psychological nature. The findings support this interpretation, which is illustrated below.

Motives associated with physical needs

Physical needs are easily identified and understood because they relate to specific symptoms such as tiredness, fatigue and stress. Several of the many variations of physical need influencing the desire to take a leisure break holiday are illustrated in the following extracts.

Primary motives are frequently associated with sources of tension and fatigue at work and in the home:

> I rarely get a chance to spoil myself. I work shifts, I work weekends, I work Christmas days . . . now and again I just like to relax in something completely different, and have total comfort . . .

Women are often more critical of the hotel experience than men. This can be explained by the domestic substitution role that the hotel must fulfil:

> for me it's a break, not so much for my husband because he's used to going out – it's part of his job, but for myself stuck at home, it is rather nice to go out and have a meal cooked for me and to be entertained . . .

Hotel leisure breaks may be used as 'recovery periods' or as an integral part of family life:

> we arrived today at 3.15 p.m. and I think we were in the pool at 3.45 p.m. I think that life today is very much for families to be together . . .

Motives associated with psychological needs

Although consumers may recognize the physical needs for a change of environment, they may also be motivated by particular psychological benefits which they expect to derive from the consumption experience. These are typically more complex and difficult for the consumer to understand and articulate. For example, the consumer may experience a feeling of well-being and security in a luxurious hotel environment:

> just the nice feeling you get whenever you walk through the place, all the walnut on the walls – it looks real walnut, it gives me a nice secure feeling. I think really that it's the sort of hotel you would stay at if you had unlimited money . . .

Consumers may also expect the hotel to provide a natural extension of their current standard of living. In this context the quality and condition of hotel furnishings and fittings may have symbolic meaning and invoke a particular psychological reaction:

> the quality of the fabric, it's a nice entrance . . . it does really make you feel good, and that's what it's all about . . . we all want for better things, we've all got nice places and nice clothes, but it's when you come into nice surroundings that you feel a lot better . . .

Although most consumers are motivated by the need to reduce the level of work-related stress they may be experiencing, or to alleviate boredom with the domestic routine, a short break may be used to focus on a particular decision or business problem:

> I wanted to get away at this time because I've got another business project that I might be buying into, in fact I might be buying outright. A rather big business, and there's an awful lot of money involved, and I just want some time to toss it around in my mind.

The primary motive may exert a strong influence on the desired type and timing of the leisure break holiday, but it is difficult to assess the effect on the decision process, or the impact of secondary motives which may be present. This is due to the inherent complexity of the motives themselves, and to the problems associated with uncovering them, as shown in Figure 3.2. It is therefore necessary to concentrate on identifying differences attributable to reported behaviour during the decision process stages of pre-purchase, consumption and post-consumption evaluation.

Consumer perceptions and the interpretation of product information

The provision of product information is an issue of some importance to consumers, who often seek tangible assurance that they are making an appropriate hotel choice. The key concerns are summarized in Figure 3.3.

The general expectation is that the brochure should provide all the necessary information. However, this has to be achieved without creating the impression that the brochure is too complicated, since this may discourage retailers and consumers from using the brochure:

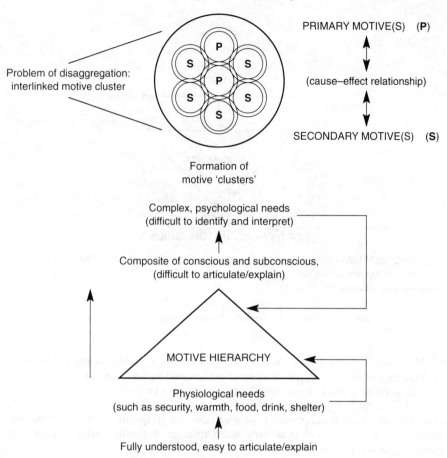

Figure 3.2 Purchase motive dynamics

you open it up and it's easy to follow, straight away you look and there's a map of England, and you've got all the hotels . . . it basically tells you all you want to know on that first page . . . I do read these pages before going any further . . .

A frequent observation is that hotels featured on a full page or more of the brochure are more attractive because they help to reduce the sense of uncertainty that the consumer may be feeling:

[On the brochure text]   To me it's the only criteria you go on, pictures do help, but without a detailed description . . . all the hotels basically offer the same core facilities, it's that extra detail that will make the diference between choosing one hotel or another.

Consumers may have some difficulty in positioning the image associations conveyed by brochures and other sources of information. If, however, the received impressions are reinforced by experience, the outcome may be an enduring sense of confidence in the brand:

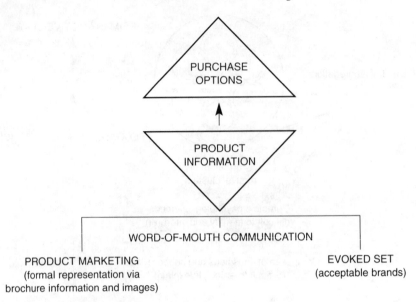

Figure 3.3 Product information influences during the pre-purchase stage

> It's a very positive image. When I first came down here, I thought they were expensive hotels . . . it's a very up-market logo, and it projects in the rooms and the feeling we have is that it's the standard we're going to keep with . . .

Incomplete or ambiguous product information is a frequent source of frustration for consumers, who often feel that they must engage in further information-gathering activities in order to satisfy their needs:

> The amount of information you get in advance enables you to make the most of the short break . . . There's nothing to tell you how to get there, or the best way of getting there, nothing about the hotel or the facilities of the hotel . . . it's sold as a package, but it doesn't have the trimmings that you would expect in a package.

The possible consequences of inadequate information are illustrated by the observations of an experienced hotel user:

> There are three places to take breakfast at this hotel at different prices . . . I would have thought that somebody unused to this kind of hotel would be slightly daunted by it all . . . if you don't know the ropes it's an extremely humiliating experience . . . people tend to hide away, and not like to say anything, and be quite unsure about what they can have, and can't have.

Word-of-mouth recommendations and risk reduction

The perceived complexity and intangibility of the hotel consumption experience suggests that consumers often need the added security of product recommendations (or cautions) from experienced hotel users:

It's very difficult to make your product stand out from somebody else's . . . I think that you've got to have a high standard of product and maintain it . . . you can do 99.9 per cent of it right, and you don't get that many mentions, people say 'Yes, that was good' – but they expect it to be good, and you get 0.1 per cent that's bad and that goes round very quickly.

Word-of-mouth communications are widely used in business communities to solve problems. For example, the cost and availability of accommodation in London is considered to be a re-occurring problem, requiring a continuous exchange of information:

staying overnight in London, how can you reduce the costs of doing so . . . it's a topic of conversation constantly . . . One is aware that you can find deals, the question is finding the right one.

When consumers feel that they have insufficient information, they may feel that they have to seek specialist advice. This is another commonly occurring source of frustration, especially if the retailer is unfamiliar with the brand:

[On a request made at the travel agency for information about the hotel] she wasn't familiar with it. She had the brochure, but I asked her several questions and she couldn't tell me anything.

A feeling of uncertainty is often more easily resolved by telephoning central or hotel reservations staff or by talking to an experienced hotel user, when received word-of-mouth recommendations can have an influential role in hotel selection:

the lady I used to work for had been here before and so that stuck in my mind . . . I don't know if I would have picked it otherwise, just on the description . . .

Product recommendations are seldom given unreservedly by experienced hotel users. This is because they recognize that the consumption situation is unpredictable:

it's a tricky thing recommending hotels, it's like recommending food or theatre – people have different anticipations, what's acceptable to me may not be acceptable to you.

The knowledge that subjective assessment of hotels will vary from one individual to another may cause consumers to identify situations where recommendations are less helpful, or even of no perceived value:

I would never take [a recommendation] for a main holiday . . . I've done that before and people have said 'Don't go there, it's an awful place' but their idea of a holiday is not necessarily my idea of a holiday . . .

The influence of prior product experience on choice behaviour

The term 'evoked set' describes the criteria used by the consumer to evaluate choice options. The evoked set consists of product attributes and brands which are important to the consumer, to the extent that an overall evaluation of the alternatives may be

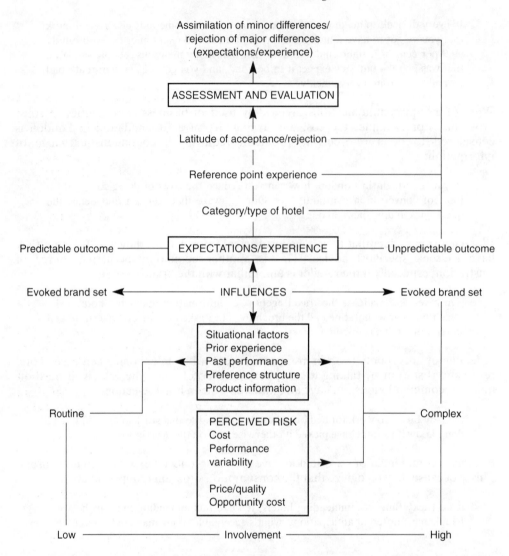

Figure 3.4 The role of decision rules

retained in long-term memory. In such situations assessment by individual attributes becomes unnecessary, since the consumer would be able to select the individual alternative with the highest perceived overall rating. These guidelines represent a form of decision rule, which may be influenced by prior experience and comparative product analysis. The factors influencing the formulation and application of a decision rule are shown in Figure 3.4.

Consumers often assess hotels or their attributes by using the closest comparison they are able to recall. Situational factors may, however, account for variations in the decision rule criteria:

[On comparisons between hotels] not that this hotel's better than that one, you just observe differences in situations if you comment on them . . . I think what you mainly remember are negatives . . . if you have a feeling that it's a reasonable standard and a reasonable price, that's fine . . .

Although choice criteria may be numerous, comparative assessment using a predetermined reference standard may have a strong influence on the development and application of a decision rule. This is because the latitude of acceptance narrows as new experience are assimilated, and the consumer's ability to differentiate between the suitability of choice option improves. More experienced consumers are able to equate acceptance with a wider experience-based understanding of hotel standards:

We've basically developed standards of hotels now . . . it has been a learning experience and the only way you can learn is to . . . you don't have to stay in the extremes but to stay in either something that's at the same level or below it or above it until you know where you are.

The interactive role of prior product experience and involvement

There are a number of factors which may influence the search and selection strategy used by the consumer prior to making a purchase decision. These include the extent of product-related experience and the degree of perceived risk associated with the decision. Ultimately, the strategy adopted by the consumer will depend upon how difficult the task is perceived to be, and how much effort and attention will be required to make an acceptable choice between purchase alternatives. A typology of three distinctive strategies – high, moderate and low involvement – was derived from an assessment of the extent and duration of pre-purchase behaviour. The characteristics of high and low levels of involvement are exemplified below.

High-involvement decision making

High-involvement behaviour is characterized by an extensive or prolonged period of search, with special importance attached to selection criteria and/or performance expectations:

[On brochure assessment procedure] We looked through them more than once or twice, we looked through them quite a lot, we marked hotels we liked on the basis of what we thought, and the text, 'No, no not that one, this one sounds all right, put a star next to it' and then we went back looking through them, to decide.

Associated activities may include telephone calls to verify information, and the consultation of intermediaries such as travel agents as well as friends, relatives and colleagues with relevant hotel experience. The final selection will be based on a careful assessment of the information gathered:

I would have phoned anyway to try and find out what the hotel was like . . . if you've phoned and found out, and it's not right, you can say 'I phoned you and you said this . . .' But if you don't phone and make contact, you've no come back.

I like to find out as much as I can. By speaking to a receptionist, you can really work out what the staff are like. If the receptionist is polite and friendly, the staff will be normally polite and friendly . . . if someone is rude towards you, you back off, don't you? If someone is warm and friendly, you come forward.

Low-involvement decision making

Low-involvement behaviour is characterized by a limited formal information search, or in some cases by none at all. Associated activities might include reference to intermediary or company information, but they more usually concentrate on obtaining brochures:

> My friends had the brochure . . . an internal sight means nothing to me at all, because I know quite readily just how easy it is to set up a photograph to give an entirely different impression . . . the friends we came with had already been here before and they said they liked it very much. They said to us that they were sure we would like it when we came down here.

Any references to selection criteria or performance expectations are likely to be assertions relating to prior knowledge or established facts:

> we have in the past got together quite a number of different brochures for different hotels . . . we've never really found anything in them that we could say would distinguish one form of hotel from another . . . usually we finish up by saying 'That is precisely where we would like to stay and it just so happens that this is the hotel nearest to it, let's try it.'

The purchase decision is likely to be dominated by personal decision-making confidence acquired from prior experience:

> it's four star . . . so you expect somewhere nice . . . I think that tells you that it's a good hotel, because it has to be to warrant its star rating, so we tend to look for things like that . . .

Role specialization is often more evident when a low-involvement strategy is used. Female-dominant activities typically begin with responsibility for initiating discussions about the timing of the break, and extend to information gathering and the screening of options:

> [On decision-making roles]   It has varied tremendously over the years, there is no way in which I could pay any pattern to it, but it's usually a higher proportion of my wife's decisions to get away . . . she says to me 'Where shall we go?' and I make several suggestions, and then we pick one . . .

The main exception to the pattern of female dominance in family decision making occurs when the male partner has extensive business travel experience of hotels. In discussions concerning familiar hotels or destinations, a higher proportion of male-dominant decisions are likely to occur:

> [On male dominance in selecting a London hotel]   I would choose it because I

know the hotel scene in London reasonably well . . . she would leave it to me on the grounds that I knew my way around a bit more . . . I would say 'Who does deals to London for a weekend? . . . let's have a look at the hotels they offer . . .'

In summary, consumers using a high-involvement strategy typically engage in extensive search to satisfy their selection criteria and/or performance expectations because they have limited prior experience of hotels. More experienced consumers may also engage in high-involvement behaviour when they attach special importance to the purchase decision.

More experienced hotel users, or consumers who feel less concerned about the return on investment risk associated with the purchase decision, will adopt a moderate or low-involvement profile. These groups of consumers may consult intermediaries during information search, but they more usually make a decision based on their own brochure appraisal. The greater the degree of confidence with which the decision is made, the more likely it is that the consumer is using an established decision rule to guide his or her choice.

Figure 3.5 highlights the differences between consumers with extensive and limited prior experience respectively, in relation to typical pre-purchase search and selection behaviour.

PRIOR PRODUCT EXPERIENCE

	Extensive	Limited
PRE-PURCHASE INFLUENCES	Established procedures for product classification and categorization facilitate close links between selection and assessment	Expectations derived from product information and personal recommendations shape assessment criteria

Figure 3.5 Extensive and limited experience in pre-purchase decision making

The purchase decision

In many cases, consumers reach a decision to purchase despite residual feelings of uncertainty. In these circumstances, the administration and the interpersonal contacts which occur during the transaction assume particular importance for the consumer. The transaction represents the initial contact with the product, during which uncertainty may be reduced or increased depending on the nature of the service encounter. If the reservation is made by telephone, most consumers expect to receive a confirmation, together with ancillary details such as directions on how to find the hotel, and further information on the services provided. Inadequacies in this provision may give rise to a renewed sense of anxiety, and may be interpreted as service inefficiency:

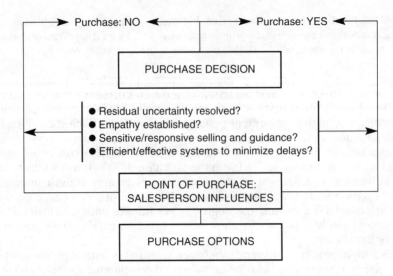

Figure 3.6   Point-of-purchase and salesperson effects

[On the booking confirmation]   there wasn't any cohesion to it, no package, unlike when you book a holiday abroad, there was nothing to give the hotel, which I felt slightly uneasy about. I had visions of arriving at the hotel and them saying 'I'm sorry, we've got no record of you, who are you, where's your voucher?' . . . we always felt a bit nervous about the arrangement, it didn't seem to be very efficient.

The critical role of the interpersonal contacts, especially by telephone, becomes apparent when an unhelpful of obstructive response occurs. The consumer may react by discounting the hotel or even hotel group at the pre-purchase stage. If, however, a reservation has already been made, the level of anxiety is likely to increase:

[On an attempt to make a restaurant reservation in advance by telephone]   I said 'Can we book for Saturday night?' 'We don't take bookings' and I said 'On the voucher it says it's advisable to book' . . . 'We don't take bookings, we don't take bookings!' and that was all I got back. That did annoy me, and when I put the phone down, I did make some comments about it . . . It made me hesitant.

Point-of-purchase contact and salesperson effects are shown in Figure 3.6.

Consumption experiences

The role of assessment criteria during consumption

In Chapter 1, the complex nature of the consumption environment for hospitality services was identified. Figure 1.1 shows the service delivery continuum, ranging from limited staff discretion over a short time period, to extensive staff discretion over a long time period. Whenever consumption occurs over a long time period – several days or more in the case of hotel leisure breaks – the consumer faces the difficult task of assessing many successive experiences to evaluate overall product satisfaction. For

PRIOR PRODUCT EXPERIENCE

	Extensive	**Limited**
CONSUMPTION ASSESSMENTS	Clearly defined role responsibilities and experience-based assessment criteria facilitate rapid and confident assessment	Imprecise role responsibilities and uncertainty about appropriate assessment criteria lead to greater dependence on the home as a basis for assessment

Figure 3.7   Extensive and limited experience in consumption assessments

consumers with limited prior experience the task is more difficult, as Figure 3.7 indicates, because role responsibilities for assessment are imprecise, assessment criteria are less certain and performance expectations are unrealistic or unknown.

The focal concern of the consumption stage is to determine how consumers use preconceived expectations and assessment criteria to measure the various aspects of product performance, both during consumption and at the post-consumption stage. The findings suggest that the consumer is able to integrate many individual assessments within a personal rating system capable of providing a moving average measure of satisfaction.

By comparing perceived ideal-product attribute ratings with experience, the consumer is able to undertake a form of cost–benefit analysis to assess 'value for money' in relation to the services received. If expectations are experience based, they may facilitate comparison against particular reference standards, enabling the consumer to assess whether the experience falls above or below their reference point standard:

> [On comparison with other recent hotel experiences]   So far there hasn't been anything that's below the standard of other hotels we've stayed at, everything is just fine.

> invariably you can find some sort of fault, or something you don't like, it's not up to your usual standards or something like that . . . but I must say that so far here, everything's been very good . . . it's the best standard of service, food and comfort that I've come across . . . you're talking about Intercontinental Hotels and places like that . . .

> I think if anybody came here first, they would come back again . . . we've compared everything with this.

The consumption environment and design effects

Atmospheric associations with physical design features sometimes described as 'warm' or 'cold' can have a powerful subconscious impact on the consumer:

> the size of a hotel seems to make no difference whatsoever . . . we've been into some hotels which are vast, and have been very happy. Others have been much smaller and like a mortuary, and I have said that this is so cold that I don't want to stay here very long . . . I think that if the hotel is cold, then the staff are cold . . .

> [On business hotel use] you're anticipating a cold situation anyway, inherently when you're on business, and you're not looking for any extraneous comforts . . . if you come into a hotel room and it's cold and it's unattractive, and your bathroom's not very nice, you finish up by saying well the best thing I can do is to jump straight into bed and ignore everything else and hope it goes away by the morning!

Although guest room assessments are subjective and therefore unpredictable, design features can be planned to convey personality and warmth. For example, the effective use of light and space will create an immediate and favourable effect:

> One of the things we generally notice is whether there are mirrors down near the entrance to the room to catch the light . . . it makes it very much more attractive . . .

> we usually find that when we come across a room set-up which is not symmetrical . . . it's far more receptive, more pleasing than if it was literally a rectangular box . . .

> what we actually said to each other was that they'd virtually thought of everything . . . it makes you feel that the people running the place are caring about it . . .

The consumer may use a formalized procedure to assess guest room facilities and standards. In this context, role specialization during assessment is commonplace, and female assessment can be rigorous, including checks for cleanliness and quality on bedding, fabrics, furnishings and fittings:

> [On female guest room assessment] I look at the towels to see how soft they are, and I sit on the bed to see what that's like . . . [Husband] I checked the electrics out . . . you obviously have to make sure that everything works, because if you're going to make any complaints, you do it the minute you get into the room, and not the next day . . .

> I think we got there and we automatically went round the room, and looked at beds, television, bathroom and things like that . . . you don't actually say it out loud, you sum it up yourselves . . .

The most widely used reference point for gauging the acceptability of the hotel, and more particularly the guest room, is the home:

> I feel when you go to an hotel it's got to be at least as good as your own home. In general décor, warmth or coolness, the atmosphere, the fittings in the rooms, the bathroom cleanliness. Things like that have got to be as good otherwise there's no point in going to a hotel.

A common expectation is that the hotel should be able to provide all of the facilities enjoyed in the home and more besides. If this expectation is not met, the consumer may feel unwelcome because the environment is perceived to be uncaring:

> if we go into a room that isn't well decorated . . . it's like the hotel doesn't care about the guests . . . you don't spend a lot of time in the hotel usually . . . but you

want a room that's going to be nice and give you a warm, welcome feeling. That's why you try to do in your home to make your guests welcome, and that's the philosophy a hotel should have.

The assessment of hotel services

The labour-intensive provision of hotel services is difficult to monitor and control, a problem that is widely recognized by experienced hotel users:

You could come into contact with fifteen or twenty staff on a weekend like this. Nineteen of them could be spot on, and one who was off-hand could tip the balance, especially if it's your initial greeting.

the sort of thing that one tends to notice is whether the staff are happy in their work or not, whether they're smiling and what kind of reception you receive . . . You can tell straight away in their voices whether they're happy in their work or not.

Service delivery is often beyond the influence or control of the consumer. If service expectations are not fulfilled, the outcome is likely to be strong consumer dissatisfaction:

We did have a problem last night. The room was far too hot, we couldn't sleep and we just couldn't seem to control the heating . . . We phoned up the hall porter and he wasn't very tactful . . . He said 'The only thing you can do is open the windows' . . . I said 'it's not very satisfactory' and he said 'Oh well, good night sir' and put the phone down. I held on to the phone . . . I was stupefied. I could have come storming down at that point . . . I thought this is dreadful, there's no way I'm ever coming back here. I think this morning I could have come downstairs and demanded my money back and left, but I don't want to spoil my weekend, everything else is fine.

Personal rating systems

In recognizing the complexity of the consumption situation, which may involve service interactions over a time period of 48 hours or more, the consumer develops a personal rating system which stores assessments as they occur:

[On assessment procedures]   I think it starts from the very beginning, and either builds or detracts . . . you come in and you've accepted the hotel because it looks appealing, and from then on the experiences you have either build on that or they detract from it, so when you finally leave, you say 'I wouldn't want to go back there again' or 'We'd like to come back here sometime'.

we were greeted by the doorman Arthur, who was very friendly and kind, and the girl at the desk was very courteous. Then we decided to have a cup of coffee, and we met the girl who serves that, she was most pleasant, so all these things kept building it up, I can't remember any particular thing that subtracted.

I think one evening in the dining room . . . I was looking for something a little different and I selected something from the à la carte which was good, but just didn't quite hit the spot, and that might have been a slight depression . . .

after the first couple of days, you tend to think it is going to tail off a bit? particularly as we'd have two good evening meals, is tomorrow night going to be the same? and it was, there was no let-up at all, it just kept to the same standard the whole way through . . .

Contrasting experiences can have an important role in the operation of the personal rating system, since positive assessments may be compared with situations which have in the past received a negative score:

immediately the car stopped and the door opened, the porter was there, the staff were very courteous, they carried everything, I was directed to a car parking space, which was fairly convenient, the receptionist told me all I had to know, no problems . . . I was staying in a hotel about a fortnight ago . . . I checked in, I was given my key and told the room was about two hundred yards down the corridor on the left . . . I asked if someone would carry my bags and I was told that there was no porter, and I had to carry them myself. That to me is not good.

Design effects may also have a psychological impact, and thereby influence how positively or otherwise the consumer feels about the consumption environment:

you feel at home, it's comfortable, it's not austere, it's not endless corridors just as though you were marching down to a prison cell. You've still got the same sort of multiple room system in here but there are noticeable differences in the corridor layout, it is not repetitive all the way down the corridor, which makes a tremendous amount of difference to an individual. I notice it only too often. When I see a long corridor where everything is absolutely identical all the way down, I shudder . . .

Figure 3.8 illustrates the integrating role of the personal rating system, which seeks to compute moving average (or transient) measures of satisfaction/dissatisfaction by assessing the totality of tangible and intangible impressions and experiences throughout the consumption stage.

PRIOR PRODUCT EXPERIENCE

	Extensive	**Limited**
CONSUMPTION ↓	Comparisons against key performance indicators provide the basis for measuring transient satisfaction ↓	Transient measures of satisfaction/dissatisfaction lead to the discovery of key performance indicators ↓
POST-CONSUMPTION EVALUATION	Predetermined task definition: enduring satisfaction/dissatisfaction evaluated against experience-based performance norms and in relation to the overall psychological impact of consumption	Reactive task definition: enduring satisfaction/dissatisfaction evaluated against learned performance indicators and psychological reactions to the consumption experience

Figure 3.8 Role of the personal rating system in measuring satisfaction during consumption

Post-consumption evaluation

During the post-consumption period, retrospective discussion and reflection are necessary in order to complete the consumption rating procedure, and calculate the overall assessment rating:

> I think at the end of the day, when we go home, we tend to mark everything out of ten . . . I think subconsciously we use some scale . . . I think it's an overall balance . . . it's something we formulate as opposed to first impressions. First impressions sometimes do stay with you, but . . . I think a couple of days after is the best time, when we say 'What did we really think about it?'

As Figure 3.8 shows, differences again emerge between consumers with extensive prior experience, who have been through this process many times before, and the instinctive but more hesitant approach generally taken by consumers with limited prior experience.

The term 'satisfaction' is used by consumers to define 'end-state' aspirations:

> I expect to leave here with the feeling that I can recommend this to someone else. If I can leave with that feeling, then I'm very satisfied with the hotel . . . My wife's saying what a nice room we have, and it's nice to go back and enjoy the room . . . it's a three-hour train ride [home] so we'll discuss the hotel and what we've done this weekend.

Strong feelings of consumer dissatisfaction usually lead to vivid recollections of the causal event or events. This is suggested by both verbal and non-verbal responses made by consumers when describing their experiences. Sources of strong dissatifaction most often relate to the disconfirmation of expectations, inefficiency or perceptions of abrupt or uncaring service:

> we were very disappointed in the room . . . it really wanted refurbishing . . . the carpets were badly stained, badly worn . . . immediately you walked through the fire doors to the family wing, you could tell, even down to the corridor carpet . . . I certainly felt like going down to reception and complaining. We'd had a long journey, we'd got my daughter who was only about four and we left it. We said 'Okay, the remedy is in our own hands, we don't come here again.' We very rarely do complain . . . we usually go, and if we don't like it, we just don't go again.

Sources of dissatisfaction are not easy to anticipate or rectify, particularly as the response of consumers is unpredictable. Most consumers do not like to complain, and so service providers must take the initiative and instigate effective procedures for monitoring service delivery:

> No matter how expert the people are, no matter what they do, you always need to take note of what people outside say and think, to enable them to see more clearly that which they've become accustomed to because it surrounds them. When it comes to doing something about it, inevitably it has to come from outside because they are constrained internally . . . I always feel slightly inhibited about filling in forms asking if you are satisfied, and how well were you treated – it was excellent, very good, good and so on . . . I mistrust it because I feel it's a way of taking the

heat out of complaints, it doesn't seem to be positive enough, it needs to be turned to advantage . . .

Implications for repeat buying

Confidence in the repurchase decision is commonly associated with shared experiences among friends and relatives, and generalized assumptions about other hotels in the group, based on experiences at one or two hotels:

> since several people, including family members, have had positive experiences . . . there's no reason to gamble any more . . . We now expect the service . . . and if it doesn't live up to it, we're going to be extremely disappointed now that the standard is established in our minds . . .

> having sampled this one, one would assume that the others are very much of the same standard. Obviously facilities vary according to the hotel, but we would probably be inclined to look at another in the same group . . . mainly because it's familiar, we've sampled one, we'll try another.

Experienced hotel users learn to accept that chain-operated hotels are not always consistent with the corporate image, or with their own personal expectations. Although they may develop customized methods of categorizing hotels, anomalies occur:

> We have been to hotels where I've complained, I've said 'This is below standard' . . . we have met quite powerful differences between hotels from one area to another, and we just say we won't come back to this hotel, but we would go to another one in the same group . . . It's difficult to say why because it's not a conscious decision, that's the big problem, you can't say without analysing what you're actually thinking at the time.

In generating repeat business, the objective for service providers must be to ensure that the expectations of consumers are met at every stage in the decision process. Given that dissatisfaction may only result in a complaint when the consumer experiences anger or frustration, the implications for product design and service delivery are important:

> The snag of the hotel and catering business is that condemnation comes quietly, people just go elsewhere, they never tell you why, you find out when it's too late. The British nature of things is not to complain, they're dissuaded from doing so. To try and encourage complaints is a difficult policy to put into practice, but should be done . . . It's a recall thing, if for example you were there when I checked into the hotel, whichever one it was . . . if I indicated to you what it was that I either liked or disliked as I went through all these various phases . . . then that would be an extremely valuable exercise . . . it's very difficult to recall everything . . .

Summary and conclusion

From the reported reactions of leisure break hotel users, it is clear that hotels with regular tourist business throughout the week are better prepared to meet the needs of the leisure break consumer. However, the situation becomes more complicated in hotels where there is a demarcation between midweek and weekend business. In contrast to the business traveller, leisure break consumers are spending their own money, and consequently their sensitivity as to what constitutes value for money is likely to be keener. As there is often a saving and investment input, the satisfaction output requirement is more clearly defined in terms of ideal mental and physical states. If hotel staff are unaware of these expectations and cannot recognize potential sources of tension relating to the consumption experience, dissatisfaction is more likely to occur.[56] This reinforces the need for continuous interpersonal skills development, especially for staff working in close contact with consumers.[57]

The examples used in the case study illustrate how consumers assess and evaluate their experiences, and indicate the importance of the consumer perspective in performance monitoring. A summary of the full consumer decision process is shown in Figure 3.9.

By recognizing that consumers consciously assess product tangibles and react subconsciously to intangibles such as design and atmospheric effects, managers can develop a more comprehensive and systematic approach to the operations audit. This issue is discussed below in the context of the research statements raised in Chapter 2.

1. The relationship between consumers with extensive prior product experience and high-involvement decision making.

The experienced hotel user is able to categorize and differentiate between hotels and leisure break brands. This is because expectations, selection criteria and procedures are well established. However, the level of involvement in decision process depends on how confidently the consumer is able to use established procedures to reduce perceived risk and assess choice options. If the primary purchase is especially important to the consumer, it may lead to the adoption of a high-involvement approach.

2. The relationship between consumers with extensive prior product experience and low-involvement decision making.

The ease with which an experienced hotel user is able to make a purchase decision is closely related to the extent of product familiarity and knowledge, personal confidence and the adoption of family decision-making roles. Product familiarity, derived from experience-based knowledge, enables the consumer to make consistent and confident decisions. In repeat-purchase situations or whenever the consumer can confidently predict hotel suitability, a low-involvement approach is likely to be adopted. There are, however, some circumstances in which a moderate-investment approach will be used. For example, a shift from low to moderate involvement may occur during brand switching or if the consumer is responsible for a booking made on behalf of, or in conjunction with, other people.

3. The relationship between consumers with limited prior product experience and high-involvement decision making.

The inexperienced hotel user may feel the need to become closely involved in the decision process in order to learn more about the product category and reduce

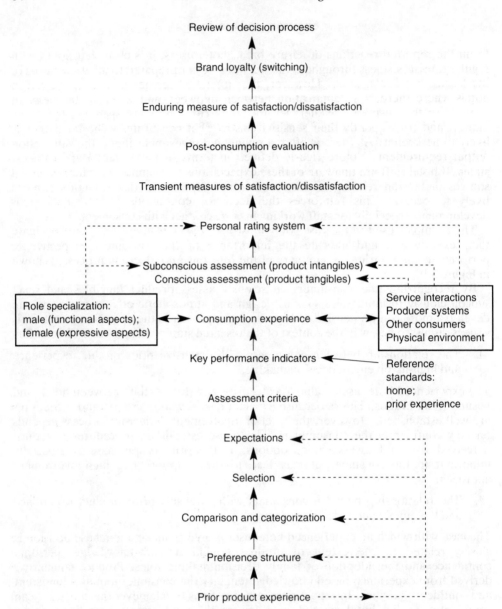

Figure 3.9   A consumer framework for assessing and evaluating hotels

Source: Teare, R., and Boer, A. (eds), *Strategic Hospitality Management: Theory and Practice for the 1990s*, Cassell, London, 1991, p. 28.

perceived risk associated with the purchase decision. As the consumer may be unfamiliar with price–quality relationships concerning standards, services and facilities available in the various grades of hotel accommodation, a more cautious approach is necessary. The ensuing activities may include consulting with travel intermediaries and experienced hotel users, and telephone enquiries made to central reservations and hotel staff.

4. The relationship between consumers with limited prior product experience and low-involvement decision making.

The inexperieced hotel user may adopt a low-involvement approach when deciding to make a return visit to a familiar hotel. This is because the decision process for a repeat purchase is not constrained by the sense of uncertainty associated with unfamiliar hotels and brands.

There are, however, occasions when a low-involvement approach may be adopted in conjunction with the selection of an unfamiliar hotel. For example, they are likely to include hotel leisure breaks motivated by the need to find a house prior to job relocation, and hotel selection motivated by the availability of indoor leisure facilities suitable for a family activity break.

In the latter example, the family may decide that the availability of indoor leisure facilities at the hotel compensates for the risks associated with using an unfamiliar hotel. This is generally because a hotel with indoor facilities is perceived to be a safer investment against the risk of poor weather than cheaper, more familiar types of short-break package offering only outdoor leisure facilities.

5. The relationship between the use of assessment criteria and prior product experience with the product category.

In general, experienced hotel users are able to detect from impressions and interactions at the beginning of the consumption period whether or not their expectations are likely to be fulfilled. This is because prior product experience provides an elaborate frame of reference against which comparisons can be made. It also provides a personal definition of acceptable standards, of which there are a number of key indicators during the initial stages of the consumption period. They . include procedures for reception and registration at the hotel, interactions with hotel staff and the assessment of guest room design and facilities.

The consumer knows from prior experience that the key indicators of service quality require careful monitoring and appraisal. In this process, relevant assessment criteria become established and are routinely used to alert the consumer to prolong sources of dissatisfaction. In this respect inexperienced hotel users are more hesitant in their approach, and in the absence of experience-based criteria, comparative assessments are likely to be made against other familiar reference points such as the home.

6. The relationship between role specialization and confidence in the joint decision-making process.

During pre-purchase, role specialization is associated with convenience and interest in the various information-gathering activities. More female than male partners are responsible for initiating discussion relating to the timing of a leisure break. This is accompanied by preparatory work such as collecting brochures and identifying possible holiday options for discussion. Where male partners have business travel experience, they tend to comment on the type and standard of hotels by referring to the brochure descriptions and photographs.

During the consumption stage, joint assessment focuses on comparisons between hotel standards and the standards of comfort at home. References to the home are frequently made by female partners, who are more dominant during guest room assessment, particularly in relation to design features and the artistic aspects of décor, furnishings and fabrics.

The assessment criteria used by male partners are more often associated with functional requirements, especially if the male partner regularly uses hotels in conjunction with business travel.

7. The relationship between expectations and prior product experience.

As noted in the context of the relationship between assessment criteria and prior experience, experienced hotel users are sensitive to perceived key indicators of service quality, and to environmental design effects. The hotel environment may be categorized as 'warm' and friendly or 'cold' and impersonal, depending on how the combined elements of atmosphere and physical design features are perceived by the consumer. If the service is efficient but impersonal, and the physical design of the building lacks personality, this may contribute to a subconscious psychological impression of coldness, evoking a feeling of detachment or even alienation.

The desirability of contrasting design features and atmospheric effects is also referred to in the context of food and beverage outlets. A common criticism of their design, especially of hotel restaurants, is that they do not have a separate identity, or manage to convey a different atmosphere from the rest of the hotel. If a hotel is considered to be impersonal, this is one of the factors which may contribute to a decision not to use its food and beverage outlets.

Inexperienced hotel users are often concerned about the kind of service they might experience at a hotel. In this respect, they are inclined to seek reassurance before making a purchase decision by telephoning the hotel beforehand. The response to the enquiry is regarded as indicative of staff attitudes at the hotel, making it an important choice determinant. If the enquiry is handled insensitively, the consumer is inclined to reject the hotel and in some cases even the leisure break brand. Interactions with hotel staff are also considered to be very important during the initial stages of consumption. When service interactions are perceived as positive and helpful, they have a confidence-building effect on the consumer.

8. The relationship between product experience and the personal rating system.

The operation of the personal rating system is related to the extent of the consumer's prior experience with the product category. In order to evaluate the overall experience, the consumer has to integrate a wide variety of individual assessments. As the assessment ratings accumulate, the personal rating system facilitates integration and aggregation to produce a transient measure of satisfaction (or dissatisfaction) which is continually updated during consumption.

As the consumer gains experience, so the personal rating system becomes more sensitive to information, and the consumer feels more confident about the processes of assessment and evaluation. The experienced hotel user has the advantage of being able to use experience-based criteria in order to make a rapid assessment of hotel suitability. This helps the consumer to detect, avoid and resolve potential sources of dissatifaction.

9. The relationship between post-consumption evaluation and assessments made during the consumption stage.

The personal rating system has two main functions. It provides a mechanism for integrating and storing assessments and impressions as they occur, and it facilitates overall evaluation at the post-consumption stage.

During post-consumption evaluation, the consumer recalls the positive and negative measures arising from assessments made during consumption. The purpose of this activity is to determine the extent to which expectations have been met, and to assess the implications for repurchasing or modified decision making in the future.

Prior product experience has a clearly identifiable role in the evaluative process, as experienced hotel users are able to evaluate a consumption experience with the aid of an established prototype for product performance. Pre-knowledge of key indicators of service quality provides a set of performance norms against which different aspects of the consumption experience can be compared. Hence, evaluation is task oriented, guided by clearly established objectives and procedures. Inexperienced hotel users are less well prepared to evaluate the consumption experience, because their frame of reference is not as detailed, or the evaluation process as well established. Consequently, evaluation is not as well focuses, and takes longer than for experienced hotel users because of the need to react to new information.

10. The relationship between post-consumption evaluation and brand evaluation.

In distinguishing between transient and enduring measures of product performance, it is important to note the influence of the final measure of satisfaction (or dissatifaction) on brand attitudes and consequent purchase behaviour. Satisfaction will reinforce positive brand attitudes, contributing to the development of brand loyalty. Conversely, dissatisfaction may lead to modifications in the approach to the decision process, with the pre-purchase stage becoming longer and more involved, especially if the consumer decides to try a different brand on the next purchase occasion.

NOTES

1. Foxall, G. R., 'Consumer theory: some contributions of a behavioural analysis of choice', *Management Bibliographies and Reviews*, vol. 12, no. 2, 1986, pp. 27–51.
2. Baker, M. J., 'The theory and practice of marketing', *Food Marketing*, vol. 2, no. 3, 1986, pp. 3–19.
3. Kelly, G. A., *A Theory of Personality: The Psychology of Personal Constructs*, W. W. Norton, New York, 1963.
4. Kuhn, T. S., *The Structure of Scientific Revolutions*, University of Chicago Press, Chicago, IL, 1970.
5. Popper, K. R., *Conjectures and Refutations*, Routledge & Kegan Paul, London, 1969.
6. Bagozzi, R. P., 'A prospectus for theory construction in marketing', *Journal of Marketing*, vol. 48 (Summer), 1984, pp. 11–29.
7. Jacoby, J., 'Consumer research: a state-of-the-art review', *Journal of Marketing*, vol. 42 (January), 1978, pp. 87–96.
8. Ajzen, I., and Fisbein, M., 'Attitude–behavior relations: a theoretical analysis and review of empirical research', *Psychological Bulletin*, vol. 84, 1977, pp. 888–918.

9. Foxall, G. R., 'Marketing's response to consumer behaviour: time to promote a change?', *Quarterly Review of Marketing*, vol. 8, no. 4, 1983, pp. 11–14.

10. Foxall, G. R., 'Consumers' intentions and behaviour', *Journal of the Market Research Society*, vol. 26, no. 3, 1984, pp. 231–41.

11. Jacoby, J., Chesnut, R. W., and Silberman, W. S., 'Consumer use and comprehension of nutrition information', *Journal of Consumer Research*, vol. 4 (September), 1977, pp. 119–28.

12. Olshavsky, R. W., and Granbois, D. H., 'Consumer decision making – fact or fiction?', *Journal of Consumer Research*, vol. 6 (September), 1979, pp. 93–100.

13. Jacoby, J., Speller, D. E., and Kohn, C. A., 'Brand choice behaviour as a function of information load', *Journal of Marketing Research*, vol. 11, 1974, pp. 63–69.

14. Jacoby, J., Speller, D. E., and Kohn Berning, C. A., 'Brand choice behaviour as a function of information load: replication and extension', *Journal of Consumer Research*, vol. 1 (June), 1974, pp. 33–42.

15. Krugman, H. E., 'The impact of television advertising: learning without involvement', *Public Opinion Quarterly*, vol. 29 (Fall), 1965, pp. 349–56.

16. Robertson, T. S., 'Low commitment consumer behavior', *Journal of Advertising Research*, vol. 16, no. 2, 1976, pp. 19–24.

17. Hunt, S. D., 'General theories and the fundamental explananda of marketing', *Journal of Marketing*, vol.47 (Fall), 1983, p. 9–17.

18. Arndt, J., 'Reflections on research in consumer behavior', in Anderson, R. E. (ed.), *Advances in Consumer Research*, vol. 3, Association for Consumer Research, Ann Arbor, MI, 1976, pp. 213–21.

19. Kassarjian, H. H., 'The development of consumer behavior theory', in Mitchell, A. (ed.), *Advances in Consumer Research*, vol. 9, Association for Consumer Research, Ann Arbor, MI, 1981, pp. 20–2.

20. Anderson, P. F., 'Marketing, scientific progress, and scientific method', *Journal of Marketing*, vol. 47 (Fall), 1983, pp. 18–31.

21. Deshpande, R., '"Paradigms Lost" on theory and method in research in marketing', *Journal of Marketing*, vol. 47 (Fall), 1983, pp. 101–10.

22. R & D sub-committee on qualitative research, 'Qualitative research – a summary of the concepts involved', *Journal of the Market Research Society*, vol. 21, no. 2, 1979, pp. 107–24.

23. Festinger, L., and Katz, D., *Research Methods in the Behavioural Sciences*, Holt, Rinehart and Winston, New York, 1966.

24. McCall, G. J., and Simmons, J. L. (eds), *Issues in Participant Observation: A Text and Reader*, Addison-Wesley, Reading, MA, 1969.

25. Roos, J. P., 'From oddball research to the study of real life: the use of qualitative methods in social science', *Acta Sociologica*, vol. 22, 1979, pp. 63–74.

26. Dean, J. P., Eichhorn, R. L., and Dean, L. R., 'Limitations and advantages of unstructured methods', in McCall, G. J., and Simmons, J. L. (eds), *Issues in Participant Observation: A Text and Reader*, Addison-Wesley, Reading, MA, 1969.

27. Hawker, R., 'The interaction between nurses and patients' relatives', PhD thesis, Department of Sociology, University of Exeter, 1982.

28. Diesing, P. R., *Patterns of Discovery in the Social Sciences*, Aldine, Chicago, IL, 1972.

29. Schatzman, L., and Strauss, A. L., *Field Research: Strategies for a Natural Sociology*, Prentice-Hall, Englewood Cliffs, NJ, 1973.

30. Bogdan, R., and Taylor, S. J., *Introduction to Qualitative Research Methods*, John Wiley, New York, 1984.
31. Miles, M. B., and Huberman, A. M., *Qualitative Data Analysis*, Sage, London, 1984.
32. Walker, R., 'An introduction to applied qualitative research', in Walker, R. (ed.), *Applied Qualitative Research*, Gower, Aldershot, 1985.
33. Glaser, B. G., and Strauss, A. L., *The Discovery of Grounded Theory: Strategies for Qualitative Research*, Aldine, Chicago, IL, 1967.
34. Glaser, B.G., *Theoretical Sensitivity: Advances in the Methodology of Grounded Theory*, Sociological Press, Mill Valley, CA, 1978.
35. Sims, D. B. P., 'Problem construction in teams', PhD thesis, School of Management, University of Bath, 1978.
36. Silverman, D., *The Theory of Organisations*, Heinemann, London, 1970.
37. Brown, G. W., 'Some thoughts on grounded theory', *Sociology*, vol. 7, 1973, pp. 1–16.
38. Trend, M. G., 'On the reconciliation of qualitative and quantitative analyses: a case study', *Human Organization*, vol. 37, 1978, pp. 345–54.
39. Turner, B. A., 'The use of grounded theory for the qualitative analysis of organizational behaviour', *Journal of Management Studies*, vol. 22, no. 3, 1983, pp. 332–48.
40. Martin, P. Y., and Turner, B. A., 'Grounded theory and organizational research', *Journal of Applied Behavioral Science*, vol. 22, no. 2, 1986, pp. 141–57.
41. Turner, B. A., 'Some practical aspects of qualitative data analysis: one way of organising the cognitive processes associated with the generation of grounded theory', *Quality and Quantity*, vol. 15, 1981, pp. 225–47.
42. Jones, S., 'Depth interviewing', in Walker, R. (ed.), *Applied Qualitative Research*, Gower, Aldershot, 1985.
43. Kelly, G. A., *The Psychology of Personal Constructs*, W. W. Norton, New York, 1955.
44. Burgess, R. G., 'The unstructured interview as a conversation', in Burgess, R. G. (ed.), *Field Research: A Sourcebook and Field Manual*, George Allen and Unwin, London, 1982.
45. Bailyn, L., 'Research as a cognitive process: implications for data analysis', *Quality and Quantity*, vol. 11, 1977, pp. 97–117.
46. Bulmer, M., (ed.), *Sociological Research Methods: An Introduction*, Macmillan, London, 1984.
47. Wind, Y., (1978) 'Issues and advances in segmentation research', *Journal of Marketing Research*, vol. 15 (August), 1978, pp. 317–37.
48. Lunn, J. A., 'Consumer modelling', in Worcester, R. M., (ed.), *Consumer Market Research Handbook*, Van Nostrand Reinhold, Wokingham, 1978, pp. 503–20.
49. Lunn, J. A., 'Some basic principles and recent developments', in *Classifying Consumers: A Need to Rethink*, European Society for Opinion and Marketing Research, Amsterdam, 1982, pp. 3–21.
50. Euromonitor, *Weekend Breaks and Day Trips*, Euromonitor Publications Limited, London, 1987.
51. Beard, J. G., and Ragheb, M. G., 'Measuring leisure satisfaction', *Journal of Leisure Research*, vol. 12, no. 1, 1980, pp. 20–33.
52. Beard, J. G., and Ragheb, M. G., 'Measuring leisure motivation', *Journal of Leisure Research*, vol. 15, no. 3, 1983, pp. 219–28.

53. Pearce, P. L., and Caltabiano, M. L., 'Inferring travel motivation from travelers' experiences', *Journal of Travel Research*, vol. 22, no. 2, 1983, pp. 16–20.
54. Laurent, G., and Kapferer, J. N., 'Measuring consumer involvement profiles', *Journal of Marketing Research*, vol. 22 (February), 1985, pp. 41–53.
55. Teare, R., and Williams, A., 'Destination marketing', *Tourism Management*, vol. 10, no. 2, 1989, pp. 95–6.
56. Teare, R., 'Generating consumer theory for the hospitality industry: an integrated approach to the treatment of practical and theoretical issues' in Johnston, R. (ed.), *The Management of Service Operations*, IFS Publications, Bedford, 1988, pp. 269–79.
57. Teare, R., Davies, M., and McGeary, B., 'The operational challenge of hotel short breaks', *Journal of Contemporary Hospitality Management*, vol. 1, no. 1, 1989, pp. 22–4.

FOUR

Closing the gap between consumers and services

A CONSUMER VIEW OF THE SERVICE ENVIRONMENT

The hotel service environment, as Chapter 3 illustrates, is characterized by many different kinds of interactions between consumers and the staff, facilities and amenities which are needed to provide services. How, for instance, do hotel users define a good hotel? Pannell Kerr Forster Associates[1] conclude:

> Hotels that will receive favourable mention from their customers will be those hotels, of whatever standard, where the rooms are clean and comfortable, the facilities modern and comprehensive and above all where the staff and the service provided is efficient, friendly and helpful. (p. 10)

The reality for hotel operations is that employees both produce and deliver services, which means that consumers are continually influenced by interactions with staff and the environment in which service delivery takes place. Although service staff may see themselves as full-time specialists in accommodation or food and beverage, they also act as part-time marketers[2, 3] because their behaviour affects consumer choice[4]. It follows, therefore, that hospitality firms wishing to close the gap between the 'ideal' service experience and the actual service that consumers receive must seek to involve all of their employees in a process of continual improvement.

This chapter focuses on the interface between the consumer and the provider of hospitality services during the consumption stage of the decision process. This has been accurately described as the 'moment of truth' for service firms[5] because every interaction represents an opportunity to impress the consumer. The logical starting point for a programme of continuous improvement is to elicit opinions from customers so that the organization becomes accustomed to listening and defining service goals in partnership with service users. A cultural change of this kind can be initiated using guest questionnaires, focus group discussions and various forms of employee feedback, but to sustain service improvement it is often necessary to deploy a wider range of research tools and techniques. There are principally two advantages of this. First, service issues can be explored from different perspectives, and in time, this may give rise to ideas for redesigning aspects of service delivery.[6]

Second, a deeper and fuller understanding of the mind of the customer provides a more effective basis for planning the next step on the improvement journey. In response to these points, the chapter opens with a review of several techniques for cognitive mapping and modelling. They facilitate reconstructions of service events by drawing on the expectations, perceptions and experiences of consumers. Ultimately, a reputation for service excellence depends on the extent to which senior management are willing to champion and encourage the full and open participation of the workforce in achieving a total customer focus.[7,8] The chapter concludes by tracing the steps taken by Scott's Hotels Limited in its quest to build and sustain a total quality culture throughout its UK hotel operations.

COGNITIVE-MAPPING AND MODELLING TECHNIQUES

Personal construct theory

Kelly[9] asserts that individuals make sense of their world through 'transparent patterns or templets' which they create and use to interpret reality. These patterns are called 'constructs' because they represent ways of construing the world around us. His personal construct theory[9, 10] consists of eleven corollaries which elaborate a central assertion which states that an individual's thinking is psychologically guided by the ways in which he anticipates events.

Kelly argues that personal constructs are organized into a hierarchical system of superordinal and subordinal relationships. The system is continually evolving to incorporate new knowledge and understanding. It also integrates factual information which the individual uses to anticipate and predict events. In this sense the construct system provides a personal theory to guide thinking and behaviour. The relationships between pesonal constructs can be explored by using a depth-interviewing technique and the analytical procedure of cognitive mapping.

Principles of cognitive mapping

The analytical technique of cognitive mapping is derived from Kelly's personal construct theory. The mapping procedure involves listening and exploring beyond the surface of the words used by the individual in an interview to describe his or her interpretation of events. The purpose of the map is to represent a person's thinking and theorizing about a part of his or her world, using the person's own language and depicting constructs or ideas and their interrelationships in his or her terms.

Jones[11] describes a manual procedure for cognitive mapping which begins with interview data in the form of either a tape recording, or notes made immediately after an interview. The aim is to code each interview so that wherever possible it can be depicted on one large sheet of paper. The coding procedure involves assigning causal or non-causal (connative) links between related constructs. Links are shown by using lines and arrow heads to illustrate the causal path. A line without an arrow head is used to show that two constructs are related, but that there is no implied direction to the link.

During the process of constructing the map, Jones uses a variety of coding aids to emphasize meaning. These include words written along the arrows and lines, and bold or dotted lines to indicate emphatic or tentative assertions made by the respondent. During the coding process, she also makes notes on apparent inconsistencies in the data, contradictory views expressed during the course of the interview and other reactions together with their significance for category development.

When all the main ideas and relationships contained in the interview have been depicted, the map is complete. From this, and with the aid of explanatory notes made on the map, it is possible to prepare summary diagrams representing clusters of ideas. The network structure of the map also makes it possible to identify loops and chains of ideas which may be helpful in theory development.

The principles of the manual cognitive-mapping technique were used in the development of a computer-based cognitive modelling program called Cognitive Policy Evaluation (COPE). The program was extensively tested, and refined during its development period,[12,13,14] and it has been used on a wide variety of research investigations. These include self-reflections and learning,[15] negotiating problem definition in groups,[16] the analysis of semi-structured interviews and qualitative market research data[17,18,19] and various organizational research studies.[20,21,22,23,24]

Computer-based cognitive modelling

COPE was originally designed to assist decision-makers and project teams with qualitative aspects of problem solving. The programmers felt that existing manage-ment science techniques were capable of supporting rational, quantitative assessments, but that their mathematical basis was better suited to the generation of solutions than creative thinking and learning around the problem itself. The intention, therefore, was to design an interactive modelling program that would bring together ideas, beliefs and attitudes associated with the objects and or people encompassed by a given problem or situation, so that the relationships could be fully explored.

The computer-based modelling procedure is a complementary form of secondary analysis because it provides a way of rebuilding semi-structured interviews using the same data. As the software program is interactive, the contents of each model can then be exported and output in the form of summary cognitive maps.

The preparation of COPE model input necessitates rereading interview transcripts and observation data in order to identify the main themes and their interrelationships. Then by working systematically through each transcript, the contents are entered into the program in the form of single lines of text, each of which represents one idea or viewpoint. The procedures used for entering data, verifying model relationships, model analysis and the interpretation of model output are outlined below and illustrated by an example, which is concerned with exploring the functions and operation of the consumers' personal rating system during service delivery.

An overview of the cognitive-modelling process

The procedure for constructing a cognitive model using an interview transcript begins by rereading the text to identify the main discussion topics and the ideas expressed in the various strands of related argumentation. One of the advantages of semi-structured interviewing is that it provides an opportunity to probe important topics in depth. However, as related ideas may have been expressed at different points during the interview, it is helpful to be familiar with the overall structure and content of the transcript before entering data and relationships into the model.

The data input used to construct a COPE model is alphanumeric, and consists of a single line of text up to a maximum of seventy-four characters in length. Each line represents one concept or idea relating to any aspect of a problem or viewpoint on the decision process. Converting a transcript to the required format is a subjective process as each idea must be summarized separately. Typically, a forty-five minute interview will contain around seventy-five ideas, which are easily contained within an individual model. To ensure that conversion is as accurate as possible, each model should be summarized on paper before rechecking and entering the ideas into the program. The program is designed to accept one line of text at a time, and each line is automatically numbered in sequence. When all the ideas have been entered, a final comparison can be made by cross-referencing the transcript with a print-out of the model contents.

Entering and verifying model relationships

The next step is to identify how the ideas contained in the model relate to each other. As a preliminary to this task it is necessary to reread the transcript, noting in the margin or on a separate sheet of paper where related ideas are located in the text. Following this, coding is undertaken by working systematically down the print-out list of idea statements from the model, using coding symbols recognized by the program to record how the ideas are related. If a section of the transcript is ambiguous, it is usually advisable to try to clarify meaning (ideally by listening to an audio tape recording of the interview again) so as to hear how a particular point had been expressed during the interview.

COPE recognizes several types of relationship, which are denoted by inserting the appropriate symbol between the related ideas. Where one idea leads to or affects another idea, this is referred to as a causal link. Causal links can be plus (+) or minus (−), and as the program accepts bipolar statements, a (+) link indicates that the first pole of one idea leads to the first pole of the related idea. The second poles of the two ideas are similarly related. For example:

49 + 50 = idea 49 leads to idea 50

This means that idea 50 is a consequence of idea 49, and also that idea 50 can be explained by idea 49.

Conversely, a (−) link denotes that the first pole of one idea leads to the second pole of the related idea. The cross-relationship also applies to the second pole of the first idea and the first pole of the second idea. This can be illustrated by referring to three ideas contained in an example model. Idea number 16 is bipolar:

16 a +ve . . a −ve: psychological impression of the guest room used on a business trip
17 intelligent design and 'warmth' created by comfort, furnishings and fittings and décor
18 the 'cold' effect of an impersonal or unattractive guest room and bath room

The relationship (18−16) means that idea of 18 leads to the (−) pole of idea 16. Hence the 'cold' effect of an impersonal or unattractive guest room and bath room leads to a

−ve psychological impression of the guest room used on a business trip.

Conversely, the relationship (17 + 16) means that idea 17 leads to the (+) pole of idea 16. Hence intelligent design and 'warmth' created by comfort, furnishings and fittings and décor leads to a + ve psychological impression of the guest room used on a business trip.

In order to code a relationship between two ideas with unspecified consequences, a full stop symbol (.) is used. This is called a non-causal or connotative relationship because the influence of one idea on the other either is unknown or has not been clearly defined. Connotative links are bi-directional, so that by entering the link (44.43) will also be automatically inserted. For example:

43 the procedure for assessing/evaluating hotels
44 experiential learning over the years . . .

In this example the relationship between the two ideas is the same, regardless of whether the relationship is shown as (43.44) or (44.43) because causal direction is not known. Hence (43.44) means that the procedure for assessing/evaluating hotels is linked to experiential learning over the years . . . which means the same as (44.43), whereby experiential learning over the years . . . is linked to the procedure for assessing/evaluating hotels.

To collect bipolar data, it is necessary to obtain the contrasting view or 'psychological opposite' to every point made by the respondent during the interview. As the format of the interviews does not always facilitate this, most of the ideas contained in the models represent single-pole (or monotonic) statements. The relationships are therefore more straighforward, using mainly connotative or causal (+) links to relate one single-pole idea with another single-pole idea.

Interpreting, listing and cross-checking the relationships for each idea statement with the meaning conveyed in the transcript is an intensive process. An average of eighty relationships per model are likely to be identified. In order to complete model construction it is therefore important to ensure that the relationships accurately represent the sense of the interview. The program has three exploratory commands which can be used for this purpose: consequences (C), explanations (E) and explore (X).

By typing the command 'C46', for example, a search for the consequences, if any, of idea 46 is activated. If the search finds that there are one or more consequences leading from idea 46, they are listed on the computer screen or print-out when the search has been completed. The listing may range from a single idea to a long chain of related ideas depending on the importance of idea 46 to the model structure. The (E) command operates in the same way, except that it activates a search for explanations of the given idea. The (X) command displays the specified idea at the centre of the output, surrounded by the ideas which are directly linked to it. Lines show non-causal links, and arrow heads indicate the direction of causal links, with (+) links assumed unless indicated by a (−) sign positioned close to the arrow head.

By using these commands to examine the relationships associated with every idea statement in each model, it is possible to check, and where necessary to amend, relationships so that potential sources of error or inaccuracy are detected prior to the analysis of model data.

Model analysis

The purpose of the modelling exercise is to create a realistic simulation of an interview so that an analysis of the model structure will report on all of the related ideas, regardless of when and in what context they were mentioned in the interview. The main task of model analysis is to identify the most influential ideas in the model structure around which key idea groups can be clustered.

COPE can generate three different analytical reports on the key ideas in the model structure. They are called cognitive centrality analysis, path analysis and trace analysis:

- Cognitive centrality analysis searches all the direct links into and out of the ideas in a model, and the report lists the ideas with the largest number of related ideas. The purpose of this procedure is to identify ideas which are important to the structure of the model.
- Path analysis reports on the most significant links or chains of argument contained in a model. The number of different routes or paths is calculated for each idea in two directions: from the head and from the tail of the argumentation. A head idea is one that has no consequences, and a tail idea is one that has no explanations. Path analysis searches and calculates the number of paths inwards from the tail of the argumentation, and outwards down the paths leading to the head ideas.
- Trace analysis looks at the way in which one idea is linked to all the other ideas. Included in the trace score for each idea are all the directly linked ideas, and ideas linked indirectly through connected paths.

By examining the reports for each model, it is possible to identify most of the key ideas, although the (C), (E) and (X) commands referred to above are also used to locate key ideas isolated from the model structure. This can happen if a particular topic has no direct bearing on the rest of the discussion topics. An average of eighteen key ideas per mode is typical, and these are identified from the reports and by using the commands as a secondary form of analysis.

The final stage of preparation necessary to produce cognitive maps from a model is the creation of key idea groups using COPE's autogrouping command. Included within a key idea group are any ideas which form part of the explanatory structure of the key idea. Prior to issuing the autogroup command, each key idea is given an identification number which can be illustrated as follows:

Examining key idea groups

G12$46 means that the key idea group 12 is centred on key idea 46.

Example list of key idea group 12 contents:

G12   differences in the operation of personal rating scale/assessment procedures $46

46   differences in the operation of personal rating scale assessment procedures
47   the circumstances of the hotel usage situation – familiar or new hotel
48   the experience of standing in a very large reception areea – unfamiliar hotel
49   an acute awareness of open space

50   the feeling of detachment from a 'cold' unfriendly environment
51   a much more critical assessment of the hotel
52   difficulty in overcoming emotional reaction – essential role for staff

The key idea group 12 (G12) is identified using the (C) and (E) commands, and as the relationships are largely self-contained within the group, it is not subordinate or superordinate to any other key idea group. In contrast the smaller key idea group 2 (G2) is part of the group hierarchical structure of the model because it has a subordinate group (G3) listed and indented beneath it, as shown below:

Examining the key idea group hierarchy

Extract from the key idea group hierarchy for an example model:

    G2   high satisfaction with the accommodation $3
    G3   a non-standard guest room (not rectangular box) $70

     3   high satisfaction with the accommodation
    7 0   a non-standard guest room (not rectangular box)
    7 1   a well-designed bathroom and entrance corridor

As successive key idea groups are created, a group hierarchy is automatically determined according to whether each new key idea group is subordinate or superordinate to existing key idea groups. By listing the complete group hierarchy for a model, it is then possible to identify which groups belong to the hierarchy, and of those which do, which groups are subsumed by others. This information provides guidance on reducing the number of cognitive maps to print, as the smaller groups that are also contained within larger groups are redundant.

Model output: a hotel personal rating system example

As noted in Chapter 3, the consumer receives and stores information from many sources during consumption, so that impressions can be assessed in relation to specific criteria and expectations. The personal rating system provides an integrating mechanism for organizing, storing and assessing experiences as they accumulate. It also provides a link with post-consumption evaluation, which draws on stored assessment ratings to determine the overall level of satisfaction. As this information increases product familiarity and knowledge, it also influences subsequent preferences, expectations and assessment criteria. This is because experience-based learning plays an important role in the refinement of the personal rating system, thereby enabling the consumer to assess and categorize hotels more accurately in the future. The following example illustrates the operation of a personal rating system to integrate subconscious reactions to the consumption environment and conscious assessments of product tangibles, such as the equipment provided in the guest room. This produces a moving average measure of satisfaction/dissatisfaction which is updated as subsequent assessments are made.

A cognitive map illustrates key idea group relationships in diagrammatic form, and a simplified example is shown in Figure 4.1. The map has a relationship grid which provides explanatory information so that lines and arrows can be drawn to link the ideas automatically positioned to facilitate this. The maps are numbered for identification purposes (Map 1). They also list the key group number (G4), the key idea statement and number ($2) and the respondent identification code (R20). The numbers to the left of the idea numbers [6, 4, 2] in the relationship grid are explanations (+2, +1, .5, .3), and those to the right are consequences (+2, .3, .5). In some maps there are explanations and consequences enclosed by brackets which refer to relationships with ideas which are not included on the map, e.g. <+23, +28>. The letters to the right of each column in the relationship grid are the reference labels for the lines linking the ideas on the map.

The map shows how the personal rating system operates, with 'subconscious assessments' (4) linked to 'the aggregation of positive and negative experiences during the stay' (2). This helps to explain how the current or 'transient measure of satisfaction' (or dissatisfaction) (6) is continually updated by new information. This is necessary in order to develop an overall impression throughout the stay (1). Conscious assessments made during discussion with others, or by comparison against expectations, are more likely to be connected with product tangibles relating to public facilities (5) and the guest room (3).

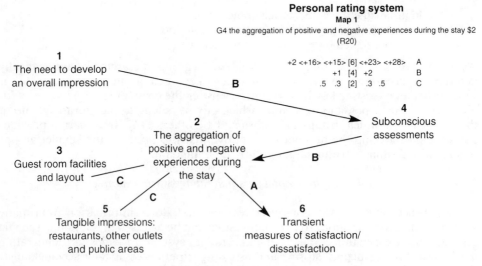

Figure 4.1 Cognitive map

A key theme of the example map is the close interrelationship between assessments made during consumption and overall evaluation at the end of the stay. If the consumer is unable to counterbalance one or more negative experiences, then overall evaluation is likely to lead to a feeling of disappointment or even dissatisfaction.[25] Clearly it is important to explore and define where, when and how negative assessments arise so that appropriate action can be taken to minimize re-occurrence. In this endeavour, cognitive mapping is a valuable enabling tool for service improvement.

Perceptual blueprinting

Perceptual blueprinting is a technique for building a snapshot picture of 'failpoints' in a service delivery system, and in this it is a powerful and effective way of involving

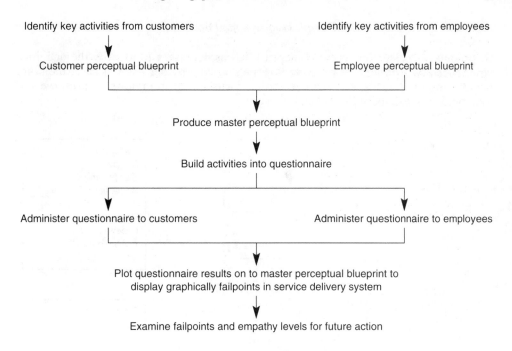

Identify key activities from customers   Identify key activities from employees

Customer perceptual blueprint   Employee perceptual blueprint

Produce master perceptual blueprint

Build activities into questionnaire

Administer questionnaire to customers   Administer questionnaire to employees

Plot questionnaire results on to master perceptual blueprint to display graphically failpoints in service delivery system

Examine failpoints and empathy levels for future action

Figure 4.2 Perceptual-blueprinting model

employees in service quality diagnosis and improvement. It was originally developed during a study of service quality issues in the UK roadside lodge sector,[26] and it draws from several established techniques such as service blueprinting[27] and perceptual gap analysis.[28] Subsequent refinements[29] have produced the extended model shown in Figure 4.2.

The principal value of the technique is that it allows for the exploration of both customer and employee perceptions of the service delivery system. This, in turn, aids the identification of potential and actual failpoints (poor service quality) in the system, thereby providing the basis of an improvement agenda.

The following example is based on work undertaken to test the final stages of a perceptual-blueprinting model for National Health Service (NHS) hotel services by obtaining a customer perceptual blueprint, an employee perceptual blueprint and a master perceptual blueprint. The work was conducted in four NHS hospitals of different type, size and location[30,31].

The customer perceptual blueprint

The key activities experienced by customers (patients) during a stay in hospital were identified via personal and focus interviews with selected respondents. The patient-respondents were asked to talk about their experiences from the moment of arrival through to departure from the hospital. Each interview constitutes an individual perceptual blueprint which can later be combined to create a composite perceptual blueprint. This represents a complete snapshot picture of the service process from the patients' perspective.

The employee perceptual blueprint

To produce a master perceptual blueprint, it was necessary to identify the activities experienced by a patient, as perceived by the service provider – in this case, the hotel service employee. This was achieved using focus group interviews to preserve the anonymity of participants and elicit honest responses.

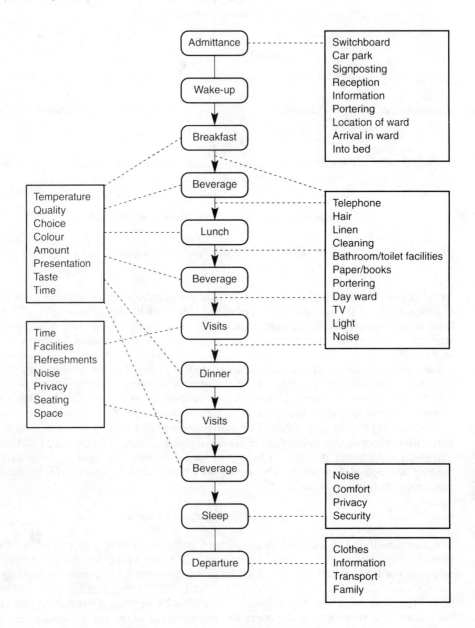

Figure 4.3   Master perceptual blueprint

The master perceptual blueprint

By aggregating the patient and employee perceptual blueprints, it was possible to formulate the master perceptual blueprint shown in Figure 4.3. This represents both common and differing variables relating to areas of service activity. The identification of perceptual differences pertaining to common variables is critical to the identification of causal factors that result in poor service.

The activities relating to the events depicted in the master perceptual blueprint can be further explored using a questionnaire for completion by a larger sample of respondents. The combination of perceptual blueprints and questionnaire responses can then be used to examine most and least common activities in the service delivery system, the location and concentration of perceived failpoints, and the differences in perceptions between and among patients and employees. Further, this information can be disseminated for discussion and resolution by quality circles and quality action teams across the NHS hotel services organization. In this way, employees can be encouraged to participate more fully in the process of continuous improvement.

THE CASE FOR A CULTURAL CHANGE IN SERVICE

In his book *Market-Led Strategic Change*[32] Nigel Piercy tells the story of the Marriott Corporation's response to a complaint he had made on a customer satisfaction questionnaire while staying in Chicago:

> on my return to the UK I received an airmail letter of apology and thanks from Bill Marriott's office, a personal letter from the hotel manager apologizing further . . . a personal airmail letter from the departmental manager apologizing . . . I have got to the stage where I am frightened to open the front door in case there are personal representatives of the catering staff from the Chicago Marriott offering yet further apologies and compensation . . . the result is . . . I am a far more loyal Marriott customer than ever before. (p. 52)

The moral of the story is that hotel companies greatly benefit from genuine attempts to identify, interpret and respond to the feelings of their customers as well as their needs. But if they are to work, it requires a fresh look at 'service' throughout the organization.

How are hotel companies responding to the market-driven need to revolutionize thinking on service? The following case study reflects the vision for and reality of an evolving hotel service culture.

CASE STUDY: TOTAL CUSTOMER FOCUS AND QUALITY SERVICE AT SCOTT'S HOTELS LIMITED

Scott's Hotels Limited (Scott's) is a wholly owned subsidiary of Scott's Hospitality Incorporated, a major Canadian corporation which has restaurant, photography and transportation operations in Canada and the USA. In the UK, Perfect Pizza is part of the Scott's Hospitality portfolio; other interests include Home Rouxl (a *sous-vide* food production facility) and Courtlands (shopping centres).

For about twenty years Scott's managed all of its hotels under a Holiday Inn brand franchise agreement. Towards the end of the 1980s, however, it was evident that the demand–supply relationship was shifting. Scott's own market research indicated that the customers' future use of a hotel brand would be determined by the satisfaction/ quality rating of their most recent stay. The evidence pointed to the need to be affiliated with a globally recognized brand, offering consistency in all its hotels and, most importantly, a company that had a system in place for ensuring total quality for its customers.

This led to signing a contract with the American-owned Marriott Corporation, which included the UK master franchise rights for two of its brands, Marriott and Courtyard by Marriott. Since 1992, Scott's has been operating Marriott core brand and Courtyard by Marriott hotels across the UK, from Aberdeen in the north to Portsmouth in the south; from Swansea in the west to Lincoln in the east. Collectively, this represents well over 2,000 guest rooms. Scott's has been pioneering the application of total quality management (TQM) in its hotel operations since 1989, and the case study aims to show how this has influenced the evolution of the company's service strategy for linking employee empowerment and continuous improvement in customer service.

Cultural synergy

The partnership between Scott's and Marriott was signed in January 1992 and conversion to the Marriott brand name took place over a comparatively short 24-week period in order to meet an operational date of 15 July 1992. On 14 July, Scott's customers went to sleep in a Holiday Inn and woke up in a Marriott hotel. This was achieved without closing the business and without using external consultants. In this, there is a powerful story to relate, a story of people involvement, determination and customer focus that demonstrates what total quality is all about.

How could Scott's be sure that the partnership with Marriott would work? The exploratory talks indicated that the companies had many things in common. Both started as entrepreunerial, family owned and managed companies, and both started with restaurants and ended up in the hotel business. Although they are now quoted on their respective stock exchanges, both have retained a very strong family influence. Above all, Marriott and Scott's share a commitment to TQM philosophy, the principles of listening to customers, adapting, improving, innovating and involving people in the process of continuous improvement. A simple example of Marriott's commitment to employee empowerment is evidenced by the tags with the inscription 'I am the boss' which form part of the name badges worn by American Marriott hotel staff. If asked, staff will explain that it is everybody's responsibility to ensure that the guest's stay is perfect in all respects. This duty of care extended beyond specific operational roles to encompass every single detail of the guests' stay.

The implementation of TQM at Scott's Hotels is underpinned by evolving structures and processes which, above all, lay emphasis on quality improvement through teamworking at every level in the organization. This has changed the culture of the organization to the extent that TQM attainments are now firmly embedded in financial month-end reports and quarterly performance reviews.

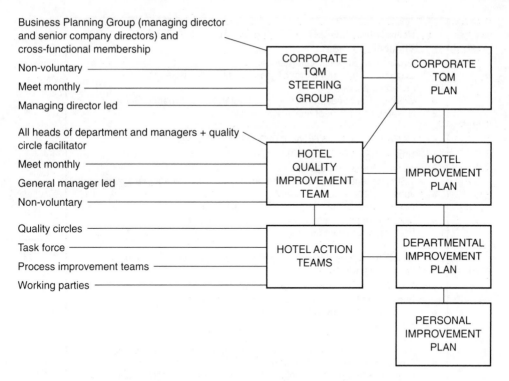

Figure 4.4 Quality improvement structure

Figure 4.4 shows the linkage between planning at the corporate TQM steering group level and the hotel quality improvement structure, which involves managers, supervisors and staff in departmental and cross-departmental team activity. The steering group, comprising company directors and representatives from quality support, operations and general management, takes responsibility for drafting the annual company TQM plan. All hotel general managers are then invited to comment on it before it is finalized and circulated so that general managers and their management teams can draw from it to construct their own hotel and departmental improvement plans.

The following two sections provide an overview of how cultural change has been achieved at Scott's through a commitment to the philosophy, structures, processes and practice of TQM. In this, a key ingredient has been and continues to be the contribution made by all employees to the process of continual improvement.

Establishing the foundations (1989–91)

The move towards TQM began to gather momentum in 1989 with the launch of the quality circles programme (see Figure 4.5). Prior to this, three of the company's senior managers had attended a one-day seminar about quality circles, and this influenced executive-level thinking about the points of convergence within the organization. A 'top-down' commitment to TQM has already been expressed by the managing director; the challenge was to capture the energy and enthusiasm of employees at unit level.

PLANNING, QUALITY CIRCLE TRIALS, AWARENESS
TRAINING (1989)
- September: Strategic Conference:
  Launch of Quality Conference (senior head office personnel; hotel
  general managers)
- October: Formation of the Corporate Total Quality Steering Group
- November: Launch of quality circles (pilot – 3 hotels)

QUALITY EDUCATION, INVOLVEMENT AND
MEASUREMENT (1990)
- March: Operations Conference:
  TQM awareness (operations managers, all hotel management personnel)
- June: Quality circles training
  Commencement of awareness days (all hotel staff)
- October: Appointment of quality support manager
  Role: to co-ordinate/facilitate the development of quality circles

CONTINUOUS IMPROVEMENT, QUALITY WEEK, QUALITY
WEEKEND (1991)
- May: Quality Circle Facilitator Workshop
  Focus on communication, relationship building
- June: Team dynamics training
  For quality circle team leaders
- July: 2-day TQM Strategy Workshops
  Implementing TQM (all hotel general managers and management teams)
- September: Strategic Conference
  Launch of Scott's 'Quality Guide for Fortune Seekers' TQM programme
  (based on the 'Wheel of Fortune' conceptual model)
- November: 'Quality Guide for Fortune Seekers'
  training/launch of Quality Week:
  Beginning of training (all staff, new employees at induction)

Figure 4.5 TQM planning and implementation, 1989–91

The quality circles pilot was conducted at three hotels (Slough, Cardiff and Glasgow), and this required the appointment of a facilitator at each location to work initially with an independent consultant on the awareness training, which took place over a two-day period for all members of staff at each unit. The intention was to form circles from groups of departmental staff attending on a voluntary basis at hotel level, and that these groups would meet on a regular basis for an indefinite period to discuss and respond to work-related issues. Following the pilot, developmental training was carried out with the support of the National Society for Quality through Teamwork (NSQT).

Some six months after the earliest quality circle has been established, the role of quality support manager was created. There were eleven Scott's hotels at that time; all had quality circles, some had four or more circles in operation, and arising from this was a need for co-ordination. Since then, the quality support manager's role has evolved so as to provide a link between the TQM leadership given by the managing director and the growing level of quality circle activity arising from the widening base of employees who had expressed a voluntary commitment to the principle of continuous improvement.

It is interesting to note that employees rapidly perceived the benefits for the organization as a whole, and for individual hotel units, of the shift towards collective responsibility for day-to-day problem solving. The programme had originally been introduced as a way of resolving work-related problems and causal factors within hotel departments. In this way, it was hoped that staff would be able to relate to a genuine attempt to release them from sources of frustration at work. In essence, it offered an opportunity to undertake basic problem solving within departments. After staff were assured that the move towards a TQM style was not transient, the majority were willing to contribute their ideas, time and energy to secure the quality circle foundations. To support circle team development and to equip members with the basic tools needed for problem solving, a training programme was implemented during 1990–1. This included sessions on communication and relationship building, team dynamics, and tools and techniques. The latter covered:

- brainstorming;
- data collection and analysis (using cause-and-effect analysis, Pareto diagrams, histograms and other formats);
- giving presentations to management;
- monitoring and observation techniques.

Improvements began to flow almost immediately, and the benefits of harnessing the collective skills and experience of specialist staff can be clearly demonstrated by referring to some of the many schemes devised by circles since the launch.

The 'Coffee Pots' quality circle

Department: Restaurant. Location: Heathrow/Slough.
The circle had identified a problem related to obtaining drinks from the dispenser bar. However, after a preliminary investigation, it was viewed as a cause rather than an effect and the project was refocused on the real problem, which was related to the cleaning and distribution of glassware. The circle began by brainstorming on to an Ishikawa (or fishbone) diagram, as shown in Figure 4.6.

Following this, data collection began in order to identify possible solutions to the problem. It was soon apparent that the journey of a dirty glass from restaurant to dishwasher and back again required closer scrutiny. It was found that the people working in areas where clean and dirty glasses are stored were often frustrated by the failure of other people to deposit glasses in the correct racks. This meant that glasses were often mixed up, which was an annoying and time-consuming problem, especially when the correct glassware was not at hand and guests were waiting. After data

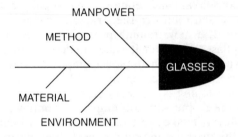

Figure 4.6 Ishikawa (fishbone) diagram

analysis, a possible solution was tested in the form of labelling. Racks were already colour-coded, but no one knew what the colours meant. The proposed solution was to add names and pictures to the glass-rack labels so that they were clearly identified, making it easier for everyone to keep the area better organized. This solution, which included a training plan and a proposal for a training video, was accepted. The 'Coffee Pots' circle implemented its plan, made the training video and monitored the situation to ensure that the problem had been fully resolved.

Other successfully completed circle projects include:

- improvements to guest breakfast service;
- a solution to storage problems for cots and rollaway beds;
- improvement in the standard of photocopying;
- staff rota system improvements;
- guest room improvements to help people with hearing difficulties.

Summarizing so far, top-down commitment was absolute and the circle programme was providing a powerful and effective vehicle for promoting improvement at unit and departmental level. However, it was becoming increasingly apparent that unit middle management were uncomfortable with the changes that were happening. Above all, they lacked the necessary training and support to enable them to make adjustments to their personal management styles, in line with the TQM philosophy that was spreading across the levels above and below them in the organizational structure. For some, the barriers to change were related to long-term industry experience; almost inevitably, those who had been working in the industry for fifteen years or more were finding it difficult to face change. Here, the most important lesson was that, for some, change can only be gradual, and it is especially important that those who can adapt more quickly are able to recognize the difficulties that some of their colleagues face.

In response to the slower rate of uptake from unit middle management, a further training input took place in July 1991. This consisted of a two-day NSQT training course to explain TQM in more detail and allow participants to explore the behavioural implications of supportive management styles. The course culminated in a planning exercise whereby participants were asked to prepare a TQM action plan for their respective hotels, drawing on the corporate TQM vision. This provided a partially successful catalyst for change; some of the participants were able to work through their objectives, and in so doing to facilitate the process of change at hotel level. However, the 1992 Marriott conversion project meant that some of the plans were no longer feasible.

The company's own 'Quality Guide for Fortune Seekers' TQM training programme has, since its launch in September 1991, been successfully implemented throughout the organization. It now forms part of the induction for all new members of staff, and in this way helps to consolidate and retain the in-company TQM knowledge base. To sustain the momentum and reinforce the strategic change arising from the Marriott conversion in July 1992, a new training programme was introduced. Marriott had previously used the phase 'Whatever It Takes' to describe the first part of its three-part TQM programme, which deals with employee empowerment (TQM1). It was felt that this was a good description of the company's TQM initiatives, particularly in relation to the development of listening skills and effective two-way communication within the organization. In essence, the aim of employee empowerment is to encourage everyone to do whatever it takes to get the customer to come back. 'Whatever It Takes' encapsulates this message and reinforces the new partnership with Marriott, so the phrase was adopted for the 1992 empowerment training programme.

Consolidating and building (1992–3)

The partnership with Marriott has several synergistic benefits, notably in the resources available for supporting TQM development. Marriott's three-phase TQM programme covers employee empowerment (TQM1), problem-solving and communication skills (TQM2) and advanced problem-solving and leadership skills (TQM3). It is interesting to note that TQM development is broadly parallel in both companies, and the next step forward is centred on the provision of more advanced tools and techniques training during 1992–3. The purpose of this is to provide a more complete form of support to quality improvement teams (QITs) and hotel action teams in the areas of process and project management (see Figure 4.7).

The training aim is to ensure that hotel-based teams can draw on the people in their own unit with the necessary skills to address complex problems and improvement opportunities. In this respect teams will be more self-contained, and it is envisaged that this will reduce the sense of frustration that can arise when teams face problem situations with the enthusiasm to find a solution, but without the means of fully exploring the range of options that they identify. The intention is to construct the tools and techniques training so that specialists within the organization can make appropriate inputs to the course. For example, the company's planning and development director is well qualified and experienced to explain and illustrate how to manage a project from inception to completion. Ultimately, this will provide a resource to address re-occurring and/or complex problems, so that hotel general managers can ask a member of management to form an action team. In consultation with the hotel general manager, the team will decide how long it needs to solve the

---

MARRIOTT CONVERSION (1992)
Key priorities:
- Managing customer care through the transition period to Marriott
- 'Quality Guide for Fortune Seekers' (continue training)
- 'Whatever It Takes' (empowerment training – all staff)
- Problem-solving training (quality circle members and leaders) (Marriott TQM3)

EXTERNAL AWARENESS (1993)
Key priorities:
- Problem-solving skills (continue training – all staff)
- Quality improvement process review (benchmarking and measurement)
- Quality circle drive (developmental process)
- Leadership skills (in collaboration with Marriott)

STRATEGIC FOCUS ON TQM AIMS (1994)
Key priorities:
- Improved customer retention
- Reduced staff turnover
- Improved profitability

Figure 4.7 TQM planning and implementation, 1992–4

particular problem, provide regular update reports to the hotel's QIT meeting, and disband when the solution has been agreed upon.

The introduction of the QIT concept led to a rethink of the circle facilitator's role, so that heads of department could be given the opportunity to take on this responsibility. Facilitators had originally been recruited on a voluntary basis from across unit operative, supervisory and managerial levels, and the role was additional to the facilitator's existing work. However, it was felt that departmental heads would wish to be involved in their department's quality circle activity, and that their level of seniority would, in turn, facilitate access to the general manager as and when the need arose.

To simply and strengthen the TQM structure, the monthly heads of department meeting concludes with a QIT meeting. All heads of department remain, and circle facilitators from among the staff who represent their respective departments are invited to attend. This has encouraged the sharing of workload and responsibility for quality initiatives and circle leadership. Although the departmental reports are still presented to the QIT by the departmental managers, one or more circle members (other than the facilitator) may attend the QIT meeting as appropriate to the nature of the circle's progress report.

The QIT concept of fully involving departmental managers in the hotel's quality improvement planning is a deliberate policy to promote collective responsibility and avoid any sense of opting out, which could occur if one person held the title of 'quality manager'.

Departmental managers should provide support and encouragement, leaving the facilitator to stimulate activity and promote the use of appropriate tools and techniques. As and when problems arise, facilitators know that it is the responsibility of their manager to seek extra support if needed, at the QIT meeting.

The principal driving force for continuous improvement now comes from the various hotel action teams. Departmental quality circles consist mainly of staff who work together and who meet regularly on a long-term basis. In so doing, they provide a sense of continuity, stability and direction because they are essentially cohesive groups with shared perspectives and a common purpose, which is to improve their part of the hotel operation. As a counterbalance, specialist and cross-departmental groups (task force, process improvement teams and working parties) are increasingly being used to take on specific improvement projects. The contribution made by these short-term project groups is increasing in direct proportion to the problem-solving experience and skills of managers and staff at hotel level. The potential for rapid and effective improvement, engineered by project groups constituted with a specific problem-solving remit, means that they provide a natural focal point for further TQM training and personal development.

In order to monitor the effectiveness of the action teams, the majority of the company's hotels are now using a cost of non-quality (CNQ) account, against which the cost of corrective action taken to resolve guest complaints is charged. Employee empowerment also requires this form of support, as staff have been encouraged to use their initiative and skill in deciding on the best way to resolve complaints the moment they arise. In some, but by no means all cases, hotel staff feel it necessary to make a charge against the CNQ account.

The cumulative account total is reviewed at the monthly QIT meeting, a procedure which involves checking the range and dispersal of complaints to see whether a pattern or trend is occurring. If, for example, complaints cluster around a particular issue or department, the hotel general manager may decide to organize an action team to investigate and resolve the problem. This is normally brought to a QIT meeting, where guidance on the discussion is provided by a checklist covering different scenarios and ways of defining and approaching the problem. The checklist is designed to facilitate a full exploration of the options available before an action team is constituted and assigned.

In summary, the company's TQM philosophy has, during its relatively short history, led to some quite radical forms of change. The whole organization works differently and in a more flexible and creative way. For example, in most Marriott hotels the servicing workload of a room attendant is sixteen guest rooms and the concept of 'self-checking' is well established. A current initiative aims to take this a stage further and break completely with the tradition of close supervision. It is envisaged that this approach will prove to be a more productive and enjoyable way of working because self-checking teams are more committed to meeting consistently the standards of cleanliness that they have helped to define.

The recession has meant that some hotels are operating with far fewer staff, and this has stimulated wide-ranging discussion about methods of working and the best ways of fully utilizing the skills and talents of the workforce. In one hotel, a group of elderly breakfast waitresses recently devised their own process flow chart (their terminology), which in its final form consisted of a carefully laid-out checklist for explaining the breakfast buffet operation. It is mainly intended to help new breakfast staff, and it provides a simple yet effective example of how this group has improved the way in which they work, introduced a form of self-checking and helped to ensure consistency in delivering customer service.

The evidence overwhelmingly shows that, if people are encouraged to take ownership of their work and to improve continually on the way in which it is organized, then they rise to the challenge, and in so doing, reinforce the total quality culture of the organization.

Sustaining the strategic focus on training for total quality

Market research undertaken prior to the Marriott conversion clearly showed that customers were fed up with and confused by the constant rebranding that has been taking place in the hotel business. In addition to the physical changes and, and in some areas, upgrading of facilities that were required by the change to Marriott, training would evidently continue to play a vital role. In fact, the training needs were closely linked to the TQM journey that the company had already embarked upon.

During the period between October 1992 and January 1993 Scott's invested a total of some 25,000 hours in training; around twelve hours for every employee. The purpose was to ensure that every member of staff fully understood the principles of total quality: namely, that all staff have a role to play, that listening to customers is key and that changes were needed to the way in which total quality techniques were practised in order to sustain continuous improvement. The company's strategic response was to devise its own six-module training programme called 'The Quality Guide for Fortune Seekers', which has become affectionately known as the Wheel of Fortune Training. This was based on the managing director's conceptual model of TQM at Scott's, which is shown in Figure 4.8.

The model depicts quality as a process of continuous improvement; this is symbolized by the use of a wheel to represent continual motion. At its centre, the words TOTAL, QUALITY and MANAGEMENT represents the three spokes of the

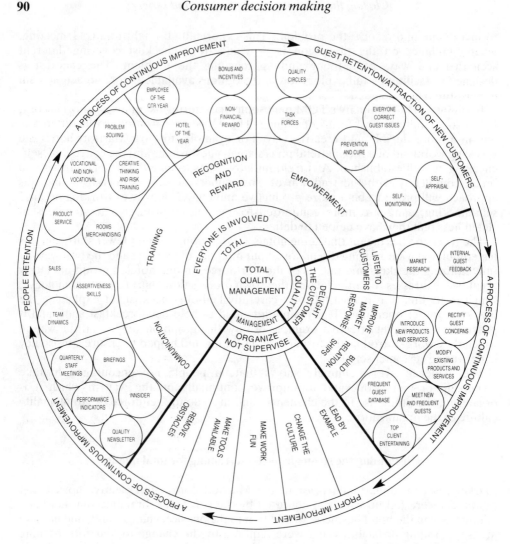

Figure 4.8 Conceptual model of TQM at Scott's Hotels Ltd

wheel. TOTAL means that everybody in the organization must be involved individually and collectively through teamwork in the organization's work output and effort to understand and respond to the needs of all customers, both internally and externally. QUALITY is synonymous with 'delighting the customer'. This means, as a minimum, ensuring that all customers receive precisely what they expect and, better still, that customer service exceeds expectations. MANAGEMENT refers to how all employees have a say in running the business; it embraces a customer-focused philosophy of organizing rather than supervising, and aiming to make things possible rather than creating barriers or resisting change. This also means that managers have to learn to let go of the things they have traditionally controlled, and give authority and responsibility to those who are closest to the decisions that need to be made. The enabling elements of the wheel are situated closer to the rim. 'Delighting the customer' through QUALITY requires listening, market responsiveness and relationship building. TOTAL involvement requires empowerment, recognition and reward, training and communication. MANAGEMENT means changing the culture, removing obstacles, making the tools for the job available, making work fun and leading by example.

The range of options for sustaining TQM year by year – in other words, the activities which can be linked to the objectives of an evolving corporate TQM plan – are shown enclosed by circles. For example, empowerment means giving people the authority and responsibility to solve problems for guests on the spot. Other methods include self-monitoring (responsibility for checking your own work), quality circles and action teams. Training includes, among other things, training in sales, product and service standards. Communication is achieved via internal company publications, staff meetings and departmental briefing meetings. Reward and recognition refers to public acknowledgement of a job 'well done', and in this, examples of positive performance are provided to encourage others. Listening is achieved by taking more notice of guest feedback. Market responsiveness deals with continuous innovation in products and services to meet customer needs. Building relationships is concerned with ensuring that frequent guests feel at home. Management methods refer to specialist training designed to help managers and supervisors adapt to new ways of managing the business. Finally, the outer rim of the wheel refers to three closely linked aims, achievable via continuous improvement. These are retaining people, attracting and retaining customers, and increasing profitability.

The company's TQM infrastructure has facilitated a much better understanding of what really is important from the guest's point of view. These issues form the basis of the service strategy, an overview of which is shown in Figure 4.9. The service strategy is centred on the contact points between customers and employees, and it is here that quality circles and action teams are concentrating their attention in an effort to maintain and improve competitive advantage through continuous improvement. This focus recognizes that sales and marketing activity can only hope to bring in new customers, and that only by serving customers and exceeding their expectations can existing customers be persuaded to come back. In this task, the 'part-time marketer' role of operations personnel is both practical and valid. As in any business situation, the TQM philosophy is equally relevant to cost management and this, combined with continuous improvement in customer satisfaction levels, aids revenue generation and, ultimately, profit performance.

A surprising number of people make a decision not to return to a hotel before they even enter the bedroom. This is linked to dissatisfaction arising from the arrival process: first impressions, the speed of check-in, the welcome, the smile, the acknowledgement, the porter service. In an effort to listen and act, Scott's has responded by devising a service strategy focused on key guest processes. The wide array of improvement action ranges from installing better soundproofing to replacing the pay movie channels with free satellite sports, movie and news channels.

The commitment to continuous, customer-focused improvement also embraces a strategy for listening to customers. This covers formal interviewing, informal discussion sessions with guests, and the gathering of ideas and suggestions made on guest comment forms. Further, eight times a year executive committee meetings are held in one of the company's hotels. The evening before the meeting, the senior management team from the hotel is invited to join the executive committee for an informal evening of leisure activity, followed by supper and an informal meeting to hear the team's views and to try to establish how to improve service support to them.

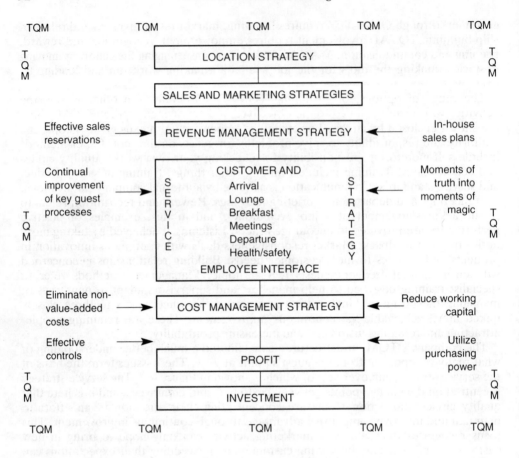

Figure 4.9 Service strategy

After the meeting, the executive committee has lunch with existing and potential customers in the locality. This helps to establish a rapport and a dialogue with customers and a better understanding of sources of guest dissatisfaction, and it enables the committee to explore their ideas and suggestions for improvement.

Empowering continuous improvement in customer service

As we have seen, the conversion to Marriott was reinforced by implementing the 'Whatever it Takes' (WIT) empowerment training programme. This, together with the training provided to ensure that employees felt comfortable with and fully understood the Marriott standards and philosophies, took up some forty to sixty hours per employee; the equivalent of forty-five person years. The key objectives are to encourage staff to look at a guest's stay from the customer's perspective; to enable them to understand the principles of internal and external customer relationships; and, above all, to re-affirm that, individually, they have a responsibility to ensure that the guest's stay is as perfect as it can be. This means giving staff the confidence to make decisions, large or small, that impact on a guest's stay. It involves enabling staff to understand who their customer is, the nature of the service that they require and the meaning of first impressions, and in parts of the training it means taking them through guest experiences using role plays. The WIT training focuses on six rules:

1. Please acknowledge that you have seen me and know that I am standing/sitting there waiting to be served.
2. Please make me feel important and like a real individual.
3. Please find out what my needs are.
4. Please look as though you enjoy working here.
5. Please know what you are doing and do it promptly.
6. Please don't bring any more hassle into my life.

To encourage and support employee development, an innovative non-vocational training scheme has been introduced. In principle, this means that all employees are eligible to receive sponsorship so that they can learn a new skill. This need not necessarily be related to their job of work or the way in which they perform their work. The idea is to promote personal growth and development through learning opportunities. In this way both the employee and the organization gain from a wider commitment to personal development. The evidence so far shows that employees perform better than ever before, and that positive feedback from guests leads to yet further performance improvement.

Ray Kroc, the man behind McDonald's, asserts that 'none of us is as good as all of us'. Scott's commitment to teamwork is sustained by quality circles and hotel action teams, and the level of employee involvement and empowerment is continuously influencing guest relations and service. The following stories illustrate the point.

Lisa, a receptionist at the Bristol Marriott hotel, dealt with a guest who claimed to have a reservation at the hotel. She was unaware that he was a senior decision-maker from a major corporation; a company that Scott's has wanted to do business with for many years. Following a series of telephone calls, Lisa located the reservation, which had been made with a rival hotel, and she then informed the hotel security manager, who took the guest in the hotel courtesy vehicle to the rival hotel. To his surprise, the security manager, who was duty manager the following morning, ended up delivering a breakfast tray to the same guest at the Marriott. On enquiring why the guest had stayed at the Marriott after all, the manager was told that the staff at the rival hotel did not appear to care: 'they did not appreciate my custom or give me the impression that I was valued'. The guest's reason for returning to the Marriott, which was undergoing building work at the time, was that 'although it [the hotel] more resembles a building site than a hotel, it has a welcome and a staff that really make a difference, so I walked out and stayed with you!'

A guest at the same hotel asked Marlene, a guest room attendant, to arrange for items of clothing to be laundered. The timing of the request meant that it would be difficult to fulfil, so rather than telling the guest this, she took the guest's laundry home and did it herself.

These and many other stories like them surface not because the staff concerned publicize them, but because the stories are retold by guests or their colleagues. It is apparent that staff derive a great deal of satisfaction from knowing that their efforts have been appreciated by the customer. In this, managers have an important role, which is to say 'thank you' in recognition of superior performance. Regardless of where people work in organizations, achievement should be recognized. In the same way, most employees have in common the following concerns about work:

- a desire to be treated with respect;
- a desire for varied and challenging work;
- recognition for the job they do and a desire to improve;
- a desire to work with people who listen;
- a preference for an environment where they are allowed to think for themselves and where they have a chance to see the outcome of their efforts;
- a desire to work for a manager who is efficient;
- a desire to be kept well informed.

These are the concerns that Scott's has sought to address during the last four years, and it is now an organization where people make decisions for themselves, take risks and, occasionally, learn from their mistakes. The company having secured the foundations of empowerment, launched a new advertising campaign that sells 'service' in 1992. It would not have been realistic to make the promises that it contains without a supportive infrastructure and the confidence of knowing that the organization as a whole will respond positively and in the manner suggested by the advertisement.

Sustaining the organizational focus on service

A consistent theme of the feedback from staff and customers is that the company's TQM programme has led to a significant cultural shift, effectively changing the 'way we do business'. It has become an organization which encourages its people to ask questions, to promote change and to challenge outdated thinking and ineffective methods. This has been achieved through staff by:

- employees providing a service that exceeds customer expectations;
- employee involvement and decision making at all levels in the organization;
- improved retention rates for employees (linked to more effective communication and feedback, training and empowerment).

Key measures are:

- quarterly improvement on a rolling annual basis of controllable employee turnover (monitored quarterly, internal);
- achievement of employee attitude survey target ratings (monitored annually, external);
- success of quality initiatives (quality circles, improvement and action teams) following external guidelines for effective quality management.

It has also been achieved through customers by:

- retention of customers (tracking/feedback and responding to guest issues);
- increasing overall market share.

Key measures are:

- attainment of service audit target scores (monitored annually, external);
- attainment of customer response ratings (from a given percentage minimum of customer base (monthly, internal);
- achievement of market share and penetration targets (monitored monthly, internal);
- attainment of performance targets in the marketplace (monitored by market audit comparisons, annually, external);

● long-term retention of key accounts (monitored quarterly, internal).

Employees now have much more involvement in operations, and they have developed further the ability to respond to guest feedback in a positive way. There is also a stronger sense of striving for excellence in the individual hotels, arising from unity of purpose and greater team involvement. This in turn has led to a better understanding and awareness of the key factors affecting the business as a whole, at every level in the organization. There is no doubt that the company's TQM philosophy will continue to provide the route to improved product-service standards and long-term profitability. The objective will remain the same: namely, to maximize revenue and improve profit by increasing efficiencies and eliminating costs that are of no direct or indirect benefit to customers. In this, coupled with total quality and continuous improvement in customer service, lies the best strategic response to managing through recession.

NOTES

1. Pannell Kerr Forster Associates, *Corporate Hotel Users in the UK*, Pannell Kerr Forster Associates, London, 1991.
2. Gummesson, E., *Marketing: A Long Term Interactive Relationship – Contributions to a New Marketing Theory*, Marketing Technology Centre, Stockholm, Sweden, 1987.
3. Gummesson, E., 'Marketing organization in service businesses: the role of the part-time marketer', in Teare, R., with Moutinho, L., and Morgan, N. (eds), *Managing and Marketing Services in the 1990s*, Cassell, London, 1990, pp. 35–48.
4. Teare, R., and Gummesson, E., 'Integrated marketing organization for hospitality firms', in Teare, R., and Boer, A. (eds), *Strategic Hospitality Management: Theory and Practice for the 1990s*, Cassell, London, 1991, pp. 144–57.
5. Carlzon, J., *Moments of Truth*, Ballinger, Cambridge, MA, 1987.
6. Teare, R., 'Designing a contemporary hotel service culture', *International Journal of Service Industry Management*, vol. 4, no. 2, 1993, pp. 63–73.
7. Hubrecht, J., and Teare, R., 'A strategy for partnership in total quality service', *International Journal of Contemporary Hospitality Management*, vol. 5, no. 3, 1993, pp. i–iv.
8. Simmons, P., and Teare, R., 'Evolving a total quality culture', *International Journal of Contemporary Hospitality Management*, vol. 5, no. 3, 1993, pp. iv–viii.
9. Kelly, G. A., *A Theory of Personality: The Psychology of Personal Constructs*, W. W. Norton, New York, 1963.
10. Kelly, G. A., *The Psychology of Personal Constructs*, W. W. Norton, New York, 1955.
11. Jones, S., 'Depth interviewing', in Walker, R. (ed.), *Applied Qualitative Research*, Gower, Aldershot, 1985.
12. Eden, C., Smithin, T., and Wiltshire, J., 'Cognition, simulation and learning', *Journal of Experimental Learning and Simulation*, vol. 2, 1980, pp. 131–43.
13. Eden, C., Smithin, T., and Wiltshire, J., *Cognitive Policy Evaluation User Guide*, Bath Software Research, University of Bath, 1985.
14. Eden, C., Jones, S., and Sims, D., *Messing About in Problems*, Pergamon, Oxford, 1983.

15. Eden, C., Jones, S., and Sims, D., *Thinking in Organizations*, Macmillan, London, 1979.
16. Eden, C., and Jones, S., 'Publish or perish? A case study', *Journal of the Operational Research Society*, vol. 31, 1980, pp. 131–9.
17. Jones, S., 'Listening to complexity – analysing qualitative marketing research data', *Journal of the Market Research Society*, vol. 23, no. 1, 1981, pp. 26–39.
18. Jones, S., 'The analysis of depth interviews', in Walker, R. (ed.), *Applied Qualitative Research*, Gower, Aldershot, 1985.
19. Jones, S., and Eden, C. 'Modelling in marketing: explicating subjective knowledge', *European Journal of Marketing*, vol. 15, no. 7, 1981, pp. 3–11.
20. Sims, D. B. P., 'Problem construction in teams', PhD thesis, University of Bath, School of Management, 1978.
21. Eden, C., 'Participating in decisions', unpublished manuscript, University of Bath, 1979.
22. Sims, D., and Jones, S., 'Making problem definition explicit in teams', unpublished manuscript, University of Bath, 1980.
23. Eden, C., Jones, S., Sims, D., and Smithin, T., 'The intersubjectivity of issues and issues of intersubjectivity', *Journal of Management Studies*, vol. 18, no. 1, 1981, pp. 37–47.
24. Smithin, T., and Sims, D., "Ubi caritas?" Modelling beliefs about charities', *European Journal of Operational Research*, vol. 10, 1983, pp. 237–43.
25. Teare, R., 'Consumer strategies for assessing and evaluating hotels', in Teare, R., and Boer, A. (eds), *Strategic Hospitality Management: Theory and Practice for the 1990s*, Cassell, London, 1991, pp. 120–43.
26. Senior, M., 'Perceptions of service quality: a study in the UK roadside lodge sector', PhD thesis, Bournemouth University, Department of Service Industries, 1992.
27. Shostack, G. L., 'Designing services that deliver', *Harvard Business Review*, January/February 1984, pp. 133–9.
28. Parasuraman, A., Zeithaml, V. A., and Berry, L. L., 'A conceptual model of service quality and its implications for future research', *Journal of Marketing*, vol. 49 (Fall), 1985, pp. 41–50.
29. Senior, M., and Randall, L., 'Hotel services in the NHS', *Managing Service Quality*, IFS Publications, July 1991.
30. Randall, L., and Tofts, A., 'NHS support services: present and future developments in training', *International Journal of Contemporary Hospitality Management*, vol. 3, no. 1, 1991, pp. 4–9.
31. Randall, L., and Senior, M. 'Managing quality in hospitality services', *International Journal of Contemporary Hospitality Management*, vol. 4, no. 2, 1992, pp. vi–viii.
32. Piercy, N., *Market-Led Strategic Change*, Thorsons, London, 1991.

PART 2

SEGMENTING TRAVEL MARKETS

Josef A. Mazanec

PART B

INTRODUCTION

Contemporary marketing theory as well as advanced marketing practice distinguish between *strategic* and *instrumental* marketing planning. The planning process occurs on two levels. Strategic decisions should be taken prior to instrumental decisions. *Strategic planning* involves two issues where marketing management is expected to take decisions. These two domains are called *product positioning* and *market segmentation*. Positioning refers to the development or selection of perceived benefits which promise to establish a competitive advantage. Therefore, they may be transformed into arguments and appeals delivered in advertising and personal selling. Segmentation is a prerequisite for selective market operation. It is based on tourist attitudes, travel behaviour and demographic or socioeconomic profiles. When targeting a marketing effort to selected segments, one can reduce the competitive pressure that would prevail if all products and services were indiscriminately offered to the same market.

The objective of *instrumental planning* is to design the appropriate 'marketing mix'. Strategy must be transfomed into action by determining product attributes, price levels, distribution channels and the communications mix (consisting of advertising, sales promotion, personal selling and public relations). Marketing planning in travel and tourism faces a particular challenge as it deals with a multifaceted, poorly standardized, highly seasonal product, and a volatile, fastidious customer. Tailoring travel products in order to satisfy tourist needs becomes a straightforward exercise once the market has been divided into segments which are homogeneous in their choice behaviour and accessible through promotional activity. Segmentation methodology has to cope with two different decision situations known as the a priori and a posteriori approaches. Chapters 5 and 6 respectively focus on each of these settings.

Chapter 5 concentrates on the use of 'a priori' explanatory models for predicting consumer behaviour and segmenting travel markets using a criterion method. Though the underlying philosophy is easily comprehensible, its transfer into marketing practice requires careful planning as multivariate tools (rather than bivariate cross-tabulations) are required in order to support management decisions. The potential value to tourism and hospitality marketers of the combined techniques of automatic interaction detection (AID) and discriminant analysis is illustrated using examples drawn from the Austrian National Guest Survey (Survey).

Chapter 6 focuses on the use of 'a posteriori' explanatory models for predicting consumer behaviour and segmenting travel markets using multivariate profiling methods. In particular, an innovative approach to segmentation methodology is introduced. This involves the development of a neural networks model which is used to recognize Survey tourist types and to classify cases with previously unknown segment affiliation.

Contemporary marketing theory treats a priori and a posteriori segmentation as if the two approaches were unrelated to each other. Chapter 7 addresses the need to find an acceptable way of combining the two concepts so as to produce recommendations that managers can act upon, Chapter 8, which takes the form of an integrated case study, describes the aims, objectives and methodology used in conjunction with the Survey, which is one of the world's largest on-going tourism surveys, and the concept of EUROSTYLES (lifestyle profiling). The final chapter in Part 2 (Chapter 9) addresses the strategic impact and practical implications for Austrian tourism of segmentation research findings.

ACKNOWLEDGEMENTS

Major parts of the research findings presented in Chapter 5 originate from empirical projects of the Institute for Tourism and Leisure Studies and of the Austrian Society for Applied Research in Tourism. Thanks are due to Ursula Vavrik for joint work on the a priori segmentation issues, to Andreas Zins for his most valuable contributions to joint work on the 1991–2 guest surveys, including the EUROSTYLES typology, and to Mark Mazanec.

FIVE

A priori segmentation

DECISION SITUATION

Travel market segmentation cannot progress in a systematic manner unless it is based on an explanatory model of consumer behaviour.[37,24,27] (The notes for Chapters 5 to 9 are grouped together on pp. 158–61.) In principle, all of the consumer characteristics appearing in these models are eligible for segmentation purposes. Any variable or construct exhibiting predictive power with respect to travel behaviour may be considered for segment description. Marketing theory recommends such variables that generate segments whose members tend to react uniformly to promotional measures taken by management. In practice, however, demographics and socio-economics are still preferred. More recently, market segmentation is increasingly relying on psychographic and behavioural characteristics.

An advanced explanatory model contains variables that are more closely associated with behaviour than sex, age, household location or income. It employs constructs like motives, attitudes or perceptions of risk, product images, etc. As a consequence, traveller segments derived from these psychographics are likely to respond homogeneously when confronted with a particular product or advertising message. However, it is costly and time-consuming to forecast behavioural response. For this reason, management often resorts to experience with past behaviour: a person who has been a frequent traveller is expected to stick to habits. The typical package tourist behaves in a different manner from the individual traveller, a camper from a luxury tourist, a cross-country skier from a snow-boarder. Each type demands a special set of tourist services from a suitable supplier.

Suppose, for example, a market analyst aims at defining segments on the basis of (past) travel behaviour. He or she would then predetermine an attribute such as type of trip, intention to repeat visit, daily expenditure, etc. as a criterion variable. Subsequently, the analyst will have to search for additional characteristics to gain a more complete consumer profile, and may consider such attributes as booking of accommodation, vacation motives or rating of resort facilities. Country of origin, age, profession, daily newspaper and preferred TV channels are other useful 'objective' descriptors to enter into selective market operation. If a single criterion variable (or a compound variable made up of several items) is fixed in advance, the task is called *a priori segmentation*, or 'criterion segmentation' (note 4, p. 229). If, however, the idea of a predetermined criterion variable is abandoned and management has no prior information as to an elementary grouping in the market (or they do not want to exploit it), the result is an *a posteriori segmentation* task. It requires the market to be divided into groups with similar multivariate profiles. The number and size of groupings previously unknown normally emerges from a clustering process (cf. 'similarity segmentation' in note 4, p. 229).

Any major tourist-receiving country faces the crucial problem of channelling demand from the peak to the shoulder seasons as well as from highly developed to less utilized tourist regions. This endeavour frequently turns out to be a market segmentation exercise. The travel products offered during off-season and in non-central tourist areas are by no means equally appealing to all customers. The same situation arises in a city hotel where the business structure varies between weekdays and weekends, and a different clientele may also patronize the same restaurant at the various meal periods. Dealing with a fragmented demand is universal in the travel and tourism business. A priori segmentation, therefore, should appear only natural to the tourism manager as a daily experience (while he or she need not necessarily be aware of management science applications to this phenomenon).

A priori segmentation will be discussed in this chapter. Its basics are easily comprehensible, but the transfer into marketing practice is not trivial. Management should seek a multivariate tool to support their decisions. It is not sufficient to work through a number of separate bivariate cross-tabulations. In the next section the technique of automatic interaction detection or AID[48,50] will be suggested. Discriminant analysis (DA) is another, more popular method for supporting a priori segmentation tasks. Both methods may be tied together to secure proper validation of AID results. The exploratory strength of AID combined with the inferential statistics of DA leads to methodological improvement in a priori segmentation analysis.

Systematic identification of market segments subject to a specific mixture of marketing variables has to include explicit objectives and hypotheses. In a priori segmentation the marketing objective automatically governs the selection of the dependent (criterion) variable(s). Assume, for example, that a tourist destination wants to increase earnings without further growth in the number of travellers to the region. Tourist spending then becomes the relevant characteristic for the target group, and marketing effort will be directed primarily to potential visitors with high daily expenditure. Where a low level of destination loyalty seems unsatisfactory, the identification of vacationists who are likely to return to the resort may be regarded as a management objective. Thus, repeat visitation represents the dependent or criterion variable. Then a set of hypotheses (a 'model') must step in to differentiate travellers with high daily expenses from those with low daily expenditure, or to spot the correlates of a strong intention to repeat the visit. Each hypothesis helps to reduce the large number of independent variables to a smaller quantity of criteria which are relevant for the analysis. Relevance implies a presumable cause–effect relationship between the criterion and the independent variables. Such a hypothesis may, for example, express the dependence of a tourist's daily expenditure on his social position or type of trip. The assumptions concerning predictors may be derived from experience, common sense ('intuitive model') or former research results. A properly designed segmentation study will always be driven by a model-based variable selection. It gives a rationale for the variables suggested as predictors, thus allowing reproducibility of results and learning by trial and error.

ANALYTICAL TOOLS

Exploring a priori segments with the automatic interaction detector (AID)

The AID technique was introduced by Sonquist, Baker and Morgan.[48] Unlike regression or discriminant analysis, it is particularly suited to nominal variables.[2] In all the following examples the dependent variable is assumed to be dichotomous, e.g. travellers with high versus low spending level, repeat visitors versus non-repeaters, etc. If more than one criterion value were to be analysed, the AID runs might be ordered sequentially: for example, 1st run, main holiday-makers versus all others; 2nd run, second and third trips versus all others; 3rd run, short trips versus all others. AID requires a sample size of not fewer than 1,000 cases. It makes no assumptions on the properties of the data, such as linearity or normal distribution of error terms. For the manager, the typical AID output of a tree diagram conveys a more illustrative description of market segments than other techniques.

A non-technical outline of the AID method in tourism market segmentation is most instructive in conjunction with a demonstration result. The following example is drawn from a study of Austrian summer guests (note 50, p. 117). The AID version, which represents a simplified version of the AID–3 algorithm by Sonquist, Baker and Morgan[48] was programmed by Vavrik.[50]

In Figure 5.1 the 'big spenders' constitute the target segments. The AID procedure divides the total sample sequentially into non-overlapping binary subgroups until fifteen two-way splits are accomplished. The output is organized as a symmetric tree diagram with five levels and thirty-one cells. Each of these cells contain two numbers, the size of the cell and its contents of 'big spenders'. The number on the top of each cell is the share of cases in the cell as a percentage of all cases. The number on the bottom of each cell is the proportion of the cases with high expenditure in the respective cell. In Figure 5.1 the 'big spenders' are defined as tourists with 'daily expenditure above average'. Before deciding on each binary split, AID examines all variables eligible for producing splits into all possible subgroups. The 'best' variable is selected. 'Best' means that the variable generates two subdivisions where the 'big spenders' accumulate as much as possible on one side while avoiding the other side.

In Figure 5.1 the starting cell 1 is divided into cells 2 and 3 by distinguishing guests in five-, four- or three-star hotels from all other categories. Cell 2 contains 3,023 respondents (46.9 per cent of 6,446) in the upper hotel categories, of whom 1,188 respondents (39.3 per cent) spent more than average. The splitting of the other cells all the way down the tree follows the same principle. The descriptive variable leading to the highest possible increase in the share of 'big spenders' becomes the next splitting criterion. The process stops if the absolute number of respondents in a mother cell falls below a critical value (of, say, fifty or thirty cases), or if the attainable improvement is negligible. Figure 5.2 provides an 'expert mode' explanation in more stringent notation.

The target segment of 'big spenders' is easily identified. In general, the cells on the bottom layer of the tree diagram with the highest cell means represent the 'hard core'

HOTEL CATEGORY

1 * * * * * * *
* 100.0* = 6,446 cases   DAILY EXPENDITURE
* 27.2* above average
* * * * * * *

5-, 4-, and 3-star hotels

2 * * * * *
* 46.9*
* 39.3*
* * * * * * *

2- and 1-star hotels or not categorized

3 * * * * *
* 53.1*
* 16.5*
* * * * * * *

HOTEL CATEGORY

5- and 4-star hotels

4 * * * * * *
* 22.3*
* 48.4*
* * * * * * *

3-star hotels

5 * * * * * *
* 24.6*
* 31.1*
* * * * * * *

TYPE OF TRIP

Short trip, other

6 * * * * * *
* 9.5*
* 28.4*
* * * * * * *

Main trip, second/third trip, business trip

7 * * * * * *
* 43.6*
* 13.9*
* * * * * * *

FREQUENCY OF PAST VISITS

Twice or more often

8 * * * * * *
* 16.8*
* 53.6*
* * * * * * *

Once, never before

9 * * * * * *
* 5.5*
* 32.6*
* * * * * * *

BOOKING OF ACCOMMODATION

No prior arrangements

10 * * * * *
* 4.6*
* 53.0*
* * * * * * *

Directly with the lessor, travel agent, local tourist office

11 * * * * *
* 20.0*
* 26.0*
* * * * * * *

DESTINATION PROVINCE

Lower Austria, Burgenland

12 * * * * *
* 1.6*
* 6.7*
* * * * * * *

Vienna, Upper Austria, Salzburg, Carinthia, Styria, Tyrol, Vorarlberg

13 * * * * *
* 7.9*
* 32.9*
* * * * * * *

CHILDREN IN THE PARTY

Yes

14 * * * * *
* 7.9*
* 3.3*
* * * * * * *

No

15 * * * * *
* 35.7*
* 16.2*
* * * * * * *

TYPE OF TRIP

Main, second/third, other

16 * * * * *
* 12.8*
* 49.7*
* * * * * * *

Short, business trip

17 * * * * *
* 4.0*
* 66.0*
* * * * * * *

FOOD ARRANGEMENTS

Full, half board

18 * * * * *
* 3.3*
* 21.9*
* * * * * * *

Else

19 * * * * *
* 2.2*
* 48.2*
* * * * * * *

CHILDREN

Yes

20 * * * * *
* 0.4*
* 28.6*
* * * * * * *

No

21 * * * * *
* 4.2*
* 55.5*
* * * * * * *

BOOKING OF ACCOMMODATION

Travel agent

22 * * * * *
* 6.6*
* 10.0*
* * * * * * *

Directly with the lessor, local tourist office

23 * * * * *
* 13.3*
* 33.9*
* * * * * * *

TYPE OF ACCOMMODATION

Hotel, pension, camping

24 * * * * *
* 1.2*
* 1.3*
* * * * * * *

Rented apartment, b&b

25 * * * * *
* 0.4*
* 21.4*
* * * * * * *

DESTINATION PROVINCE

Vienna

26 * * * * *
* 0.6*
* 70.3*
* * * * * * *

Tyrol, Vbg, Styr, Car., Upper A., Salzbg

27 * * * * *
* 7.3*
* 29.9*
* * * * * * *

AGE

>50

28 * * * * *
* 0.9*
* 12.5*
* * * * * * *

<50

29 * * * * *
* 7.0*
* 2.2*
* * * * * * *

FOOD ARRANGEMENTS

Full board, self-cater.

30 * * * * *
* 8.9*
* 8.4*
* * * * * * *

Half board, other

31 * * * * *
* 26.9*
* 18.8*
* * * * * * *

Figure 5.1   Locating the 'big spenders'

Source: Note 50, p. 117.

Performing the binary splits in the AID tree

The two parameters of each cell in the AID tree diagram are the cell size *N* and the cell mean of *Y*. *N* is the relative frequency of cases in the cell as a percentage of all cases. *Y*, the dependent variable, is dichotomous with values 0 and 1. Thus, mean(*Y*) is the portion of the cases in the respective cell that have a value of 1 for the dependent variable. In Figure 5.1, where the dependent variable is defined as 'daily expenditure above average', 1 means 'yes' and 0 means 'no'. Before deciding on a binary split, all variables eligible for splitting are examined to calculate the means of all possible subgroups. If, for example, a potential splitting criterion like 'country of origin' has four values (categories), there are ten combinations with two non-empty subgroups that must be examined: four possible splits with one country versus the rest of three, and six splits into two different country pairs. With two parameters (cell size and cell mean) the explained sum of squares (*ESS*) is given by the formula:

$$ESS = N_1 * \mu \, (Y_1)^2 + N_2 * \mu \, (Y_2)^2$$

For each split, the pair of subgroups attaining the highest value of *ESS* is selected. In Figure 5.1 the independent variable 'hotel category' performed best. The whole sample (cell 1) is divided into cells 2 and 3 by distinguishing guests in the three upper hotel categories from all other hotels (lower category or hotels not categorized). 'Hotel category' still remains one of the independent variables for usage on the succeeding levels of the diagram. Both of its subgroups may be divided further (e.g. category 5 plus 4 stars versus 3 stars). Working down the segmentation tree follows the same rule. The descriptive variable yielding the highest increase in the variance explained of the dependent variable becomes the next splitting criterion. As the maximization of variance explained corresponds to minimizing the predictive error, the iterative algorithm may be said to apply a least-squares principle.

Figure 5.2   Performing the binary splits in the AID tree

of the target group. If they turn out to be of small size, more cells may be added. In Figure 5.1 guests in five- and four-star hotels with two or more past visits to Austria are the most attractive travellers (16.8 per cent of the great universe). A small fraction (4 percentage points) of these guests on short or business trips even contains two-thirds of 'big spenders' (cell 17). And also guests in three-star hotels are likely to spend more than average, if they make no prior reservations and travel without children (cell 21; 4.2 per cent of all guests). Altogether, a segment totalling about one-fifth of the guest population may be composed, where the likelihood of finding a 'big spender' has doubled compared to the master sample.

An AID analysis answers questions on the usefulness of target segment descriptors, on the size of the target group to be reached by promotional activities, and on the expected accuracy of selective market operation. There are no restrictive statistical assumptions. The data may contain non-linearities, correlations or interaction effects. Concerning the scaling level, all types of variable may enter the analysis. As AID is particularly designed for qualitative data (nominal and ordinal), quantitative variables (interval and ratio-scaled) have to be 'downgraded'. This means that a personal attribute like age (a ratio-scaled variable) must be categorized into age groups (an ordinal variable). AID is expected to identify the best descriptors of a target group. Membership in the target group is the dependent (or criterion) variable. As one either belongs to the target group or not, this is a dichotomous variable (with value 1 or 0).

AID's major advantages are its exploratory strengths and its ease of interpretation. In itself, of course, it is not a method of inferential statistics. Therefore, a statistical validation of AID results using discriminant analysis is strongly recommended (note 50, p. 119).

From the decision-maker's point of view, AID represents a basis for constructing more sophisticated models with a decision support function. AID makes no definite segment proposals and does not automatically optimize market operations. It is not a decision or optimization model. AID serves as an instrument for multivariate descriptions of a priori segments. Validation with a subsequent discriminant analysis refines the technique.

Validating AID results with discriminant analysis (DA)

AID enables the marketing practitioner to evaluate consumer characteristics and better to define the profile of tourist target segments. But it is still questionable whether these characteristics will pass a statistical test. As AID is an exploratory method, discriminant analysis (DA) is applied to verify the AID results and to draw statistical inferences. DA examines the predictive power of the tourist characteristics suggested by AID. Prior to DA processing, all variables describing the target segments are (re)coded into dichotomous (zero/one) data. AID results assist in optimal coding for the DA because the tree diagram exhibits the dividing point for each variable's values. For example, the variable 'hotel category' in Figure 5.1 showed up best with the two values '5- and 4-star hotels' and the remaining lower categories. 'Type of trip', 'frequency of past visits', 'destination province' and 'children' are dichotomized into dummy variables (coded 1 or 0) accordingly. To avoid bias a DA should spare some part of the sample (divided randomly); the other part (the hold-out or validation sample) is preserved for testing purposes.

The most convincing test requires the construction of a classification matrix. The matrix in the demonstration example exhibits two subgroups of either observed or predicted above- and below-average spenders. The percentage of the cases correctly classified (%CC) is a practical and intuitively appealing measure for the amount of information extracted from the independent variables. To compare the %CC with random classifications, the proportional and the maximal chance criteria $Cpro$ and $Cmax$ (note 36, p. 323) may be calculated. If, out of 6,446 guests, 27.2 per cent are travellers with a high spending propensity, the $Cmax$ value would be 0.73 (i.e. all cases are classified as poor spenders). This value, however, is not feasible here. It completely neglects the target group. The $Cpro$ value recognizes both groups, the 27.2 per cent big spenders as well as the 72.8 per cent poor spenders. $Cpro$ assumes that 27.2 per cent of the cases are randomly selected and assigned to the big spenders' group, and that 72.8 per cent are randomly selected and allocated to the poor spenders' group. The %CC value expected from such a random allocation is the probability of really being a big spender multiplied by the probability of being allotted to the big spenders' group (i.e. 0.272 * 0.272), plus the analogous product for the poor spenders' probabilities (i.e. 0.728 * 0.728). In short (if **2 denotes raising to the second power), $Cpro = 0.272**2 + 0.728**2 = 0.60$, saying that 60 per cent of all guests might be correctly classified into either of the two spending categories just 'by chance'. A DA run with the characteristics 'hotel category', 'frequency of past visit', 'type of trip', 'children', and 'booking of accommodation' (as inferred from the tree structure in Figure 5.1) results in a %CC of 73.4 (note 50, p. 116). Thus, the improvement in classification amounts to 13.4 points. It is attributed to the appropriate selection and coding of independent variables suggested by the AID analysis.

The exploratory technique of interaction detection was introduced as a practical segmentation tool for the marketing manager in tourism. AID represents a technique better suited to target group selection than common bivariate cross-tabulations. The assets of AID include easy interpretation of results and a feasible ratio of information gain and analytical investment. It is important from the inferential statistics point of view that AID findings are subject to discriminant analysis as a method of validation.

SIX

A posteriori segmentation

DECISION SITUATION

The a posteriori approach to market segmentation rests on a very simple and plausible assumption. Subgroups in the consumer population may be homogeneous in terms of motives, attitudes or activities. Therefore, they may be expected to react to product offerings and promotional efforts in a similar manner. The most popular concept to fit such a decision situation is called *benefit segmentation*. It was introduced in 1971 by Russell Haley.[14] His argument was that consumer groups with a markedly different pattern of benefits sought should be considered to be 'natural' segments in the market. From a behavioural science point of view, the notion of 'benefit' relates to the more prominent concept of 'attitude'. Benefits desired or expected reveal attitudes towards particular consumption goals (cf. the Rosenberg model of attitude measurement).[41] For example, a traveller who seeks a 'friendly host population' when choosing a destination attaches high salience to the quality of social contact with locals. He holds a strongly favourable attitude towards this attribute of a tourist destination, which may become a dominant item in his overall judgement of a receiving country or tourist region.

Policy-makers in tourism often want to have travel behaviour traced back to its underlying *motives*. This is not easy to achieve in a typical mass survey. Motives are conceived as a state of arousal with no distinct directional effect towards a particular means of satisfaction (cf. questionnaire items such as 'to change pace', 'relax'). A closer look at routine travel surveys shows that many of the questions pretending to measure motives contain an evaluation of some attribute of a (real or ideal) tourist product. Thus they are attitude rather than motive items. Where a validated measuring instrument for capturing travel motives is available, it may also be subject to a posteriori segmentation. The similarity of the motive structure then determines the allocation of travellers to segments. Lifestyle (see Chapter 7) and value systems[18] are gaining importance in travel segmentation theory and practice. Motivational and attitudinal variables related to various domains of everyday life are combined to yield lifestyle and value types.

Travel and vacation *activities* are another type of base material for constructing a posteriori segments.[16] Asking about activities is customary in commercial travel or guest surveys. The definition of 'tourist roles' as suggested by Yiannakis and Gibson[61] is also closely linked to travel activities. Tourist activities easily lend themselves to segmentation purposes. Considerable improvement may be gained over a trivial single-item classification (apline skier, cross-country skier, mountaineer, etc.) if the multivariate nature of activity patterns is taken into account. In benefit segmentation it is the benefit *bundle* which constitutes a segment. Activities are also regarded as arising in typical combinations.

A posteriori segmentation is not that easily understood in tourism marketing practice. Why search for customer groups where there seems to be no compelling reason to do so? The concepts of benefit segmentation of lifestyle, however, should be instructive enough intuitively to justify tourism management becoming involved in traveller typologies and cluster analysis. There is always a chance of coming across something new, a hitherto unexplored combination of motives, attitudes and activities, anything that may evolve into a commercially viable specialization strategy. Innovations in segmentation research are brought forward in two ways: they come along with improved predictive ability of behavioural models and with more sophisticated data manipulation.

The a posteriori variant of segmentation hides behind a different name, since the usage of terminology varies with a writer's scientific origin. Consumer types (psychology), market segments (marketing science) and clusters (quantitative methods) are all different names for the same phenomenon. The theoretical concepts are not new, but only with the advent of more sophisticated techniques of cluster analysis and more powerful computer assistance during the 1970s has a posteriori segmentation become a widespread marketing practice.

ANALYTICAL TOOLS

A non-hierarchical clustering method

A priori segmentation does not necessarily require a multivariate data technique. The segments are already installed, and a more complete description with additional ('passive') variables may be achieved more or less successfully with conventional cross-tabulation. A posteriori segmentation cannot succeed without a multivariate method. The whole pattern of motives, attitudes and activities accounts for the mutual similarity of segment members.

The clustering methodology recommended is not new and has been fairly successful over the years. It was tailored to handle binary data and to cope with a large sample size. The method was cross-validated with the advanced model of latent class analysis, proving that in spite of being much simpler it could detect 'structure' in the data quite reliably. Since the working principles and program are documented elsewhere,[12,25,26] it may suffice to give a brief outline here. Raw data usually arrive in multidimensional scale batteries or item lists from questionnaires or personal interviews. A complicated scale is not needed. Instead, a simple response such as 'yes/no', 'agree/disagree', 'important/unimportant', which can be coded with 1 and 0 (dichotomous data), is sufficient. Variables with more than two categorical values (polytomous data) and ordinal data may be transformed into binary format. For example, a variable like 'country of origin' with values 'UK', 'France' and 'Germany' becomes a set of three 'artificial' binary variables 'UK', 'France' and 'Germany' each with values 1 = 'yes' or 0 = 'no'. Each respondent is represented by his or her response pattern (a 0–1 vector). Identical patterns collected from various respondents are weighted by their frequency and treated jointly during clustering. Depending on the number of variables, this transformation may reduce computing time enormously. Clusters are constructed by sorting respondents according to their mutual similarity. Similar cases become members of the same cluster; dissimilar ones are attributed to different clusters. Expert knowledge about the computation of similarity measures is not necessary to understand the results of the cluster analysis. For those readers interested in a brief outline of how to derive dissimilarities, Figure 6.1 has the details.

The BINCLUS clustering program performs a partitioning (not a hierarchical) procedure. This means that a (tentative) number of clusters has to be fixed in

---

How to derive similarity and dissimilarity values

A similarity measure is needed to express the information inherent in the data vector with 0–1 reactions. A simple matching coefficient or the Tanimoto measure seems to be preferable. The first measure counts all 1 and 0 matches as a proportion of the total number of variables. The Tanimoto coefficient recognizes a contribution towards similarity of a pair of guests/tourists only from 1–1 matches (not from 0–0 matches). If, for example, tourists i and j both want to play golf, they are considered to be similar; if neither of them does, they are not. A sample computation of the similarity coefficients with 10 variables in the response patterns proceeds in the following manner:

Item number : 1 2 3 4 5 6 7 8 9 10

Respondent i: 1 1 1 0 0 1 0 0 1 0

j: 1 1 0 1 0 1 1 1 1 0

The number of 1–1 matches divided by the number of items (not tied in a 0 match) gives a similarity value with upper and lower bounds of 1.0 and 0.0 respectively.

	Respondent j		Matching coeff.
	1	0	= (4 + 2)/10
			= 0.6
	1	4 + 1 = 5	
Respondent i		+	Tanimoto coeff.
	0	3 + 2 = 5	= 4/(10 – 2)
			= 0.5
	= 7	= 3 10	

1.0 less the similarity value can be regarded as a metric distance which quantifies dissimilarity. For a number N of response patterns, there are $N*(N – 1)/2$ pairwise distances. The sum of (squared) distances portrays heterogeneity within a segment. When it is accumulated over segments, an overall measure of heterogeneity results.

Figure 6.1 How to derive similarity and dissimilarity values

advance. Starting with an initial random grouping, response patterns are reallocated and exchanged between clusters until overall heterogeneity drops to a minimum. Consecutive solutions are produced for, say, 2 to 6 clusters. The heterogeneity of cluster solutions is bound to decrease with a growing number of clusters. Sometimes a sudden decline (an 'elbow' effect) in the heterogeneity function indicates that a further increase in the number of clusters only leads to a poor improvement in homogeneity. Given no such indication, one has to rely on the face validity of the frequency distributions of the segment-defining variables. But, according to the experience of numerous clustering studies, an inconclusive situation rarely occurs, unless the variables have been compiled rather deliberately (with no underlying explanatory model in mind). Cross-tabulation of cluster membership by demographic, socioeconomic and behavioural criteria (so-called 'passive' variables) concludes the series of data-processing steps.

Neural network (NNW) models

The classification of consumers into market segments closely resembles a pattern recognition problem, which is one of the basic issues of artificial intelligence research. AI technology, therefore, can be exploited for segmentation purposes. In particular, it has been demonstrated that neural network models are a new promising data-processing technique for handling segmentation projects.[29,30]

Inspiration from the neural 'hardware' in the human brain is only one aspect of network modelling. There are an increasing number of applications to data-processing tasks very different from human perception and reasoning where network models seem to be appropriate problem-solvers. In their pioneering work, McClelland, Rumelhart and Hinton (note 34, p. 10) discuss neural networks under the name of parallel distributed processing (PDP) models. This name emphasizes the new method of storing information which is completely different from 'normal' computer-assisted procedures. As in the human brain, one cannot spot the precise location where a particular knowledge domain resides. Knowledge in a network becomes implicit. It is represented in the connectivity structure rather than in particular processing units. Storage and processing are no longer separated as in conventional programming and computing procedures (note 49, p. 355; see Figure 6.2 for the items that make up a network model).

Inventory of network model components

A network model consists of:
- a number of units ('neurons') where information processing occurs in parallel;
- a pattern of relationships among these units (weighted connections) along which information flows through the network;
- a state of activation and an output function for each unit;
- a propagation rule determining the strength of activation passed on to the other connected units;
- an activation rule for processing all inputs reaching a unit and preparing an output from this unit;
- a learning rule for modifying the weight structure depending on new experience;
- links to the outside world to read input and to write output (note 43, p.46).

Figure 6.2   Inventory of network model components

A detailed discussion of NNW case studies is postponed to Chapter 7. To illustrate the methodology, however, classification of travellers with an NNW model is demonstrated here. In one of the case studies in Chapter 7, four traveller types (segments) will be constructed by clustering respondents according to their importance ratings for a list of twenty-four benefits. Each type is characterized by the relative frequencies of his 1 ratings (expressing 'important', while 0 = 'unimportant'). A network model that has been trained on these four frequency distributions can be used to allocate new cases with their 0–1 patterns into one of the four psychographical segments. A pattern classifier model may be constructed with the InstaNet facility of

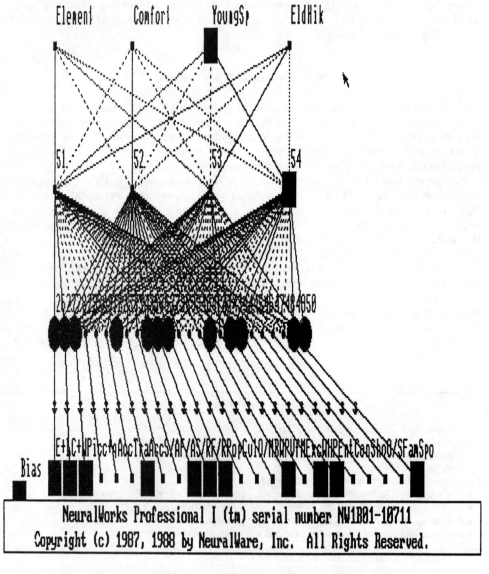

Figure 6.3   A benefit segment classifier network

Source: Note 51, p. 27.

Counterpropagation network architecture

Figure 6.3 employs a so-called counterpropagation architecture with four layers of processing elements:
1. An input layer with 24 input units, corresponding to a person's importance ratings for each of 24 benefits.
2. A normalizing layer, transforming the input vectors to unit length.
3. A nearest-neighbour classifier, where the processing units compete with each other in such a way that only one single 'winning' unit produces an output ('competitive layer').
4. An output layer, which learns to reproduce the correct segment affiliation depending on the element activated in layer 3 (note 38, pp. 466–70).
As the number of clusters to be learned by the network is four, there are four units in the competitive and the output layers. 24 + 1 units are necessary to implement the normalizing step in layer 2. It is apparent from Figure 6.3 that units of neighbouring layers 2, 3, and 4 are completely interconnected. Each connecting line marks a weight applied to the output from the sending ('firing') unit before processing by the receiving unit. The network's experience is stored in this weight pattern (its associative memory).

Figure 6.4   Counterpropagation network architecture

the NeuralWorks software package (NeuralWare, Inc. 1988). Figure 6.3 shows the overall structure. The benefit data of a respondent are fed into the network from the bottom, and are transformed and propagated upwards to output a segment prediction on the top layer. A manager need not know the details of the network's architecture to use its predictions. Figure 6.4 offers some additional remarks for the methodologically interested reader.

Table 6.1   Frequency of benefits considered important (%)

	Benefits	1	2	3	4
1.	Environment, countryside	79	98	86	94
2.	Climate and weather	65	98	94	79
3.	Picturesqueness of town	23	93	71	73
4.	Peace and quiet	44	81	36	62
5.	Accessibility (transport)	17	69	27	29
6.	Local traffic conditions	5	62	12	11
7.	Furnishing, pleasantness	29	90	59	93
8.	Service/accommodation	17	83	26	92
9.	Catering/accommodation	15	77	29	83
10.	Service in restaurants	12	86	69	42
11.	Catering/restaurants	11	85	73	36
12.	Friendliness of the locals	55	96	82	79
13.	Cultural life	11	56	23	19
14.	Opening hours of museums	2	28	1	2
15.	Bad weather programme	6	56	27	12
16.	Value for money	21	97	62	34
17.	Scope for excursions	41	89	48	60
18.	Hiking paths	50	75	52	68
19.	Entertainment facilities	11	68	53	21
20.	Conference meeting facilities	2	6	0	0
21.	Shopping facilities	17	85	39	21
22.	Opening hours of shops	9	69	33	5
23.	Family orientation	13	38	13	14
24.	Range of sports facilities	17	38	66	13

A network has to be trained, which implies the repetitive presentation of a desired output (traveller type) together with a particular pattern of input data (benefits sought). Learning occurs by a continuous adaptation of the weights contingent upon the size of error generated in each trial output. In this demonstration, the input consists of four series of twenty-four frequency values each (one series for each segment; see Table 6.1), while the output desired is one of the data vectors $(1,0,0,0)$, $(0,1,0,0)$, $(0,0,1,0)$ and $(0,0,0,1)$ for each of the four traveller types. After 4,000 training cycles the network has learned to output each of the four types correctly when shown the respective frequency data. Now it is prepared for 'recall': that is, forecasting the cluster affiliation of a person by checking his or her importance ratings for twenty-four benefits. If the total sample of 499 respondents (with known cluster numbers) is classified, the network operates reasonably well in reproducing 444 cases or 89 per cent correctly (Table 6.2). There might be some bias because, owing to the smallness of the sample, a training and a hold-out (validation) subsample were not separated.

Table 6.2   Classification matrix for four
benefit segments(%)

Actual segment	*Predicted segment by network*			
	1	*2*	*3*	*4*
1	93	0	1	7
2	0	89	2	9
3	7	1	75	17
4	3	0	4	93

Cases correctly classified: 89%.

SEVEN

Hybrid segmentation

DECISION SITUATION

Contemporary marketing theory treats a priori and a posteriori segmentation as if the two approaches were unrelated to each other. Management, however, needs a recommendation as to which segmentation approach should be pursued given a particular strategic background, or how to combine both concepts. As yet there is no data technique capable of dealing with both segmentation strategies simultaneously. Neural networks seem to be a promising methodology in terms of practising an a priori and an a posteriori segmentation approach within a single model. In this chapter the outline of a general network structure suited to capture both segmentation concepts is followed by an empirical demonstration study in the field of travel behaviour.

Marketing theory seems to put up with a division between a priori and a posteriori segmentation. Figure 7.1 outlines the logical structure of the segmentation approaches and the data techniques used in the preceding case examples.

Why worry about the twin worlds of segmentation? Contemporary marketing science shifts the responsibility to the marketing manager. He or she is supposed to take the right option either with a predetermined classification of consumers or with an attempt to detect a new partition of the market. Apparently, the basic separation of a priori and a posteriori segmentation reveals an explanatory deficit in segmentation theory. This shortcoming may be removed in either of two ways:

- Recommendations to rely on a priori segments or to adopt an a posteriori approach must explicitly be made dependent on the conditions and characteristics of the decision situation.
- New methodology for measuring typical a priori and a posteriori variables is introduced, enabling the manager to couple both segmentation approaches in a single study.

115

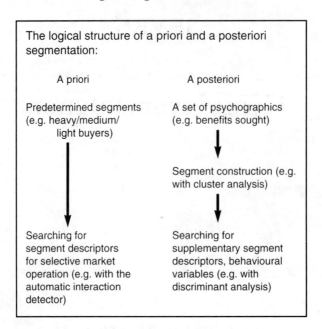

The logical structure of a priori and a posteriori segmentation:

A priori	A posteriori
Predetermined segments (e.g. heavy/medium/ light buyers)	A set of psychographics (e.g. benefits sought)
	Segment construction (e.g. with cluster analysis)
Searching for segment descriptors for selective market operation (e.g. with the automatic interaction detector)	Searching for supplementary segment descriptors, behavioural variables (e.g. with discriminant analysis)

Figure 7.1 A priori and a posteriori segmentation

There is a convincing rationale to favour the second solution. In spite of the more sophisticated a posteriori approach, the fanciest typology and the most elaborate benefit segmentation finally serve a marketing objective. The psychographic segments have to be examined with respect to their behavioural patterns. They turn out to be conducive to reaching marketing goals if significant behavioural differences (purchasing, media usage) emerge. Therefore, one might conjecture that the two worlds of segmentation exist because so far no data technique has managed to cover simultaneously the ('hybrid') tasks of segment identification and description.

ANALYTICAL TOOLS: THE GENERAL ARCHITECTURE OF A NEURAL NETWORK 'HYBRID' MODEL

A very brief and non-technical outline of the 'hybrid' model will be given here. The reader interested in more computational details is referred to the neurocomputing literature: Aleksander and Morton[1] and Wasserman[54] are recommended as introductory texts; Freeman and Skapura[13] provide an introduction for readers with some background in engineering; and Simpson[46] succeeds in compressing extremely instructive material into fewer than 200 pages. The discussion here is limited to drafting a back-propagation network which accommodates all sorts of variables inherent in a 'hybrid' segmentation project.

The network consists of three layers of processing units. Figure 8.15 in the following chapter contains a sample network which exhibits the architecture of units, layers and

Specifics of a 'hybrid' network

Neighbouring layers are fully connected to each other in the standard version of a three-layer feedforward network. It is the purpose of *m* hidden units to extract and to compress the information arriving from *n* input units ($m < n$). In the 'hybrid' network, however, the number of connections is reduced as they are guided by explicit hypotheses. According to these hypotheses, the hidden units share responsibility for only a subset of input units. They fulfil a function similar to unobservable constructs in a causal model (of the LISREL type; 17,3). A number of m_1 hidden elements are interconnected with a number of n_1 input units ($m_1 < n_1$), m_2 hidden elements to n_2 input units ($m_2 < n_2$), etc., where $m_1 + m_2 + ... = m$ and $n_1 + n_2 + ... = n$.

Figure 7.2   Specifics of a 'hybrid' network

connections. The processing elements on the bottom layer represent the demographic, socioeconomic, psychographic and behavioural attributes of the consumers under study. Only those variables intended to fulfil the 'a priori' mission are excluded. They are located on the top (output) layer, where they deliver each consumer's segment affiliation predicted by the network. The intermediate layer is made up of 'hidden' elements with no direct relationship to the outside world. Figure 7.2 explains the difference between a 'normal' network and the 'hybrid' model for the experienced reader.

Data processing occurs in each unit. The inbound flow of information arriving along the input connections consists of weighted output values of the units on the preceding layer. It gets accumulated (usually by a simple summation function) to represent a unit's activation potential. A unit's actual state of activation and, therefore, its outbound information depend on how it treats the summated input, i.e. on the type of transfer function employed. Usually one prefers a non-linear function because it enables the network to learn relationships of any complexity between the input data and the desired output. For the methodologically advanced reader, Figure 7.3 has computational details on activation, transfer and learning in more rigorous terms.

Learning occurs in training cycles. Each training cycle entails a forward pass through the network (from bottom to top) for calculating (trial) output and errors, and a subsequent backward pass (top to bottom) for the weight updates (hence the term *back*-propagation). Convergence has been proven for infinitesimally small corrections of the weights. For weight updates with reasonable magnitude to be achieved within a finite number of iterations, various improvements of the basic estimation procedure have been suggested to prevent the gradient procedure from getting trapped in local minima and to accelerate convergence (see 54, pp. 55ff.). In traditional classification terminology, the network estimates the a posteriori probabilities of belonging to an output class given the input attributes,[53] thereby approximating the Bayes optimal discriminant function.[42] This means that the activation of the output units indicates the 'degree of confidence in class membership'.[45] Classification ambiguity for each case thus becomes apparent. An input vector resulting in one dominant output unit reveals a high degree of confidence. A rather uniform activation level on the output layer is typical for a case with a weak relationship to any class.

To examine a network's performance and practical relevance, the same prediction criteria as are customary in discriminant analysis may be applied. The contextual interpretation refers to the weights denoting the strength of connections between

---

Activation, transfer and learning

If the transfer function is non-linear (a logistic curve, or a hyperbolic tangent), the unit's state of activation varies between the boundaries 0 and 1 or −1 and 1. A hidden layer in conjunction with a non-linear transfer function enables the network to mimic any continuous mapping function of any (unknown) complexity. Non-linearities and interactions are implicitly taken into account.

In more stringent notation, for the elements on the hidden layer:

$$p(i) = \sum_{j=1}^{n} w(i, j) \, x(i, j) \tag{1}$$

where $p(i)$ is the activation potential of unit i
$w(i,j)$ is the weight for input from preceding unit j
$x(i, j)$ is the activation transferred from unit j
n is the number of units on the preceding (input) layer connected to unit i.

$$a(i) = \frac{1}{1 + \exp(-p(i))} \tag{2}$$

where $a(i)$ is the actual state of activation of unit i.

The 'knowledge' that a network acquires about the outside world rests in its associative memory, made up of the weight vectors. Adjustment of the weights occurs through training, i.e. repetitive exposure to training examples (consumers with their a priori, a posteriori and accompanying descriptive attributes). Back-propagation is a powerful method of network training and weight estimation. On the top (output) level, the difference between a desired output $o(i)$ and an actual output $a(i)$ of unit i enters a least-squares error function:

$$E = \frac{1}{2} \sum_{k} (o(i, k) - a(i, k))^2 \tag{3}$$

Then a weight update amounts to

$$\Delta w(i, j) = -\eta \, \frac{\delta E}{\delta w(i, j)} \tag{4}$$

where learning constant $0 < \eta < 1$ and
the derivative $\delta E / \delta w$ of the error function.

As the hidden layer has no direct links to observable values, a difference $o(i,j) - a(i,k)$ is not available for updating the hidden units. The generalized delta rule typical for weight updates in a back-propagation network, therefore, relies on the accumulated error involving all output units connected to a hidden unit (note 44, pp. 322 ff.)

Figure 7.3 Activation, transfer and learning

input variables (input units), constructs (hidden elements) corresponding to types or clusters, and the network output. In contrast to the traditional segmentation methodology, all the weight estimatres serve one final purpose: to reproduce the desired a priori classification. The a posteriori portion of the network is no exception to this rule; it is also governed by the overall input–output mapping principle. Thus, the results do not just correspond to a data reduction or clustering solution derived from an external optimality criterion (e.g. to render consumers homogeneous within and heterogeneous between types/clusters). Typological results (the a posteriori subsystem) are not attained through the 'hybrid' model unless they relate to consumer attributes relevant for selective market operation.

EIGHT

Case examples

IDENTIFYING THE 'REPEAT VISITOR' AND THE 'MAIN HOLIDAYMAKER' AS A PRIORI SEGMENTS

Marketing objectives

'Repeat guests' in this study are defined by a strong intention to come to visit the same tourist resort again within the next two to three years. The intention criterion relates to the degree of satisfaction with tourist services offered by a destination. Give the well-known recommendation to build on customer loyalty,[15] it is an appropriate variable with which to define a priori segments where marketing efforts are likely to be successful.

A breakdown by type of trip is a standard routine for many travel and guest surveys (see, for example, the German travel survey developed by the Studienkries für Tourismus, Starnberg, which is one of the widely used data sources for tourism managers in Europe). The trip categories involve a distinction between main holidays, second/third trips, and short trips (two to four days). Main holidays do not necessarily have the longest duration, but they are subjectively rated as being the 'most important' trip in a calendar year. Thus, a family would be hesitant to sacrifice their 'main holiday' if there were a need to cut household expenses. A second or third trip, or a short trip, might be skipped more easily.

During the 1980s Austria (and other European receiving countries) suffered from a continuing trend in favour of second/third and short trips, while the share of main holidays diminished gradually. If a national tourist office is considering ways of counteracting these tendencies, the first step must be to take a closer look at the profile of the typical main holiday-maker.

Raw data

This analysis of Austrian inbound tourism is based on the GBÖ, the Austrian National Guest Survey.[28] Bivariate cross-tabulations produced from this survey form the basis for the hypotheses underlying the application of AID. The GBÖ master sample consists of 6,760 cases with 257 variables each. The number of characteristics was reduced to 28 for the AID demonstration. The AID sample runs are taken from.[51] The observed and some factorized variables are listed in Table 8.1. The dependent (criterion) variables are 'intention to repeat the visit' and the 'type of trip'. They are coded with 1 and 0, where 1 indicates a strong intention to repeat the visit and a main holiday, while 0 collects all the other visitation and trip categories.

Table 8.1   Variables and their values

Variables	*Values*
1. Intention to repeat visit	Almost certainly, probably, hardly
2. Type of trip	Main holiday, second/third holiday, short trip, congress/business trip, other
3. Age	<30, 30–49, >50
4. Booking of accommodation	With a travel agency, the lessor, a local tourist office, left to chance
5. Children	Yes, no
6. Size of home town	$<20,000$ inhabitants, 20, 001–50,000, $>50,000$
7. City traveller	Austria, FRG, Netherlands, UK, Belgium, other
9. Daily expenditure	$\geq$ AS658, $<$AS658 (i.e. above/below average)
10. Hotel category	***** and ****, ***, ** and *, not categorized
11. Meal arrangements	Full board, half board, breakfast and restaurant, breakfast and self-catering, self-catering
12. Motives 'pleasure, fun'	Yes, no
13. 'new experience'	
14. 'relaxation'	
15. 'health'	
16. 'hiking'	
17. 'sports'	
18. Number of prior visits to Austria	Never before, once, twice or more
19. Profession	Chief employee, white-collar, blue-collar, self-employed, housewife, student
20. Province visited	Vienna, Lower Austria and Burgenland, Upper Austria and Salzburg, Carinthia and Styria, Tyrol and Vorarlberg
21. Rating of resort facilities	Very good, moderately good, neutral, moderately bad, very bad
22. Tour group	Yes, no
23. Type of accommodation	Hotel, pension bed and breakfast
24. Factor 1: 'satisfaction with recreation facilities'	Yes, no
25. Factor 2: '. . . with accommodation'	Yes, no
26. Factor 3: '. . . with price/value ratio'	Yes, no
27. Factor 4: '. . ., with quality of restaurants'	Yes, no
28. Factor 5: '. . . with traffic situation'	Yes, no

Source: Note 51, p. 11.

Correlations among predictors were examined and all cases with missing values were excluded from the analysis. The 'factors' mentioned in the table are condensed data. Twenty-four rating variables were reduced to five factors by principal components analysis. As the rating variables are sensitive with regard to missing values, the number of valid cases for the AID run is only 1,265. In the second example, then, the database is much larger, with a sample size of 6,421 respondents.

Deriving the 'repeat guest' profile

The bivariate analyses performed in the standard guest survey report revealed remarkable relationships between the tourists' intention to repeat their visit and their nationality ('country of origin') as well as the 'province visited'. To these two predictors a number of characteristics were added: age, booking of accommodation, city traveller, number of prior visits to Austria, hotel category, type of trip. Six motive variables and five factorized attitudinal variables also entered the analysis to examine the role of psychographic influences.

The tree diagram of the AID run (Figure 8.1) reads as follows. Cell 1 marks the starting point, indicating that 39.4 per cent of 1,265 guests have the intention to visit their Austrian resort again. The history of binary splits in the tree suggests that booking of accommodation, the 'new experience' motive, country of origin and age should be considered as descriptive criteria. The selected criteria values portray the typical repeat visitor as a person who:

- books accommodation directly with the lessor;
- does not aspire to experience something new;
- originates from Austria, the FRG, the UK and Belgium;
- is aged more than fifty years.

If arrangements for accommodation are made directly with the lessor, the share of repeat guests rises from 39.4 to 56.8 per cent. After adjustments for the next three splitting variables, the portion of repeaters amounts to 71.2 per cent. Travellers who did not book directly with their place of accommodation are only 25 per cent likely to intend a repeat visit. Cell 29 is small but nevertheless interesting. It consists of only 5.8 per cent of the 1,265 travellers, but 68.5 per cent of them show a strong intention to repeat the visit. The guests in this group:

- book their accommodation with a travel agent or tourist office, or prefer a trip without any prior reservations;
- attach great importance to good restaurants and have been satisfied with restaurant services;
- like hiking;
- appreciate recreation facilities.

If all these traveller characteristics were combined, the resulting 'core' segment would account for 30 per cent of the total market. In this segment, there is a 70 per cent probability of meeting a strong 'intention to repeat visit'. The exploratory strength of the AID analysis becomes apparent. Between cells 1 and 22, the percentage of repeaters grows by more than 30 points. The use of information gained through AID results enhances the accuracy of promotional efforts directed to the target segment of repeat visitors. In addition, a number of new variables hitherto not seen in connection with the repeat guest are identified. There is an improvement over simple 'report reading' and over purely bivariate analyses for segmentation purposes.

1******
* 100.0* = 1,265 cases
* 39.4* INTENTION TO REPEAT VISIT almost certainly
******

BOOKING OF ACCOMMODATION

Directly with the lessor | Travel agency, local tourist office, left to chance

2******
* 45.5*
* 56.8*
******

3******
* 54.5*
* 25.0*
******

MOTIVE 'NEW EXPERIENCE'
Yes | No

4******
* 6.5*
* 25.6*
******

5******
* 39.1*
* 61.9*
******

SATISFACTION WITH RESTAURANT SERVICES
No | Yes

6******
* 31.9*
* 18.6*
******

7******
* 22.6*
* 33.9*
******

COUNTRY OF ORIGIN
Austria, Belgium, UK, Netherl. | Netherlands, other countries

8******
* 3.7*
* 10.6*
******

9******
* 2.8*
* 45.7*
******

10*****
* 3.2*
* 30.0*
******

COUNTRY OF ORIGIN
Austria, Germany, Belgium, UK | Netherlands, other countries

11*****
* 35.9*
* 64.8*
******

BOOKING OF ACCOMMODATION
Left to chance | Travel agency, local tourist office

12*****
* 14.9*
* 29.3*
******

13*****
* 17.0*
* 9.3*
******

MOTIVE 'HIKING'
Yes | No

14*****
* 9.2*
* 54.7*
******

15*****
* 13.4*
* 19.5*
******

COUNTRY OF ORIGIN
Austria, UK, Belgium | Germany, Netherl., other

PROVINCE VISITED
Vorarlb., Tyrol | Vienna, Lower A., Burgenld, Upper A., Carinthia, Salzbg, Styria

COUNTRY OF ORIGIN
France, other | Austria, Belgium, UK, Netherl.

16*****
* 3.2*
* 5.0*
******

17*****
* 0.5*
* 42.9*
******

18*****
* 0.8*
* 90.0*
******

19*****
* 2.0*
* 28.0*
******

TYPE OF TRIP
2nd/3rd trip, other | Main, short, business trip

20*****
* 0.5*
* 0.0*
******

21*****
* 2.6*
* 36.4*
******

AGE
>50 | <50

22*****
* 25.8*
* 71.2*
******

23*****
* 10.1*
* 48.4*
******

HOTEL CATEGORY
5, 4, 2, 1-star hotels | 3-star, not cat.

24*****
* 6.6*
* 47.0*
******

25*****
* 8.3*
* 15.2*
******

TYPE OF TRIP
Main, 2nd/3rd, short trip | Business trip, other

26*****
* 15.4*
* 7.2*
******

27*****
* 1.6*
* 30.0*
******

SATISFACTION WITH RECREATION FACILITIES
No | Yes

28*****
* 3.5*
* 31.8*
******

29*****
* 5.8*
* 68.5*
******

COUNTRY OF ORIGIN
Austria, UK, Belgium | Germany, Netherl., other

30*****
* 1.9*
* 41.7*
******

31*****
* 11.5*
* 15.9*
******

Figure 8.1 Identifying the repeat visitor

Source: Note 51, p. 10.

Deriving a profile for the 'main holiday'-maker

The second example analyses the typical guest on a main holiday in Austria. The dependent variable 'type of trip' is dichotomized and differentiates travellers on a main holiday from travellers on other types of trip. A further exploration of hypotheses concerning potential predictors of main holiday making is again inspired by simple cross-tabulations. Judging from these tables, there is a positive correlation between type of trip and a number of associated variables: daily expenditure, profession, age and province visited. An AID run should now examine these relationships under a multivariate model. More personal and trip-related variables can be added: age, children, size of home town, number of prior visits to Austria, booking of accommodation, and motives of 'pleasure, fun', 'new experience', 'health', and 'sports'.

Figure 8.2 displays the tree structure. The share of the travellers on a main holiday amounts to 61 per cent in the mother cell. AID calculates 86.9 per cent for the share of main holiday-makers in cell 28. This corresponds to an increase of more than 25 points. The appropriate splitting criteria extracted in the tree diagram are country of origin, daily expenditure, hotel category, and the dominant motive of 'relaxation'.

A typical guest on a main holiday:

- originates from abroad;
- does not spend much during his or her holiday;
- prefers accommodations not categorized;
- considers relaxation the primary motive for his or her vacation.

Cell 30 introduces a slightly different type of traveller on a main holiday, whose third and fourth attributes relate to:

- usage of categorized accommodations;
- a preference for hiking.

Cell 25 adds a subgroup of vacationists who:

- are prepared to spend more than average;
- take holidays mainly for the purpose of relaxation;
- belong to the social middle class (cf. white-collar, blue-collar, housewives).

Given the target group profile outlined above, a well-directed marketing effort could reach about 40 per cent of the total market with an 80 per cent chance of encountering a potential main holiday-maker. The same results cannot be gained from simple bivariate analyses. Again AID uncovered some new relationships between the dependent variable and segment identifiers.

Validating with discriminant analysis

AID yields exploratory results that should be subject to a subsequent statistical test. For processing with DA, all variables are dichotomized into dummy variables in such a way that the variable category or categories separated by AID become the 1 or 0 values. Take the example of 'booking of accommodation'. The category 'direct booking with the lessor' receives the value 1 and all the other forms of reservation are accumulated under value 0. Both samples are divided randomly. Discriminant function estimates stem from the analysis samples. Classification matrices are

```
1******
* 100.0* = 6,421 cases
*  61.0* TYPE OF TRIP = main holiday
******
```

COUNTRY OF ORIGIN

Austria
```
2******
* 24.7*
* 35.4*
******
```

Abroad
```
3******
* 75.4*
* 69.4*
******
```

MOTIVE 'RELAXATION'

Yes
```
4******
* 15.3*
* 44.9*
******
```

No
```
5******
* 9.3*
* 20.0*
******
```

DAILY EXPENDITURE

Above average
```
6******
* 19.9*
* 52.5*
******
```

Below average
```
7******
* 55.4*
* 75.4*
******
```

INTENTION TO REPEAT VISIT

Hardly
```
8******
* 2.0*
* 17.6*
******
```

Almost certainly, probably
```
9******
* 13.4*
* 48.8*
******
```

HOTEL CATEGORY

5-, 4-, 3-star hotels
```
10****
* 5.2*
* 9.9*
******
```

2-, 1-star hotels, not categorized
```
11****
* 4.2*
* 32.6*
******
```

MOTIVE 'RELAXATION'

Yes
```
12****
* 21.7*
* 69.9*
******
```

No
```
13****
* 16.3*
* 49.2*
******
```

HOTEL CATEGORY

Not categorized
```
14****
* 18.7*
* 83.9*
******
```

5-, 4-, 3-, 2-, 1-star h.
```
15****
* 18.6*
* 71.8*
******
```

TYPE OF ACCOMMODATION

b&b, Hotel, pension, apartment, farm
```
16****
* 0.2*
* 66.7*
******
```

Hotel, pension, apartment, farm
```
17****
* 1.8*
* 12.4*
******
```

PROVINCE VISITED

Lower A., Burgenl., Upper A., Salzbg
```
18****
* 6.1*
* 38.9*
******
```

Vienna, Carinthia, Vorarlbg., Styria, Tyrol
```
19****
* 7.2*
* 57.2*
******
```

TYPE OF ACCOMMODATION

Hotel, camping
```
20****
* 4.8*
* 7.1*
******
```

Pension, apartment, b&b, farm
```
21****
* 0.4*
* 47.8*
******
```

MEAL ARRANGEMENTS

Half board, self-cat.
```
22****
* 1.0*
* 62.5*
******
```

Full board, breakf., breakf. & self-c.
```
23****
* 3.2*
* 23.2*
******
```

PROFESSION

Chief employee, self-employed, student
```
24****
* 6.6*
* 57.4*
******
```

Housewife, white-collar, blue
```
25****
* 15.1*
* 75.4*
******
```

DAILY EXPENDITURE

Above av.
```
26****
* 8.6*
* 38.4*
******
```

Below av.
```
27****
* 7.7*
* 61.3*
******
```

'RELAXATION'

Yes
```
28****
* 14.6*
* 86.9*
******
```

No
```
29****
* 4.1*
* 72.9*
******
```

HIKING

Yes
```
30****
* 10.5*
* 78.5*
******
```

No
```
31****
* 8.1*
* 63.1*
******
```

Figure 8.2 Identifying the main holiday-maker

Source: Note 51, p. 14.

established for the hold-out samples. %*CC*, the percentages correctly classified, are a practical and plausible measure to assess the quantity and relevance of information extracted from the independent variables. Table 8.2 has computational details for the methodologically interested reader. It shows that 59.2% of the repeat visitors and 80.4% of the non-repeaters are correctly classified, while 40.8% of the repeat visitors and 19.6% of the non-repeaters are misclassified. In a similar vein, 84.9% of the cases known to be main holiday-makers and 48% of the non-main holiday-makers are correctly recognized, while 15.1% of the main holiday-makers and the majority of non-main holiday-makers (52%) are erroneously attributed to the wrong subgroup.

Table 8.2   Classification matrices and discriminant coefficients

(a) *Classification matrix for repeat visitors*

		Predicted	
		Repeat visitors	Non-repeat visitors
Observed	Repeat visitors	59.2%	40.8%
	Non-repeat visitors	19.6%	80.4%

%*CC* = 71.9%   *Cpro* = 51.8%   *Cmax* = 59.6%

(b)   *Classification matrix for main holiday-makers*

		Predicted	
		Main holiday-maker	Non-main holiday-maker
Observed	Main holiday-maker	84.9%	15.1%
	Non-main holiday-maker	52.0%	48.0%

%*CC* = 70.4%   *Cpro* = 52.2%   *Cmax* = 60.6%

(c)   *Standardized coefficients of discrimination*

	For identifying	
Variable	Repeat visitors	Main holiday-makers
Country of origin	0.24	0.68
Booking of accommodation	0.56	
Motive 'relaxation'		0.37
'new experience'	0.35	
Factor 'satisfaction with		
restaurant services'	0.30	
Age	0.30	
Daily expenditure		0.29
Profession		0.29
Motive 'hiking'	0.14	0.24
Hotel category		0.20
Factor 'satisfaction with		
recreation facilities'	0.10	

For the two a priori segmentation tasks, the overall percentages correctly classified (%*CC*) amount to 72 and 70. The observed %*CC* values are compared to random values in order to judge their magnitude. Morrison's *Cpro* and *Cmax* coefficients are calculated for this purpose. As the %*CC* exceeds *Cpro* by about 20 points or more, AID can be said to have detected tourist attributes which contribute significantly to identifying repeaters and main holiday-makers.

The DA results indicate how much the independent variables contribute towards differentiating main holiday-makers from other vacationists, and repeat visitors from non-repeaters. This information rests in the standardized coefficients of discrimination. The values are listed in Table 8.2. Booking of accommodation, the 'new experience' motive and satisfaction with restaurant services are the most predictive splitting criteria for repeat visitors. Country of origin, the 'relaxation' motive and daily expenditure correlate highest with main holiday-making. Both findings are in accordance with the AID tree structures. To sum up, the DA confirmed the AID results reasonably well. The repeater and main holiday-maker profiles prove to be conducive to segment-specific market operation.

USING THE EUROSTYLES AS A PRIORI SEGMENTS

Lifestyle segments

It may be worthwhile to consider consumer lifestyle types as potential market segments for travel and tourism marketing. During the 1970s lifestyle criteria became popular in consumer segmentation studies.[55,56,57] Tourism and leisure research followed suit;[23,5] see [52] for a critical comment. In the early 1990s the lifestyle concept experienced its renaissance in international marketing research for tourism. The Austrian National Tourist Office, among others, started to work with the lifestyle data available from the Europanel group.[22,59] This group is an association of fifteen European commercial market research institutes. The lifestyle data originate from consumer panels in the tourism-generating countries. The lifestyle types apply to many different product classes and services. Information on travel behaviour is limited. On the other hand, plenty of travel and vacation data are known about the guests staying in Austria from the Austrian National Guest Survey. In 1991–2 this survey adopted the EUROSTYLES methodology to examine the lifestyle structure of travellers to Austria during the summer and winter seasons.[31,32]

Marketing objectives

The two databases of the EUROSTYLES and the guest survey data on actual tourist behaviour collected in the resorts should be combined to relate the lifestyles to guest characteristics. In doing this marketing managers can assess the strengths and weaknesses of the EUROSTYLES typology for tourist market segmentation. The question arises of whether the EUROSTYLES qualify as 'prefabricated' market segments. If a tourist belongs to a particular lifestyle segment, what does this mean in terms of consumer choice behaviour, activities or spending habits? Does a lifestyle transfer its idiosyncrasies into a comparable vacation style and vice versa? As tourism marketers at the national level are primarily concerned with generating countries, they expect the EUROSTYLES typology to assist in evaluating the market potential. The overall aim is to attract more or more wealthy travellers with tourist services tailored to their value systems.

The basics of EUROSTYLES

It is not the purpose of this case study to discuss the construction of the EUROSTYLES typology at length. Instead, the assumption has to be verified that individual STYLES or groups of STYLES ('socio-targets') contribute to the advancement of tourist marketing.

The EUROSTYLES system[11,21] is a multinational lifestyle typology developed by the Centre de Communication Avancé (CCA) of the Havas-Eurocom group. Since 1989 the system has been in commercial use in fifteen European countries. It covers five principal domains of lifestyle:

- objective personal criteria;
- behavioural attributes;
- attitudes;
- motivations and aspirations;
- sensitivities and emotions.

Through continuous measurement, the system allows the monitoring of socio-cultural trends ('socio-waves').[6]

The EUROSTYLES system comprises sixteen different lifestyle types, resulting from a series of multivariate analyses (factor, correspondence, cluster analysis). The sixteen STYLES are the same in each European country and for all sectors of activity (e.g. politics, advertising, media habits, purchase and consumption of products and services).

Figure 8.3 portrays the EUROSTYLES system on a two-dimensional map. The horizontal axis bridges two opposing poles named 'settlement' on the right and 'movement' on the left. The vertical axis connects the 'valuables' (pleasure) pole in the north with the 'values' pole in the south. Percentages in parentheses are the portions of the European population located in the right or left and the upper or lower hemispheres.

The settlement hemisphere is characterized by values such as priority to the individual's defence and survival, preservation of the current social status, adherence to habits and traditions, group protection, and obedience to the rules of life. In contrast, movement means dynamism, freedom of criticism, priority to the individual, and scepticism *vis-à-vis* social norms, law and authorities. The northern hemisphere is characterized by values of pleasure, sensuality and hedonism. It is strongly associated with tangible values, money and material assets, spending and waste. Each lifestyle type in Figure 8.3 bears a label for easy reference.

The diameters of the circles in Figure 8.3 indicate the shares of the 16 STYLES in all fifteen countries. The major types in Europe are the Rocky (13.5 per cent), the Defence (8.5 per cent), and the Romantic (7.8 per cent). The size of each style varies by country.

Figure 8.4 exhibits the distribution of the EUROSTYLES for ten European countries. The Rocky type dominates the sociocultural scene particularly in the Netherlands, Great Britain, France and Switzerland. The Moralist and the Romantic attain high shares in Germany, Austria, Belgium and Switzerland. The Pioneer type appears fairly frequent in Denmark and Sweden.

A particular strength of the EUROSTYLES system is the interlacement of the lifestyle findings with the wealth of national consumer panel data. Once a target segment has been defined, the market researcher obtains supplementary information on media habits, communication styles and themes, images and preferences.

The direct usage of individual STYLES fails

Management would employ the EUROSTYLES typology in a *direct* manner if they were to accept the STYLES as ready-made market segments. Before choosing this

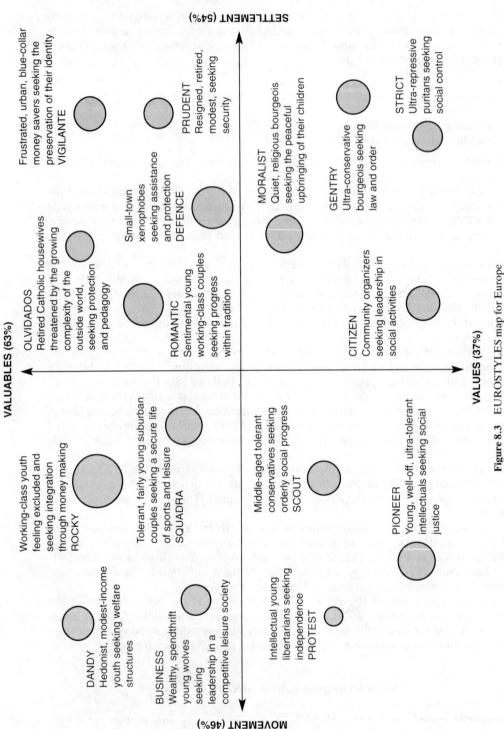

Figure 8.3 EUROSTYLES map for Europe

Source: CCA/EUROPANEL.

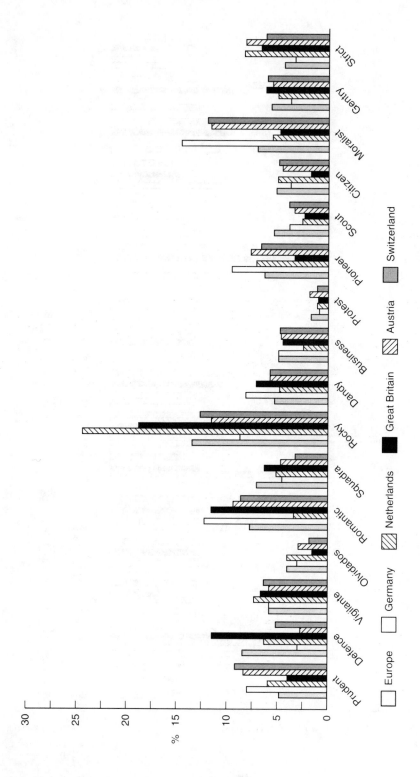

Figure 8.4 EUROSTYLES in various European countries (continued overleaf)

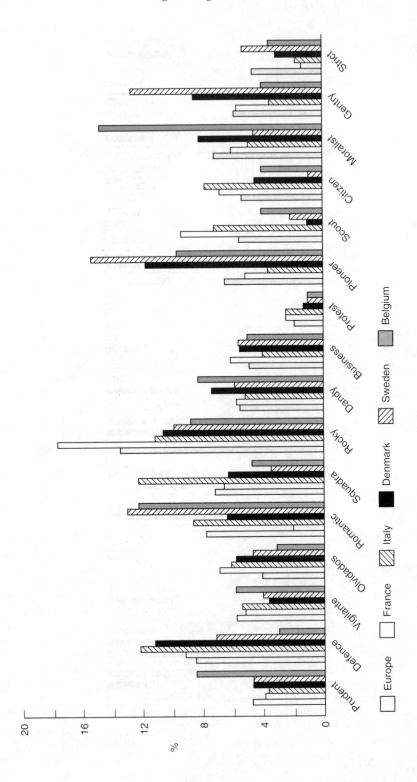

Figure 8.4 (continued)

alternative, however, one must check whether the STYLES prove to be homogeneous within and heterogeneous between types in terms of tourist behaviour. An affirmative result would justify selective market operation. If sufficient disparities are not detected among the STYLES, there is a second option. Market segments are constructed by means of other, more discriminating traveller characteristics. Some of these segments may have an over-proportional share of one or more particular EUROSTYLES. In this case the supplementary lifestyle descriptors may lead to improving promotional messages channelled to potential visitors in their home countries.

Any EUROSTYLE qualifies as a ready-made market segment on condition that its members differ significantly from those of other STYLES in terms of travel-related attributes such as:

- main trip versus second/third or short trip;
- number of visits, travel experience;
- travel motives and expectations;
- actual usage of tourist services;
- preferred activities;
- amount and composition of daily expenditure;
- satisfaction, intention to repeat visit, loyalty.

An examination of the differences regarding these behavioural criteria was not convincing. Lifestyle turned out to be a poor predictor for the components of guest behaviour. But these findings need not be taken as a failure. It is evident that travellers' choice of a particular destination must have a 'smoothing' or filtering effect. The guests surveyed within Austria are likely to have more homogeneous psychographics and behaviours than respondents preferring various destinations and questioned in their home countries.

Individual STYLES may be merged into socio-targets according to their mutual similarity. The location of the two-dimensional EUROSTYLES map is just one aspect of such a merger. Alternatively, the sixteen original STYLES may be hierarchically clustered with a similarity measure based on benefits sought, motives or activities.

Grouping EUROSTYLES into socio-targets

The common approach of merging STYLES into socio-targets is based on motivational, attitudinal or behavioural differentiation. Therefore, the aggregation of the sixteen EUROSTYLES into socio-targets was based on travel motives and activities.[33] A hierarchical cluster analysis processed eleven motives (recreation, pleasure, new experiences, cultural interest, etc.) and ten activities (playing tennis, golf, exercising, water sports, relaxing, shopping, visiting museums, concerts, theatres, etc.) as active variables and the sixteen STYLES as objects. Five clusters were retained for interpretation. Figure 8.5 depicts the configuration of the sixteen EUROSTYLES on the two-dimensional map. The diameters of the circles denote the relative share of each STYLE in Austria's 1991 guest population. The hatched areas in the map demonstrate how each STYLE becomes associated with one of the five socio-targets that are homogeneous in terms of travel motives and activities.

The first socio-target comprises six STYLES (with an aggregate share of 47 per cent). Its relevant motives and activities are recreation and health, doing nothing, and hiking. The second segment combines two neighbouring STYLES with an aggregate

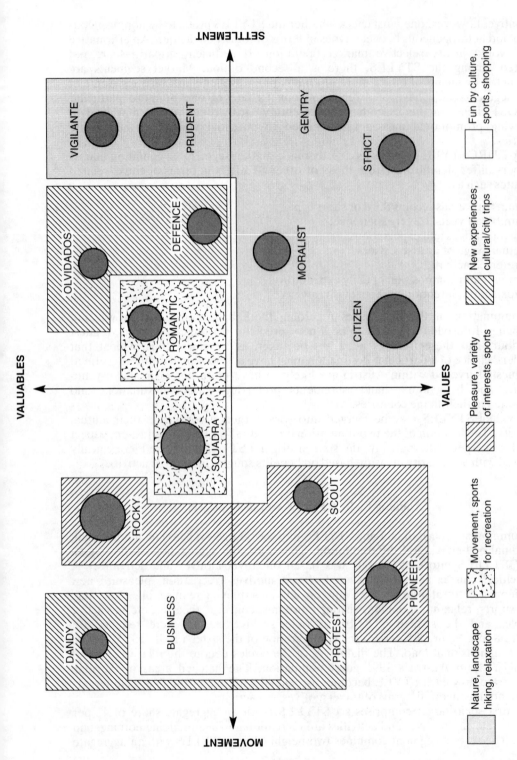

Figure 8.5 Condensing 16 EUROSTYLES into 5 socio-targets: target segments by travel motives and activities

Source: Note 33, p. 208.

share of 16 per cent. Its members like to indulge in activities such as cycling, swimming, horse-riding or sun-bathing, in a colourful surrounding offering variety and change. The third socio-target occupies the western region of the sociocultural map and ties three STYLES together (resulting in a share of 21 per cent). Pleasure and sports (tennis, cycling, water sports, golf) in combination with mental training are the prevailing motives.

The fourth cluster seeks cultural events but is uninterested in sports and physical strain. It can be found in the north-east and the far west of the movement–settlement axis, accounting for a share of 14 per cent. The remaining unassigned STYLE represents outsiders of about 2 per cent of the guest mix. They are interested in sports, culture and shopping for having fun.

Socio-demographics (e.g. age, profession, size of home town, household income) as well as behavioural and travel-related variables (e.g. party size and composition, intention to repeat visit, length of stay, accommodation and boarding, purpose of travel, benefits sought, spending pattern) reveal significant differences between the five socio-targets (see Table 8.3).

The five socio-targets are a promising basis for segmenting the European travel market. They are constructed from EUROSTYLES with an overt preference for Austria as a destination country. As the EUROSTYLES are known all over Europe, the same merging process may be repeated for each generating country. Thus, the STYLES serve as a gateway from the guest survey within a receiving country to the panel data collected in the guests' home countries.

An indirect use of the EUROSTYLES for strategic planning

Identifying the loyal visitor potential is a crucial issue in the design of marketing strategies. The differentiation of lifestyles favourable and unfavourable to repeat visitation may be helpful. The stronger the intention to repeat the visit, the better the prospect of gaining loyal tourists. The analysis starts with guest survey data. To strengthen the contrast only two groups of EUROSTYLES are formed. STYLES with an average share of repeat visitors are ignored. The five EUROSTYLES with the strongest and the five STYLES with the weakest intention remain in the analysis. 'Strong' means at least 4.5 percentage points above average (i.e. 39 per cent). This is true for the following STYLES (31 per cent of all guests): Prudent, Vigilante, Olvidados, Citizen and Moralist. 'Weak' means at least 5.7 points below average, involving the following STYLES (26 per cent of all guests): Rocky, Dandy, Protest, Pioneer and Scout.

The two resulting groups exhibit significant differences for a number of relevant guest attributes:

- age (52 versus 40 years on average);
- share of retired persons (33 versus 13 per cent);
- share of city travellers (8 versus 15 per cent);
- preferred activities;
- advance bookings and arrangements;
- daily expenditure per capita ($74 versus $82);
- average length of stay (13 versus 10 nights);
- benefits sought.

Table 8.3 Selected attributes of the five socio-targets

Variable	Average	Socio-targets 1	2	3	4	5	F-ratio	Chi-square	Sig.
Share of all guests in %	47	47	16	21	14	2			<0.001
Age of travel party in years (average)	47	52	44	41	46	42	161.05		<0.001
Size of town of residence <100.000 in %	60	61	64	58	65	51		50.09	<0.001
Profession of respondent:								237.42	<0.001
Self-employed	14	13	9	16	13	15			
Employed	59	51	72	68	59	60			
Retired	27	36	19	16	28	25			
Share of repeat visitors in %	74	77	74	72	70	67		7.72	<0.001
Main trip of the year in %	60	63	62	56	54	46		11.15	<0.001
Party size	2.1	2.1	2.3	2.1	2.0	2.0	17.73		<0.001
Accompanied by children under 14 in %	13	11	18	14	11	11		9.09	<0.001
Lodging in hotels and pensions in %	65	66	56	68	69	83		14.21	<0.001
Length of stay in Austria in days	12.3	13.6	11.6	11.4	10.8	9.9	25.41		<0.001
Expenditures per day and capita in US$	64	61	57	67	71	85	13.19		<0.001
Shopping exp. for whole party and trip in US$	227	231	217	190	270	222	2.58		0.0355
Benefits sought in %:									
Walking/hiking paths	73	79	77	65	62	53		44.24	<0.001
Calmness of the resort	72	80	71	65	63	54		41.58	<0.001
Variety of landscapes	62	66	65	55	57	40		21.07	<0.001
Value for money	63	67	65	57	55	53		18.37	<0.001
Service in accommodation	62	67	57	57	59	63		15.12	<0.001
Service in restaurants	63	67	61	55	61	61		13.26	<0.001
Reachability	52	55	56	45	48	45		12.98	<0.001
Environmental quality	92	93	93	90	89	79		11.80	<0.001
Friendliness of locals	78	82	77	75	75	63		11.66	<0.001

Source: Note 33, p. 209

Analysis of the guest data suggests that there are some tourists who might be transformed into loyal visitors more easily than others. The EUROSTYLES typology provides a tool for assessing the loyalty potential in all generating countries where the frequency distribution of the STYLES is known.

Both the strong and the weak loyalty group assist in condensing EUROSTYLES and generating countries into a single portfolio diagram. A generating country accommodates a typical mixture of EUROSTYLES each with a particular amount of affinity for Austria as a tourist destination. Suppose that tourism managers are rather conservative in their segmentation policies, and thus want to cater for the loyal visitors. In this case they are likely to focus on the EUROSTYLES which show a strong intention to repeat their visit when asked during their stay in an Austrian resort.

The EUROSTYLES called Prudent, Vigilante, Olvidados, Citizen and Moralist were already identified as the most sympathetic towards Austria. Comparing the share of all loyal STYLES in the respective country of origin X with the share among guests from X results in one of four possible outcomes. The share lies:

- above average in the home country and above average in Austria;
- below average in the home country and above average in Austria;
- below average in the home country and below average in Austria;
- above average in the home country and below average in Austria.

Adopting the pictorial representation common in portfolio models,[8,58,35,9] generating countries are portrayed in four quadrants (see Figure 8.6).

The first quadrant (north-east) contains those markets where Austria has already exploited its opportunites ('success markets'): 'Austria-prone' lifestyles are over-

Figure 8.6 Constructing a portfolio of loyal markets

represented within the origin population as well as among the visitors to Austria. A weak representation of Austria-prone STYLES in an origin country, combined with high frequency of these STYLES among the guests, implies a high degree of market saturation ('empty markets').

A less than proportional frequency of Austria-prone STYLES at home and among the guests in Austria is indicative of a market with doubtful opportunities ('risk markets'). A 'full market' offers a large share of its population belonging to Austria-prone STYLES combined with a small share of these STYLES among the tourists actually travelling to Austria.

Merging the Europanel results with the guest survey findings produces a portfolio chart of generating countries for Austria (see Figure 8.7). It depicts Austria's market opportunities in terms of EUROSTYLES. The size of the circles denotes each country's contribution to the total volume of guests recorded in Austria. Germany, Switzerland and Austria itself offer the most promising chances, which are already utilized. The marketing climate is somewhat less favourable in France, Belgium Denmark, the Netherlands and Italy. From France, however, Austria could extract more than its fair share. Great Britain and Sweden are rather brittle in terms of Austria-prone lifestyles, with the UK showing a markedly better transformation rate of potential visitors into actual guests.

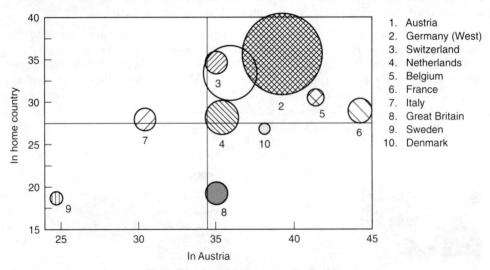

Figure 8.7   Austria's strong loyalty portfolio

Summary

A standardized lifestyle typology like the EUROSTYLES facilitates a priori segmentation provided that certain amendments are applied. The original consumer lifestyle types have to be merged into groups of types (socio-targets). The grouping process must employ a travel-related and behaviourally relevant set of criteria such as travel motives or activities. Once a grouping of STYLES has been found, it lends itself to segmentation purposes at an international (i.e. European) level. Besides the opportunity to define segments across borders, management will benefit from a multitude of data accumulated during normal panel operation.

Socio-targets are not new entities, but consist of well-known components. Thus, they are easily portrayed in terms of consumption patterns, shopping habits or media usage for increased marketing efficiency. The evaluation of tourism-generating countries is a routine task in any National Tourist Office where strategic thinking guides the marketing planning process. A standardized a priori classification like the EUROSTYLES contributes to this effort, if it gets associated with a fundamental indicator such as visitors' loyalty.

USTYLES: 'EXPORTING' THE EUROSTYLES TO THE USA

Marketing objectives

In future, Euro-marketers will have to deal with consumer typologies from more than one source. This means that not all data will be available for all countries. A well-established typology, therefore, should be portable from one survey or database to another. The EUROSTYLES concept was introduced in the preceding case study, where a link between the European database and the Austrian National Guest Survey (GBÖ) was established. The GBÖ collected the EUROSTYLES lifestyle variables (about 100 items) necessary to reconstruct the EUROSTYLES system. The wording of the lifestyle questions, however, is unsuited for visitors from overseas. Thus, an important guest nation like the USA was not included in the lifestyle analysis. On the other hand, it would have been an intriguing exercise for a European tourism manager to ascertain the mixture of comparable lifestyle types for the USA. It is the aim of this case study to adapt the EUROSTYLES system for usage within the USA, and to extract the American counterparts of the European STYLES.

Raw data

These stem from a sample of 858 US air passengers headed for Europe and other world regions. Field work during May 1992 was organized at the two sample points of New York JFK (two-thirds) and Dallas-Forth Worth (one-third) international airports. A number of adaptations in the questionnaire were indispensable to account for the differences in language and thought pattern. For instance, a proxy for 'Europe' had to be introduced into the cosmopolitanism questions ('United Nations'); and expressions like 'saloon' were replaced by 'sedan' in the car preference question.

Data techniques

A neural network approach is expected to master the lifestyle transfer task in an elegant manner. In particular, only half the number of variables (forty-nine) is needed. This turns out to be a valuable advantage given the time pressure in the interview situation at the airport transit zones. Moreover, the complicated scales can be replaced by simple yes–no questions. The EUROSTYLES classification is kept secret by the Europanel market research institutes. Nevertheless, it is not prohibited to recapture the STYLES by means of a 'reverse engineering' procedure with advanced methodology. A neural network (NNW) model (cf. the back-propagation model in Figure 8.8) was trained with the Austrian data where the EUROSTYLES classification had been purchased from a commercial supplier. With only half the number of variables, the NNW model attains a percentage correctly classified at 67 per cent (the standard classification with about 100 variables does not exceeed 80 per cent of the types correctly classified). A split-half procedure for the guest survey sample (50 per cent training data set and 50 per cent hold-out sample for testing) was applied. This means that the network had to classify respondents whom it had never seen before into lifestyles types. The results are satisfactory for all practical purposes, since a minority of poorly reconstructed STYLES (49 per cent in the worst case) faces a majority of types with an excellent fit (up to 80 per cent).

Results

Figure 8.8 exhibits the network model in a state of activation (the blown-up units or 'neurons') elicited by a particular respondent. The bottom layer inputs the yes–no reactions for each of forty-nine lifestyle variables (a mixture of opinions, consumption and leisure preferences, and values). The output layer on the top represents the sixteen lifestyle types, now called USTYLES. The RMS (root mean square error), the confusion matrices and the frequency diagram are diagnostical tools for monitoring the network during training. A large number of repetitive presentations of

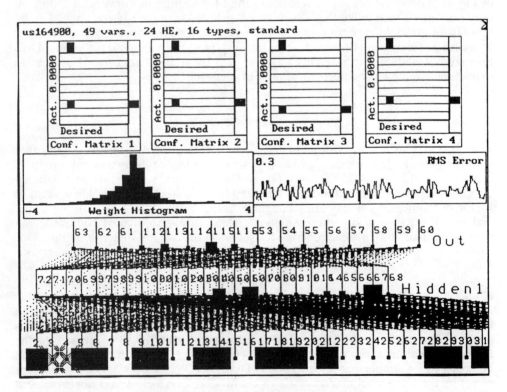

Figure 8.8   Reconstructing the USTYLES

respondents (about 400,000 iterations) with their lifestyle attributes and their STYLES affiliation led to the appropriate set of weights (the connections in Figure 8.8). During training the weights were modified according to an optimization principle (called the generalized delta rule, discussed briefly in Chapter 7, p. 118), until the best possible STYLES reproduction quota was reached. Then the network was prepared for 'recall': that is, classification of new cases (with previously known type affiliation for testing, or unknown affiliation for 'prediction').

Network models are capable of 'generalizing' by extracting the stable and 'typical' features of data configurations. As a consequence, even a considerable number of missing observations does not harm the quality of prediction seriously. This is particularly useful in a situation where respondents are unwilling to react to questions invading their privacy. And with a set of lifestyle variables, such effects cannot be avoided easily.

A segmentation task involves an interplay between 'customer response profiles' and a search for 'identifiers'.[10] The lifestyle classification is part of such a 'profile'. Similarity in terms of lifestyle is supposed to lead to similar travel patterns. A second step then asks for the 'externals', such as age, gender, profession and income.

Table 8.4 Comparison between European and US lifestyle (%)

STYLE	EUROSTYLES	USTYLES
1. Prudent	4.8	7.6
2. Defence	8.5	0.8
3. Vigilante	5.8	7.5
4. Olvidados	4.1	10.0
5. Romantic	7.8	0.5
6. Squadra	7.2	1.2
7. Rocky	13.5	10.1
8. Dandy	5.5	3.5
9. Business	4.9	23.4
10. Protest	1.9	3.5
11. Pioneer	6.5	2.7
12. Scout	5.5	19.5
13. Citizen	5.3	4.8
14. Moralist	7.2	3.3
15. Gentry	5.8	0.8
16. Strict	4.6	0.9

Figure 8.9 summarizes the results. The lifestyle map contains the sixteen USTYLES comparable to their European counterparts. The 'centre of gravity' in the map has shifted to the movement hemisphere (see Figure 8.3). The size of the 'movement-driven' STYLES is even more remarkable if one compares them with the distribution of lifestyles among the visitors to Austria (see Figure 8.10). A numerical comparison between Europe and the USA in terms of lifestyles (see Table 8.4) detects the dominant roles of the Business and the Scout types in the USA. Other STYLES appearing more frequently in Europe (Defence, Romantic, Squadra, Pioneer, Gentry, Strict) are rather scarce. It is obvious that the 'conservative corner' (south-east in the lifestyle map) is not a popular location for US citizens. The difference is accentuated if the lifestyle map for guests in Austria is considered. This country seems to appeal to the 'settlement' people all around Europe in a very peculiar way. (Of course, this is not an astonishing result, but the striking proof has some news value.)

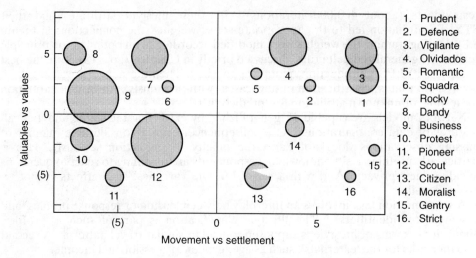

Figure 8.9 USTYLES among travellers from the USA

What about the behavioural characteristics of the USTYLES going on vacation to Europe, and to Austria in particular? It comes as a surprise that the American Rocky is the prevailing STYLE among the travellers from the USA. A more in-depth deliberation, however, lends face validity to this finding. The Rocky is an outsider STYLE. He or she is inclined to go to rather 'exotic' destinations. Thus, a receiving country like Austria is not particularly attractive to the European Rocky. Austria is far from playing the role of an 'exotic' destination within Europe; for a long-haul traveller, however, the country assumes a good deal of exoticism. The American Business and Scout are equally remarkable. Both STYLES not only represent a large segment potential but are also prepared to visit Austria more frequently than the average US traveller.

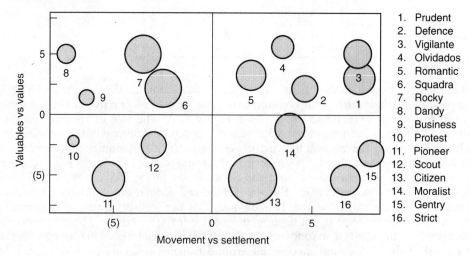

Figure 8.10 EUROSTYLES among guests in Austria

The Rocky is largely motivated by recreation ('relax', 'change pace'). The Business seeks 'new experience'. He or she is likely to engage in sports activities such as tennis, water sports and horse-riding. The Scout is rather ambitious with respect to education and seeing works of art.

What about the identifiers? Consider age and profession. According to a breakdown by age, the Rocky accumulates in the 40–9 and 50+ age brackets. Aiming at the Business, one must take care of the travellers aged less than forty. Marketing strategy thus may rest on two pillars: target groups homogeneous in terms of lifestyles; and traveller segments sufficiently differentiated by age.

Profession is of less help. Because of his or her age, the Rocky correlates with senior executives and the retired. Working with lifestyles, one should always keep in mind that the underlying dimensions are mainly psychographic. The European and the corresponding USTYLE, such as the Rocky, have a similar psychographic profile. The 'external' identifiers, however, may deviate significantly from each other. To cite another example, the Business STYLE is found among the self-employed as well as among blue-collar workers.

Summary

There is a lesson to learn from 'exporting' the EUROSTYLES to the USA. A transatlantic transfer is possible and it makes sense. Of course, the US market does not offer the accompanying range of panel data that is available for Europe (there are various other lifestyle systems with plenty of consumption data). A European tourism manager who is trained in handling EUROSTYLES, however, may draw on this experience while planning for the American overseas travel market. Above all, the size of the lifestyle segments that may be attracted to Europe is encouraging.

Nevertheless, there are some caveats:

- The psychographics and lifestyle categories based on value systems, attitudes and preferences are transferable; the 'external' identifiers are not.
- On the US market, a European destination like Austria assumes an 'out-of-the-ordinary' position quite in contrast to its role within Europe.
- All of a sudden, the lifestyle segments where Austria has not been successful within Europe become the target groups.
- The symbolic labels for EUROSTYLES or USTYLES may arouse misunderstandings because of their brevity. Managers are advised to mistrust the conciseness and to look into the type-generating attributes more thoroughly.

IDENTIFYING BENEFIT SEGMENTS FOR TOURIST RESORTS

Marketing objectives

The 'Europa-Sport-Region' comprises the two prominent tourist resorts of Kaprun and Zell am See in the Austrian province of Salzburg. The region is famous for winter sports and has a second season during summer. The carrying capacity approaches its ceiling, thus compelling local tourism managers to evaluate carefully the current 'guest mix and to decide on the type of tourists they should continue to attract. A benefit segmentation approach was chosen to clarify the structure of guest expectations, their interrelationships and to what degree they might be met by the local tourist services.

Raw data

The benefits sought are operationalized by means of importance ratings for destination attributes. The database of the Austrian National Guest Survey contains a sufficiently large number of cases for the Europa-Sport Region. This survey measures the attitude towards a tourist resort using a list of twenty-four attributes in two steps. At first its sorts out the resort attributes that the respondent holds to be important:

1. 'In the following evaluation of tourist assets, please say what is important to you during your present stay here.'

For the items marked as important it then asks for the degree of satisfaction on a four-point rating scale:

2. 'How satisfied are you with those features that you find important?'

The importance judgements may be considered as indicative of benefits sought. Emphasis is on tourist expectations rather than satisfaction. The aim is to segment by consumption goals rather than by the goal-satisfying capabilities of the particular tourist region visited. It is hypothesized that tourists, though being on vacation in the same region, are still heterogeneous in terms of benefits sought. The data collection by personal interviewing yielded 499 cases within the Europa-Sport Region.

Deriving the benefit segments

A BINCLUS run processes the total sample of 499 respondents with satisfaction ratings for each of twenty-four resort attributes. The homogeneity value gained by increasing the number of clusters rises steadily, which gives no hint as to the 'right' number of segments (Figure 8.11). Ease of interpretation speaks in favour of the four clusters solution. Each of these four clusters or segments, accompanying between 92 and 172 respondents, exhibits a very typical profile of benefits.

In Figure 8.12, dark cells refer to benefits rated highly important, grey cells mark medium importance, and white cells indicate below-average or no importance at all. Many items are not of much attractiveness to segment 1. It appears to be very modest in its expectations. Segment 2 exhibits the highest aspiration level. Segment 2 members stick to their high expectations with the exception of sports facilities. This item ranks top for segment 3 together with entertainment facilities. The standard of catering in restaurants other than in the place of accommodation seems important to segment 3. Segment 4 is very much concerned with accommodation-related items and seeks peace and quiet. Hiking also receives much attention among segment 4 members. Checking the columns one gets the impression that segment 3 members must be of lower age than those in segment 4.

The pie chart in Figure 8.13 visualizes the share of the benefit segments in the guest sample. A short label is introduced for each segment. The 'elementary vacationer' is driven by very basic needs catered for in any tour package or travel destination. The

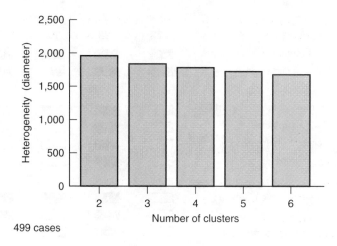

Figure 8.11 Homogeneity indicator

'comfort seeker' is sophisticated in his or her need structure. (However, it will become apparent later that this person may be reluctant to have an above-average daily expenditure.) The 'young sports vacationer' and the 'elderly hiking tourist' are indeed closely linked to different age groups.

Profiling with demographic, socioeconomic and behavioural descriptors

An identification of psychographical (i.e. benefit) traveller/guest segments is of limited use, unless segments are described 'objectively' with additional geographic, demographic, socioeconomic, behavioural and lifestyle criteria. Without such descriptors management can only hope for the travellers themselves to respond selectively to a segment-specific promotional programme ('customer self-selection').

In the Europa-Sport Region study, cross-tabulation of segment membership with various demographic, socioeconomic and trip-related criteria reveals substantial correlations. Personal characteristics where some segments are significantly over-represented are itemized in Table 8.5. The average age of male as well as female guests differs markedly. There is some connection with profession, type of trip (main holiday, second/third trip, short trip), number of persons in the travelling party, arrangements for food, and preferred type of accommodation. For instance, a large proportion of 'holiday apartments' and 'camping' prevails in segment 3. This explains its low interest in accommodation-related benefit items.

As far as daily expenditure is concerned, the gap between segments 1 versus 2 and 3 versus 4 is enormous. Segment 1 with the lowest aspirations also has a tight spending pattern. Segment 2 spends more but, by far, does not match its aspirations with its spending habits. Daily expenditure does not vary between segments 3 and 4 which, on the other hand, are of great psychological dissimilarity.

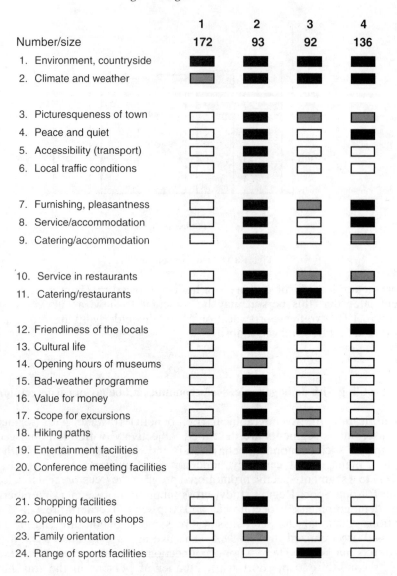

Figure 8.12 The importance of benefits

Source: GBÖ, 1988.

Implications for selective market operation

The a posteriori segments are distinct enough to justify selective market action. First of all, tourism managers in the Europa-Sport Region have to determine whether they should continue to cater for each of the four segments in the long run. The young sports vacationer and the elderly hiking tourist are attractive prospects owing to their spending levels. Their vacation styles, however, are rather incompatible (sports and

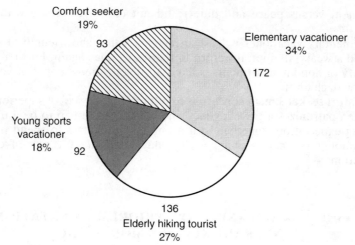

Figure 8.13 Four benefits segments

Table 8.5 Selected segment characteristics

	Segment			
	1	*2*	*3*	*4*
Average age in years:				
Male	41	48	34	51
Female	44	48	31	54
Total	42	48	33	52
Profession (overrepresented)	Blue-collar, housewife	Senior exec./civil servant	Self-employed	White-collar
Type of trip		Main holiday	Short holiday	Second/third
Party size/structure	Family, children		Alone	Group
Travel motives			Sport	New experience
Yes				
No				
Information from		Travel agent		
Meal arrangements				Full board
Accommodation	Apartment		Apartment, camping	Bed and breakfast, hotel
Means of transport				Bus, train
Number of persons	2.1	2.2	1.8	1.9
Daily expenditure in AS	601	660	890	890
Duration of stay in days	8	12	9	11
Type of landscape preferred			Sea, lakes	Mountain
Intention of repeat stay	Low		High	

entertainment versus peace and quiet) and not easily reconciled within the same resort.

The elementary vacationer is least attractive, with a short length of stay, a small budget and a weak intention to return to the resort once again. Further extension of the capacity of holiday apartments is likely to favour this segment of young families travelling with children.

The comfort seeker's main concern is to obtain 'full service' of superior quality. He or she often patronizes a travel agency and considers the trip to be a main holiday. High-flying expectations together with a limited willingness to spend more than an average amount per capita and per day may aggravate the risk of criticism and dissatisfaction.

UNIFYING A PRIORI AND A POSTERIORI SEGMENTATION WITH NEURAL NETWORK MODELLING

Marketing objectives

The Austrian National Guest Survey supports the National Tourist Office (ANTO) and other tourist organizations and businesses in their marketing decision making. In 1991–2, when the study was commissioned for the fourth time, special emphasis lay on guest attributes related to lifestyles. With a mixture of psychographic and behavioural variables the EUROSTYLES (see pp. 126–37) were reconstructed. Given a sample size of 7,000 respondents, there are ample opportunities to experiment with various segmentation techniques.

The traditional approach towards constructing vacation types implies a set of psychographics and/or activities subject to a clustering or factorization procedure (note 7; note 47, pp. 52–62; pp. 108–13 in this book). Only afterwards are the resulting types (a posteriori segments) evaluated as potential target markets. Contrary to routine this case study attempts to perform the data reduction task while maintaining a direct relation to a marketing objective. Management was primarily concerned about the guests' intention to repeat their visit. Apparently, the examination of potential vacation styles is not an end in itself, but part of a strategy to identify and better to understand travellers with a high likelihood of returning to their summer 1991 destination.

Neural network implementation

The 'a priori' part of the hybrid model requires a classification into travellers with a strong ('almost certainly') versus a weak ('probably not') intention to repeat the visit within the next three years. The intermediate category ('probably') was skipped in order to accentuate the contrast. Cherishing customer loyalty is a prominent objective in the marketing of services and an outstanding characteristic of the 'breakthrough companies'.[15] Also in this example the 'probably not' repeaters were not considered a target group. They only serve the purpose of detecting excitatory and inhibitory relationships. (One should emphasize, however, that tourism marketing for an entire receiving country may be slightly different in its treatment of fluctuating demand. The 'once-and-never-again' guests have their merits. They spend significantly more than the repeaters, and their seasonal preferences are more balanced. Thus, the tourism industry also has to cater for the presumble non-repeaters and a National Tourist Office is expected to include them in some of its marketing strategies.)

The 'a posteriori' part of the hybrid model rests on two sets of items, travel motives and activities ('relevant things to do on a summer holiday'). This is where data reduction must step in to account for the mutual dependencies within each variable set. Motives as well as activities arrive in symptomatic combinations. Looking into them individually may be misleading. Given six motives and eight activities, it was hypothesized that not more than three motivational types and four activity types would emerge. Therefore, seven hidden elements ('constructs') are specified. The three motivational elements are fully connected to the six input units for motive items (main 'reasons for staying here'). The same applies to the four activity units and their eight observables (see Figure 8.15).

In addition to the multi-item attributes, eight univariate descriptors were admitted. These criteria correspond to the 'passive' variables in the traditional terminology. They are helpful in converting segmentation strategy into action. Their main purpose is to characterize repeaters and non-repeaters for selective exposure to marketing influence. One single hidden element is specified to absorb the predictive power of these attributes. All input variables are dichotomous. Table 8.6 contains the complete list with the abbreviations employed in the network graphs.

For all subsequent analyses a random split of the sample was used. Out of 4,557 cases, 2,285 are retained for validation purposes, and, 2,272 cases are subject to discriminant as well as network estimation procedures. A linear discriminant analysis (DA) including all twenty-two variables (canonical correlation = 0.62, Wilks' lambda = 0.61) leads to an overall percentage of cases correctly classified (in the hold-out sample) of 75.4. Travellers with a weak intention to repeat their visit are recognized more easily (81.2 per cent) than those with strong intentions (69.7 per cent) (see Table 8.8). Not surprisingly, the variables that are highly correlated with the canonical discriminant function are frequency of past visits (0.79) and direct prior arrangements/ booking at the place of accommodation (0.51). Motivational criteria like 'seeing works of art' (−0.26), going on a 'tour/round trip' (−0.23), and activities such as 'visiting museums' (−0.23), or 'visiting historical sites/places' (−0.23) follow next. The DA results are of practical value compared to a proportional chance (and also a maximal chance) criterion of 50 per cent correctly classified.

The improvement expected here from a neural network model does not relate primarily to classification performance. (As the network involves more parameters and a (non-linear) mapping function of arbitrary complexity, it should never perform worse than the traditional linear model). Instead, the criticism is a conceptual one. The DA specification cannot accommodate the a posteriori element in the overall segmentation scheme. In DA the motivational and activities variables are treated separately without exploiting their interrelationships for the generation of consumer types.

An NNW model is constructed with the Backpropagation Builder of the NeuralWorks Professional II/Plus Package.[39] Figure 8.14 quotes some of its technical details.

Figure 8.15 and Table 8.6 present NNW results after 200,000 iterations with the training sample. If the NNW model is fed with new cases in the hold-out sample (not yet used for training), 75.2 per cent are classified correctly (Table 8.8). It is easier to detect non-repeaters (82.4 per cent) than repeat travellers (67.9 per cent). Without

Table 8.6 Variables, hidden units, weights (before pruning)

Input variables (abbreviation)	Connection weights for hidden units (types)							Descriptive variable group unit
	Mo1	Mo2	Mo3	Ac1	Ac2	Ac3	Ac4	
INPUT to HIDDEN LAYER								
Motives/reasons:								
Pleasure, fun (Pl)	-1.04	-0.55	1.01					
Visit friends (Fr)	1.00	-0.69	-0.72					
Hiking (Hi)	0.37	-1.51	-0.97					
Education/studies (Ed)	0.10	-0.61	-0.55					
Seeing works of art (Ar)	-1.29	1.14	1.00					
Tour, round trip (Ro)	-0.90	1.48	2.08					
Activities:								
Playing tennis (Te)				0.36	-0.14	1.07	0.54	
Cycling (Cy)				0.22	-0.16	0.70	-0.55	
Horse-riding (Ho)				1.14	-0.04	1.49	-0.48	
Sun-bathing (Su)				0.57	-0.38	-0.57	-2.10	
Visiting historical sites/places (HP)				-0.74	-0.63	-1.34	-0.43	
Going to concerts (Co)				0.53	-0.02	0.38	-0.42	
Visiting museums (Mu)				0.07	-0.35	-0.42	1.44	
Going to the theatre (Th)				1.76	-0.06	0.51	-0.77	
Descriptors:								
Country of origin, Germany and Austria versus rest (Or)								-0.38
Advance arrangement directly with the place of accommodation (Di)								-0.86
Information from travel agent (TA)								0.43
Personal informants (PI)								-0.50
No information required (NI)								-0.22
Frequency of past visits, 2 or more (3x)								-2.14
Age, < 30 years (29)								0.98
30–59 years (59)								0.65
HIDDEN LAYER to OUTPUT								
Connection weights for a priori classes:								
Intention HI	0.62	-0.59	-0.14	0.65	-0.22	0.63	-0.93	-2.12
Intention LO	-0.61	0.59	0.16	-0.64	0.24	-0.65	0.91	2.11

Table 8.7 Variables, hidden units, weights (after pruning)

Input variables (abbreviation)	Connection weights for hidden units (types)					Descriptive variable group unit
	Mo1	Mo2	Ac1	Ac3	Ac4	
INPUT to HIDDEN LAYER						
Motives/reasons:						
Pleasure, fun (Pl)	-1.18					
Visit friends (Fr)	0.91					
Hiking (Hi)		-1.65				
Education/studies (Ed)		-0.84				
Seeing works of art (Ar)	-1.25	1.25				
Tour, round trip (Ro)	-0.97	1.69				
Activities:						
Playing tennis (Te)				1.28	0.76	
Cycling (Cy)				0.86	-0.60	
Horse-riding (Ho)			1.19	1.68	-0.60	
Sun-bathing (Su)			0.53	-0.58	-2.00	
Visiting historical sites/places (HP)			-0.49	-1.30		
Going to concerts (Co)			0.64			
Visiting museums (Mu)					1.27	
Going to the theatre (Th)			1.70	0.49	-0.86	
Descriptors:						
Country of origin, Germany and Austria versus rest (Or)						
Advance arrangement directly with the place of accommodation (Di)						-0.93
Information from travel agent (TA)						0.56
Personal informants (PI)						
No information required (NI)						
Frequency of past visists, 2 or more (3x)						-2.00
Age, < 30 years (29)						0.84
30–59 (59)						0.60
HIDDEN LAYER to OUTPUT						
Connection weights for a priori classes:						
Intention HI	0.64	-0.70	0.68	0.77	-0.89	-2.27
Intention LO	-0.64	0.71	-0.67	-0.79	0.87	2.25

Some hints on network specification and training

The type of transfer function, the learning scheme and the instruments for monitoring the learning process need a few comments. Considering the experience collected in many other applications, a hyperbolic tangent is chosen as transfer function, squeezing the output of the processing elements into the [−1, 1] interval. Learning is faster in the beginning and slows down in the later stages. This means that the learning constant decreases gradually with the number of iterations. But there are differences between the layers to speed up the overall learning effect. The hidden layer makes greater adjustments than the output layer in the early stages of the learning process (40). Three instruments are used to monitor the learning process. The weight distribution shows the frequency of connection weights of varying magnitude. In Figure 8.15 the weights spread out over a range from −2 to +2. The root mean square error denotes the goodness of fit between the expected and the predicted network output. It moves downward continuously during effective learning. The confusion matrices show a reasonable degree of correlation between the observed and the predicted affiliation of respondents with the 'hi' or 'lo' intention subgroups.

Figure 8.14 Some hints on network specification and training

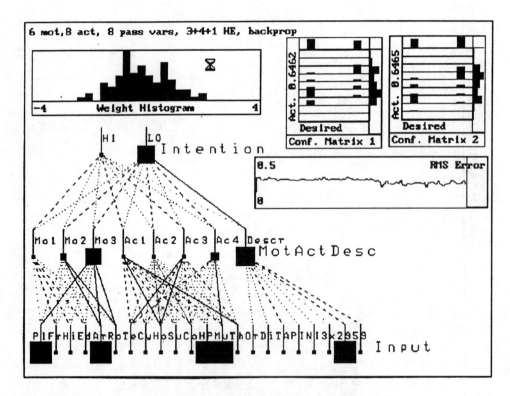

Figure 8.15 A neural network model for 'hybrid' segmentation

the demographic and trip-related descriptors (age, country of origin, frequency of past visits, arrangements made prior to starting the trip, information behaviour) the percentage correctly classified drops to 62.4 per cent.

Results

The examination of the weight structure compares large values in Table 8.6 (corresponding to solid connections in Figure 8.15) with small values (or dotted lines). It reveals that the motivational and activity types Mo1, Ac1 and Ac3 are closely linked to a strong intention to repeat the visit. Types Mo2, Ac2 and Ac4 are likely to be non-repeaters. If the descriptive hidden unit Descr becomes highly activated, it enforces a 'lo'-intention output. Compared to the other hidden units, Mo3 and Ac2 have only weak connections to the output layer. These elements are candidates for elimination during a 'pruning' exercise. Such a simplification of a network is desirable because a less complex network is expected to generalize better when exposed to new input data (19; 39, p. 78). In two pruning phases, connection weights of less than 10 per cent (up to 400,000 iterations) and then less than 20 per cent (until 440,000 iterations) of the maximum (absolute) weight value are removed.

Table 8.7 and Figure 8.16 present the simplified network. (The pruning effect also becomes visible in the weight histogram after removal of the small weights around

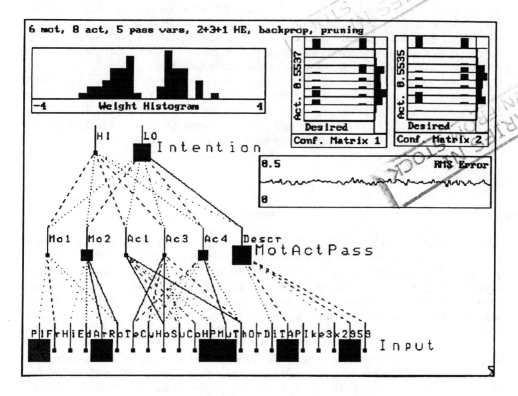

Figure 8.16   The 'hybrid' model after pruning

Table 8.8 Percentage correctly classified (hold-out sample)

Observed group membership	Predicted group membership							
	Discriminant analysis with all variables		Network without descriptors before pruning		Network with descriptors before pruning		Network with descriptors after pruning	
	HI	LO	HI	LO	HI	LO	HI	LO
Intention:								
HI	69.7	30.3	61.4	38.6	67.9	32.1	70.2	29.8
LO	18.8	81.2	36.9	63.1	17.6	82.4	19.0	81.0
% correctly classified	75.4		62.4		75.2		75.7	

zero.) The classification power improves slightly (Table 8.8). Conclusions are based on robust relationships and are easily verified. Only two motivational types are important in terms of repeat behaviour. A strong interest in 'works of art' in conjunction with a 'round trip' characterizes the prototype non-repeater, in particular if it is not accompanied by a 'hiking' motive. In contrast, a single dominant purpose to 'visit friends and relatives' motivates a most likely repeater.

At the same time the travellers are subject to a classification in terms of activities. There are two activity types prone to repeat their visit. Ac1 prefers to go to the theatre (and concert); horse-riding is the only sports activity worth mentioning. Ac3 is a sports-lover; tennis and cycling add to this person's list; sun-bathing – more a 'passiveness' than an activity – and historical sites do not fit into the activity pattern capable of increasing repeat visitation. Ac4 is a non-repeater mostly occupied with visiting museums; playing tennis would fit into the pattern but a typical preoccupation of a main holiday-maker such as sunbathing would definitely not.

Frequency of past visits among the complementary descriptors exerts a considerable influence strong enough to override the psychographic and lifestyle effects. Direct booking and age are also well represented in the overall descriptive unit. Information from a travel agent and the younger age brackets coincide with low intention; two or more past visits and direct arrangements with the place of accommodation inhibit the descriptive unit in getting activated, thus preventing it from firing 'lo'-intention ammunition.

Summary

The connectionist findings outlined above differ from a more traditional segmentation treatment in several ways. On the hidden layer of typology formation (the a posteriori subsystem), consumers are not classified into exhaustive and mutually exclusive clusters. A person may be ambiguous with respect to motivational and/or activity types. In network terminology this means that more than one hidden element gets activated and induced to fire into the output layer. Consequently, no information is lost if a case does not fit nicely into a typological straitjacket. Moreover, the typologies extracted are not complete. The hidden units (i.e. type equivalents) cannot survive a pruning process unless they contribute to the final classification target (the a priori subsystem). There, on the output layer, the amount of excitation of the 'lo'- and 'hi'- intention units may be interpreted as a posteriori probabilities (not yet normalized) in the Bayesian sense. The allocation of cases follows the maximum probability rule because the output unit with the highest activation indicates the segment affiliation.

Outlook

A next step in exploring NNW models for 'hybrid' segmentation will be to detach the a posteriori subsystem from the a priori classification during an initial stage and to combine the two subsystems afterwards. In particular, the so-called 'self-organizing maps'[20] are worth experimenting with. Under the SOM paradigm a two-dimensional layer of hidden units ('Kohonen' layer) performs the typology formation of the a posteriori segmentation task. The search for types always implies some sort of data compression: for example, many individual travel activities into few activity types, or a long list of benefits sought into a much smaller number of benefit types. The Kohonen layer in an SOM network also accomplishes a data reduction by transforming input vectors of arbitarary dimensionality into a two-dimensional mapping. The transformation preserves order in such a way that input vectors (cases) similar to each other tend to stimulate neighbouring units on the hidden layer (a task related to cluster analysis). Thereby, the typological information is visualized, just as brand evaluation becomes apparent in a perceptual mapping model.

The second phase of weight estimation relates typology results and complementary descriptive attributes to an output layer of desired a priori classes. Compared to the feedforward model outlined above, the typology formation will not be 'disturbed' by any predetermined partitioning. The idea sounds very familiar to market researchers normally applying a clustering approach. First let the types evolve themselves, and then have them assessed in terms of consumption criteria. It remains open to discussion what kind of approach will develop more appealing features for marketers and researchers in the long run.

NINE

Strategic impact and practical implications of segmentation results in Austrian tourism

OVERVIEW

Results of modern segmentation projects have influenced the policies of the Austrian National Tourist Office (ANTO) and of provincial and regional offices since the early 1980s. The most spectacular outcome of market segmentation decisions is the ANTO's long-term strategy of establishing so-called special-interest groups of tourist services. The concept of *special-interest tourism* was introduced to provide a number of submarkets, which are homogeneous in their leisure or travel activities, with a tailor-made tourist product. This would not be particularly innovative unless the process was accompanied by an effort to encourage a number of individual small and family-operated businesses to co-operate under such a marketing 'umbrella'. This makes the difference compared to product planning customary with the large tour operators.

Any business seeking to become a member has to fulfil a number of service-level and specialization criteria to match with the profile of the group. Prominent examples of special-interest tourism groups are:

- Golf Green Austria (20 golf clubs, 77 hotels, 8,300 hotel beds);
- Kinderhotels Österreich (specializing in families with children; 80 members, 6,300 beds);
- Multitennis Austria (comprising 69 businesses with approx. 6,000 hotel beds);
- Reitarena Austria (specializing in horseriding; 60 hotels, 5,000 beds);
- Round Table-Konferenzhotels (specializing in organizing meetings and conventions; 80 members, 12,200 beds);
- Slim & Trim in Austria (48 hotels, 5,300 beds);
- Vinoveritas Austria (94 members in famous wine-growing regions);
- Wassererlebnis Österreich (specializing in aquatic sports; 40 hotels, 3,200 beds).

These groups are complemented by co-operation initiatives specializing in a particular country of origin, such as:

- Austria per l'Italia (145 members, 12,200 hotel beds);
- Autriche pro France (146 members, 11,700 beds).

Each group of tourist services formed by tourists' special interests or countries of origin produces its own catalogue and participates jointly in the distribution networks, including membership in one of the Austrian hotel reservation systems (AOL – Austria, On-line; MEHR – Mondial Elektronische Hotelreservierung) accessible through the European Computerized Reservation Systems (CRS) Galileo and Amadeus. Market segmentation principles have contributed to improve the competitive positions of small and medium-sized businesses, to counterbalance the scale revenues of international hotel chains, and to exceed the 'critical mass' necessary for international market operation.

Some of the a priori segmentation exercises reported in the preceding application sections have led the NTO managers to look into tourist and guest data in a more sophisticated manner than before. The multivariate nature of tourist or guest profiles is now recognized to require more than naïve reading of (bivariate) cross-tabulations in a typical market research report. Take the typical *main holiday-maker* as an example. If the present trend continues, main holiday-makers are bound to become a rare species among vacationists in Austria. Tourism marketing policies in the past, however, have escalated the long-term tendency rather than mitigated it. The fashionable concern of tourism marketers to shape their destinations into 'adventure' and 'active vacation' style regions cannot at the same time accommodate the main holiday-maker motivated by less conspicuous claims like relaxation or hiking.

A similar rationale applies to the objective of attracting *repeat visitors* (Chapter 8, pp. 119–26). Managers have learnt that repeat visitation also implies a danger of senescence and limited ambition to experience something new. There has to be some rotation in a destination's guest mix to balance the risk of ageing and of getting trapped in a product life cycle. One of the lessons becomes apparent in the selection of messages for international tourist advertising. Though there must still be focus in advertising content, the time of one single dominant appeal or proposition (the reader may remember Austria's famous and long-lasting 'hiking campaign') is over. Great variety, more change, shorter intervals and a different approach for neighbouring and long-haul markets have emerged and are now prevailing.

It was a logical consequence of the special-interest movement that ANTO became preoccupied with *lifestyle and value systems*. Austrian tourism was among the first industries to adopt the new EUROSTYLES typology. The analyses outlined in Chapter 8 (p.126–37) were not ready when ANTO decided to condense the original sixteen styles into five socio-targets. The vicinity in the lifestyle map arranges this grouping into five *'vacation style' types* (Figure 9.1). They are labelled:

- the prudent relaxation-seeker;
- the young family;
- the young hedonistic vacationist;
- the demanding adventure-seeker;
- the classic culture-seeker.

In addition to the strategic evaluation of tourism-generating countries, the EUROSTYLES are particularly useful in *educational programmes*. ANTO has been in charge of marketing education for local and regional managers for many years.

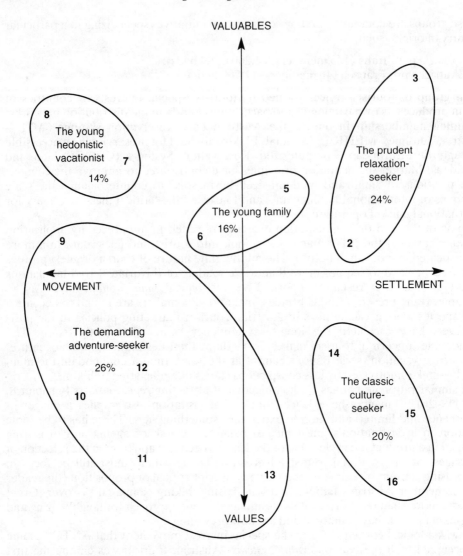

Figure 9.1 Five vacation types constructed from 16 EUROSTYLES

Source: Mazanec, J., and Zins, A., *Gästebefragung Österreich, EUROSTYLE-Bericht, Sommer 1991*, Austrian Society for Applied Research in Tourism, Vienna, 1991.

Recently, the lifestyle types and the vacation styles in particular turned out to be an extremely successful instrument for demonstration purposes. The five styles are portrayed with a lot of pictorial elements such as typical clothing, preferences for car makes, newspapers read, TV channels watched and leisure activities pursued. This helps greatly in educating a novice at marketing, and in conveying that markets are made up of individuals and of target groups that might need a different treatment while staying in a particular resort.

The experiment of *'exporting' the EUROSTYLES to the USA* (Chapter 8, pp. 137–41)

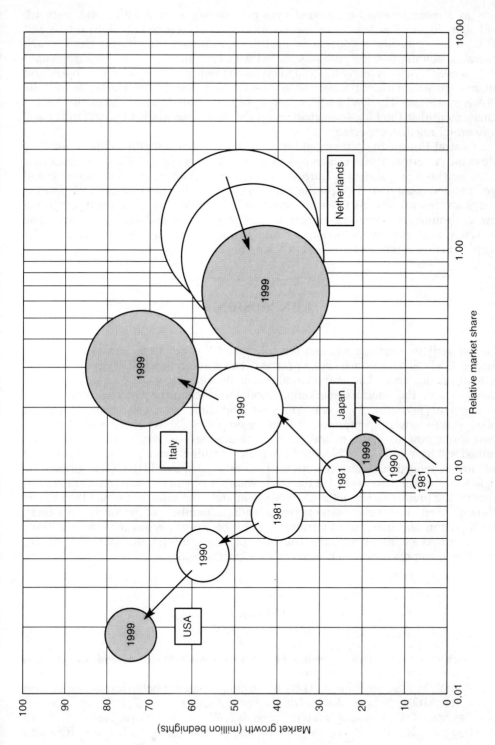

Figure 9.2 Trends in Austria's strategic position

Source: Note 60, p. 128.

also has a more serious background than just playing around with neural network modelling. Figure 9.2 clearly explains the reasons. The Netherlands, Japan, Italy and the USA are featuring in a 'dynamic' growth–share matrix. The trajectories for each generating country link the positions of 1981 with 1990 and extrapolate the trend until 1999. While Austria is likely to strengthen its competitive position in the Italian and Japanese growth markets (evidenced by an increase in the relative market share), the USA is in decline. The USTYLES results have contributed to convincing the ANTO management that the long-term chances on the American market are still intact and more promising than expected.

A Central European destination, however, has to accept that it fulfils an outsider role in the American traveller's consideration set. In contrast to the market conditions in the neighbouring states of Europe, the management faces a more movable and open-minded consumer. The psychographic profiles of the most attractive US target groups are heavily shifted towards motives and attitudes like movement, exploring new environments, exposing oneself to new experience and changing pace. The marketing management is forced to adapt to these challenges and to practise the 'proper' market conduct of a long-haul destination.

CONCLUSION

It is too early to conclude whether the concept of *'hybrid' segmentation* reported in Chapter 8 will survive in marketing practice. The marketing scientist experiences the well-known dilemma. The market reality, on the one hand, is always much more complex than the fanciest marketing model can capture. On the other hand, management practitioners, owing to cost and time restraints, have a limited willingness to indulge in mysterious decision-support systems. There is still much to learn about how to make neural network results easy to digest. Presumably, the method will have to remain 'hidden' from the user (this is the 'black-box' approach of the most advanced commercial software packages, such as 4THOUGHT offered by Right Information Systems Ltd in the UK). Another way to get management involved relies on the predictive strengths of an NNW model. The rationale would then run as follows: given a traveller target group with a number of particular personal, psychographic and trip-related attributes, will it be a repeater segment, a spendthrift group, etc? As a consequence, the TourMIS marketing information system of ANTO intends to incorporate more advanced 'what-if' methodology.

NOTES

1.   Aleksander, I., and Morton, H., *An Introduction to Neural Computing*, Chapman & Hall, London, 1990.
2.   Assael, H., 'Segmenting markets by group purchasing behavior: an application of the AID technique', *Journal of Marketing Research*, vol. 7, 1970, pp. 153–8.
3.   Bagozzi, R. P., *Causal Models in Marketing*, Wiley, New York, 1980.
4.   Bagozzi, R. P., *Principles of Marketing Management*, Science Research Associates, Chicago, IL, 1986.

5. Bernard, M., 'Leisure-rich and leisure-poor: leisure lifestyles among young adults', *Leisure Sciences*, vol. 10, 1987, pp. 131–49.
6. Cathelat, B., *Styles de vie*, Vols 1 and 2, Editions d'organisation, Paris, 1985.
7. Darden, W., and Darden, D., 'A study of vacation life styles', in Travel and Tourism Research Association, *Proceedings of the 7th Annual Conference*, Salt Lake City, Utah, 1976, pp. 231-6.
8. Day, G. S., 'Diagnosing the product portfolio', *Journal of Marketing*, vol. 41, 1977, pp. 29–38.
9. Day, G. S., *Analysis for Strategic Market Decisions*, West Publishing Co., St Paul, MN, 1986.
10. Day, G. S., *Market Driven Strategy: Process for Creating Value*, The Free Press, New York, 1990.
11. Europanel, 'Euro-styles: Eine europaweite Landkarte mit 16 sozio-kulturellen Typen', *Marketing Journal*, vol. 22, 1989, pp. 106–11.
12. Formann, A. K., Mazanec, J. A., and Oberhauser, O. C., *Numerische Klassifikationsprobleme in 'großen' Datensätzen der demoskopischen Marktforschung: Ein numerischer Methodenvergleich von Latent Class- und Cluster-Analyse*, Arbeitspapiere der absatzwirtschaftlichen Institute der Wirtschaftsuniversität Wien, Orac, Vienna, 1979.
13. Freeman, J. A., and Skapura, D. M., *Neural Networks, Algorithms, Applications, and Programming Techniques*, Addison-Wesley, Reading, MA, 1991.
14. Haley, R. J., 'Benefit segmentation: a decision-oriented research tool', *Journal of Marketing*, vol. 32, 1968, pp. 30–5.
15. Heskett, J. L., Sasser, W. E., and Hart, C. W. L., *Service Breakthroughs*, The Free Press, New York, 1990.
16. Hsieh, Sh., O'Leary, J. T., and Morrison, A. M., 'Segmenting the international travel market by activity', *Tourism Management*, vol. 13, 1992, pp. 209–23.
17. Jöreskog, K. G., 'The LISREL approach to causal model-building in the social sciences', in K. G. Jöreskog and H. Wold (eds), *Systems under Indirect Observation*, Part I, North-Holland, Amsterdam, 1982, pp. 81–99.
18. Kamakura, W. A., and Novak, Th. P., 'Value-system segmentation: exploring the meaning of LOV', *Journal of Consumer Research*, vol. 19, 1992, pp. 119–32.
19. Karnin, D. D., 'A simple procedure for pruning back-propagation trained neural networks', *IEEE Transactions on Neural Networks*, vol. 1, 1990, p. 239–42.
20. Kohonen, T., *Self-Organization and Associative Memory*, Springer, Berlin, 1984.
21. Kramer, S., *Europäische Life-Style-Analysen zur Verhaltensprognose von Konsumenten*, Dr Kovac, Hamburg, 1991.
22. Kreutzer, R., 'Länderübergreifende Segmentierungskonzepte – Antwort auf die Globalisiergung der Märkte', *Jahrbuch der Absatz- und Verbrauchsforschung*, vol. 37, 1991, pp. 4–27.
23. Mayo, E. J., and Jarvis, L. P., *The Psychology of Leisure Travel*, CBI, Boston, MA, 1981.
24. Mazanec, J., *Strukturmodelle des Konsumverhaltens*, Orac, Vienna, 1978.
25. Mazanec, J., 'Deterministische und probabilistische Klassifikation in der Konsumverhaltensforschung: ein empirischer Anwendungsversuch der Quervalidierung clusteranalytischer Verfahren für qualitative Daten mit der Latent Class-Analyse', in Fandel, G. (ed.), *Operations Research Proceedings 1980*, Springer, Berlin/Heidelberg/New York, 1980, pp. 296–305.
26. Mazanec, J., 'How to detect travel market segments: a clustering approach', *Journal of Travel Research*, vol. 23, 1984, pp. 17–21.

27. Mazanec, J., 'Consumer behavior in tourism', in Witt, St. F., and Moutinho, L. (eds), *Tourism Marketing and Management Handbook*, Prentice-Hall, Englewood Cliffs, NJ, 1989, pp. 63–8.

28. Mazanec, J., and Mikulicz, H., *Gästebefragung Österreich, Österreich-Bericht, Sommer 1988*, Austrian Society for Applied Research in Tourism, Vienna, 1989.

29. Mazanec, J., 'Market segmentation once again: exploring neural network models', in *Tourist Research as a Commitment*, Association Internationale d'Experts Scientifique du Tourisme, St Gall, 1990, pp. 36–53.

30. Mazanec, J., 'Classifying tourists into market segments: a neural network approach', *Journal of Travel and Tourism Marketing*, vol. 1, 1992, pp. 39–59.

31. Mazanec, J., and Zins, A., *Gästebefragung Österreich, EUROSTYLE-Bericht, Sommer 1991*, Austrian Society for Applied Research in Tourism, Vienna, 1991.

32. Mazanec, J., and Zins, A., EUROSTYLES and SOCIO-TARGETS as guest segments: selected findings, a brief outline of the EUROSTYLES typology', *Revue de Tourisme*, 2/1992, pp. 5–8.

33. Mazanec, J., and Zins, A. 'Tourist behaviour and the new European lifestyle typology', in Theobald, W. (ed.), *Global Tourism: The next decade*, Butterworth-Heinemann, Oxford, 1994, pp. 199–216.

34. McClelland, J. L., Rumelhart, D. E., and Hinton, G. E., 'The appeal of parallel distributed processing', in Rumelhart, D. E., and McClelland, J. L. (eds), *Parallel Distributed Processing: Explorations in the Microstructure of Cognition*, Vol. 1: *Foundations*, MIT Press, Cambridge, MA, 1986, pp. 3–44.

35. McNamee, P., *Tools and Techniques for Strategic Management*, Pergamon, Oxford, 1985.

36. Morrison, D. G., 'On the interpretation of discriminant analysis', *Journal of Marketing Research*, vol. 6, 1969, pp. 156–63.

37. Moutinho, L., 'Consumer behavior in tourism', *European Journal of Marketing*, vol. 21, 1987, pp. 3–44.

38. NeuralWare, Inc., *NeuralWorks Professional*, Pittsburgh, PA, 1988.

39. NeuralWare, Inc., *Reference Guide, NeuralWorks Professional II/Plus*, Technical Publications Group, Pittsburgh, PA, 1991.

40. NeuralWare, Inc., *Neural Computing, NeuralWorks Professional II/Plus*, Technical Publications Group, Pittsburgh, PA, 1991.

41. Rosenberg, M. A., 'Cognitive structure and attitudinal effect', in Fishbein, M. (ed.), *Readings in Attitude Theory and Measurement*, Wiley, New York, 1967.

42. Ruck, D. W., Rogers, St. K., Kabrisky, M., Oxley, M. E., and Suter, B. W., 'The multilayer perceptron as an approximation to a Bayes optimal discriminant function', *IEEE Transactions on Neural Networks*, vol. 1, 1990, pp. 296–8.

43. Rumelhart, D. E., Hinton, G. E., and McClelland, J. L., 'A general framework for parallel distributed processing', in Rumelhart, D. E., and McClelland, J. L. (eds), *Parallel Distributed Processing: Explorations in the Microstructure of Cognition*, Vol. 1: *Foundations*, MIT Press, Cambridge, MA, 1986, pp. 45–76.

44. Rumelhart, D. E., Hinton, G. E., and Williams, R. J., 'Learning internal representation by error propagation', in Rumelhart, D. E., and McClelland, J. L. (eds), *Parallel Distributed Processing*, Vol. I: *Foundations*, MIT Press, Cambridge, MA, 1986, pp. 318–62.

45. Shoemaker, P. A., 'A note on least-squares learning procedures and classification by neural network models', *ILEE Transactions on Neural Networks*, vol. 2, 1991, pp. 158–60.

46. Simpson, P. K., *Artificial Network Systems*, Pergamon, New York, 1990.
47. Smith, St. L. J., *Tourism Analysis: A Handbook*, Wiley, New York, 1989.
48. Sonquist, J. A., Baker, E. L., and Morgan, J. N., *Searching for Structure*, 2nd edn, Survey Research Center, Ann Arbor, MI, 1973.
49. Valentine, E. R., 'Neural nets: from Hartley and Hebb to Hinton', *Journal of Mathematical Psychology*, vol. 33, 1989, pp. 348–57.
50. Vavrik, U., *Marktsegmentierung mit dem automatischen Interaktionsdetektor: Methodische Fortschritte – Reflexe im Tourismus*, Service Fachverlag, Vienna, 1990.
51. Vavrik, U., and Mazanec, J., *A-priori and A-posteriori Travel Market Segmentation: Tailoring Automatic Interaction Detection and Cluster Analysis for Tourism Marketing*, Cahiers du Tourisme, Série C, No. 62, Aix-en-Provence, 1990.
52. Veal, A. J., 'Leisure, lifestyles and status', *Leisure Studies*, vol. 8, 1989, pp. 141–53.
53. Wan, E. A., 'Neural network classification: a Bayesian interpretation', *IEEE Transactions on Neural Networks*, vol. 1, 1990, pp. 303–5.
54. Wasserman, Ph. D., *Neural Computing: Theory and Practice*, Van Nostrand Reinhold, New York, 1989.
55. Wells, W. D., and Tigert, D. J., 'Activities, interests and opinions', *Journal of Advertising Research*, vol. 11, 1971, pp. 27–35.
56. Wells, W. D. (ed.), *Life Style and Psychographics*, AMA, Chicago, IL, 1974.
57. Wells, W. D., 'Psychographics: a critical review', *Journal of Marketing Research*, vol. 12, 1975, pp. 196–213.
58. Wind, Y., Mahajan, V., and Swire, D., 'An empirical comparison of standardized portfolio models', *Journal of Marketing*, vol. 47, 1983, pp. 89–99.
59. Winkler, A. R., 'EURO-STYLES in panel analyses', *Europanel Marketing Bulletin*, 1991, pp. 8–11.
60. Wöber, K. W., 'Systementwurf und Realisierung eines Entscheidungsunterstützungs-Systems für eine nationale Tourismusorganisation unter besonderer Berücksichtigung von Expertenschätzungen', doctoral thesis, Vienna University of Economics and Business Administration, 1993.
61. Yiannakis, A., and Gibson, H., 'Roles Tourists Play', *Annals of Tourism Research*, vol. 19, 1992, pp. 287–303.

GLOSSARY OF TECHNICAL TERMS

Automatic interaction detecting/detector (AID): A data technique and computer program to find the relationships between a dependent variable and several independent variables where all variables are qualitative (i.e. measured on nominal level, such as 'country of origin', or on ordinal level, such as 'social class').

Back-propagation network: A neural network with three or more layers of processing elements ('neurons') where the error between model output and observed data is calculated on the top layer and 'propagated back' to the preceding layers for revision of the connection weights between elements.

Bayes optimal discriminant function (for classifying consumers): A weighted sum of consumer attributes (variables) which allows the best possible prediction of the classes (segments) that the consumers belong to.

BINCLUS clustering program: A non-hierarchical cluster analysis program for binary data (0–1 variables), which partitions a set of objects into a given number of clusters, thereby minimizing the overall degree of heterogeneity (expressed as the sum of squared pairwise distances).

Canonical correlation: Correlation (coefficient) between two weighted sums (or linear combinations) of variables.

Cases correctly classified (%CC): The share of cases (respondents) correctly attributed to a known class by exploiting the information residing in a set of explanatory variables (characteristics); a quality criterion for the results of classification methods (e.g. discriminant analysis).

Chi-square: Value of a density function for the sum of squared variables following a normal distribution; used in statistical significance tests for cross-tabulations.

Cluster analysis: A generic name for a large number of various cluster algorithms with the common aim of sorting objects into classes depending on their similarity.

Discriminant analysis (DA): A multivariate data technique for determining the discriminating power of explanatory variables (attributes) and their ability to predict class membership.

Explained sum of squares: Portion of the total variation of a variable (attribute) that could be reproduced by another variable or a combination of other variables (independent or explanatory variables, predictors).

F-ratio: A quotient of two variances following the F-distribution; used for statistical significance testing in correlation and regression analysis and in ANOVA (analysis of variance).

Generalized delta rule: A method of revising the connection weights in a neural network model where the amount of weight updates corresponds to the back-propagated error (see Back-propagation network).

Hold-out sample: Part of a (master) sample which is not used during an analysis but is reserved for statistical significance testing to prevent the bias that would result if analysis and testing were applied to the same data.

Latent class analysis: An advanced probabilistic method of analysing the interrelationships in a set of qualitative variables (attributes).

LISREL: A method and computer program performing parameter estimation in causal models incorporating unobservable constructs and (observable) indicators.

Maximal chance criterion (CMax): Percentage correctly classified by chance if all objects are allocated to the largest subgroup (or class) (see Proportional chance criterion).

Neural network modelling: One of the mainstreams of artificial intelligence research, building models according to the principles believed to underlie the operation of the human brain (parallel processing, robustness *vis-à-vis* distorted or incomplete data input, ability to generalize).

Parallel distributed processing: Synonymous with neural network modelling.

Polytomous data: Data made up of qualitative variables with more than two values or categories (cf. binary or 0–1 or dichotomous data if only two categories are involved).

Principal components analysis: A popular data reduction technique condensing a large number of variables into a much smaller set of their underlying dimensions; used for generating perceptual maps needed in product-positioning models.

Proportional chance criterion (CPro): Percentage correctly classified by chance if the objects are allocated to subgroups (or classes) according to the size of these subgroups (see Maximal chance criterion).

Regression analysis: A multivariate data technique to reproduce a dependent variable by exploiting the explanatory power inherent in a set of independent variables: e.g. used in market response models for estimating demand functions.

Root mean square error: A popular measure of the goodness of fit calculated as the square root of the average squared difference between observed and predicted values.

Segmentation:

A posteriori segmentation (similarity segmentation): A market segmentation strategy where consumer segments are not known beforehand, but result from a clustering process applied to a set of motivational, attitudinal, activity-oriented or lifestyle attributes.

A priori segmentation (criterion segmentation): A market segmentation strategy employing a predetermined partitioning of the market (e.g. heavy, medium and light buyers) and seeking the most distinctive descriptions of these already-defined segments with additional attributes.

Hybrid segmentation: A new segmentation strategy attempting to combine a priori criteria and a posteriori variables in the same model; this is not manageable with traditional segmentation methods, but may be achieved with neural network modelling.

Self-organizing maps: A variant of neural networks where a multidimensional input is compressed into a two-dimensional representation; the network learns to mimic a given input which may be important for various pattern recognition tasks.

Tanimoto measure/coefficient: A measure ranging between 0 and 1 expressing the degree of similarity between two objects with dichotomous attributes where non-existent attributes in both objects do not add to the overall similarity.

Variables:

Compound variables: A combination of two or more variables (e.g. stage in the family life cycle, made up of criteria like number of persons in the household, number and age of children, age of parents).

Criterion variable: Synonymous with dependent variable.

Dependent variable: Synonymous with criterion variable; a variable (consumer attribute) with values that are believed to depend on one or more influential factors (e.g. other personal attributes, characteristics of the goods and services bought, the purchase situation; see Independent variables).

Dichotomous variables: Variables with two values, mostly coded with 0 and 1; the variables may correspond to 'natural' attributes (e.g. gender) or to 'dichotomized' attributes (e.g. country of origin X – yes, no, country of origin, Y – yes, no . . .; see Dummy variables).

Dummy variables: Non-dichotomous variables artificially dichotomized into a set of 0–1 variables (see Dichotomous variables).

Independent variables: Variables (consumer attributes) which are believed to exert an influence on one or more other (dependent) variables (see Dependent variable).

Nominal variable: Variable measured on the lowest measurement level, consisting of a number of unordered categories (e.g. type of profession, country of origin).

Wilk's lambda: A significance measure ranging between 0 and 1 used in discriminant analysis where values approaching 1 denote a poor predictive power of the independent variables selected for the DA (see Discriminant analysis).

PART 3

NEW PRODUCT RESEARCH AND DEVELOPMENT

Simon Crawford-Welch

INTRODUCTION

Part 3 of the book is founded on the premise that, in today's volatile, dynamic and complex hospitality industry, an unwavering organizational commitment to product and service* development is not an option, it is a prerequisite for survival. Chapters 10 to 12 seek to provide a structured, sequential and self-contained view of product development in the lodging and food service segments of the hospitality industry. A wide array of approaches are discussed, including 'new-to-the-world' products, new product lines, product line extensions, product repositioning and product cost reductions.

Chapter 10 considers the overall importance of product development to the hospitality industry and describes, with examples, the role of different types of research in the product development process. The chapter also outlines the 'traditional' approach to product development and offers a framework for achieving improvements in the effectiveness and efficiency of the product development approach.

Chapter 11 outlines the development of the Courtyard by Marriott concept with specific reference to the research techniques employed to test the product concept. Multivariate and inferential research techniques were used, and these are discussed in relation to the support provided to designing, developing and successfully launching the lodging chain concept.

Chapter 12 focuses on a methodology for developing and introducing new products in the foodservice industry. The purpose is to explain and illustrate the research and planning stages needed to ensure that millions of dollars of development funding are secured against product development plans which have been properly formulated and implemented.

*Throughout Part 3, references to 'product' are equally applicable to 'service' development.

TEN

Product development in the hospitality industry

There is nothing more difficult to take in hand, more perilous to conduct, or more uncertain in its success, than to take the lead in the introduction of a new order of things.

Machiavelli, *The Prince*

INTRODUCTION

The one constant in today's hospitality environment is change. Change in the hospitality industry can be categorized into two kinds: evolutionary change and revolutionary change. The former comes from within and the latter comes from without. To be leaders in the industry and maintain a sustainable competitive advantage, hospitality organizations must design, control and implement their own change. Otherwise, change will be imposed on them by the external world in an uncontrollable manner. A structured, coherent and sequential approach to product development goes some way to adopting an evolutionary, as opposed to revolutionary, approach to change.

Robert C. Hazard, Jr, President of Choice Hotels International, maintains that the 1990s will be the most competitive decade in the history of the lodging industry, and suggests that every hotel and lodging company must become more market driven, improving their product to create a unique, sustainable competitive advantage in their local marketplace and a perception of greater value among their guests. Success in today's cut-throat global hospitality industry often depends on being the first to pinpoint a consumer trend, develop and introduce new products, and capitalize quickly upon ever-changing consumer needs and desires. For example, the development and introduction of extended-stay all-suite hotel concepts in the lodging industry was the result of a consumer need for a place to stay which was more 'homely'; while the introduction of McDonald's 'McLean' Burger and KFC's roll-out of its 'Lite 'n Crispy', a skinless fried chicken product, were a direct result of increased consumer concern for health and nutrition.

The 1980s saw a tremendous emphasis on new product development in the lodging and food service industries as organizations attempted to cater for the increasingly diversified needs of the marketplace. In a recent survey of 4,000 lodging and restaurant organizations in North America, over 77 per cent of responding organizations stated that new product development was moderately to very important as a method of maintaining a competitive advantage in the marketplace. However, over a third of respondents viewed conducting consumer research as unimportant, which offers some credence to the argument that much of the product development in the hospitality industry is not market oriented but product oriented. The emphasis on new product development and introduction in the hospitality industry was, in essence, a response by corporations to the plurality of the marketplace and the diverse price/ value needs of multiple market segments. In today's hospitality industry there is no such thing as a mass market. Mass markets are a vestige of the past. Both lodging and foodservice companies are faced with the task of finding product line additions that will maintain their profitability during downturns in the economy while improving profit potential in growth periods. This is a highly complicated task.

Successful product development may require peeling back multiple layers of consumer, technological, manufacturing and other variables before the product is successfully positioned in the marketplace. The failure rate of new product introductions is indicative of just how complicated the process can be. Although the rewards of success with new product introductions are great, the costs of failure are also high. One rule of thumb predicts that only one product in ten ever makes it as far as a consumer testing, and only 10 per cent of those ever make it to market. This risk is compounded when major hospitality corporations tend to forgo much of the battery of consumer tests in order to beat their competitors to the marketplace. Other estimates suggest that, of one hundred new product ideas generated, only fifteen survive the screening phase, six survive the product development phase, and only two survive the commercialization phase – a 2 per cent success ratio! New products fail for many reasons, but some of the major barriers to success include the lack of a relationship to the mission of the firm; the adoption of a product orientation as opposed to a market orientation; a lack or misuse of market research and market analysis; poor sales forecasting; poor product design and quality; poor pricing structures; and insufficient distribution channels. In general terms, it has been suggested that new products fail in the marketplace in large part owing to the lack of an appropriate product development process integrated with an adequate marketing strategy.

The purpose of this chapter is to offer an overview of the historical and current state of research and product development practices in the North American hospitality industry. Specifically, the objectives of this chapter are:

- to outline the importance of product development in today's hospitality industry;
- to describe, with examples, the vital role of different types of research in the product development process;
- to outline the 'traditional' approach to product development in the hospitality industry;
- to offer a framework for a more effective and efficient approach to product development.

THE IMPORTANCE OF PRODUCT DEVELOPMENT

The development of new products in the hospitality industry is important for several reasons. New products often create excitement, build commitment and make a company a more exciting place to work, while simultaneously enabling companies and salespersons to strengthen customer relationships and to build new ones. The pull-through effect of important new products on an organization's entire product mix is often significant, and almost always underrated. In today's hospitality industry, a steady stream of successful new products is essential to avoid decline and to fuel continued growth. The R & D associated with new product development also serves as a barrier to entry into the marketplace by competitors as well as lending companies flexibility in the form of a talent base and infrastructure that can be brought into play as needed.

TYPES OF NEW PRODUCT

There are generally considered to be six categories of new product, as shown in Figure 10.1.

1. 'New-to-the-world' products are products that create an entirely new market, and they constitute approximately 10 per cent of total new product introductions.
2. New product lines are new products that allow a company to enter an established market for the first time, and these constitute approximately 20 per cent of total introductions.
3. Line extensions are new products that supplement an organization's established product line, and they constitute approximately 26 per cent of total new product introductions. Line extensions include 'upgrade products', 'economy products' and 'additional feature products'. Since many forecasters predict that new products will have decreasing chances of success in the 1990s, line-extension-based development has accelerated dramatically, particularly as a percentage of overall new product development efforts. However, a very real danger with line extensions is the cannibalization of the parent brand. In the late 1980s many hospitality organizations, eager for quick success, introduced line extensions to a major brand without due regard for the long-term effect on the parent brand. The pattern has become fairly standard: the 'line extension' manager launches the new product, diverting resources away from its parent; the extention achieves its sales objectives and the manager is rewarded; eventually, top management detects signs of the parent's slow decline, and the post-mortem reveals cannibalization as the cause of the parent's illness. One method of avoiding the pitfall of cannibalization is for organizations to conduct a simulated test market (STM) of the proposed product. The process of STMs is discussed later in this chapter.
4. Improvements and revisions also constitute approximately 26 per cent of new product introductions. They are new products that provide improved performance of greater perceived value, and which replace existing products.

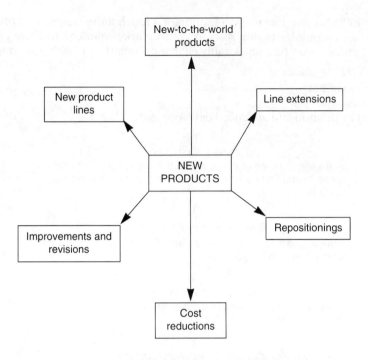

Figure 10.1 Types of new product

5. Repositionings are existing products that are targeted to new markets or market segments, and they constitute approximately 7 per cent of the total.
6. Finally, cost reductions are new products that provide similar performance at a lower cost, and they constitute 11 per cent of total new product introductions.

THE NEW PRODUCT DEVELOPMENT LIFE CYCLE

There is no single process for the development of new products. Some companies use six stages in the process of new product development. These stages are:

- genesis;
- preliminary evaluation;
- early development;
- advanced development;
- introduction;
- in-market evaluation.

However, in today's dynamic hospitality environment some companies are emphasizing shorter developmental time lines and getting to market more quickly. In the 1970s and for much of the 1980s, for example, the product development process was highly structured and dependent on research (although not always sound research) at each stage. In the 1990s we are seeing the adoption of a much more fragmented process, as some companies emphasize taking risks to get to market quickly. In these cases, the development process may be considerably changed, consisting of only four stages:

- genesis and evaluation;
- early development;
- introduction;
- in-market evaluation and advanced development.

BUSINESS STRATEGY
State major goals of the firm and the plans for achieving these goals. Define what business the firm is in or wants to be in.

↓

NEW PRODUCT STRATEGY
Outline goals for new products and define boundaries within which they can be developed.

↓

IDEA GENERATION
Search for new product ideas that are consistent with the organization's objectives.

↓

SCREENING AND EVALUATION
Reduce the number of ideas by developing and applying criteria to eliminate the impractical ones; also develop a product concept for surviving ideas by expressing them in meaningful user terms.

↓

BUSINESS ANALYSIS
Evaluate surviving ideas according to the firm's requirements for sales, market share, profits and return on investment.

↓

DEVELOPMENT
Transform the idea into a prototype model to ensure that it is technically and commercially feasible; in addition, tentatively develop the other marketing-mix elements.

↓

TESTING
Evaluate the product and marketing programme under actual or user conditions.

↓

COMMERCIALIZATION
Launch the new product and thereby incorporate it into the firm's product mix.

Figure 10.2 Stages of new product development

Source: *New Products Management for the 1980s*, Booz, Allen & Hamilton, New York, 1982.

For some companies and some products, the process of product development occurs over a period of years; for other companies and products, it can take as little as a few months. The elapsed time from initial product concept until the new product is commercially available is called cycle development time. A shorter cycle time, other things being equal, raises the competitive value of the new product.

Figure 10.2 outlines the various generic stages of new product development. These stages may be labelled differently depending upon the organization, but the basic stages are the same across organizations. Product development begins in earnest at the idea generation stage of Figure 10.2. Naturally, each stage of product development is accompanied by related strategies. Each of these stages is discussed in greater depth below.

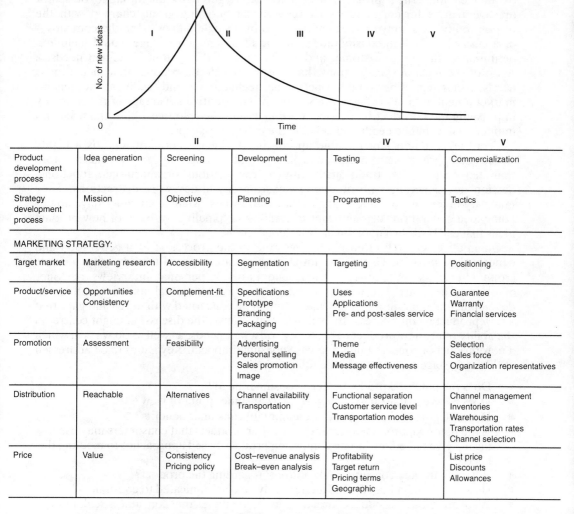

	I	II	III	IV	V
Product development process	Idea generation	Screening	Development	Testing	Commercialization
Strategy development process	Mission	Objective	Planning	Programmes	Tactics

MARKETING STRATEGY:

	I	II	III	IV	V
Target market	Marketing research	Accessibility	Segmentation	Targeting	Positioning
Product/service	Opportunities Consistency	Complement-fit.	Specifications Prototype Branding Packaging	Uses Applications Pre- and post-sales service	Guarantee Warranty Financial services
Promotion	Assessment	Feasibility	Advertising Personal selling Sales promotion Image	Theme Media Message effectiveness	Selection Sales force Organization representatives
Distribution	Reachable	Alternatives	Channel availability Transportation	Functional separation Customer service level Transportation modes	Channel management Inventories Warehousing Transportation rates Channel selection
Price	Value	Consistency Pricing policy	Cost–revenue analysis Break–even analysis	Profitability Target return Pricing terms Geographic	List price Discounts Allowances

Figure 10.3   Product development life cycle

Source: Kortge, G. D., and Okonkwo, P. A., 'Simultaneous new product development: reducing the new product failure rate', *Industrial Marketing Management*, vol. 18, 1989, pp. 301–6.

Figure 10.3, a linkage matrix, shows a five-stage strategy development process which can be used to provide the marketing manager with a systematic means of evaluating the long-term feasibility of introducing a new product into the marketplace. As can be seen in the diagram, each stage of the product development process should be accompanied by certain marketing strategies geared towards enhancing the success of the introduction over the long term.

Idea generation

The idea generation stage generally includes the identification and initial refinement of an idea for a new product. This may be triggered by an initiative of senior management, a formal planning exercise by an on-going group charged with the responsibility, or simply an idea championed by a single individual in the company – or a customer. Typical considerations in the idea generation stage would include a definition of the target customer and an overview of the customer's unmet needs; a sense of the technological options that exist to develop a product that meets those needs; issues regarding suitable operational technologies and facilities; the general market potential for a product of this type; the competitive advantage of the company in pursuing the introduction of such a product; and the resources, both financial and human, that would be needed to develop the product concept.

There are a number of possible approaches to idea generation. One is a highly structured approach using a trained facilitator and a group that generally has no more than ten participants, traditionally drawn from various organizational functions. Sessions are generally held off-site, away from day-to-day work distractions. They may vary in length from a few hours to an entire week. Many companies have an on-going idea generation stage in order to establish a 'pipeline' or bank of new product ideas that can be drawn upon on an 'as needed' basis.

Qualitiative research often plays a big role in the process of idea generation and concept development. Generally, initial concepts are exposed to consumers in focus group interviews, mini-groups, triads and in-depth personal interviews or 'one-on-ones'. There are two kinds of interview: developmental and evaluative. In developmental interviews, the discussion might be concerned with needs and gaps that a new product might address. In evaluative interviews, the discussion might centre on the ability of the new product to meet key consumer needs, as well as on ways in which a new product or concept might increase consumer appeal. Key issues to be addressed at this early stage might include the following:

- Does the potential product meet a consumer need?
- Does it have a 'reason for being' from a consumer point of view?
- Does the potential product offer meaningful consumer benefits?
- Is the potential product different from other products that consumers may use to meet a given need, including competing product-based approaches to meeting the need?
- What are the key consumer 'hot buttons' regarding the product?
- How can product benefits most effectively be communicated to consumers?
- What are the key product characteristics or attributes that consumers seek in such a product?
- What are the general issues involved in the consumer's price/value considerations?

Screening

The screening stage can often be divided into two phases: preliminary evaluation and volumetric estimation.

Preliminary evaluation utilizes various approaches which examine either the absolute appeal of the new product concept or the comparative appeal of the new concept. The former kind of appeal is measured using a monadic rating, in which the concept is not compared to other concepts or products, but the intrinsic concept appeal itself is measured. Alternatively, the appeal of the new product concept as compared to other new product concepts and existing products can be measured. This comparative measure may be used to screen a number of potential ideas and select the most promising candidate(s), or it may assess the appeal of individual new product concepts relative to proven concepts or existing products. A control concept or concepts, known to be of either strong or weak consumer appeal, is generally included to measure the relative strength of the new product concept. Often, major corporations have norms, or hurdle rates, for concept testing or screening, which set a minimum threshold for concept appeal.

A final pre-market step in consumer research is volumetric estimation, which involves the use of quantitative concept testing within a mathematical model to predict the year 1 in-market volume.

Development

The development phase usually consists of preparing a business opportunity plan (BOP), the contents of which would normally include:

- a forecast of customer preferences (including the relevant market research data);
- an analysis of the competitive status of the company if this product is successfully introduced (an 'impact' analysis);
- an outline of major design requirements for the product (such as features, functions, reliability, size) and the associated 'manufacturing' process;
- an analysis of competitive threats and responses;
- a marketing plan including sales and market share forecasts;
- a product/service development plan or 'blueprint' (costs, timing, and organizations to be involved);
- a financial analysis to justify the new product introduction.

Resources are allocated to identifying the performance potential and aesthetic attributes of the product. The BOP should also encompass a feasibility study which should focus on both technical and marketing feasibility.

Technical feasibility is concerned with the technological requirements (both 'hard' and 'soft' technology) necessary to ensure the successful introduction of the product. All questions as to what the product will do, what it will look like, and how it will be used must be addressed and answered. In appropriate situations, this is also when patent protection is sought and potential issues of environmental impacts are identified and described. The goal of this phase is to achieve a design release for the new product.

Marketing feasibility is assessed in terms of business strategy, marketing and sales objectives, marketing tactics, and the associated resource requirements and product launch schedule. Consumer acceptance and sales estimates are also projected at this phase.

Testing

There is a saying among market research practitioners that 'It's better to fly a new product simulator than crash the real thing.' The testing stage is specifically concerned with the use of research techniques to:

- provide information to reduce risk and improve the odds of success;
- facilitate the new product introduction process.

The information role of consumer research is both developmental and evaluative. In its development aspect, it is concerned with the key consumer issues, needs and benefits; and the key product features and attributes important to consumers. As an evaluation aid, it considers questions such as: does the product address consumer issues, needs and benefits? and is the product different from other means by which consumers may address needs, get benefits, etc.?

Test marketing is often used as a predictive research tool for new product introductions. It uses mathematical models to project forecasts of sales and market share as well as to make recommendations for improving pricing, advertising or promotion. Simulated test marketing research is the best way for a company to reduce risk when launching a new product, or restaging or repositioning an existing product. Possible testing methods include simulated test markets (STMs), minimarket testing or controlled market testing, and fully-fledged test markets. During the test market phase the complete product is produced in low-volume pilot runs and is tested under various conditions that approximate the full range of typical customer usage environments. The basic purpose is to discover any defects that could be modified before volume production occurs. There are several advantages to conducting simulated test marketing research.

First, it reduces risk. These risks include the costs of marketing and sales as well as the capital risk. Second, it increases efficiency by allowing organizations to determine projects with the greatest return. Third, STMs maintain security by allowing organizations to test a product without competitors engaging in unrealistic overt action to drown the new product before it is born. Fourth, an STM can also save time by delivering results in three to six months, compared with a wait of more than a year for the results from an in-market test.

The better STM systems today represent the offspring of a marriage between sophisticated mathematical models of the new product marketing mix and less sophisticated, but undeniably clever, simulated test market research systems. These better systems integrate marketing science modelling, automated intelligence technology, historical databases and simulated test marketing research.

Historically, STMs used five-component multiplication models. The old models' methodologies were based on taking a year-end awareness number (component 1) and multiplying it by an awareness-to-trial (component 2) and distribution estimate (component 3) to forecast penetration. The penetration figure, coupled with repeat-purchase (component 4) and usage-rate (component 5) data, helped the company forecast sales. The problem with the five-component model stemmed from the primitive manner in which marketers estimated or guessed at these five different parameters.

In contrast, today's better STMs capture every important component in the marketing mix, from media weight and schedule to promotion, product and positioning, and assess the effect of any plan on brand awareness through to market share and profitability. Figure 10.4 shows the input and output components for some of today's more sophisticated STM models. Some STM systems used today can go beyond volume forecasting and answer such questions as 'What would happen if media spending were reduced by 25 per cent?' or 'What would happen if consumer promotion were increased by 10 per cent?' In addition, some of the very new STMs can capture competitive response by projecting what will happen, for example, if competitors decrease their price by 10 per cent when the new product is introduced.

Another technique used in STMs is critical attribute analysis. This enables a marketer to assess the attributes and benefits that affect a buyer's purchasing decision the most. It provides insights into the factors that contribute to or inhibit product trial, and it permits a company to evaluate how well a product fulfils the buyer's pre-purchase expectations. Critical attribute analysis, unlike traditional research and

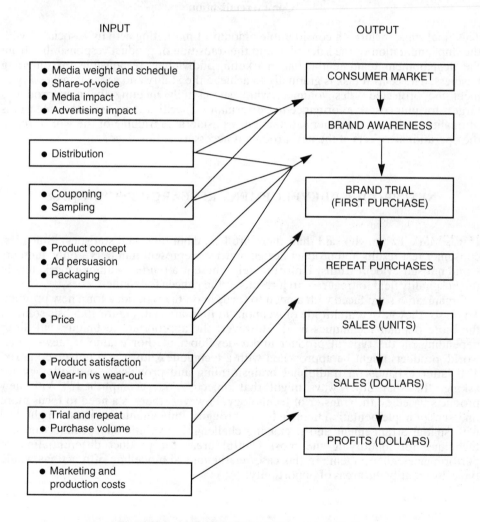

Figure 10.4   Marketing-mix model for a new product

Source: Schulman, R. S., and Clancy, K. J., 'It's better to fly a new product simulator than crash the real thing', *Planning Review*, July/August, pp. 10–17.

analysis, goes beyond the buyer's self-reported behaviour to estimate the true impact of features on brand preferences and purchasing behaviour. By taking a multi-dimensional approach, linking motivating powers of features with brand perceptions, the analysis identifies product strengths, weaknesses and opportunities. Once a company has this information it can build upon the product's strengths, work to minimize its weakness and take advantage of any opportunities.

In sum, the main objective of simulated test marketing research today is not to obtain a volume forecast. The objective is to provide diagnostic insight designed to help improve the likelihood of success.

Commercialization

This final stage includes a considerable amount of marketing activity associated with the implementation of the sales plan and the transition of product responsibility from the development team to the line marketing individuals responsible for on-going business. The central task is gradually to achieve the ability and capacity necessary to meet the projected sales volumes, while successfully meeting the new product's targets for unit cost, conformance to performance specifications, and other measures of quality, including customer satisfaction. Considerable training of the workforce in the operational aspects of the new product is necessary at this stage.

NEW PRODUCT DEVELOPMENT RESEARCH TECHNIQUES

It was Mark Twain who said that 'there are lies, damn lies, and statistics'. Statistics, consumer test results and product design matrices represent numbers – only numbers – and not self-evident truths. Unfortunately, there is a tendency among marketers in the hospitality field to treat research results as the pancea for all their woes.

Organizations are faced with a need to focus in on the right idea for a new product. To do so, they have a multitude of weapons in their arsenal. Figure 10.5 lists some of the more popular techniques used. However, the appropriate technique will differ depending on the type of product under development. For example, 'new-to-the-world' products might be approached with a technique known as a universe matrix. The latter expands on traditional brainstorming and provides a methodology for asking, 'In what other ways might that objective be accomplished?' With new products based on the transfer of technology, however, there is a need to focus more on issues of implementation than on breakthroughs. Implementation issues might deal with spatial arrangement and packaging challenges. Evolutionary products need a technique for identifying the most fruitful areas for product differentiation or performance enhancement. In this case, mathematical modelling of functions would typically identify the areas of opportunity.

Focus groups	A small group of about ten members led by a moderator through an in-depth discussion of issues useful to new product development. The interplay of ideas stimulates group members to reveal information helpful in the new product development process.
Brainstorming sessions	A small, diverse group led by a moderator who can control behaviour without inhibiting the group. There are two major principles of brainstorming: quantity of ideas is preferred over quality, and judgement of ideas is deferred until a later time.
Surveys	Structured questionnaires which can be administered in any of three ways: mail, telephone or personal.
Personal interviews	In-depth, face-to-face interviews on a particular subject. The interview may be semi-structured or unstructured. Benefits include quality of information and the ability to probe for underlying motives, beliefs and attitudes.
Product-use tests	Tests conducted by research personnel, experts and/or customers. The purpose is to get ideas for product improvement, learn modes of use, verify product claims and expose product weaknesses.
Competitive intelligence	There are a variety of legal and ethical methods used to obtain competitive information. These methods include: published material, trade shows and exhibits, financial reports, market surveys and analyses of competitors' products.

Figure 10.5   New product development research techniques

Source: Adapted from Crawford, M. C., *New Products Management*, Irwin, Homewood, IL, 1987.

PRODUCT DEVELOPMENT IN THE HOSPITALITY INDUSTRY

Approaches to product development in the hospitality industry can be categorized into two types: 'traditional' approaches, and the newer more sophisticated inferential and multivariate approaches. In addition, we have begun to see the use of database-related techniques in the development and introduction of hospitality products and services. Each is discussed in turn.

'Traditional' approaches to product development

Traditional approaches to product development in the hospitality industry have been largely descriptive in nature. The industry has tended to concentrate on the gathering and interpretation of descriptive marketing data as they relate to product development. Unfortunately, descriptive data by their very nature are of little analytical worth. For example, knowing that a potential target market has an average household income of

$100,000 does not provide any insight into how the household spends that income and whether they will even entertain the thought of purchasing the proposed product. Descriptive statistical categories, such as age ranges, income ranges and stage in the family life cycle of the segment to be targeted, are not capable of inferring individual or group values; nor are they capable of inferring the reasons behind purchase decisions. Therefore, descriptive research approaches to product development, when used in isolation, are not capable of meeting the main objectives of new product development research outlined in this chapter.

Historically, the approach adopted to product development in the hospitality industry has been product- as opposed to market-oriented. The practice of product segmentation in the hospitality industry is indicative of a preoccupation with the product and not the market in the product development process. An example of a product approach to new product development can be seen in the all-suite segment of the lodging industry, which has been divided into limited-service all-suites, full-service all-suites, and extended-stay all-suites. Within each of these respective sub-segments, lodging firms have attempted to develop distinct branded products in the hope of creating perceived differentiation in the mind of the consumer.

Unfortunately, differentiation may be moot when it occurs within the same product class, such as the all-suite segment. It could be argued that the practice of attempting to create differentiation through the development of a product brand has become somewhat meaningless in the lodging industry, since such differentiation may not relieve customer confusion and create product awareness and loyalty, but rather may only serve to enhance such confusion. This problem has arisen partly because firms pursuing a strategy of differentiation through product branding have not developed a strong market-positioning strategy.

As a result of what is a largely product-oriented approach to development, many lodging chains have experienced limited success in their attempts to market multiple products. Success in developing multiple products under a single umbrella corporation depends on creating, and more importantly maintaining, a clear differentiation in the mind of the consumer. Lodging organizations have often failed to create a strong statement of differentiation for each of their products because each product does not stand for a unique combination or package of goods and services. With only a few exceptions, the advertising and promotion that have been initiated on behalf of new product concepts have failed to communicate clearly or convincingly the basis of the differentiation.

For example, what began as a fairly straightforward idea – a limited-service hotel geared to business travellers, with the main attraction being a home-like two-room suite priced competitively with standard guest rooms – has burgeoned into a multi-tiered segment encompassing a number of hotel classifications and target markets. There are said to be at least thirty-five companies with hotels in the all-suite segment today, including economy, moderate, upscale and luxury properties. It is questionable whether the plethora of market segments for which these products were designed really exists.

Inferential approaches to product development

To be of real value to the management decision process, new product development research must make use of inferential and multivariate techniques and approaches to gauge the potential success of a product in the marketplace. Multivariate research techniques, such as conjoint analysis, multiple discriminant analysis (both discussed in Chapter 11) and multidimensional scaling, are capable of analysing the associations among three or more variables. The multivariate approach to new product development allows the researcher to gain a whole array of potentially more fruitful knowledge than could ever be obtained through traditional descriptive approaches. In addition, the use of inferential statistics allows the researcher to draw conclusions about a population on the basis of evidence from the sample (for example, a test market). Perhaps one of the best examples of the benefits of using sophisticated multivariate statistical research techniques is the development and introduction of the Marriott Corporation's 'Courtyard by Marriott' concept, which is discussed in detail in Chapter 11.

Database models and product development

If a product launch is unsuccessful, it is tremendously costly in money and opportunity cost terms, and it can also do tremendous damage to a company's position and prestige in the marketplace. Through utilizing a database in the launch of new products, hospitality organizations can go some way to avoiding such failures.

A hospitality organization's database is a ready-made research laboratory, test market and target market at the organization's fingertips. Database marketing makes the difference between reactive marketing, where companies think they understand what customers need, and pro-active marketing, based on real customer knowledge.

With today's technology it is relatively simple and inexpensive to develop a relational database capability, linking multiple transaction databases from different locations: for example, mail-order marketing, telemarketing, event marketing, customer periodical mailings, order processing, accounts receivable and customer service. Information on a given customer that resides in any of these discrete databases can be assessed and combined with data from other databases across a company's worldwide network. The system can also be designed to provide tools for identifying groups of customers with common attributes and to predict their buying behaviour.

A database can be used to aid in the gereration of ideas for new products by examining the preferences of current customers. Research can be used to target select groups within a company's database, which can produce a finely tuned understanding of current customers' receptivity to a new product and the attributes of the most likely buyers. Such an understanding can then be extrapolated beyond an organization's customer base. Researching current customer needs helps organizations to identify likely targets and to determine how to test a new product – price, medium and message – before conducting a costly roll-out.

A second way in which databases can be used is in the sales area once products have been introduced. Because database marketers know which share of the market they own, they can reach base-line levels of distribution and sales faster than would otherwise be possible. For example, with the aid of a database a product could be designed that 'warms up' a segment of the database that is not as active as the most responsive segment. In other words, new product launches have the potential of opening new niches within the database if the launch is uniquely suited to the requirements of the targeted audiences. Such an approach uses the database as a strategic tool and respects the database as a dynamic market. Simply targeting top-responding groups with the same offer in the same time frame misses the potential of database and information-based marketing. It is also possible for marketers to find and purchase outside lists with characteristics matching the target prospects in their customer database.

One hospitality organization that has realized the importance of databases in new product development is ITT Sheraton. Since 1986 ITT Sheraton has been building a unique database of frequent travellers – business customers willing to pay $25 annually to belong to its frequent-traveller club (the fact that these travellers self-qualify by paying $25 sets Sheraton apart from most other frequent-traveller progams).

At the heart of the program is a sophisticated member database built upon Sheraton's worldwide reservation system. Every time a customer reserves a hotel room and gives his or her identification number to the reservationist, the transaction is recorded in detail. This information is used to customize monthly promotions to each member based on known hotel usage patterns and preferences.

The 600,000 active-member database also helps ITT Sheraton to develop and roll out service enhancements. For example, it recently rolled out 'Club Cheques', which transform club points into 450 'cheques' easily usable at Sheraton facilities, without any reservations. EXpressPass is another recent enhancement which gives customers what they value the most – time. Participating customers register their credit card number with Sheraton. When they call for a reservation, they do not have to go through the billing information with the reservations operator. When they get to the hotel they just show their identification card and are given their room key. They can check out without signing the bill and their receipts are mailed to them within twenty-four hours. This offer was introduced at thirty-five high-traffic hotels and mailed to 140,000 members. From the database, club travellers were chosen who frequent hotels or who come from feeder cities, and who may therefore have opportunities to go to these hotels.

Database product and service launches are often driven by competitive forces, but they also serve to support other business objectives – such as offsetting declining revenues by identifying new revenue streams. However, database marketing is not just about minimizing risk. It is about maximizing creative potential and opportunity. The real power of the database comes to firms that have a pro-active, strategic attitude towards their customer relationships, and which use their database as a marketing tool.

CONCLUSION

In today's fast-paced, fiercely competitive world of product development, speed and flexibility are essential. Companies are increasingly realizing that the old, sequential approach to developing new products simply will not get the job done. Instead, companies are using a holistic approach. Sports analogies have been widely used to distinguish these two approaches. The more traditional sequential approach is portrayed as a relay race, in which only one player runs at a time and a baton is passed in one direction from one runner to his or her successor. If any one runner falters, or if the hand-off is bungled, the entire effort is delayed. A holistic approach, in contrast, is likened to a game of rugby. Here, the entire team runs down the field at the same time, repeatedly passing the ball back and forth among the players. A holistic approach requires considerable on-going interaction and is at all times a team effort.

For hospitality organizations truly to take advantage of today's technology in their new product development process, they must not only adopt a sequential approach to development, but also enjoy the more sophisticated research techniques in their quest to identify gaps in the market. Chapter 11 shows how one organization, the Marriott Corporation, used several sophisticated research techniques to identify a gap in the market and develop a successful and profitable product for the lodging industry.

BIBLIOGRAPHY

Crawford, M. C., *New Products Management*, Dow-Jones Irwin, Homewood, IL, 1987.

Frand, E. A., *The Art of Product Development*, Dow-Jones Irwin, Homewood, IL, 1989.

Graf, E., and Saguy, I. S. (eds), *Food Product Development: From Concept to Marketplace*, Van Nostrand Reinhold, New York, 1991.

Hall, J. A., *Bringing New Products to Market: The Art and Science of Creating Winners*, American Management Association, New York, 1991.

Kortge, G. D., and Okonkwo, P. A. 'Simultaneous new product development: reducing the new product failure rate', *Industrial Marketing Management*, vol 18, 1989, pp.301–6.

Rosenthal, S. R., *Effective Product Design and Development: How to Cut Lead Time and Increase Customer Satisfaction*, Business One Irwin, Homewood, IL, 1992.

Schulman, R. S., and Clancy, K. J., 'It's better to fly a new product simulator than crash the real thing', *Planning Review*, July/August 1992, pp.10–17.

ELEVEN

The development of Courtyard by Marriott*

INTRODUCTION

The development of Courtyard by Marriott is an excellent example of how useful and insightful multivariate and inferential statistical analysis can be in the development and launch of hospitality products. Since the launch of Courtyard by Marriott, the chain has been a thriving success, and from three test hotels in 1983, the chain currently boasts in excess of 200 units.

The research techniques used allowed Marriott to identify a niche in the mid-level market which was not being filled by any concept at the time. The introduction of the Courtyard concept was the catalyst which led to the restructuring of the entire mid-price level of the lodging industry in North America. For example, at least half a dozen Courtyard by Marriott clone chains have been introduced by competing lodging groups in an attempt to ride on the coat-tails of Courtyard's success. In addition, older competing hotels in the Courtyard by Marriott price range were losing market share, and market forces led them to upgrade their properties or reduce prices to compete. The alternative to upgrading was of course to sell out, which some chains in fact did. Courtyard's impact on the industry was not solely confined to the older chains, since relatively new hotels in the Courtyard price range decided to refurbish early, to reduce rates on competitive business, or to add popular features available at Courtyard by Marriott. Thus the impact of Courtyard by Marriott on the North American lodging industry was significant.

Marriott management set three criteria which had to be met in the design of the Courtyard concept. These criteria were:

• to assure that the new concept offered consumers good value for money;

*This chapter draws extensively on Wind, J., Green, P. E., Shifflet, D., and Scarbrough, M., 'Courtyard by Marriott: designing a hotel facility with consumer-based marketing models', *Interfaces*, vol. 19, no. 1 (January/February), 1989, pp. 25–47.

- to minimize cannibalization of their other hotel offerings;
- to establish a market position that offered management a substantial competitive advantage.

THE MANAGEMENT QUESTIONS

Marriott management essentially had five questions to address in the research design. These were:

- Does sufficient demand exist for a new hotel concept aimed at the low business and pleasure segment to meet growth and financial return objectives?
- What is the best competitive positioning for the new hotels?
- Of the various hotel features and services available, which combination should be offered?
- What should be the pricing strategy for rooms in the new hotels?
- What should be the location strategy for the new hotels?

In essence, Marriott wanted to develop the optimal hotel chain. To answer these questions Marriott adopted a seven-step development process.

THE DEVELOPMENT PROCESS

The steps in the Marriott development processes were not dissimilar to the processes outlined in Chapter 10. They were:

- selection of a product-development team;
- environment and competitor analysis;
- customer analysis;
- idea generation;
- product refinement;
- product positioning;
- monitoring of results.

Selection of the product development team followed two guidelines. First, the team had to be of a relatively small size to maintain functional efficiency, yet it also had to encompass a diverse combination of expertise and experience. Second, the team was formed to include several product champions whose enthusiasm and commitment to the project would guide the process through the difficulties and barriers encountered.

The environment and competitor analysis followed a traditional 'SWOT' (strengths, weaknesses, opportunities, threats) analysis of the competition in all lodging segments including budget, mid-price and luxury. The analysis revealed considerable unmet demand in both the pleasure and business markets for a cheaper hotel product priced $2 to $3 below the typical Holiday Inn.

The customer analysis was extensive and consisted of focus group interviews and a segmentation study which took over a year and $300,000 to conduct. One of the major findings of the consumer analysis was the categorization of customers into two main types: 'security seekers' and 'functional roomers'. The former wanted secure locks on doors, well-lit interior corridors and fire safety features, while the latter wanted rooms that could facilitate both business and social activities.

The information from the above steps led to the idea generation phase, which consisted of brainstorming dozens of possible products, only a handful of which were retained for further investigation and research.

The product refinement phase was extensive, and the remainder of this chapter discusses in depth the research approach and technique used to refine the final product. Use was made of sophisticated preference and trade-off models using conjoint and cluster analysis as the primary research tools. The goal was to obtain the optimum mix of features and attributes in the new product as seen from a consumer's point of view. Conducted among 601 consumers selected from the four metropolitan areas of Atlanta, Dallas, San Francisco and Chicago, the study asked respondents to choose from 150 attributes, each with a price attached. From the product refinement phase Marriott generated a basic conceptual framework for the product which met the following criteria:

- It would be tightly focused for the transient mid-priced market segment.
- It would be relatively small (150 rooms or fewer) to project a residential image.
- It would serve a limited menu, and it would offer less than competitors in the way of public space and amenities.
- It would be a standardized product managed in clusters (i.e. five to eight hotels in one area).
- The Marriott name would be attached for recognition and a 'halo effect'.

In 1982 the first prototype was constructed with movable walls. Three possible room configurations were shown to hundreds of consumers to get their input. One piece of information generated from consumer viewing concerned the length of the room and led Marriott to make adjustments which resulted in an estimated $80,000 saving per hotel property constructed.

Marriott then developed a product positioning statement for the hotel concept, which stated that the Courtyard product, as it was now being called, was to serve business travellers who wanted moderately priced hotels of consistent high quality, and pleasure travellers who wanted an affordable room that was a safe base of operations.

The test market for the Courtyard by Marriott product was Atlanta, Georgia, and the first Courtyard opening in 1983. The test market led to some final 'tweaking' of the product. For example, the size of the rooms was reduced and closet doors were placed on closet areas, a feature not usually found in mid-price hotels. The occupancy level for the first six months of operation was in the ninetieth percentile range with little cannibalization of existing Marriott brands.

Finally, the results-monitoring stage was as detailed and thorough as prior stages. Marriott, to this day, consistently keeps a pulse of the market's reaction to even the smallest of changes in the Courtyard concept.

The remainder of this chapter focuses on exactly how Marriott conducted the product refinement stage. The research techniques used will be discussed, followed by an outline of the research process, the research analysis and, finally, the research results for the product refinement stage.

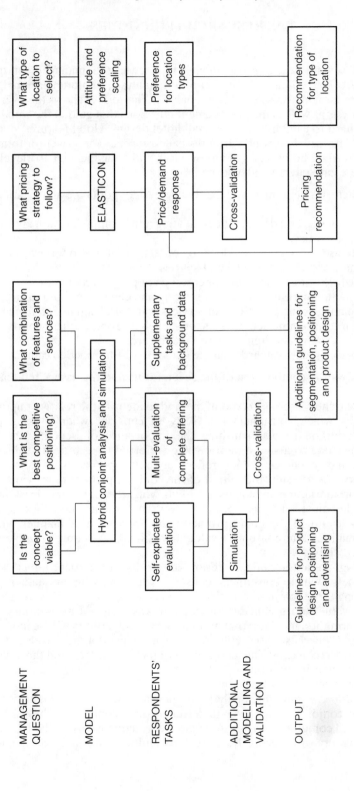

Figure 11.1 Overall study design

Source: Wind, J., Green, P. E., Shifflet, D., and Scarbrough, M., 'Courtyard by Marriott: designing a hotel facility with consumer-based marketing models', *Interfaces*, vol. 19, no. 1 (January/February), 1989, pp. 25–47.

THE RESEARCH TECHNIQUES

Marriott used several research techniques to answer the management questions described above, including a hybrid conjoint analysis, multidimensional scaling, multiple discriminant analysis and cluster analysis. Figure 11.1 shows the overall study design and analysis as well as the management questions that guided the study.

Marriott wanted to establish the 'optimal' hotel design. Hotel features investigated were grouped into seven sets of attributes called facets. There were a total of fifty factors that described hotel features and services and an associated 167 levels. These fifty factors were categorized under seven facets:

- External factors – building shape, landscape design, pool type and location, hotel size.
- Rooms – room size and décor, type of heating and cooling, location and type of bathroom, amenities.
- Food-related services – type and location of restaurant, room service, vending services and stores, in-room kitchen facilities.
- Lounge facilities – location, atmosphere, type of people (clientele).
- Services – including reservations, registration and check-out, limo to airport, bellman, massage centre, secretarial services, car rental and maintenance.
- Facilities for leisure time activities – sauna, exercise room, squash courts, tennis courts, games room, children's playroom and yard.
- Security factors security guards, smoke detectors, 24-hour video camera.

Figure 11.2 shows the composition of the seven facets and the associated feature and service levels.

Marriott researchers used the conjoint method to identify the relative importance of various benefits which consumers are likely to consider when making purchase decisions. In addition to distinguishing the importance of benefits, the conjoint procedure allows one to assign a metric value (referred to as a utility value or part-worth) to alternative choices which reflect possible options available under each benefit category. As a result, the output of the conjoint procedure provides valuable information for marketing managers by identifying the most and least important benefits and the most and least preferred option for each benefit desired. This information is useful in designing products and services in a manner which best captures the qualities that consumers value most highly. A simple example will help clarify this discussion.

In purchasing an automobile, exterior colour has been determined to be an important benefit which consumers consider when making an actual purchase decision. Among three colour alternatives provided as options, white was assigned the highest utility value and green the lowest; red was assigned an intermediate-level value. This information indicates that automobile manufacturers will be more likely to increase customer purchase satisfaction (and sell more cars) if they produce white cars rather than red or green cars. The least satisfaction to customers (and the lowest levels of sales) would occur in the situation where the production of green automobiles was predominant over other colour options.

Marriott's use of conjoint analysis is perhaps the most sophisticated and comprehensive conjoint design ever undertaken on a commercial basis. The study included a hybrid conjoint analysis task, a price elasticity task using the ELASTICON model and a variety of other analyses, such as multidimensional scaling and cluster

EXTERNAL FACTORS
Building shape
  L-shaped w/landscape
  Outdoor courtyard
Landscaping
  Minimal
  Moderate
  Elaborate
Pool type
  No pool
  Rectangular shape
  Free form shape
  Indoor/outdoor
Pool location
  In courtyard
  Not in courtyard
Corridor/view
  Outside access/restricted
    view
  Enclosed access/
    unrestricted view/
    balcony or window
Hotel size
  Small (125 rooms
    2 storeys)
  Large (600 rooms, 12
    storeys)

ROOMS
Entertainment
  Colour TV
  Colour TV w/movies
    @ $5
  Colour TV w/30 channel
    cable
  Colour TV w/HBO,
    movies, etc.
  Colour TV w/free movies
Entertainment rental
  None
  Rental cassettes/in-
    room Atari
  Rental cassettes/stereo
    cassette playing in
    room
  Rental movies/in-room
    BetaMax
Size
  Small (standard)
  Slightly larger (1 foot)
  Much larger (2½ feet)
  Small suite (2 rooms)
  Large suite (2 rooms)
Quality of decor (in
  standard room)
  Budget motel décor
  Old Holiday Inn décor
  New Holiday Inn décor
  New Hilton décor
  New Hyatt décor
Heating and cooling
  Wall unit/full control
  Wall unit/sound proof/
    full control
  Central H or C (seasonal)
  Central H or C/full
    control
Size of bath
  Standard bath
  Slightly larger/sink
    separate
  Much larger bath w/
    larger tub
  Very large/tub for 2

Sink location
  In bath only
  In separate area
  In bath and separate
Bathroom features
  None
  Shower massage
  Whirlpool (jacuzzi)
  Steam bath
Amenities
  Small bar soap
  Large soap/shampoo/shoe
    shine
  Large soap/bath gel/
    shower cap/sewing kit
  Above items + toothpaste,
    deodorant, mouthwash

FOOD
Restaurant in hotel
  None (coffee shop next
    door)
  Restaurant/lounge combo,
    limited menu
  Coffee shop, full menu
  Full service restaurant,
    full menu
  Coffee shop/full menu
    and good restaurant
Restaurant nearby
  None
  Coffee shop
  Fast food
  Fast food or coffee shop
    and moderate restaurant
  Fast food or coffee shop
    and good restaurant
Free continental
  None
  Continental included in
    room rate
Room service
  None
  Phone in order/guest to
    pick up
  Room service, limited
    menu
  Room service, full menu
Store
  No food in store
  Snack items
  Snacks, refrigerated items,
    wine, beer, liquor
  Above items and gourmet
    food items
Vending service
  None
  Soft drink machine only
  Soft drink and snack
    machines
  Soft drink, snack and
    sandwich machines
  Above and microwave
    available
In-room kitchen facilities
  None
  Coffee maker only
  Coffee maker and
    refrigerator
  Cooking facilities in room

LOUNGE
Atmosphere
  Quiet bar/lounge
  Lively, popular bar/lounge

Type of people
  Hotel guests and
    friends only
  Open to public – general
    appeal
Lounge nearby
  None
  Lounge/bar nearby
  Lounge/bar w/
    entertainment nearby

SERVICES
Reservations
  Call hotel directly
  800 reservation number
Check-in
  Standard
  Pre-credit clearance
  Machine in lobby
Check-out
  At front desk
  Bill under door/leave key
  Key to front desk/bill
    by mail
  Machine in lobby
Limo to airport
  None
  Yes
Bellman
  None
  Yes
Message service
  Note at front desk
  Light on phone
  Light on phone and
    message under door
  Recorded message
Cleanliness/upkeep/
  management skill
  Budget motel level
  Holiday Inn level
  Non-convention Hyatt
    level
  Convention Hyatt level
  Fine hotel level
Laundry/valet
  None
  Client drop-off and
    pick-up
  Self-service
  Valet pick-up and
    drop-off
Special services (concierge)
  None
  Information on restaurants,
    theatres, etc.
  Arrangements and
    reservations
  Travel problem resolution
Secretarial services
  None
  Xerox machine
  Xerox machine and typist
Car maintenance
  None
  Take car to service
  Cars on premises /bill to
    room

Car rental/airline
  reservations
  None
  Car rental facility
  Airline reservations
  Car rental and airline
    reservations

LEISURE
Sauna
  None
  Yes
Whirlpool/jacuzzi
  None
  Outdoor
  Indoor
Exercise room
  None
  Basic facility w/weights
  Facility w/Nautilus
    equipment
Racquet ball courts
  None
  Yes
Tennis courts
  None
  Yes
Game room/entertainment
  None
  Electric games/pinball
  Electric games/pinball/
    ping-pong
  Above and movie theatre,
    bowling
Children's playroom/
  playground
  None
  Playground only
  Playroom only
  Playground and playroom
Pool extras
  None
  Pool w/slides
  Pool w/slides and
    equipment
  Pool w/slides, waterfall,
    equipment

SECURITY
Security guard
  None
  11 a.m. to 7 p.m.
  7 p.m. to 7 a.m.
  24 hours
Smoke detectors
  None
  In rooms and throughout
    hotel
Sprinkler system
  None
  Lobby and hallways only
  Lobby/hallways/rooms
24-hour video camera
  None
  Parking/hallways/public
    areas
Alarm button
  None
  Button in room, rings
    desk.

Figure 11.2 Fifty factors that describe hotel features and services, and the associated 167 levels categorized under seven facets

Source: Wind, J., Green, P. E., Shifflet, D. and Scarbrough, M., 'Courtyard by Marriott: designing a hotel facility with consumer-based marketing models', *Interfaces*, vol. 19, no. 1 (January/February), 1989, pp. 25–47.

analysis, related to consumers' demographic and psychological characteristics, attitudes and usage of hotels.

Hybrid conjoint models adopt a procedure which entails the prior consideration of a type of self-explicated utility task, where respondents evaluate the levels of each attribute (one attribute at a time) on some kind of desirability scale. This is followed by an evaluation of the attributes themselves on an importance scale, and the collection of data on each respondent's evaluation of a limited set (usually eight or nine) of complete (all-attribute) stimulus profiles. These stimulus profiles are, in turn, drawn from a much larger master design (usually ranging between 64 and 256 profiles) that permits statistical estimation of all main effects and selected two-way interactions. Moreover, profiles are 'balanced' (to prevent bias) within respondents by means of various blocking designs. The respondent evaluates each complete stimulus profile on a likelihood of purchase or intentions-to-buy scale.

The results of the study provided specific guidelines for selecting target market segments, positioning the hotel within the market, and designing an improved facility in terms of physical layout and services.

THE RESEARCH APPROACH

To answer the five management questions, four tasks had to be completed.

Task 1a: the concept

The first task was to address the concept issue or combination of attributes. The goal was to produce individual utility functions using hybrid conjoint analysis, which could then be input into a computer simulation that allowed management to assess any desired combination of attributes in terms of the potential market share and source of business (i.e. cannibalization or from competitors). It would then be possible to develop the optimal attribute combinations for each market segment targeted by the proposed concept.

A questionnaire was administered to respondents to find out which predetermined characteristics they prefer in hotels. Each respondent was given seven cards, one at a time. Each card dealt with one of the seven facets (external factors, rooms, food, lounge, services, leisure and security). Figure 11.3 shows the rooms facet. Respondents were asked to think about their usual hotel stay (for business purposes or pleasure), and to mark with a cross the triangle in each row that best described the hotel they currently used. Next, the respondents supplied one of three possible responses for each amenity–price combination:

- The combination is completely unacceptable.
- The combination is completely preferred.
- The combination is acceptable.

Respondents were also asked to rank the various factors within the facet in terms of their relative importance. The process was repeated for all seven facets. Because of the large number of attributes and attribute levels (over 160 levels) pictures were used, where appropriate, to describe the various attribute levels.

ROOMS

'X' the TRIANGLE (△) in the block that comes closest to describing your current hotel (ONLY 'X' ONE)
'X' the CIRCLE (O) in the block(s) that you find completely unacceptable (YOU MAY 'X' ONE OR MORE THAN ONE)
'X' the SQUARE (□) in the block that represents what you want and are willing to pay for (ONLY 'X' ONE)

Enter price of wanted block

FEATURES — ALTERNATIVE DESCRIPTIONS

Feature	Alt 1	Alt 2	Alt 3	Alt 4	Alt 5
Entertainment	Colour TV (.00) △O□	Colour TV with movies which are 9 months ahead of HBO. $5 each. (.00) △O□	Colour TV with 30 channel cable (.25) △O□	Colour TV with HBO movie channel, sports news channel (.40) △O□	Colour TV with free in-room movies (choice of 3) (2.50) △O□
Entertainment/ rental	None (.00) △O□	Rental cassettes available for use with in-room Atari or intelevision (.40)+ △O□	Rental cassettes available. In-room stereo cassette player (1.35)+ △O□	Rental movies, in-room video cassette player (BetaMax) (1.35)+ △O□	
Size and furniture	Small–typical size motel/hotel room △O□	Somewhat larger – 1 foot longer △O□	Much larger – $2\frac{1}{2}$ feet longer △O□	Small suite – 2 rooms △O□	Large suite – 2 rooms △O□
Quality of décor (in standard room)	Similar to Days Inn and other budget motels △O□	Similar to older Holiday Inn, Ramada, Rodeway △O□	Similar to newer and better Holiday Inns △O□	Similar to newer and better Hilton and Marriott △O□	Similar to Hyatt Regency and Westin Plaza hotels △O□
Heat/cooling	Through-wall unit. Full control of heating and cooling year round △O□	Through-wall unit (soundproofed). Full control of heating and cooling year round △O□	Either central heating or cooling (not both), depending on season △O□	Full control of central heating and cooling year round △O□	
Bath size	Standard bathroom and tub/shower as in most hotels. Sink in bathroom only △O□	Somewhat larger bath and stand-ard tub/shower. Sink in separate area outside bathroom △O□	Much larger bathroom with large tub/shower △O□	Large bathroom w/sunken tub for 2 △O□	
Sink location	Sink in bathroom only △O□	Sink in separate area outside bathroom △O□	Sink in bathroom and a sink outside bathroom △O□		
Bathroom features	None △O□	Shower massage △O□	Whirlpool (jacuzzi) △O□	Steam bath △O□	
Amenities	Small bar of soap △O□	Large soap, shampoo packet, shoe-shine mitt △O□	Large soap, bath gel, shower cap, sewing kit, shampoo, special soap △O□	Large soap, bath gel, shower cap, sewing kit, special soap △O□	Large soap, bath gel, shower cap, sewing kit, special soap, toothpaste etc. △O□
Importance ranking					TOTAL

Figure 11.3 Example of a stimulus card used by Marriott researchers

Source: Wind, J., Green, P. E., Shifflett, D. and Scarbrough, M., 'Courtyard by Marriott: designing a hotel facility with consumer-based marketing models', *Interfaces*, vol. 19, no. 1 (January/February), 1989, pp. 25–47.

Once the respondents had evaluated all seven facets, they were asked to add the total incremental costs of the features and services they selected. If the total of the charges plus the base room price were higher than they were willing to pay on a regular business (or pleasure), trip, they were asked to go back and select the enhancements they were willing to forego in order to arrive at an acceptable total room price.

Task 1b: the product offering

This involved obtaining a multifaceted evaluation of 'complete' hotel offerings. Respondents were shown five cards, one at a time, each containing a full-profile description of a 'complete' hotel offering. Figure 11.4 shows an example of a full description profile developed using a fractional factorial design. Each set of five cards was drawn from a possible fifty cards and was balanced within subject. Factorial designs ensured that respondents would receive various combinations of a total of fifty profiles. The researchers used what is termed a 'fractional orthogonal main effects plan', which helped management determine the qualities that respondents preferred in a hotel, given the trade-offs they have to make for comfort versus price.

Task 2: the ELASTICON model

The second task addressed the pricing question and aimed to determine respondent's price elasticity among various hotel concepts (various combinations of attributes). The ELASTICON model was used to evaluate hotels likely to compete with the proposed concepts. The hotel concepts were first described in terms of price, external factors, rooms, food and beverage services, entertainment, recreation and other services, and security. Each respondent received five cards. Each card listed four existing hotels and two new hotel concepts, each at a specific price. Respondents were asked to allocate 100 points among the hotel–price combinations based on how likely they would be to stay at each hotel at the given price.

Task 3: the location

The third task addressed the location question. Researchers asked respondents to allocate 100 points among a set of locations based on their importance in selecting a hotel. The locations were defined in terms of closeness to business, shopping, sightseeing, night life, theatre, airport, major highways, and so forth.

Task 4: additional information

The final task involved the use of additional research techniques and supplied management with additional information such as:

- the various segments' perception and preference for various hotel features and services;
- the key discriminating characteristics of the various segments.

ROOM PRICE PER NIGHT IS **$45.85**

BUILDING SIZE, BAR/LOUNGE
Large (600 rooms) 12-storey hotel with:
• Quiet bar/lounge
• Enclosed central corridors and elevators

LANDSCAPING/COURT
Building forms a spacious outdoor courtyard
• View from rooms of moderately landscaped courtyard with:
– many trees and shrubs
– the swimming pool plus a fountain
– terraced areas for sunning, sitting, eating

FOOD
Small, moderately priced lounge and restaurant for hotel guests/friends
• Limited breakfast with juices, fruit, Danish, cereal, bacon and eggs
• Lunch – soup and sandwiches only
• Evening meal – salad, soup, sandwiches, six hot entrées including steak

HOTEL/MOTEL ROOM QUALITY
Quality of room furnishings, carpet, etc. is similar to:
• Hyatt Regencies
• Westin 'Plaza' Hotels

ROOM SIZE AND FUNCTION
Room 1 foot longer than typical hotel/motel room
• Space for comfortable sofa-bed and two chairs
• Large desk
• Coffee table
• Coffee maker and small refrigerator

SERVICE STANDARDS
Full service including:
• Rapid check-in/check-out systems
• Reliable message service
• Valet (laundry pick-up/deliver)
• Bellman
• Someone (concierge) arranges reservations and tickets, generally at no cost
• Cleanliness, upkeep, management similar to:
– Hyatts
– Marriotts

LEISURE
• Combination indoor–outdoor pool
• Enclosed whirlpool (jacuzzi)
• Well-equipped playroom/playground for kids

SECURITY
• Night guard on duty 7 p.m. to 7 a.m.
• Fire/water sprinklers throughout hotel

'X' the ONE box below which best describes how likely you are to stay in this hotel/motel at this price:

Would stay there almost all the time	Would stay there on a regular basis	Would stay there now and then	Would rarely stay there	Would not stay there

Figure 11.4   One of the 50 full-profile descriptions of a hotel offering developed by a fractional factorial design of the seven facets each at the five levels

Source: Wind, J., Green, P. E., Shifflet, D. and Scarbrough, M., 'Courtyard by Marriott: designing a hotel facility with consumer-based marketing models', *Interfaces*, vol. 19, no. 1 (January/February), 1989, pp. 25–47.

Researchers also asked respondents for demographic information and conducted a secondary conjoint on seven additional design factors including room size, quality of décor, type of heating and cooling unit, bathroom features, and the amenities and type of entertainment available in the room. In addition, to help Marriott management select the hotel name, respondents were asked to indicate how much they liked each of eleven names, and following this to rank the names that best fit the hotel concept. Courtyard by Marriott was one of the eleven names.

THE RESEARCH ANALYSIS

Figure 11.5 shows the step-by-step analysis adopted by the Marriott researchers.

Technique: Categorical conjoint analysis
Purpose:　 Run on each of the seven facets to determine consumer utility functions

↓

Technique: Compute respondent's self-explicated utility
Purpose:　 To obtain a set of predictor variables

↓

Technique: Calculate hybrid conjoint model parameters
Purpose:　 To determine residuals for each cluster of respondents

↓

Technique: Regress residuals on price
Purpose:　 To determine whether including a specific price accounted for significant variance in the residuals

↓

Technique: Computer choice simulation
Purpose:　 To determine market attractiveness of various bundles of features and services

↓

Technique: Secondary conjoint analysis
Purpose:　 Run on additional features to provide guidance in selecting hotel features

↓

Technique: Multi-dimensional scaling
Purpose:　 Run on the 16 secondary features to provide further guidance in selecting hotel features

↓

Technique: ELASTICON model
Purpose:　 To determine price elasticity

↓

Technique: Multiple discriminant analysis
Purpose:　 To determine segment profiles

↓

Technique: Cross-tabulations and preference mapping
Purpose:　 To help name, position and locate the proposed concept

Figure 11.5　 Research analysis process for Courtyard by Marriott

THE RESEARCH RESULTS

The study showed that some business and pleasure travellers were dissatisfied with current hotel offerings. Some hotels cost too much and offered features not valued by the traveller, while others that cost less offered too few of the desirable features. Both types of hotel also tended to lack the personalization of features that travellers sought. Thus, the Marriott researchers developed a new hotel concept tuned to travellers' needs at an acceptable price.

The study revealed that consumers wanted 'a special little hotel at a very comfortable price'. The hotel most preferred by pleasure and non-business travellers was 'an informal, quiet, relaxing hotel or motel with charm and personality'. The study provided extremely detailed guidelines for the selection of close to 200 features and services. Table 11.1 is an example of the output that the study provided for various external features or facilities. It suggests how powerful the study was in directing the design of the hotel. The attributes selected for the hotel are those that are numbered in bold type – the ones with the highest utility for the target segments.

Similar output and patterns of implementation were found for the other six sets of attributes. The simulation also provided management with a clear idea of the following:

- The likely share (of nights) that any hotel concept (presented as a specific combination of features and services) would get by any target segment(s).
- The source of business – the hotels from which the new hotel would be most likely to draw business, including the likelihood of cannibalization of the Marriott.

Table 11.1   Part worths for external factors/facilities attribute levels

Attribute	Level	Description	Part worth
Hotel size	**1**	Small (125 rooms) 2-storey hotel (0.00)	1.06
	2	12-storey (600 rooms) with large lobby, meeting rooms, etc. (7.15)	0.00
Corridor/view	1	Outside stairs with walkways to all rooms. Restricted view. People walking outside window. (0.00)	0.00
	2	Enclosed central corridors and stairs. Unrestricted view. Rooms have balcony or large window. (0.65)	1.85
Pool location	1	Not in courtyard (0.00)	0.00
	2	In courtyard (0.00)	1.37
Pool type	1	No pool (0.00)	0.61
	2	Rectangular pool (0.45)	1.25
	3	Freeform pool (0.50)	0.29
	4	Indoor/outdoor pool (0.85)	0.00
Landscaping	1	Minimal landscaping (0.00)	0.81
	2	Moderate landscaping (0.50)	0.97
	3	Elaborate landscaping (0.50)	0.00
Building shape	1	L-shape building with modest landscaping (0.00)	0.00
	2	Building forms an outdoor landscaped courtyard for sitting, eating, sunning, etc. (0.45)	0.37

*Figure in parentheses after each description = price premium.

Source: Wind, J., Green, P. E., Shifflet, D., and Scarbrough, M. (1989), 'Courtyard by Marriott: designing a hotel facility with consumer-based marketing models', *Interfaces*, vol. 19, no. 1 (January/February), 1989, pp. 25–47.

- The characteristics of the specific segment attracted to the specific configuration of attributes and services.

The results of the ELASTICON tasks and analysis included the following:

- The expected share for each of the concepts tested by each price versus their current competition.
- The likely source of business for the concept.
- The self-elasticity and cross-elasticity of demand for the concept. This most critical information for each segment was presented in a table, and the price–demand relationship for each segment was also presented graphically.

CONCLUSION

The resulting hotel followed almost to the letter the recommendations of the study. Every one of the features and services offered were among those valued highest by the consumer. The important differences identified for the Courtyard by Marriott product led Marriott to create an operating division separate from Marriott hotels.

In addition, the study showed:

- Products and services can, and should, be developed using targeted consumer perception, preference and attitudinal inputs.
- Complex and large products, such as hotels (with close to 200 attribute levels), can be studied effectively using creative conjoint designs.
- Categorical hybrid conjoint analysis models can be used in commercial applications.

Marriott's experience shows the tremendous benefits that can be reaped from the use of sophisticated research techniques in the product development process in the hospitality industry. It is unrealistic, however, to expect the average hospitality organization to have either the financial resources or the human expertise to engage in such sophisticated, time-consuming and expensive research prior to new product introduction. More often than not, hospitality organizations will still cling to the 'trial and error' approach. Chapter 12 shows how even the smallest of foodservice organizations can conduct more effective and efficient product development through a more structured method.

BIBLIOGRAPHY

Feltenstein, T., 'New product development in food service: a structured approach', *Cornell Hotel and Restaurant Quarterly*, November 1986, pp. 63–71.
Wind, J., Green, P. E., Shifflet, D., and Scarbrough, M., 'Courtyard by Marriott: designing a hotel facility with consumer-based marketing models', *Interfaces*, vol. 19, no. 1 (January/February), 1989, pp. 25–47.

TWELVE

Product development in the foodservice industry*

INTRODUCTION

Like the lodging industry, in an attempt to compete in what is becoming an increasingly cut-throat competitive environment, many foodservice companies are turning to the new product, development bandwagon in an attempt to establish and sustain a strategic competitive advantage. New product introductions have become a way of life in the foodservice industry as a means of both maintaining and expanding market share. The past decade has seen an abundance of new products launched in the foodservice area.

For example, the standard McDonald's menu has thirty-three items, not counting various size permutations; that is 25 per cent more than in 1980. Its size is still growing. Recent introductions include McDonald's McPizza, McLean Burger and Burritos. McDonald's openly admits that the key element in its campaign to lure homebodies into its restaurants is new products. KFC (Kentucky Fried Chicken), in its quest to lure convenience-minded lunch and snack patrons, is focusing a lot of attention on a new line of sandwiches such as the recently rolled out Lite 'n Crispy chicken, a skinless fried chicken product. KFC is just one of many operators attacking with new products on all fronts. Other recent introductions include Chicken Littles and the Colonel Chicken Sandwich.

The future will see no decline in the rate of new product introductions. In mid-1992, for example, McDonald's announced that it is test marketing the broadest range of new menu items in its history, including breakfast burritos, chicken fajitas, Italian dinner entrées and several turkey products. However, the launch of new products is not solely limited to menu items. McDonald's is also test marketing a new Golden Arches Café concept and a McDonald's Express concept, which is a

---

*The structure of this chapter is founded on Feltenstein, T., 'New product development in food service: a structured approach', *Cornell Hotel and Restaurant Quarterly*, November 1986, pp. 63–71.

prefabricated building with scaled-down drive-thru-only operations.

But as in the lodging industry, the introduction of new products in the foodservice industry is expensive. In 1985 Burger King spent nearly $50 million to announce its Croissan'wich, and the new Whopper and Church's spent $5 million introducing catfish to selected regional markets. Wendy's spent $14 million to announce its breakfast menu, which was a failure and threw the entire organization into a financial and operational tailspin in the mid-1980s. TGI Friday's toyed with the introduction of several $2 million-a-unit 'Dalts', which was a stylish concept with mahogany booths, marble bars, imported tile floors, over 125 menu items and a vast variety of beer from around the world. The concept was not well planned or thought out, and despite volumes exceeding $2 million, profits were scarce and the concept ultimately underwent considerable modification. As of September 1992 there were eleven units with sales in excess of $26 million, with a mix of 85 per cent food and 15 per cent liquor and an average bill of $7.50.

The purpose of this chapter is to outline a method for developing and introducing new products in the foodservice industry, which, if adopted, goes some way to ensuring that millions of pounds and dollars are not spent on new products without the necessary research and planning.

NEW PRODUCT DEVELOPMENT IN FOODSERVICE

One approach to product development in the foodservice industry is the structured approach. This helps to determine whether new products result in some form of synergy with a foodservice organization's existing product mix, or whether they result in cannibalization or the ineffective and inefficient use of scarce resources. A six-step procedure to new product development in the foodservice industry can be suggested which is similar to the stages outlined in Chapter 10. These six steps are shown in Figure 12.1.

Assemble a new product task force

The composition of the new product task force is perhaps one of the most important elements of the new product development process. Team members should be harnessed from as diverse backgrounds as possible to ensure that suggestions and product leads are not overly narrow in their focus. While chefs and cooks may be amply qualified to suggest new menu items, they are not equally qualified to determine the new product's market acceptance (a marketing function), the cost of the new product (an accounting function), or the implications for the design of kitchens (an operational function). It thus makes logical sense to involve individuals from each functional area of the organization in the development of new products from the earliest stage to the final stage. A co-ordinator should be appointed to the task force. The role of the co-ordinator is to guide the members of the task force and facilitate progress so that they are as productive as possible. The co-ordinator's role is akin to the role of a moderator in a focus group setting. It is not the role of the co-ordinators to impose his or her will on the group.

1. Assemble a new product task force

2. Set new product priorities
   A. Review corporate goals
   B. Audit current test items
   C. Determine candidates for deletion or redevelopment
   D. Examine new product roles
   E. Conduct SWOT analysis

3. Generate new product ideas

4. Screen and select ideas
   A. Develop screening methodology
   B. Qualitative analysis
   C. Quantitative analysis
   D. Select ideas to be developed

5. Develop products
   A. Recipe formulation
   B. Operational specification
   C. Unit operational testing
   D. Preliminary market testing
   E. Market testing

6. Plan marketing and roll-out campaigns

Figure 12.1 Procedures for new product development in food service

Source: Feltenstein, T., 'New product development in food service: a structured approach',
Cornell Hotel and Restaurant Quarterly, November 1986, pp. 63–71.

Set new product priorities

There are five steps in the setting of new product priorities. First, a review of corporate goals should be conducted to ensure that the new product is not counterproductive to the overall mission of the organization: in other words, there has to be some degree of synergy between the new product and existing products. If, for example, it is the overall mission of the corporation to increase the frequency of customer visits to a restaurant, then it would make little sense to allocate all resources to a new product which would bring in new customers and not increase the frequency of existing ones. The 'fit' of the new product with existing corporate philosophies and goals should be examined in depth.

Many foodservice organizations have introduced seemingly worthy products only to find that they did not have any level of synergy with the existing menu mix. It has been argued that McDonald's introduction of the McPizza was one such error. The McPizza was first introduced in 1984 and was really a calzone – an envelope of dough, stuffed with tomato, cheese and sausage, delivered frozen to restaurants and then fried. Unfortunately, the product had two problems. The filling kept falling out in the delivery trucks and people did not think it looked like a pizza. Appearance problems also doomed the second McPizza, introduced in 1986. It could be argued that many of the problems encountered with the McPizza are the result of McDonald's attempting to enter a market (the pizza market) in which it has no expertise and which is out of the realms of its traditional 'meat and potato' menu mix.

The second and third steps in the setting of new product priorities is the audit of current test items to determine which ones should be maintained and which ones should be put on the back-burner while valuable resources are re-allocated to more deserving new product candidates. Some foodservice companies prefer to allocate what few new product development resources they have to two or three major products, while others, like Jack in the Box, prefer to have up to 25 new products undergoing various stages of development at any given time. Objective criteria should always be established for determining whether a new product is maintained or dropped. Measures used often include sales levels, profit margins, contribution margins, market saturation level, and economies of scale achieved.

The fourth step in setting new product priorities is the determination of new product roles. It is suggested that there are basically three types of new product in foodservice: entrées, side-dishes and new categories products (Feltenstein, 1986). Each type plays a different role on the menu.

A new entrée expands, extends or enhances the menu, without departing from the operation's basic concept. It maintains a menu's competitiveness, especially when it matches a competitor's product offering. An example of this would be McDonald's introduction of its McDLT to defend itself against Burger King's Whopper. Any new entrée should ideally achieve three goals:

- bring in additional customers;
- increase the average bill by trading up customers;
- increase the frequency of customer visitors by providing variety on the menu.

In addition, any new product should avoid cannibalization. For example, it would not have benefited McDonald's in the long run if the introduction of the McDLT had taken away from sales of Big Macs and Quarter Pounders. In this case, the McDLT was sufficiently different from any existing product not to cannibalize them, yet it still did not depart from McDonald's basic 'meat and potato' menu concept. The balance between introducing new products that do not depart from existing menu concepts and ensuring that cannibalization does not occur is a delicate one. For example, KFC initially tried to attack the sandwich market by rolling out bite-sized, fried chicken sandwiches called Chicken Littles, but these mini-sandwiches cannibalized bill averages, and thus roll-out was delayed and franchise acceptance was hard to achieve.

A side-dish should usually extend or enhance the current menu. The purpose of a new side-dish is to increase the average bill by adding to existing entrées or to differentiate an operation from direct competitors. For example, McDonaldland cookies, Popeye's corn on the cob, and KFC's baked beans are examples of side-dishes that differentiate one fast-food restaurant from another.

Finally, new category products are products outside the scope of the current menu, but they address important consumer needs that the restaurant has not met. The purpose of introducing a new category product is to broaden the customer base and increase the visiting frequency of existing customers. Examples include Chicken McNuggets and McPizza.

The final step in the second phase of procedures for new product development is SWOT analysis. SWOT analysis is the systematic identification of the strengths, weaknesses, opportunities and threats faced by an organization, and the strategy that reflects the best match between them. It is based on the logic that an effective strategy maximizes a business's strengths and opportunities, but at the same time minimizes its weaknesses and threats. SWOT analysis can be used systematically to compare key external opportunities and threats to internal strengths and weaknesses in a structured approach. In this manner, four distinct patterns will emerge in the match between an organization's internal and external situations. These four patterns are represented by the four cells in Figure 12.2.

Cell 1 is the most favourable situation, with the organization facing several environmental opportunities and having numerous strengths that encourage pursuit of such opportunities. This condition suggests the development of new products whose main objective is expansion. Cell 4 is the least favourable situation, with the organization facing major environmental threats from a position of relative weakness. The foodservice organization should clearly rethink its involvement with all new products being developed, since they are relatively weak and are subject to major environmental threats. Cell 2 represents an organization with key strengths facing a unfavourable environment. In this situation, strategies should use current strengths to build long-term opportunities in other products. The strategy to pursue in this cell might be menu diversification through extension and/or enhancement. Finally, Cell 3 represents an organization which faces impressive market opportunity but is constrained by several internal weaknesses. Foodservice firms which find themselves in this cell should attempt to eliminate internal weaknesses in order to pursue market opportunity more effectively. This condition calls for strategies that reduce or redirect

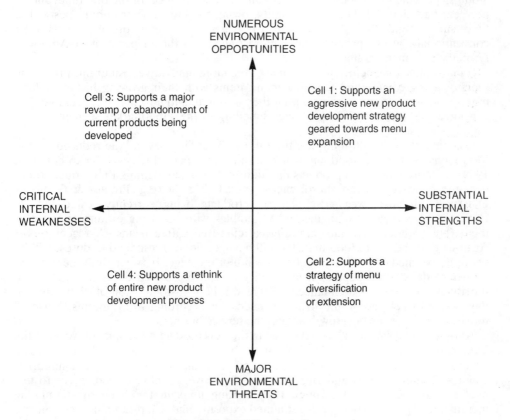

Figure 12.2 SWOT analysis diagram

resources in the existing development process so that new products can be developed.

SWOT analysis will reveal internal strengths and weaknesses which are different between and among organizations; it will also reveal 'generic' external opportunities and threats that impact on all foodservice organizations within a given segment of the industry. For example, the 1980s saw six areas which afforded prime opportunities for new products. These were:

- breakfast foods;
- light or nutritious foods;
- new taste sensations (e.g. ethnic or regional recipes);
- foods that cannot be prepared easily at home;
- foods that lend themselves to takeaway;
- delivered food.

The 1990s will see new products in the foodservice industry continue to revolve around the health issue, but there will also be additional product research and development in the area of engineered-for-health foods. There can be little doubt that the entire food industry will become a healthier industry.

Burger King, for example, has test marketed, with some success, Weight Watchers' pre-packaged, low-calorie entrées and snack foods. Organic foods are no longer a fringe interest; they are mainstream. A 1990 Harris poll found that in the last year alone 19 per cent of respondents had bought organic produce for the first time, and 30 per cent had changed their eating habits, owing to news concerns about pesticides. One survey said that 84 per cent of Americans prefer organic foods over conventionally grown produce, but, interestingly, less than 1 per cent of American farmland is farmed organically.

It may not be long before we see some of the more innovative restaurants producing their own ingredients and labelling menu items with their growing history: where ingredients were grown or raised, what they were fed, and how they were treated. We can already see the beginning of such labelling in the supermarket segment of the retailing industry.

Engineered-for-health foods are the future, expanding beyond the reduced-calorie food industry (the diet food and drink business is expected to reach $49.6 billion in 1994), to more innovative products like fluoridated chocolate milk that reduces tooth decay in children, no-cholesterol cheese, and fatless fat (e.g. Procter & Gamble's Olestra, and NutraSweet's Simplesse). Products being currently tested include cholesterol-free eggs, bio-engineered vegetables with the same protein quotient as meat (but without fat), and naturally caffeine-free coffee beans. A recent report suggests that the entire food industry will change. Food, prescribed in doses, will be preventative medicine. 'Foodaceuticals' will blur the edges between drug therapy and nutrition; daily-dose soups or drinks will give you prescribed doses of anti-disease nutritives, or even mood-enhancers. There will be a customization of diets – by the day, by the week, according to mood needs, or according to symptoms. Personal nutrition advice is the big growth area in the service business.

Another trend which will be pervasive in the new product development world of the foodservice industry in the 1990s is what can be termed 'cross-product branding'. For example, America's second largest pizza company and its second largest hamburger chain – Domino's Pizza and Burger King respectively – have joined forces to test market the sale of pizza through Burger King units in the hope of stimulating incremental sales. Domino's will get added exposure and will pick up new customers, while Burger King will gain incremental sales through a new product. From a competitive stance it also gives Burger King some advantages, in that it has made an alliance with a recognized pizza expert, as opposed to McDonald's which is trying to create the product from scratch. Other examples of co-branded products include 7-Eleven convenience stores' experiment to sell both Church's Fried Chicken and Hardee's hamburgers; Wendy's attempts to sell Baskin Robbins' products; and the Stop N Go convenience store chain making and selling Mrs Field's Cookies.

Generate new product ideas

Once new product priorities have been established, new product ideas can be generated through several of the techniques outlined in Chapter 10. Brainstorming is perhaps the most popular form of new product idea generation.

Screen and select ideas

The purpose of the idea generation phase was to generate as many ideas as possible, regardless of their quality. The emphasis was on quantity as opposed to quality. This fourth stage of the new product development process concentrates on the quality of new product ideas by:

- developing a screening methodology;
- conducting qualitative analysis;
- conducting quantitative analysis;
- selecting ideas to be developed.

There are as many screening methodologies as there are foodservice organizations. Different measures are used and different hurdle rates established depending on the internal requirements of the individual organization. Feltenstein (1986) offers examples of generic qualitative and quantitative methods which are often used in the screening process. These are shown in Figure 12.3 and 12.4.

Once the ideas have been screened, the most promising new products should be selected. As discussed in Chapter 10, the failure rate of new products is high, so it makes sense to select more than a few new products for concentration and resource allocation. The task force should set development strategies, objectives and tactics for each new product being developed, with specific allocation of responsibilities, established time frames and action steps. Figure 12.5 is an example of a new product development action plan.

Develop products

As shown in Figure 12.1, Feltenstein suggests five steps in the development of products. The first step of recipe formulation obviously involves determining every ingredient that the proposed product requires, and the quality and quantity of the ingredient. Use is often made of consumer taste panels in this step. The second step involves determining the operational specifications for the menu item. The cost of each ingredient and the cumulative cost of the product, including labour and overheads required in its production, are determined. In addition, research should be conducted into possible pricing strategies, and calculations conducted to determine the menu item's contribution margin and its potential impact on the menu and profitability mix of the operation. The final three steps all involve some form of testing: a unit specific test market, a limited test market, or a fully fledged test market. These three test steps have been receiving less and less emphasis over the past few years as organizations forgo the benefits of conducting such in-depth tests in an attempt to get to market sooner.

---

1. Proposed new product _____
2. General description _____
3. Company objectives it will meet _____
4. Role it will play: ___ new entrée   ___side dish ___new product
5. Key strengths or opportunities _____
   _____
6. Key weaknesses or threats_____
7. Expected impact on sales: ____increase traffic ____trade up
      ____ increase frequency   ____ increase av. check
      ____ new customers
8. Yearly sales goal_____   Profit impact goal_____
9. Items it will cannibalize _____ To what degree_____
10. Target customers _____
11. Day part(s) affected _____
12. Target price _____   Target portion size_____
13. Key ingredients_____
14. Estimated food cost _____
15. Expected production requirement _____
16. Current equipment required _____
    _____
17. New equipment required_____
    _____
18. Space required _____
19. Labour required_____
20. Additional employees required _____
21. Special training required _____
    _____
22. Negative impacts on current production _____
23. Negative effects on staff _____
24. Similar competitive items _____
25. Likely competitive response _____
26. Key benefits _____
27. Key disadvantages_____
28. Required for development: _____
    a. facilities _____
    b. budget_____
    c. personnel _____
    d. special expertise _____
    e. tlme _____

Figure 12.3   Qualitative screening worksheet

Source: Feltenstein, T., 'New product development in food service: a structured approach', *Cornell Hotel and Restaurant Quarterly*, November 1986, pp 63–71.

CRITERIA	RATING (A)	RATING (B)	TOTAL (A×B)
Image			
Menu approach			
Overall company goals			
Company strengths			
Company opportunities			
Desired role			
Level of quality			
Pricing			
Current customers			
Targeted customers			
Services			
Specialities			
Menu voids			
Day-part voids			
Production procedures			
Labour content			
Equipment			
Space availability			
Suppliers			
Developmental capabilities			
Total			

Note: Each new product idea is rated on a scale of 1 (low) to 5 (high) on each of the criteria. Then a weight of 1 to 5 is assigned to each criterion. The product of the rating and the weight gives a total score for the product on each criterion. The sum of these scores gives a final grand total for comparison with proposed products.

Figure 12.4 Quantitative screening worksheet

Source: Feltenstein, T., 'New product development in food service: a structured approach', *Cornell Hotel and Restaurant Quarterly*, November 1986, pp. 63–71.

For example, McDonald's, in an attempt to rekindle cholesterol-wary Americans' appetite for hamburgers, rushes its new McLean Deluxe low-fat burger into all domestic units, bypassing the lengthy process that usually precedes a product roll-out. However, while the market test process was limited and short, the development process was not. McDonald's developed the McLean Deluxe with Auburn University researchers with funding by the National Livestock and Meat boards. The development process took three years and cost $2 million, while the test market took a mere four months.

The hamburger chain Jack in the Box focuses on new product introduction by taking the unorthodox step of compressing the time spent on research, development and roll-out. A new product's gestation at Jack in the Box averages nine months, as compared to two or three years for its rivals. At any one time, Jack in the Box has twenty new products in various stages of research and development, and in the past seven years the chain has introduced twenty-five products system-wide.

To speed up the development and market-testing process, Jack in the Box starts with three or four brainstorming sessions held each year. Executives from all departments attend the brainstorming sessions. Ultimately, one member each from marketing, operations and R & D is picked to 'drive the product to town'. Use is made of food technologists to ensure a sound nutritional base. A 'sensory panel', a group trained much like wine-tasters, judges the product's flavour and texture. Consumer focus groups are then conducted, and afterwards employees are trained in the production of the new product.

Plan marketing and roll-out campaigns

The sixth and final stage of the new product development process are the marketing and roll-out campaigns. The planning behind these campaigns is meticulous and detailed. The more sophisticated foodservice organizations make use of marketing campaign tracking systems which can monitor new product activity on a weekly, daily and even hourly basis in stores where the product is being launched. When a product is launched, specific time frames, responsibilities and action plans must be formulated and strictly implemented. Figure 12.5 is an example of the format of an action plan that a new product can follow.

CONCLUSION

One of the few guarantees that can be given in foodservice product development is that the marketing and roll-out campaigns will not be static. They will be dynamic. In other words, the campaigns will constantly be undergoing modification, change and adjustment. Today's dynamic and volatile foodservice environment married to unpredictable competitive reaction ensures that a marketing and roll-out campaign will need adjustment almost before the ink has dried on the plan. Change is a constant in the world of new product development in the foodservice industry.

Objective/goal _____

Strategies

A. _____

B. _____

C. _____

Action steps	Person responsible	Begin date	End date	Estimated cost
———	———	———	———	£ ———
———	———	———	———	£ ———
———	———	———	———	£ ———
———	———	———	———	£ ———
———	———	———	———	£ ———
———	———	———	———	£ ———
———	———	———	———	£ ———
———	———	———	———	£ ———
———	———	———	———	£ ———
———	———	———	———	£ ———
———	———	———	———	£ ———
———	———	———	———	£ ———
———	———	———	———	£ ———
———	———	———	———	£ ———

Total cost   £ _____

Amount of risk/return   Other individuals involved in
                                 action programme:
Estimated return £ _____   _____
                                 _____
                                 _____
                                 _____

Figure 12.5 New product development action plan

BIBLIOGRAPHY

Feltenstein, T., 'New product development in food service: a structured approach', *Cornell Hotel and Restaurant Quarterly*, November 1986, pp. 63–71.
Popcorn, F., *The Popcorn Report*, Doubleday Currency Publishing, New York, 1991.

GLOSSARY OF TECHNICAL TERMS

Conjoint analysis: A survey-based technique for measuring consumers' trade-offs among product* attributes. It is typically used to identify the most desirable combination of features to be offered in a new product. Respondents are generally told about the various combinations of features under consideration and are asked to indicate the combination they most prefer, to indicate the combination that is their second preference, and so on. The information provided by conducting a conjoint analysis is invaluable in designing a product which best captures the qualities that consumers value most highly.

Cluster analysis: A research technique which identifies different groups (or clusters) of respondents, such that the respondents in any one cluster are similar to each other, but different from the respondents in the other clusters.

Cross-elasticity: The relationship between two or more variables (e.g. particular hotel chains) along two attributes (e.g. price and demand). For example, if XYZ hotel is priced at $38, add 7.8 points to XYZ's market share and subtract 3.3 points from ABC's share; or if XYZ is priced at $50, subtract 12.4 points from XYZ's market share and add 9.2 points to ABC's share.

ELASTICON model: A type of conjoint analysis in which the respondent sees not one supplier's profile or attribute levels but a composite profile that explicitly shows each competitive offering and its associated price. The respondent's task is to indicate, under the stated price conditions, what share of his or her choices would go to each alternative.

Fractional factorial design: A technique used to determine interactive effects between attributes being studied. If two attributes are being studied, each may have a main effect (impact), but when combined they may have an interactive effect which would otherwise not have occurred. In the Courtyard by Marriott case, each of the seven facets being studied was treated as an experimental factor with five levels each. A large range of combinations resulted (five to the seventh power) which resulted in a complex experimental design (the 5 to the 7th full-factorial design), called a fractional orthogonal main effects plan.

Hybrid conjoint analysis (models): Statistical techniques which are based on 'traditional' conjoint models, but which are somewhat more complex. They are generally used when the number of product attributes is high, as in the case of the Courtyard by Marriott concept. The term 'hybrid' is used to denote the fact that the

*The references to 'product' throughout the glossary are also applicable to 'service' attributes.

technique incorporates both compositional and decompositional procedures to obtain utility functions.

Inferential statistics: Statistical techniques which allow the researcher to draw conclusions, or make inferences, about a population on the basis of evidence from a sample.

Multidimensional scaling: A group of analytical techniques used to study consumer attitudes, particularly attitudes relating to perceptions and preferences. These techniques attempt to identify the product attributes that are important to consumers and to measure their relative importance. Generally, multidimensional scaling considers three questions. These are (a) how many dimensions (product attributes) underlie the consumer's perceptions of a given product? (b) what is the actual configuration of the consumer's perceptions of the products – which products are the more alike and which the least? (c) what are the actual attributes underlying the configuration?

Multiple discriminant analysis: A technique used to generate dimensions (product attributes) that discriminate or separate the products as much as possible. Discriminant analysis identifies clusters of attributes on which products differ. If all products are perceived to be similar with respect to an attribute, that attribute should not affect preference. The extent to which a product attribute tends to be an important contributor to a dimension depends on the extent to which there is a perceived difference among the products on that attribute.

Multivariate analysis: Statistical analyses can be broadly categorized into three main types. These are (a) univariate analysis, which examines the properties of a single variable in isolation; (b) bivariate analysis, which analyses the association between two variables; (c) multivariate analysis, which analyses the association between three or more variables.

Self-elasticity: The relationship between two attributes (e.g. price and demand) of a variable (e.g. a particular hotel chain). For example, if XYZ hotel is priced at $38, add 7.8 points to XYZ's market share, or if XYZ is priced at $50, subtract 12.4 points from XYZ's market share.

Stimulus profile: A composite of all attributes being studied. It is the 'big picture', a full description of the product being researched. If a large number of attributes are being studied, each with three or more levels, as in the case of the Courtyard by Marriott concept, it is simply not feasible to present respondents with all possible profiles. Rather, selected composite profiles, drawn from a master design and balanced by blocking designs to prevent bias, are presented to respondents who evaluate each complete stimulus profile on some type of likelihood-of-purchase or intention-to-buy scale.

PART 4

STRATEGIC MARKETING COMMUNICATION

Stephen Calver

INTRODUCTION

Marketing research is becoming an essential support for the decision-making process in hospitality organizations, complementing the intuition and entrepreurial ability that have been responsible for the success of the industry in the past few decades. Chapter 13 examines the unique contribution that attitude research can make to the management of hospitality operations. The hospitality industry is a complex amalgam of subproducts and yet represents a single brand or service concept to the consumer. Understanding consumer perceptions of hospitality services requires a careful unravelling of consumer attitudes and beliefs in order to develop meaningful and effective strategies. A brief case study is used to illustrate the application of research to a complex corporate problem.

Communication, the focus of Chapter 14, is the major strategic tool at the disposal of most established hospitality organizations and the main influence on consumer attitudes discussed in Chapter 13. For small operators, the role of communication is even more important and may be regarded as an essential part of the product offering. The indistinct nature of the unbranded hospitality service means that communication in terms of design, advertising and public relations represents the tangible presence of the hospitality product in the marketplace and the essential precursor of sales promotion, personal selling and direct marketing. For branded hospitality services, the role of communications in positioning products relative to the competition is a crucial component of strategic development.

Chapter 15 provides the context and direction for developing communications and product positioning in the long term. The hospitality industry is confronted by a series of relatively novel challenges. A period of unprecedented growth over almost three decades, where demand for the core products of food and accommodation has been supplemented by extraordinary levels of property and asset appreciation, has ended dramatically. Uncertainty in overseas markets, increased competitive activity, reduced consumer demand and a massive asset portfolio have meant that the industry as a whole needs to consider its options very carefully for the long term. The challenge facing the hospitality industry is the reconciliation of the need to consolidate its service offerings to the consumer and maintain a market position with the need to remain flexible enough to respond to changes in its trading environment. The service element and the staff which provides it are the core of the hospitality product and yet are notoriously resistant to change. The chapter examines approaches to strategy development within the parameters set by the hospitality industry.

ACKNOWLEDGEMENTS

The case material contained in Chapers 13 and 14 draws extensively upon interviews with Crispian Tarrant of Business Development Research Consultants, London, and Geoffrey Breeze, Vice-President, Corporate Marketing, Hilton International. The material in Chapter 13 also refers to a paper by Crispian Tarrant and Geoffrey Breeze delivered at the Market Research Society Conference in Birmingham, February 1993. Many thanks for their time and effort in providing valuable insights.

THIRTEEN

Attitude measurement and the hospitality consumer

INTRODUCTION

The hospitality industry is confronted by a series of profound challenges now and for the foreseeable future. Many of these challenges, such as increased foreign and domestic competition, saturated demand and the search for brand identity, were features of the late 1980s. The new decade has brought its own agenda of issues, involving reduced demand in most sectors. Poor business confidence and poor economic performance throughout the Western world have made the trading environment a more perilous place with few straightforward options for the business community. Because of this challenging trading environment, many commentators and analysts have stressed the need for more accurate information to reduce the risks inherent in business decision taking. The risks associated with the widespread practice of devoting resources mainly to product research and staff training, with only superficial regard for the marketplace, have been made apparent by recent failures in the business community. The dramatic losses incurred by IBM in 1993 were partly due to the company's focus on product issues such as the development of mainframe computers, ignoring the demand for individual or networked personal computers.

Making decisions based on an assessment of market trends is a risky business, but ignoring the marketplace and pursuing a product-led policy is even riskier. The need for thorough, continuous research as a response to the conditions facing the hotel sector has been expressed by Tarrant[1] as follows:

> To respond to the challenge of the context of a changing hotel scene, there is a need for the hotel industry both to understand what motivates hotel guests to buy a particular product and to anticipate their future demands so that the hotel product can be adapted and developed accordingly. It is in these areas that the contribution of research can be most telling.

The following issues were identified as the subject of various ongoing surveys:

- assessment of overall market size, structure and segmentation;
- nature of the buying decision/hotel choice process;
- review of customer requirements of hotel services and facilities;
- tracking of new developments, e.g. incentive schemes, restaurant themes;
- monitoring individual hotel group marketing performances;
- emergence of identifiable, branded hotel products;
- concept testing.

This chapter is not intended as a comprehensive account of market research techniques. It emphasizes the role of consumer attitudes within a hospitality context, and the approaches to measuring attitudes as they may apply to any of the above survey types. The intention is to provide an awareness of the issues relating to attitude research and its relation to consumer behaviour in a hospitality context. Later in this chapter a case study is included to explain the contribution of market research to the specific issue of brand building.[2]

Consumer attitudes represent a distillation of an individual's personality, experience, education, culture, family values and socialization, including the assimilation of marketing messages over a lifetime as a consumer. Attitudes and their component beliefs will regulate the individual's behaviour and motivation, influencing his or her willingness to purchase products and services. If these attitudes can be identified and clustered to form viable and accessible target markets, it means that appropriate product modifications, communication plans and differential pricing policies can be developed.

A caveat must be applied to the use of attitude research and other forms of consumer marketing research. The extent to which these methods can actually assist the marketer in developing products and markets is contentious: some researchers believe that assessing customer needs is a complete waste of time, especially with complex products such as hotels, because it is unlikely that the customer actually knows what he or she wants. There are many marketing departments that could give examples of well-researched products that did not succeed in the marketplace even though consumers had a positive attitude toward them.

Various studies have been conducted to examine the relationship between attitudes and likely behaviour, none of which has satisfactorily established the nature of the relationship. This fact, combined with the expense of applying the most effective of these techniques, means that marketers should use them as a means of risk reduction in making any particular decision, and must certainly use their own expert judgement and experience in applying research results.

However, despite the potential shortcomings of attitude research, it can provide invaluable insights into the consumer's view of the brand and possibly identify a positive link between attitudes, beliefs and behaviour. By examining the relationship between brand attitudes and purchase behaviour, marketers can identify consumer needs and evaluate competing products and brands.

First, the chapter examines the role of 'descriptive' methods of attitude measurement that provide the marketer with a series of measures to assess the strength of attitudes and their component beliefs along several parameters. Further, the chapter explores the use of 'predictive' models, which attempt to relate attitudes to a likely behavioural outcome: for instance, the purchase of a product or service.

Petty[3] acknowledges that 'There is now widespread agreement among psychologists that the term *attitude* should be used to refer to a general and enduring positive or negative feeling about some person, object, or issue. This view originates from the work of Gordon Allport in 1935 and his definition of attitudes as 'learned predispositions to respond to an object or class of objects in a consistently favourable or unfavourable way'.[4] This treatment of attitudes is extremely important for marketers. The fact that attitudes are learned means that companies and organizations can significantly influence the attitudes of their target markets regarding goods, services and ideas, using effective communications strategies – they can, in effect, 'teach' patterns of consumption. Attempts to educate the target market and establish favourable attitudes towards a particular product or service may, of course, be offset by competing communications, by other information sources such as consumer interest programmes in the general media, or by regulating authorities such as government agencies.

The enduring nature of attitudes means that marketers can study them for the purpose of developing short- to medium-term strategies. This presupposes that attitudes can first be measured and then clustered to represent viable and accessible market segments. Gordon Allport called attitude 'the most distinctive and indispensable concept in contemporary social psychology'. This claim could also be made for the use of attitudes in order to identify discrete market segments and product offerings. The use of attitude research to anticipate or even predict individual and group behaviour provides the marketer with an invaluable tool.

The distinction between attitudes and beliefs is as important to market researchers as it is to social psychologists. A consumer's overall attitude towards a particular hotel group will consist of many beliefs which are related to behaviour in terms of willingness to purchase or patronize a product. For instance, beliefs relating to a hotel may include ease of access, speedy check-in and check-out procedures, attractive locations and other issues that incrementally form a positive or negative attitude towards the company or unit. The aggregate of these beliefs may be translated into bookings, depending upon the relative perception of the consumer regarding competitive offerings. Attempts by marketers to change or manipulate attitudes and behaviour must therefore involve consideration of individual beliefs.

ATTITUDES AND THE DEVELOPMENT OF HOSPITALITY MARKETING STRATEGY

Most hospitality organizations may be regarded as dealing with high-involvement products. Even highly branded, standardized, fast-food operations will involve some *active* learning by the consumer, and some brand evaluation will probably take place after the purchase decision has been taken. With more complex, composite products such as hotels, leisure operations or holidays, the extent of pre-purchase learning might be considerable and might take place over an extended period. The complexity of the decision-making process, involving, from the consumer's point of view, high-risk, mainly intangible products, results in the formulation of strongly held beliefs (when compared to many fast-moving consumer goods) and attitudes about product groups and brands. For instance, 'I believe that hamburgers are cheap, convenient and taste good' or, alternatively, 'I believe that McDonald's hamburgers are not good for my children and are environmentally questionable' represent beliefs about the relative value, nutrition and ethics pertaining to this product which would have been carefully considered by the consumer before purchasing for themselves or their families. High-involvement products have several implications for marketers investigating attitudes:

- Consumers seek to overcome the high perceived risk of hospitality services by more vigorous information gathering. This means that the marketer seeking to identify attitudes and likely behaviour patterns will encounter more firmly established, identifiable beliefs based on more rational and deliberative thought processes than they might find with low-involvement goods.
- Because these attitudes are likely to be closely related to the individual's value system and lifestyle, they are likely to be enduring and long term, enabling the marketer to plan and track the changes as they occur. For instance, a business traveller will seek to replicate *at least* the comforts and standards that he or she experiences at home.
- Identifying strongly held beliefs will enable the marketer to develop more effective communication plans, although if the intention is to try and change behaviour, this may prove to be more difficult owing to the reluctance of service consumers to ignore the learning experience that has led to their present consumption patterns.

The way in which consumers evaluate brands by the interaction of brand beliefs and consumer needs has been described by Assael.[5] The degree to which a brand has the attributes consumers' need is called *perceived instrumentality*. If this is positive then there could be a strong intention to buy.

These three components – brand beliefs, brand evaluation and intention to buy – have also been referred to as:

- the cognitive component (beliefs, knowledge of the brand);
- the affective component (brand evaluation, emotional response to the brand);
- the conative component (action or intention to buy).

This approach was illustrated by Woodside *et al.*,[6] who compared the results obtained from measuring brand attitudes on a multidimensional basis with ratings of the brand's attributes and those obtained on a one-dimensional basis by an overall evaluation of the brand. The results indicated that the multidimensional measure of brand attitudes predicted intention to buy much better than the narrower single measure.

Attitudes can therefore usually be measured and analysed, but what are their strategic uses? The marketer can utilize data obtained from attitude analysis in several ways:

- to identify market opportunities;
- to anticipate consumer behaviour;
- to assess marketing strategies;
- to describe target market segments.

Identifying market opportunities

Market opportunities or gaps are increasingly difficult to identify owing to the high level of competition in most hospitality markets and the low growth in market demand. Attitude research can assist the marketer in identifying areas of possible demand not yet serviced. For instance, in a survey carried out in the early 1980s it was apparent that many visitors to a south-coast resort believed that many of its characteristics were consistent with resorts further west, which they rated highly as a holiday destination. Subsequent marketing of the resort through West Country tourist agencies was received well by target markets in the main visitor-generating areas of the United Kingdom. The study further indicated that some significant groups, mainly users of the marine amenities, sailboard enthusiasts, yacht owners and others. felt that they needed specialized hotel accommodation and restaurant facilities.[7,8]

The use of attitude research to identify market opportunities within the hospitality industry is particularly appropriate. Often, because of the complexity of hospitality products, it is difficult for producer and consumer to understand the full potential of different attractions and facilities. It is only through careful study and analysis of existing and potential consumers, using various methods including attitude testing, that the full market potential can be realized.

Anticipating consumer behaviour

As previously noted, there is likely to be a relatively high, positive correlation between attitudes and behaviour for high-involvement hospitality products. The higher perceived risk associated with most hospitality services involves more deliberate information seeking. Therefore the formulation of an attitude may take longer, as will the formation of particular behavioural patterns. Once behavioural patterns associated with a particular type or brand of hospitality operation have been established, it is difficult for competitive operations to change that behaviour without significant marketing effort. Consumers, however, tend to have an 'itinerary' of different hospitality operations from which they can choose. Hospitality products may have more brand-loyal customers than fast-moving consumer goods, although such loyalty may be caused by an awareness of the perceived risk involved in trying a different type of hospitality product rather than by a commitment to the tried and tested choice.

Assessing marketing strategies

Attitude measurement and brand evaluation can provide useful diagnostic measures for:

* identifying new products and test marketing;
* establishing ratios for measuring the effectiveness of a product;
* testing advertising messages before and during use.

The measurement of attitudes towards complex hospitality products can provide a vital tool in the positioning of a particular operation or brand. For instance, different markets will demonstrate different collective attitudes towards guest registration procedures, billing, restaurant service, room design and the many other features that define a customer's experience of a hospitality operation. Attitude research can be used to track product effectiveness over time and to provide useful pointers for management action.

Hilton International's quality assurance programme was based upon the collation of guest questionnaires that were left in the guest rooms, individual guest interviews and an analysis of guest correspondence. Consumer attitudes towards most guest services were analysed and random follow-up questionnaires were distributed for anonymous completion by previous guests (sampling frame criteria included frequency of visit, purpose of visit, length of stay and expenditure characteristics). Attitudes towards individual products, rooms, bars and restaurants were analysed on a monthly basis and comparisons made with previous years. The results of this analysis were discussed during departmental meetings in order to assess likely implications for present policy and future planning. An aggregate ratio of positive/negative comments to total comments was calculated for each hotel unit. In the long term an acceptable ratio could be established (usually a 70 per cent positive ratio was accepted as the norm) and monitored on a monthly basis.

A survey investigating the effectiveness of advertising for a local arts centre demonstrated the complex and long-term issues relating to hospitality products and consumer attitudes. While respondents were able to express attitudes towards the arts centre and its 'products' (cinema, theatrical productions, concerts, exhibitions, bar, restaurants, meeting/conference facilities), the source of information which assisted in the formulation of these attitudes was difficult to establish. The study implied the long-term, incremental effects of promotion. There was no apparent direct relationship between advertising, public relations activity and design issues (functional and aesthetic) and subsequent levels of sales, but these promotional activities provided an essential support for merchandising, sales promotion, direct mail and personal selling where a more direct link could be established with sales.

Describing target segments

Attitudes can be used to describe consumer segments. This approach is particularly important as narrower market parameters need to be identified in order to refine competitive activity. For instance, saturation in the business travel market for hotel accommodation is leading many hotel groups to search for niche markets. Attitudinal research has indicated that clustered beliefs and attitudes relating to such need criteria as proximity to main road routes and town centres, plus internal facilities such as business centres and working areas in guest bedrooms, provide the parameters of viable market segments which are as yet largely undeveloped.

Segments may be described by these need criteria or brand attitudes, which may influence perception of a particular brand. However, a positive influence towards a particular brand may not necessarily result in a sale. The consumer may want to remain loyal, but the product may not be available or may be too highly priced. Wind[9] terms these consumers 'a vulnerable segment' because they may be prone to switch from their existing brand due to their positive attitudes towards competing brands. The relationship between attitudes and predicted behaviour, and the durability of this relationship, are crucial where substantial investment is to be undertaken. Therefore the survey and analysis of attitudes must obviously be rigorous.

ATTITUDES AND BEHAVIOUR

The previous discussion of the uses of attitude research presupposes that there is a direct and provable link between attitudes and behaviour, but as stated earlier, this link has been the subject of much controversy. Soon after attitude scales were first introduced, their relative usefulness was brought into question.

LaPiere[10] tested the link between attitudes and behaviour by investigating racial prejudice, which was presumed to be a phenomenon based on strongly held beliefs. La Piere travelled across the United States with a Chinese couple, stopping at sixty-six hotels and restaurants, and was refused service at only one establishment. A survey carried out shortly after the journey indicated that 92 per cent of hotel and restaurants *would not* serve or admit Chinese people. This example demonstrates the discrepancy that may exist between attitudes and actual behaviour. It was unfortunate that the survey could not identify whether the hotels and restaurants that responded were the same establishments visited, but many subsequent surveys have found only a tenuous link. Wicker[11] in 1969 concluded that 'taken as a whole, these studies suggest that it is considerably more likely that attitudes will be unrelated or only slightly related to overt behaviours than that attitudes will be closely related to actions'.

This apparent disillusion with the whole concept of attitude measurement was reflected elsewhere, and by the mid-1970s the study of attitudes by social psychologists had declined dramatically.[12]

The role of attitudes and attitude research was reconsidered during the 1970s following the contribution of researchers looking at the *structure* of attitudes. The research conducted by Fishbein and Ajzen[13, 14] led to a more confident reappraisal of the relationship between attitudes and behaviour. Ajzen and Fishbein[14] noted that behaviour can be viewed as consisting of four elements:

- the *action* performed (eating);
- the *target* at which the action is directed (snack, main meal, social eating);
- the *context* in which the action is performed (at home, restaurant);
- the *time* component (New Year, lunch, birthday).

By combining these components – for example, eating a snack in a restaurant at lunchtime – the researcher is able to describe the behaviour specifically. In order to predict behaviour, Ajzen and Fishbein argue that the overall attitude measure should correspond to the behaviour on the action, target, context and time categories. If the values do not correspond, there is unlikely to be a positive correlation between behaviour and attitude.

A study of attitudes towards holidays in the West Country (Dorset, Devon and Cornwall) demonstrates the point. The objective of the study was to predict whether families would take their holiday in the impending summer vacation. Table 13.1 demonstrates how well different attitude measures predicted selected families taking their holidays in the West Country.

The attitude towards holidays in the United Kingdom does not predict behaviour very well. The target group may have had positive feelings towards holidays in the West Country (tinged possibly with feelings of loyalty to the idea of taking holidays in the United Kingdom), but not towards devoting time or money to the activity. By adding the action and time components, however, prediction accuracy is increased.

The example above demonstrates the relationship between a specific behaviour and a specific attitude measure. During extensive research, Ajzen Fishbein and others

Table 13.1   Poole Tourism Survey of 180 families in NW England, 1985

Attitude measure	Correlation with behaviour
Attitude towards holiday in United Kingdom this summer	0.072
Attitude towards holidays in the West Country this Summer	0.147
Attitude towards taking a holiday in the West Country this summer	0.438
Attitude towards paying a deposit on a holiday in the West Country this month for this summer	0.533

were able to demonstrate that a general attitude measure should be able to predict a general behavioural pattern. For instance, measuring the attitudes of business people towards the act of staying in a particular type of hotel using the target, context and time components should demonstrate a positive correlation between attitude scores and behaviour. In this case it is highly probable that business people will stay in the defined hotel type at some stage in the future rather than at a specified time.

In addition to measuring the correlation between attitude and behaviour, two other issues have been found to affect the ability to predict behaviour from attitudes.

The first issue is the amount of time that elapses between the attitude and the behavioural measurement. This poses a problem for marketers in the hospitality industry. As stated earlier, attitudes towards service products are formed over a longer period than is the case with low-involvement products; information gathering is more intensive and thorough, and potential customers are therefore more exposed and vulnerable to competitive communications for a longer period. Brand loyalty is also more difficult to establish. The time that elapses between a consumer demonstrating a positive attitude towards a hospitality service and actually using it may be the subject of intensive marketing effort by competitors, which may influence the potential customer significantly in his or her final choice. This particular issue may become irrelevant if the consumer actually experiences the product or has experienced it before being surveyed. There is likely to be a more positive correlation if an attitude is based upon experience.

A less predictable influence on the attitude/behaviour correlation is the extent to which the individual is focused on his or her 'inner' and established beliefs. Respondents may indicate a positive response to taking an expensive holiday until they reflect on their belief in simple pleasures that may have helped them through previous decision processes. This dissonance between the stated belief and the respondent's true internal feelings may eventually prevent the purchase taking place.

ATTITUDE MEASUREMENT: QUANTITATIVE METHODS

Attitudes can provide useful guidelines for marketing action. Generally, researchers use several techniques to measure attitudes that provide the raw data for decision making. None of the techniques described is totally satisfactory in describing the relationship between attitudes and behaviour. Researchers use various scaling techniques and less structured, qualitative techniques in order to assess the salience of attitudes towards a particular product or issue. Decisions regarding the relationship between attitudes and behaviour are left to management experience or intuition.

The structure of the survey is important for the final result. For instance, if a respondent is asked to agree or disagree with a proposition, a degree of distortion may arise if the proposition is irrelevant to the consumer. Asking shoppers whether a fast-food operation is appropriate to their needs may force an opinion, whereas asking respondents about their ideal eating arrangements at lunch-time may prompt a different response and indicate the priorities of the target group.

An important aspect of consumer market research is the extent to which comparisons can be made between different groups – for instance, long-stay and short-stay hotel guests. In order to make valid comparisons, it is important to be able to measure the representatives of each group on the relevant attitude *dimension*, such as ease of booking, in order to measure how they feel about it. This dimensional concept underlies all the main techniques of attitude measurement.

Scaling methods

The most frequently used tool in attitude measurement is the rating scale, where respondents are asked to identify their position on several dimensions of opinion which are scored and collated. Thus, instead of learning whether or not a respondent is favourably inclined on an issue, as represented by responses to specific questions, a reasonably accurate measure is obtained of the respondents' position on the attitude continuum. Several types of scaling technique are discussed as a basic introduction to the subject.

These scaling techniques, with the exception of semantic differential techniques, use a series of common procedures, although they differ in their application depending upon the technique used. Most scaling techniques require the compilation of sets of items (statements) from which the final scale for inclusion on a questionnaire will be constructed.

Qualitative techniques are invariably used to elicit a suitably large item bank. These techniques, which are discussed later, may include individual depth interviews or group interviews, and may be structured or very informal. Statements made during unstructured interviews can be a valuable source for an item pool because they have the advantage of being expressed in terms that are commonly used by the respondents themselves rather than suggested in the less familiar terminology of the researcher. Unstructured interviewing also encourages the respondent to deal with items according to his or her beliefs, rather than according to what the respondent understands to be contemporary opinion or fashion.

Having assembled the item pool, the next stage is to choose the items to be included in the final survey. It is important to ensure that, while the removal of unsatisfactory items takes priority, the full range of opinions is included in the scale.

Thurstone's differential scale

One of the earliest scaling procedures was developed by Louis Thurstone, who in 1928 published a paper entitled 'Attitudes can be measured'.[15] The theory evolved out of scaling perceptions of such sensory stimuli as light and sound, and Thurstone concluded that emotionally involving stimuli may be measured using the same techniques. The method of preparation is as follows.

1. The first step is to collect a large number of items or statements on the subject of the survey: for instance, attitudes towards fast food as a family meal. These

statements should range from one extreme of favourableness to another. They are first of all reduced by cutting out ambiguous items, duplicates and items that do not discriminate between respondents. For instance, the item 'Fast food should be cheap' would probably be supported by most respondents.

2. Each item is transferred to a separate card or database and a number of 'judges', perhaps between thirty and sixty, are asked independently to assess the items. The judges use objective criteria rather than their own judgement, and sort them into a set number of piles according to their perceived degree of favourableness regarding the issue in question. For instance, 'Fast food is a reasonable alternative to home-cooked meals at lunch-time' may be included in pile 3 on a 7-point scale where 1 is positive and 7 negative, whereas 'Fast food is not as nutritious as home-cooked food' may rate 7 on the same scale. The number of 'piles' can range between seven and eleven, with the middle pile being neutral. Better results are often obtained from fewer piles where the judges do not have to discriminate over such a wide range. The whole process can be facilitated by the use of computer technology where the judges simply record their score on the screen. Sorting procedures can also be carried out efficiently, as well as the final production of a questionnaire.

3. Sortings by judges that are obviously flawed – for instance, having no correlation with other scores – can be eliminated from the outset. The remaining items can be scored depending upon the pile that they represent (i.e. an item in pile 1 scores 1 and so on). Items will tend to be scattered over several piles. If the scatter is too great then the item should be eliminated because it does not discriminate adequately. A median value is calculated where half the judges give the item a lower position and half higher, with an interquartile range that measures the scatter of judgements. The list of items is now reduced by:

- discarding items with a high scatter;
- selecting from the remainder some twenty or so statements which cover the entire range of attitudes and appear to be equally spaced (as judged by the medians).

4. The items are then included in a questionnaire in random order. Respondents are asked to indicate the items with which they agree, the average value indicating agreement represents the respondent's score.

From the respondent's point of view this is a straightforward process which requires agreement or disagreement. However, various criticisms of this scaling technique have been expressed. First of all, the judges may not be representative of the respondents whose attitudes are to be scaled, and this may affect the scale values. There is conflicting evidence regarding this point, but studies have demonstrated reassuring evidence that the scale values are often independent of the judges' own attitudes. It may also be difficult (or expensive) to obtain the co-operation of a large number of individuals. Empirical evidence has shown that reliable scales for statements can be obtained from a relatively small number of judges. The laboriousness of the technique and the mathematical procedures involved are often cited as further disadvantages of this method, although computer technology can reduce the amount of time invested in the various procedures.

Likert summated scales

Although the Thurstone scale is rather difficult to construct, it does allow a fairly precise estimate of where a person stands on an attitude dimension. In most commercial research, however, this level of precision is not required. It is often sufficient to know how people can be ranked relative to each other without the assumption of 'equal appearing intervals' implicit in the Thurstone technique. In 1932 Rensis Likert published a paper entitled 'A technique for the measurement of attitudes'[16] that described a verbal rating scale where respondents are asked not to decide just whether they agree or disagree with a statement, but to choose between several response categories, indicating various strengths of agreement or disagreement. The following procedure is used.

1. Statements relating to a particular issue or product are assembled using qualitative techniques.

2. The statements are then compiled as a draft questionnaire and respondents, who are representative of the target group, are asked to indicate their level of agreement or disagreement with each statement. Five categories of response are normally provided, but three or seven can be used. An even number of responses may also be used to avoid the 'central tendency' that may occur when respondents wish to avoid committing themselves on an issue, although this is largely discounted in most surveys. Response categories may include:

- strongly disagree;
- disagree;
- unsure;
- agree;
- strongly agree.

The responses are then scored 1, 2, 3, 4 and 5, where 1 = strongly disagree. The scale can be reversed, depending on whether 'strongly disagree' indicates a positive attitude or a negative attitude. Some items on the scale will be expressed positively, so that the response 'strongly agree' denotes a favourable attitude: for instance, 'fast food can provide an alternative to home-cooked meals' or 'My family enjoys the occasional fast-food meal'. Others will be expressed negatively, so that the 'strongly agree' response denotes an unfavourable attitude: for instance: 'Fast food is not as nutritious as home-cooked food' or 'Fast food is not as tasty as home-cooked meals'.

In order to make the score meaningful, positive and negative items must be scored in a consistent way throughout the questionnaire.

3. The scores for statements and individuals are then calculated. If a questionnaire with twenty statements scores 5 on each, the total will be 100. If an individual's score is equal to 80 or above this represents a favourable attitude.

4. When selecting the statements for inclusion on the final questionnaire, three considerations should be borne in mind:

- Extreme statements are not very useful because the purpose of the scale is to spread responses across all categories.
- Neutral items do not work well in Likert scales.
- It is advisable to have a roughly equal number of negative and positive statements.

The scores of individual statements should be correlated with the total of all statement scores. Those with the highest correlations should be included in the final questionnaire. Scores that do not discriminate between respondents with high and low total scores should also be eliminated.

Unlike the Thurstone scale, construction and administration can be accomplished with the same type of respondents who will eventually feature in the survey. Further, the Likert scale is easier to construct than the Thurstone scale and has a higher level of reliability. Likert scales are also relatively easy for the respondent to understand.

Because Likert scaling techniques are relatively straightforward, they are prone to misuse: for instance, any questionnaire can look convincing with a number of statements plus an agree–disagree scale. Care should also be taken in the selection of words such as 'some', 'considerable' and 'moderate' to avoid misunderstanding. Researchers will establish their own databank of words to achieve effective discrimination, but this does require a lot of time and careful analysis.

Table 13.2 Likert scale: scoring statements

	Strongly agree	Agree	Uncertain	Disagree	Disagree strongly
There is a lot to do and see (+)	5	4	3	2	1
The children did not enjoy their trip (−)	1	2	3	4	5

Semantic differential scale

In an attempt to understand the dimensions and meanings of words, Osgood *et al.*[17] developed a convenient way to assess attitudes towards a wide variety of subjects and issues. Research demonstrates that three factors account for most of the meaning that is attributes to different words. These are:

- evaluation – relative goodness or value;
- potency – relative strength of intensity;
- activity – relative speed or excitability.

The first factor may be regarded as an attitude, and Osgood proposed that it could be measured by having respondents rate the attitude object on bipolar adjective pairs (Figure 13.1). This represents the evaluative dimension of meaning. Respondents are asked to indicate the blank that best fits their attitude towards the brand of product under consideration, by marking it. The procedure is flexible and easier to use and

McDonald's Hamburgers

Tasty	— — — — — — — —	Bland
Inexpensive	— — — — — — — —	Expensive
Large	— — — — — — — —	Small
Fast	— — — — — — — —	Slow

Figure 13.1 Example of an Osgood scale

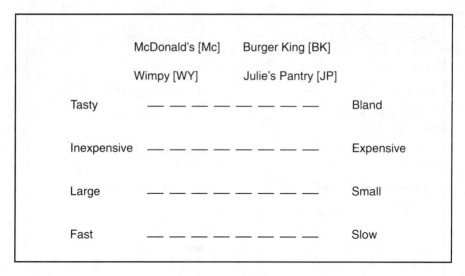

Figure 13.2 Osgood scale showing several brands on one sale

understand than other scaling methods. It is also reasonably reliable, and because of this, it is the most frequently used attitude scaling device in marketing research.

The format of the semantic differential test has been varied by many researchers to improve the results of their surveys. One such alteration is to have several brands or products rates on the same scale (Figure 13.2). Respondents are asked to insert the initials of the different brands on the scale to indicate relative attitudes.

A variation that does not restrict attention to the evaluative factor, and which uses descriptive phrases instead of bipolar opposites, is particularly useful for hospitality research where the product or service is too complex to be represented by a single word. Significant market groups can be compared using this technique, providing a profile of the brand image (Figure 13.3) is used as a template.

Hotels could be profiled using the dimensions shown in Figure 13.4.

A simplified version of the semantic differential scale is represented by the Stapel scale, which is a unipolar rating scale using a range of intervals (Figure 13.5). The Stapel scale uses just one adjective to describe the concept in question. The scale in Figure 13.5 may be used in measure attitudes toward a leisure centre.

Chisnall[18] has commented on the fact that Osgood's scales have been used successfully for marketing research investigations into consumer attitudes dealing with corporate image, brand and advertising image, and in other areas where it is often difficult for consumers to articulate their feelings.

The hospitality industry may benefit from similar applications where many of the issues relating to consumer acceptance of the product are intangible and complex, and consumers experience difficulty in explaining their attitudes. Some researchers[19] have suggested that a 5-point scale may be preferable because it is better understood by respondents and easier for the interviewer to explain.

CONSCIENTIOUS EATER CONCERNED ABOUT 'ISSUES'	CAREFREE EATER UNCONCERNED ABOUT 'ISSUES'
Contemporary	Traditional
Liberal views	Conservative views
Price/product sensitive	Price/brand sensitive
Extensive information search	Limited information search
Resistant to overt promotion	Sensitive to promotion
Feminine	Masculine
Positive health food image	Negative health food image
Service factors less important	Service factors important
Location less important	Location more important
Profound interests	Less profound interests

Figure 13.3 Osgood scale using descriptive phrases

'Standard' layout	Unique layout
Modern	Old
Tourist	Business
Budget market image	Luxury market image
Easily accessible from motorway	Less easy access from motorway

Figure 13.4 Hotel brand profile

The repertory grid technique

Many of the techniques discussed have been criticized for their failure to communicate in the language of the consumer, and for their limited appreciation of consumers' needs. A more comprehensive approach to attitude measurement was developed by George Kelly[20] based on a repertory grid method of measurement. For most commercial purposes, the repertory grid technique varies very little from the original

Clean	— — — — — —
Helpful staff	— — — — — —
Well equipped	— — — — — —
Well maintained	— — — — — —
Safe	— — — — — —
Clear instructions	— — — — — —
Easy to use	— — — — — —

Figure 13.5   Stapel scale

approach developed by Kelly. Individuals are required to respond to a number of stimuli which may take different forms, such as:

- advertising copy or images;
- products such as hamburgers and pizzas;
- lists of statements;
- brand concepts and story boards.

These stimuli (the number may range between five and thirty) may be presented in different formats – videos, photographs, statements, actual products and other ways. Having removed from the list any items that the respondent has not used, visited or heard of, three stimuli are usually presented. The respondent is asked to describe one way in which two of them are alike and yet different from the third. For instance, three photographs of different lager-can labels may be shown to the respondent, who may respond that two of them are 'easy to drink' and the third is 'gassy'. The basis for similarity (relative easiness to drink) is termed the emergent pole and the difference ('gassiness') is termed the implicit pole. These are recorded, and the remaining stimuli are then sorted between the implicit and emergent poles. Another three stimuli are then presented and the respondent is asked to repeat the process. The market researcher continues to present the respondent with different randomly selected combinations of three stimuli until the respondent exhausts the reasons why two stimuli are different from the third.

The repertory grid technique requires careful preparation and execution by the researcher. It is also extremely tiring for the respondent, who may react against the testing nature of the grid technique. A significant operational problem posed by the repertory grid interview is its tendency to encourage some responses which may be too general or irrelevant: for instance, 'Those two pizzas are round, that one is rectangular', 'Those two hamburgers are made by McDonald's, that one is made by

Burger King' or 'I like those two, I don't like that one'.

However, given a response such as 'those pizzas are crispy, the other one is not', a scale can be formed using 'crispy' and 'not crispy' (although according to Kelly this would not represent a proper construct, whereas 'crispy'/'soggy' would). A good deal of editing and rephrasing usually has to take place without obscuring the meaning as it is understood by a particular target group.

Figure 13.6 is an example of a single repertory grid sheet, which would usually be accompanied by between ten and fifty similarly prepared sheets. It was used as part of a research programme examining consumer attitudes towards fast-food products. The results of the research can be entered directly on to a computerized spreadsheet or statistical package in order to carry out correlation analysis of the entries on the grid, thus indicating the way in which the respondent's constructs are related to each other. The collection of items is often later used to form attitude scales.

Thomas[21] is one of the few researchers to point out the application of the repertory grid techniques to marketing analysis – especially in the field of communication, where an understanding of how consumers interpret words and images is essential to the effective use of advertising, public relations and other forms of promotion.

This point is acknowledged by Francis Harmer-Brown:[22]

Piz. = Pizza   Ham. = Hamburger   KCH = Fried chicken
Mex. = Mexican   BP = Baked potato   Bg = Filled baguette

	Piz.	Ham.	KCH	Mex.	BP	Bg

EMERGENT POLE	IMPLICIT POLE
Nutritious	Not nutritious
High in calories	Low in calories
Easy to eat out	Difficult to eat out
Replaces main meal	Does not replace main meal
Spicy	Not spicy
Family meal	Not a family meal
Can be vegetarian	Cannot be vegetarian
Easy to carry	Difficult to carry
Filling	Not filling
Easy to make at home	Difficult to make at home
Value for money	Not value for money
Fattening	Not fattening
Can eat any time of day	Cannot eat at any time of day
Enjoyed by children	Not enjoyed by children

Figure 13.6   Repertory grid exploring takeaway fast-food products

Advertisements are today quite an important part of the mass of data that a person has to organise and control in order to predict future events. It would be extremely interesting to know what constructs in this area, different sub groups of people have in common; and in what way these sub groups are related to existing media groups, for example. Repertory grid analysis on a group of respondents using as data a series of different advertisements in a related product field, would, I think, yield fascinating results. But as far as I know, this has not yet been done. Instead, the advertising business has ignored almost completely, Kelly's theories of human behaviour and has rushed to apply repertory grid techniques in areas for which they are totally unsuitable, simply because the techniques are objective, scientific and statistically respectable.

The relationship between attitudes and behaviour

The various scaling techniques discussed above give a valuable insight into the possible attitude constructs of consumers. As mentioned earlier, more comprehensive theories have been formulated in an attempt to identify the likely behaviour of individuals and groups. Most of these theories draw upon a number of social science disciplines which are too complex to provide a direct basis for consumer modelling. However, modified versions of these models can be of considerable practical value to the researcher, since they may indicate ideas and concepts which might be utilized in consumer surveys.

One example explains the concept of the evoked set.[23,24] This distinguishes those brands in a product field which a consumer would consider buying from those which either are not known or would not be considered. The scope and detail of the evoked set may vary in the long term due to such factors as experience and confidence. The concept is particularly useful in researching attitudes towards hospitality services, since consumers tend to choose from a personal itinerary of different hospitality products.

The Fishbein model

Fishbein[25,26] devised a multi-attribute model for marketing application in order to focus on the attitude towards the act of purchasing a brand rather than simply on the attitude towards the brand. This model allows for consideration not only of the beliefs about the brand, but also of normative beliefs: that is, how respondents believe they should behave with regard to those around them.

Fishbein's model, in common with other multi-attribute models, regards attitudes as a function of consumer beliefs about the attributes of brands. Beliefs are also weighted according to the importance of these attributes to the consumer. For instance, a consumer who perceives Travelodge as providing facilities for young children, and who places a high value on hotels that provide facilities for young children, will have a positive attitude towards the brand and will be likely to patronize it. This relationship can be defined as:

Attitude toward the object (Ao) = The sum of beliefs about the object on various attributes (bi) × the value placed on each attribute (ai)

or:

$Ao = å\ biai$

Because multi-attribute models aggregate responses to the brand under investigation in order to evaluate an overall attitude, weakness on one attribute may be compensated by strength on another. The disaggregated scores indicating weakness or strength can be used to develop marketing strategy for the brand.

Brand A

Replaces home-cooked meal __ _x_ __ __ __ __ __   Does not replace home-cooked meal

Brand B

Replaces home-cooked meal __ __ __ __ __ __ _x_   Does not replace home-cooked meal

Brand A

Bite-sized pieces __ __ __ __ __ _x_ __   Not bite-sized pieces

Brand B

Bite-sized pieces __ __ _x_ __ __ __ __   Not bite-sized pieces

Indicate how satisfied you would be:

If you replaced a home-cooked meal with A or B

Very satisfied   __ _x_ __ __ __ __ __   Very dissatisfied

If you replaced a home-cooked meal with bite-sized pieces of chicken

Very satisfied   __ _x_ __ __ __ __ __   Very dissatisfied

Figure 13.7   Compensatory nature of the Fishbein model

Figure 13.7 demonstrates the compensatory nature of multi-attribute models. While Brand A does not come in 'bite-sized pieces', the preferred option for this respondent, it may be compensated by the fact that it is perceived as a replacement for a 'home-cooked meal' and therefore may be preferable to Brand B.

Multi-attribute models are based on the assumption of a hierarchy in which the beliefs about a brand and the evaluation of these beliefs result in an overall evaluation of the brand. This ultimately results in a positive or negative intention to buy (*BI*) (see Fig 13.8), and may result in purchasing or other positive behaviour (*B*). Fishbein offered several modifications of his basic model in an attempt to explain better the formation of brand attitudes and purchase intentions.

An attempt to resolve the relationship between a consumer's attitude towards an object (*Ao*), as opposed to his or her attitude towards the act of purchasing or behaving in a particular way towards an object, was the subject of further investigation. For instance, consumers could have a very positive attitude towards staying in a particular hotel, but lack the necessary funds to do so. The attitude towards the act (*Aact*) of staying in the hotel may therefore be a more legitimate consideration. The distinction between these two aspects reflects the marketer's probable view that it is more meaningful to evaluate the consumer's attitude towards purchasing or consuming than simply to the consumer's general attitude towards a product or brand.

Another important modification to the multi-attribute model introduced by Fishbein involves the influence of the group on the individual consumer – for instance, family and/or friends (*SN*). It was assumed that the consumer did not act in isolation but either actively sought advice on purchases or had an indirect response to their perceived needs or attitudes. This particular aspect is of considerable significance when researching hospitality markets. Consumers often make joint decisions about pubs, restaurants, hotels or leisure activities, and business travellers will be regulated by corporate policy and decision processes determined by departments or committees. Fishbein also suggested a qualifying variable to take account of the individual's likely

$$B \gg BI = w_1(Aact) + w_2(SN) + w_3(MC)$$

B	= Behaviour
BI	= Behavioural intention
Aact	= Attitude towards the act
SN	= Subjective norm
MC	= Motivation to comply
w_i	= weights representing the relative influence
	of *Aact*
	and *SN/MC* respectively

Figure 13.8 Extended Fishbein model

The subjective norm:

My family thinks that I should buy Brand A as an alternative to a home-cooked meal

True ____   ____   ____   ____   ____ False

The motivation to comply:

I will buy Brand A
because my family
thinks that I should ____   ____   ____   ____   ____

I will not buy Brand A
even though my family
thinks that I should

Figure 13.9   Examples of the subjective norm and the motivation to comply

motivation to comply (*MC*) with the views of these 'significant others'. The notation for Fishbein's extended model is given in Figure 13.8. Examples of the subjective norm and the motivation to comply are given in Figure 13.9.

Various researchers[27] have suggested that the extended Fishbein model is a better measure of behavioural intentions than the original model, which measured attitude towards the object. The implications for the better understanding of what influences the consumer's intentions to behave in a particular way are also significant. The disaggregated model can enable a diagnosis of reasons for behaviour and suggest alternative marketing strategies.

Assael[5] has suggested the following strategic implications of multi-attribute models:

- To identify the strengths and weaknesses of the company's brand in relation to the competition. For instance, the belief component may indicate that Sheraton hotels are considered more exclusive and prestigious than competing hotels.
- To identify the needs of segments of the market based on the value component. Sheraton hotels would be in a strong position to optimize the market opportunities among those consumers appreciating an exclusive product, but may be vunerable in a business market requiring a less prestigious product but higher perceived efficiency.
- To determine the need for product positioning.
- To identify the determinant attributes for strategic purposes.
- To identify new product opportunities.

The Fishbein model and other expectancy value models offer substantial benefits to marketers. Most of all, there is the analysis of *reasons* for consumer preferences, even though these may not always translate into actual sales. The component beliefs can be used to develop promotional messages and adapt service elements to the needs of specific markets. The cost and complexity of the models' implementation are likely to be prohibitive for most commercial applications, but the techniques and approach to survey design can be built into consumer research in an attempt to access behavioural probability.

QUALITATIVE RESEARCH

The previous discussion focused upon various methods of quantifying attitudes with the aim of identifying target groups and specific marketing propositions. The remainder of this chapter will examine qualitative research techniques as a further means of evaluating consumer attitudes.

The common problem with quantitative methods is that they often force the respondent to choose between given alternatives: for instance, whether a product is nutritious, very nutritious or not very nutritious. These alternatives may not reflect the shades of opinion that a single consumer may have; nor do they begin to describe the underlying reasons for and circumstances of an opinion. The problem is further aggravated when the results are compiled and aggregated. One consumer may rate a product (−2) on a scale and another (+4), but the aggregate (+2) does not represent the view of either consumer. Careful analysis of the data and a full explanation can, of course, mitigate this problem, but even this is open to the researcher's interpretation.

Direct questioning for a calculable response may be difficult for other reasons:

- The complexity of hospitality products and services means that consumers may not have a clear idea of their motivations, intentions and beliefs.
- Many hospitality markets are international, and problems of translating questionnaires or explaining questionnaires in one language can introduce bias.
- Potentially embarrassing questions relating to income, leisure activity, and disposable income may not receive a willing or accurate response.
- A categorical response does not provide the understanding of context or circumstances that may be necessary for marketing decision marking.

Qualitative research, on the other hand, has a long tradition in the social sciences and in consumer motivation research. The Market Research Society[28] commented that qualitative research has 'long since extended from its original function of uncovering consumers' motivations to that of providing the constant conceptual link between consumer and decision maker in marketing and advertising development'. Sampson[29] has identified ten common examples of the use of qualitative research:

- To investigate the background of a particular issue or problem. This is particularly important when dealing with complex issues such as use of leisure time.
- To identify concepts such as disposable income.
- To analyse behaviour patterns, beliefs, opinions and motivations.
- To determine the priority that may exist among beliefs, opinions and attitudes. For instance, how does the family holiday relate to other demands upon expenditure?
- To identify problems, or to outline an issue for further investigation. For instance, when a particular market declines it is important to get as much information as possible regarding the possible reasons.
- As a preliminary screening process. For instance, in developing a questionnaire for a large-scale survey, a large number of possible questions may be reduced to a few pertinent examples which still cover the main issues.
- As a means of obtaining a large amount of data about a subject.
- Conducting post-research. Quantitative surveys often create several further areas of investigation. For instance, a survey may reveal that a large proportion of a hotel's summer visitors originate from the north-west of England. This fact, while useful, needs to be investigated to find out the possible reasons.

- To pilot questionnaires and other survey material to ensure that it is understood by the target sample production.
- To investigate potentially sensitive subjects such as income level.

Qualitative research may not be as 'scientific' as quantitative research, which is based on statistical sampling theory and enables researchers to comment on the statistical probability of results. However, the examples given above are evidence of the overall usefulness of qualitative research to the market researcher as a diagnostic, exploratory technique. McIver[30] commented that 'when it is affordable, a combination of qualitative and quantitative research is usually more informative than either by itself'. But the reluctance of clients to accept qualitative research data without the support of a quantified survey is sometimes groundless and is often caused by overconfidence in the apparently more objective statistical approach.

There is also a mistaken belief that, because the techniques of qualitative research appear to be easily understood, there is little skill involved. The reverse is actually true.

The use of qualitative research in Europe has grown significantly in recent years.[31] It is estimated that it now represents 20 per cent of all market research and is the main research technique in such marketing activities as new product development, concept research and advertising pre-testing.

Qualitative techniques

The rules and methods of qualitative research are not as well established as those relating to quantiative techniques. Many of the methods derive from other disciplines, usually in social sciences that bear little relation to consumer research. The success of qualitative methods depends almost entirely upon the skill of the researcher, who must have the ability to use the right form of probing questions and to interpret the responses appropriately.

The techniques used are varied and often quite specific to a particular researcher, who has found certain methods to be effective. Methods include depth interviews, individual or group interviews, usually with a maximum of fifteen participants, and structured or unstructured interviews. Focus groups, extended creativity groups, sensitivity groups, brainstorming, role playing and many other methods may also be used. Critics of some of these techniques, and of qualitative research in general, point to the fact that while the results may be interesting, the objective of providing information for marketing decision making should not be overlooked.

Sampling

Crude sampling techniques can be applied to the selection of individuals or groups to ensure that they have a similar profile to the market under investigation, or at least that the main subgroups are represented. The selection of participants can also involve a screening process to ensure that they possess certain knowledge or experience.

The following example was taken from an investigation of the market for pizza restaurants in the United Kingdom. Six extended group discussions of two hours' duration were to be taped. Information about the six groups is provided in Table 13.3.

Table 13.3 The six discussion groups

Group no.	Age	Sex	Social class	Lifestage	Location
1	18–23	M	BC1	Single	Ipswich
2	18–23	F	C1C2	Single	Hull
3	24–30	M	C1C2	No children	Watford
4	24–30	F	BC1	No children	Watford
5	31–40	M	BC1	With children	Exeter
6	31–40	F	C1C2	With children	Exeter

The following selection criteria were used:

- All had visited pizza restaurants regularly.
- All had been to a pizza restaurant within the last two months.
- Mix of outlets: at least four Pizza X, Pizza Y.
- Spread of times of day.
- Two groups had tried home delivery.
- Two groups had tried takeaway.

The following stimulus material was used in the group discussions:

- Collage boards: atmosphere, food imagery, chefs, customers.
- Photographs: competing outlets.
- Menus: Pizza Co. X, Pizza Co. Y, Pizza Co. Z.
- Sort cards: pizzas, interiors, additional pizza items (anchovies, etc.).
- Advertising: television, the press.

The results of this survey enabled the company to develop a new integrated concept which included interior design, menu selection and staff training.

Having determined the composition of the sample, various approaches can be adopted to extract information from the participants.

Depth interviews

The interviewer does not usually have a set of specified questions, although he or she may have a list of points. The interview may commence by discussing broad issues (e.g. travelling on business) and then progress by focusing on more specific issues (e.g. suites for businesspeople in hotels). The interviewer has the freedom to probe and follow a line of enquiry as the respondent is encouraged to talk about the subject under investigation. These interviews may take place in groups or as individual sessions.

The American Marketing Association makes the distinction between depth interviewing, which it defines as the study of one individual, and group depth interviewing, which studies either the interaction of the group members or the reaction of the group to an individual. The latter is of particular significance because, as we have seen, the interaction of individuals in cohesive groups such as families influences the decision-making process.

One major international hotel company keeps lists of individuals who are representative of different user groups. These people may be invited to group interview sessions, usually lasting up to three or four hours. Occasionally, independent research organizations may be used to ensure the objectivity of the findings.

Extended creativity groups combined with depth interviews have been developed within the area of consumer market research. These sessions involve a combination of different stimuli that may include cartoons, story boards or other projective techniques. The purpose of these sessions is to use varying 'prompts' to investigate the motives and attitudes of respondents that may otherwise be obscured during conventional interviews.

However the sessions are organized, it is important to have trained and experienced members of the research team who are familiar with some of the psychological problems that can occur. Group or individual interviews will put the respondent(s) under some pressure, which can become intolerable, especially for the less articulate. The session organizer or an assistant should be familiar with the early signs of unreasonable stress and be able to manage the situation in such a way that the participants are not left with any residual negative feelings or anxiety.

Projective techniques

The use of projective techniques in clinical psychology has a proven track record as a means of indirectly obtaining information on issues that may cause distress or embarrassment to the respondent. There has been some criticism that the techniques may be misunderstood by the subject, who may be tempted to give an inappropriate response either to satisfy the interviewer or for their own motives. The application of projective techniques to consumer research, where they may be used by untrained and inexperienced staff, is even more controversial. The results obtained by such methods are open to interpretation and must therefore be the subject of careful scrutiny before decisions are based upon them. Oppenheim[32] described the benefits of using projective techniques:

- They can help to penetrate the barrier of awareness – people are often unaware of their own motives and attitudes, and particularly so with complex products and services.
- The barriers of irrationality can be breached – people often feel that they must justify their decisions with rational argument.
- The barrier of inadmissibility may be broken – people are loath to admit to some kinds of 'non-ideal' behaviour. For instance, in a survey investigating petty (but expensive) theft of hotel towels, hangers and furnishings, discussing other people's motives, using story boards, was obviously more constructive than discussing the participants' own possible motives.
- The barrier of self-incrimination is penetrated – this is related to the previous point and refers to the participants' understanding of how other people may regard their behaviour and attitudes.
- They can breach the barrier of politeness – some forms of behaviour may be considered impolite or socially unacceptable by respondents. Projective techniques may assist discussion of this behaviour.

The techniques that may be used include the following:

- word association test;
- thematic apperception test;
- sentence completion test;
- Rorschach ink blot test;
- psychodrama;
- cartoons;
- third person test;
- story completion test.

Word association tests are probably the best-known tests and have even been reinterpreted as a parlour game. Respondents are given a single word to which they must respond with the first unconsidered word that enters their head. Where hesitation occurs for more than two or three seconds, this is often due to a strong emotional connotation of the word, which may not be suitable for promotional purposes if the response is common to the group. The words used in the tests relate to the product or service under investigation, although neutral words are often dispersed throughout the list in order to overcome defensive tactics.

In *thematic apperception tests* the respondent is shown a series of illustrations and asked to describe the situations shown, what led up to the events depicted and what followed. This technique was used to good effect during an investigation of petty theft by guests. A cartoon was prepared of a person being apprehended at an airport with a suitcase full of hotel towels, and participants were asked to describe the events implicit in the illustration.

Sentence completion tests are similar to word association tests. Their value lies in the spontaneity of the answers. Examples may include: 'a mother who serves fast food to her family for lunch is . . .' and 'The nutritional value of fast food is . . .'

Rorschach ink blot tests rely on respondents describing abstract shapes, often formed by ink blots, as objects or animals. A drop of ink squeezed between two pieces of paper is often used. The technique is controversial because it depends on the subjective evaluation of the respondent being subjectively interpreted by the researcher.

The effective use of *psychodrama* in psychotherapy does not translate easily into consumer research for the same reasons as the Rorschach ink blot tests: the difficulty of interpretation. Participants are asked to act out a buying process, such as booking a holiday, in order to identify the sequence of events that forms the behaviour and some of the emotional issues that influence the process.

Cartoons frequently involve a sketch showing two people talking, their speech represented by empty balloons. For instance, the illustration may show a guest standing at a reception desk talking to a receptionist; one or both of the balloons are empty and the respondent is asked to fill them in. This type of technique has been used successfully in investigating customer service requirements, such as checking-in and checking-out procedures.

In *third-person tests*, participants are required to give their opinion on the behaviour of a third person, such as in their choice of holiday accommodation. The opinions given may reflect a view that would otherwise be difficult to express for reasons stated earlier. The early claims made for these techniques have been investigated by several researchers,[33] who question whether they can indicate user characteristics.

Story completion tests are an extension of sentence completion tests. The respondent can give more information about an issue and the possible sequence of events that leads to a particular form of behaviour: for instance, booking a meal for a social occasion. It is therefore useful in identifying significant stages in the buying process that may be influenced by promotional effort by the supplier.

New product development and consumer research

The use of consumer research in the development of new products is open to question, and the results should be interpreted with care. For example, consumer research indicated the potential consumer demand for healthier food in restaurants, and that salad bars were a highly desirable component of the menu. Many hotels installed elaborate salad bars only to find that customers rarely patronized them, preferring more traditional, less healthy fare. It seems that consumers will often:

- feel obliged to 'please' the researcher by telling him or her what the consumer feels that the researcher wants to hear;
- give an answer that represents the consumer's preferred behaviour rather than his or her actual behaviour.

There is no doubt that, given the high rate of new product failure and the perishability of existing products, consumer research has a role to play in the decision-making process. However, the methods used and the results obtained must be scrutinized carefully and tested in several ways to improve the reliability of the data.

Interpretation of results

> Analysis brings moments of terror that there's nothing there and times of exhilaration from the clarity of discovering ultimate truth. In between are long periods of hard work, deep thinking, and weightlifting volumes of material.[34]

The aim of qualitative research is to produce data that can be used in the decision-making process. Unlike quantitative data, there are no tests of validity and significance that can assist the process. Perhaps one of the few canons that applies to the interpretation of qualitative research is the need for full disclosure as to how the conclusions were reached, in order that method and results can be thoroughly evaluated. Described below are some of the approaches that Patton[34] identifies for the interpretation of qualitative data:

- Focusing the analysis. This which involves identifying the aims of the research and the analysis.
- Organizing the data. Qualitative research generates a considerable amount of data, often with no obvious pattern or structure. It is important at this stage to ensure that the data, voluminous as they are, cover the objectives of the survey.
- Content analysis. Researchers develop their own techniques of analysing the content of the results: for instance, coding responses (G = group opinion, I = individual opinion), or computerized data processing (e.g. rating comments 1 = very negative, 2 = negative and so on). There are several sophisticated programmes that can be used in the analysis of qualitative data, but they should be tailored to the individual aims of the survey.
- Developing case studies. Case studies can be used to provide a narrative account of behaviour which may be a composite of several individual or group accounts. Thus the case may not represent an individual session but summarizes the significant aspects of several.
- Inductive analysis. This implies that main themes emerge from the data rather than being imposed by the objectives of the study. Even within a large mass of data, common themes may emerge that are not exactly replicated by all participants, but which nevertheless provide an important indication of the principal issues. Respondents may refer in various ways to the intimidating nature of some hotel receptions (e.g. impersonal nature, unfriendly receptionists, poor signage), and these represent different comments on a similar theme.

The distillation of a large amount of apparently featureless material into a form that provides guidelines for decision making takes a great deal of skill and patience. The time and resources that must be devoted to qualitative research if it is to provide meaningful results are often a deterrent for commercial organizations. However, complex hospitality products may benefit from investment in qualitative techniques. As competitive pressure increases and demand slows, greater insight is required into consumer motivations and buying decisions in order to retain market share. Carefully conducted qualitative research can provide the necessary clues to assist in effective decision making to meet this contemporary challenge.

CASE STUDY: MARKETING RESEARCH APPLICATIONS AT HILTON INTERNATIONAL

This case study demonstrates an application of some of the research techniques discussed in this chapter. It also acts as an introduction to some of the issues of communication and strategy discussed in Chapters 14 and 15.

In September 1987, Ladbroke announced that it was to purchase Hilton International. On completion of the deal Ladbroke became the operator of more than ninety Hilton hotels with in excess of 35,000 bedrooms in forty-four countries. Before the takeover Ladbroke had been the second biggest operator in the United Kingdom, but with an ill-defined brand presence. Hilton had the distinction of being one of the most established hotel brands in the world. The benefits of the takeover were apparent in the press release issued by Ladbroke shortly afterwards:

> The Hilton name is synonymous with hotels . . . Ladbroke's Hotels in the United Kingdom and Europe will benefit from rebranding. The Hilton name will enhance the revenue and capital values of Ladbroke's Hotels.

A further statement went on to say:

> Ladbroke also intends to create a new circuit of hotels in the United Kingdom . . . to be called Hilton Inns, rebranding a number of Ladbroke's existing hotels. The Hilton Inns concept will provide . . . an opportunity to expand . . . in major provincial and commercial centres.

When Ladbroke acquired Hilton, it brought into a conventional and conservative service culture. Massive attention had been paid to the traditional craft elements of the hotel keeping, but the brand was now being challenged by competent and vigorous international competition from the likes of Sheraton, Hyatt, Marriott and Intercontinental, as well as having to face the changing demands of increasingly sophisticated consumers worldwide.

Ladbroke wanted to establish as a priority what was the state of the Hilton brand. Very little research had been conducted by Hilton International for over a decade, so Ladbroke instigated a research programme in key markets – the USA, the UK, Germany, Australia and Japan – under the direction of NOP.

The quantitative study of international and frequent-staying business travellers provided reassuring results. There were, however, variations in the countries with a

Hilton presence. Hilton was particularly strong in the USA and Japan, while weaker in Germany and Australia. The strength of the Hilton name was apparent, with approximately one-third of travellers attributing their selection of Hilton to some aspect of the brand, such as familiarity or reputation. The research also revealed two weaknesses:

- The sub-brand names of Hilton International and Hilton National performed less well in terms of the awareness of the Hilton name.
- The Hilton International logo was the least well known of seven hotel logos tested.

Hilton was rated first in key brand image areas of prestige, business orientation and efficiency, but was also considered unfriendly and a little traditionalist, with a tinge of complacency.

A worldwide postal survey of employees was also conducted, the results of which included firm views on the following:

- Hilton International should become customer oriented.
- There should be an increase in staff training.
- The presence and personality of the brand should be re-asserted.

The new management of Hilton International responded to these findings and developed a customer-oriented communications programme. This featured a new corporate identity to re-establish the presence of the Hilton name, and included a new logo. The global 'Take me to the Hilton' campaign was also launched. The message was that Hilton is the natural and proper choice of seasoned, discerning travellers worldwide.

These changes were accompanied by major internal developments. The realization among senior management that meeting the guest's needs relies on the individual employee emphasized the prevailing management culture as the main barrier to the achievement of guest satisfaction objectives. This general issue is dealt with in more depth in Chapter 15, which considers the development of strategy in hospitality organizations.

In addition to relaunching the Hilton corporate brand, the company also developed new products targeted at specific markets:

- The Hilton Club has access to a detailed, centralized guest history database. This offers special services to frequent travellers in order to develop loyalty.
- Hilton Meeting 2000 is a business service aimed at the organizer of small meetings.

In early 1991, Hilton International repeated part of its 1988 research, managed by BLM in the Japanese, German and Australian markets (the UK was covered by the annual British Hotel Guest Survey, and the USA was not subject to the advertising campaign).

The results of this research indicated that, in all three markets, Hilton had broadly maintained its business and prestige orientation, while the new advertising and logo achieved consistently high recall levels. These trends were in contrast to the downward trend for its key international competitors.

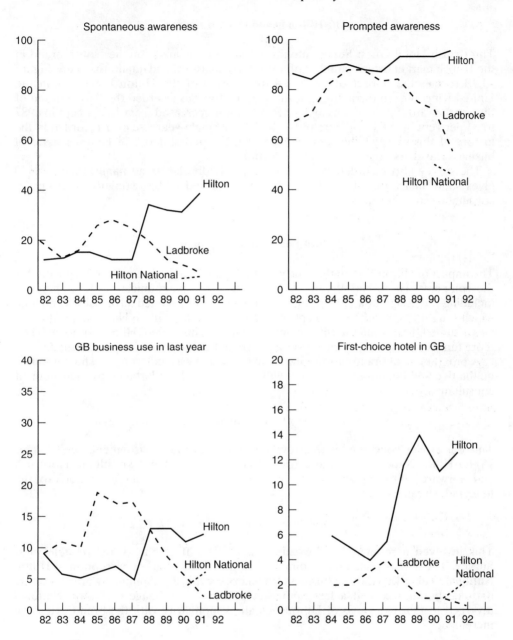

Figure 13.10 British business travellers

Source: British Hotel Guest Survey (NOP/BDRC).

The Hilton brand in a UK market

The British Hotel Guest Survey monitors the progress made by the Hilton brand in the British market using a number of attitudinal measures and qualitative data. Figure 13.10 reveals the impact of increased distribution of the Hilton brand within the United Kingdom. In the autumn of the 1988 Hilton was awarded the 'Hotel brand of the year' award. Spontaneous awareness of Hilton increased from 12 per cent in 1987 to 34 per cent in 1988, which remains the largest single-year rise ever recorded in the history of this survey. The same is true of the 6 per cent rise in Hilton's share of business travellers' first-choice hotel selection.

The survey also recorded the demise of the Ladbroke brand name. Figure 13.10 gives some indication of the time taken for a brand to be extinguished from the consumer's consciousness.

Positioning Hilton National

The impact of Hilton National on the generic Hilton brand was a matter of concern for the company. There had already been a number of communication developments, including the design of a Hilton National logo and an image-led advertising campaign which sought to extend the concept of Hilton style to the Hilton National product. It was assumed that, while the International brand was image led, Hilton National had a more functional aspect and the positioning would be product and experience led.

A programme of brand-positioning review research was undertaken. This combined qualitative and quantitative research with desk research undertaken by management consultants.

Desk research

This was largley concerned with a review of the operating environment (see Chapter 15) for Hilton National, and was carried out by the independent consultants Horwarth and Horwarth. It examined factors which included the macroeconomic outlook for the hotel industry in Britain.

Preliminary consumer market exercise

This involved a re-analysis of existing image data from the British Hotel Guest Survey. The data revealed that, compared to the overall market perception of Hilton National (Table 13.4), those business travellers specifically claiming awareness of the national brand accord it a less upmarket position. The image of Hilton National diverged further from that of Hilton overall as familiarity with the brand extension increased.

Qualitative research

This was carried out by Context Research among business travellers, leisure travellers, training managers and conference organizers. The results of the qualitative research emphasized that within the hotel marketplace the Hilton brand has a distinct image which is one of its key strengths, and which differentiates it from other hotels. The research also indicated that Hilton had failed to communicate the brand in a positive and motivating way to its target market.

Table 13.4   The imagery of Hilton in Great Britain

A hotel used by . . .	1987 Hilton	1991 Hilton
The Chairman of ICI	+54	+27
Marketing director	+30	+26
Marketing executive	0	+6
Junior manager	−23	−10
Sales representative	−26	−15
Conference attenders	−7	+1

A hotel used by . . .	Ladbroke	Hilton National
The Chairman of ICI	−6	+7
Marketing director	−1	+10
Marketing executive	+3	+3
Junior manager	+1	−2
Sales representative	+2	−5
Conference attenders	+6	+1

Note: Scores, either negative or positive, represent the extent of variation away from the expected score for each individual hotel group, which is derived from the average score for all hotel groups assessed.

Source: British Hotel Guest Survey (NOP/ARC 1987, NOP/BDRC 1991).

Quantitative research

To investigate the Hilton branding issue further, a quantitative survey was conducted with resident guests at nine hotels spread across three 'levels' of Hilton:

- secondary/provincial Internationals;
- good core brand nationals, as defined by management;
- weaker Nationals.

The results showed that the guest profiles in the first and second groups were broadly similar, indicating that these hotels appealed to much the same markets. The weaker Nationals attracted an older, more downmarket customer base, who were more likely to consider mid-market hotels as an alternative. Overall, the Hilton name was the third most important influence on hotel selection after location and price. The research also identified a series of specific delivery standards that consumers regarded as appropriate differentiators of the Hilton International and National products.

Review

The results of various types of market research have been applied to a complex and strategically important issue: the relaunch of a world brand and its extension to new, domestic markets. Further research has indicated the success of the strategies developed with regard to the perceptions of the consumer. However, the ultimate measure for any business must be the business performance of the brand. During its five years of ownership Ladbroke has not only built the brand with consumers, but also improved its operating margins.

- Occupancy rose by 6 per cent from 1986 to 1990, just prior to the Gulf War. Even during 1991 Hilton International achieved occupany higher than recorded in 1986.

- The average achieved room rate rose by 41 per cent between 1986 and 1991.
- Total revenues in the same period increased by 97 per cent.
- The gross operating profit margin widened by 28 per cent during the period, reflecting both cost economies and the improved leverage generated by the Hilton brand.
- Gross operating profit advanced by 147 per cent between 1986 and 1991.

The difficult decisions necessary to achieve these results have been supported by a research programme that has been carefully co-ordinated, and which has drawn upon new and existing markets and staff for its findings. While management skill, intuition and entrepreneurial flair have undoubtedly been the lodestar of Ladbroke's success, market research has made a significant contribution to a complex problem.

NOTES

1. Tarrant, C., 'Understanding the hotel guest: the role of research in the development of hotel marketing and segmentation programmes' anticipating and responding to change', *Proceedings of the ESOMAR Seminar*, Nicosia, Cyprus, May 1988. Dr Crispian Tarrant is Director of British Development Research and Consultancy, Sydney Mews, London.
2. Tarrant, C., and Breeze, G., 'Capitalizing on the brand: Ladbroke's development of the Hilton brand', Market Research Society Conference, Birmingham, February 1993.
3. Petty, R. E., and Cacioppo, J. T., *Attitudes and Persuasion: Classic and Contemporary Approaches*, Publishers WCB, 1981.
4. Allport, G. W., 'Attitudes', in Murchinson, C. (ed.), *Handbook of Social Psychology*, Vol. 2, Clark University Press, Worcester, MA, 1935.
5. Assael, H. *Consumer Behavior and Marketing Action*, 3rd edn, PWS, Kent, 1987.
6. Woodside, A. G., Clokey, J. D., and Combes, J. M., 'Similarities and differences of generalized brand attitudes, behavioural intentions and reported behaviour', in Schlinger, M. J. (ed.), *Advances in Consumer Behaviour Research*, Vol. 2, Association for Consumer Behaviour, Ann Arbor, MI, 1975.
7. Calver, S., *Tourism Volume and Income for the Borough of Poole*, unpublished report, Bournemouth University, 1984.
8. Calver, S., *Attitude Survey: Poole as a Tourist Destination*, unpublished report, Bournemouth University, 1986.
9. Wind, Y., 'Brand loyalty and vulnerability', in Woodside, A. G., Sheth, J. N., and Bennett, P. D. (eds), *Consumer and Industrial Buying Behaviour*, North-Holland, New York, 1977.
10. LaPiere, R., *Attitudes versus Actions*, Social Forces, New York, 1934.
11. Wicker, A. W., 'The relationship of verbal and overt behavioural responses to attitude objects', *Journal of Social Issues*, vol. 25, 1969, pp. 41–78.
12. Lambert, J., *Social Psychology*, Macmillan, New York, 1980.
13. Fishbein, M., and Ajzen, I., *Belief, Attitude, Intention and Behavior: An Introduction to the Theory and Research*, Addison & Wesley, Reading, MA, 1975.
14. Fishbein, M., and Ajzen, I., 'Acceptance yielding and impact: cognitive

processes in persuasion', in Petty, R. E., Ostrom, T. M., and Brock, T. C. (eds), *Cognitive Responses in Persuasion*, Erlbaum, Hillsdale, NJ, 1981.

15. Thurstone, L. L., 'Attitudes can be measured', *American Journal of Sociology*, vol. 33, 1928, pp. 529–44.
16. Likert, R. A., 'A technique for the measurement of attitudes' *Archives of Psychology*, vol. 140, 1932, pp. 1–55.
17. Osgood, C. E., Suci, G. J., and Tannenbaum, P. H., *The Measurement of Meaning*, University of Illinois Press, Urbana, IL, 1957.
18. Chisnall, P. M., *Marketing Research*, 4th edn, McGraw-Hill, New York, 1992.
19. Morton-Williams, J., 'Questionnaire design', in Worcester, R., and Downham, J. (eds), *Consumer Market Research Handbook*, Van Nostrand Reinhold, New York, 1978.
20. Kelly, G. A., *Psychology of Personal Constructs*, Vol. 1, W. W. Norton, New York, 1955.
21. Thomas, R., 'Marketing processes and the personal construct theory', *Advertising Quarterly*, no. 20, summer 1969, pp. 27–8.
22. Harmar-Brown, F., 'Constructing Kelly – the lure of classification', *Advertising Quarterly*, no. 18, winter 1968–9; reprinted in Chisnell, P. M. (ed.), *Marketing Research*, McGraw-Hill, New York, 1992.
23. Lunn, T., 'Consumer modelling' in Worcester, R., and Downham, J. (eds), *Consumer Market Research Handbook*, Van Nostrand Reinhold, New York, 1978.
24. Howard, J. A., and Sheth, J. N., *The Theory of Buyer Behavior*, John Wiley, New York, 1969.
25. Fishbein, M., 'A behavior theory approach to the relations between beliefs about an object and the attitude toward the object', in Fishbein, M., (ed.), *Readings in Attitude Theory and Measurement*, John Wiley, New York, 1967.
26. Azjen, I., and Fishbein, M., *Understanding Attitudes and Predicting Social Behaviour*, Prentice-Hall, Englewood Cliffs, NJ, 1980.
27. For instance, Richard, L., Oliver, R., and Berger, P. K., 'A path analysis of preventative health care decision models', *Journal of Consumer Research*, September 1979; Ryan, M. J., and Bonfield, E. H., 'The Fishbein extended model and consumer behaviour', *Journal of Consumer Research*, September 1975.
28. Market Research Society, 'Qualitative research – a summary of the concepts involved', Research and Development Sub-Committee on Qualitative Research, *Journal of Market Research Society*, vol. 21, no. 2 (April), 1979, pp. 36–45.
29. Sampson, P., 'An examination of exploratory research techniques', ESOMAR Congress, 1969.
30. McIver, Colin, *The Marketing Mirage: How to Make It a Reality*, Mandarin, London, 1990.
31. Cooper, Peter, 'Comparison between the UK and US: the qualitative dimension', *Journal of the Market Research Society*, vol. 31, no. 4 (October), 1989, pp. 43–6.
32. Oppenheim, A. N., *Questionnaire Design and Attitude Measurement*, Heinemann, London, 1969.
33. Anderson, James, C., 'The validity of Haire's shopping list projective technique', *Journal of Marketing Research*, vol. 15, no. 4. (November), 1978, pp. 649–56.
34. From 'Halcolm's laws of evaluation research à la Murphy', in Patton, M. Q., *Qualitative Evaluation and Research Methods*, 2nd edn, Sage Publications, London, 1990, p. 371.

FOURTEEN

Communication and the hospitality industry

Chapter 13 examined the role of attitudes in marketing decision making. Communication is the principal means by which marketers can influence attitude change and thereby secure and develop market opportunities; it also enables the hospitality operator to define clearly to the consumer the nature of the service which, because of its intangible nature, might otherwise be misconstrued. This chapter will examine some of the unique problems that confront the hospitality marketer when developing communication strategy.

THE NATURE OF HOSPITALITY COMMUNICATIONS

The complexity of many hospitality industry products and the subsequent problems of consumer interpretation emphasizes the importance of clear, unambiguous communications. Customers, shareholders, personnel, management, 'the community' and others all need information for different purposes, often from different parts of the organization, thereby creating potential for conflicting and potentially damaging situations. Studies have indicated the important role of communication in either confirming or confounding the consumer's perception of service quality.

Parasuraman, Berry and Zeithaml[1] suggest that consumers' perceptions are influenced by a series of five distinct gaps occurring in organizations. Figure 14.1 is a modified version of their model. The five gaps can be described as follows:

1. Differences between consumer expectations and management perceptions of consumer expectations.
2. Differences between management perceptions of consumer expectations and service quality specifications.
3. Differences between service quality specifications and the service actually delivered.

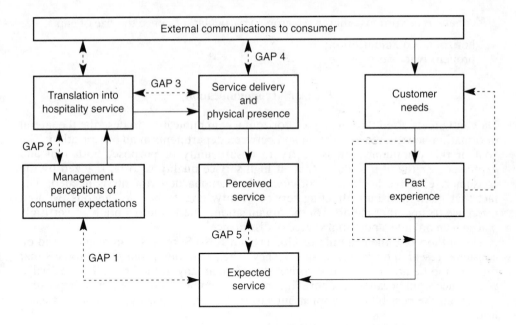

Figure 14.1   Conceptual model of service quality

Source: Adapted from Parasuraman, A., Berry, L. L., and Zeithaml, V. A., 'Service firms
need marketing skills', *Business Horizons*, 26 November 1983.

4.   Differences between service delivery and what is communicated about the
     service to the consumer.
5.   Differences between the perceived and expected service.

The last gap creates problems for strategy definition in hospitality operations because
it is difficult to evaluate and requires careful analysis via continuous research. Often
the consumer approaches the hospitality product with only a vague notion of the
priorities that direct him or her to that particular product. For instance, a visit to a
coffee shop may be because it is lunch-time, not because the customer is hungry or
even finds the food in a particular operation agreeable (although it is unlikely that it
will be disagreeable). Or the coffee shop may simply be a refuge from adverse
weather while waiting for an appointment or train.

   In these circumstances, customer expectations are likely to be minimal, and
communication in the form of design, merchandising and staff/management contacts
is crucial. On subsequent occasions, during more formal decision-making processes
(e.g. choosing the venue for a birthday party), the 'core' product (a cup of coffee) is
unlikely to have had a large impact, but the augmented product and the way in which
the operation has communicated itself may have an important influence.

   Because of the vagueness of consumer expectations regarding hospitality products
(or any other product where the motivation is not based on a degree of tangible need),
a clear statement in the form of advertising copy, a display stand, a news release or
internal décor is crucial in helping consumers to form an understanding of the nature
of the hospitality experience.

Zeithaml *et al.*[2] propose that two factors in particular influence the size of gap 4:

- horizontal communication;
- propensity to overpromise.

Horizontal communication

Daft and Steers[3] used the concept of horizontal communication to describe the lateral information flows that occur within and between departments in an organization. The goal of this communication is to try to ensure unity of purpose, both real and expressed. Zeithaml postulates that, if high service quality is to be realized by the consumer, effective horizontal communication among departments is needed. The fact that many decisions affecting service quality have to be spontaneous, without reference to any other member of the organization, whether horizontally or vertically placed, can provide a potential source of dissonance.

The authors cite the example of Holiday Inn's 'No Surprises' campaign, based on consumer research by an advertising agency. The promotion promised customers that there would be no unpleasant surprises during their stay in the hotel. The campaign was unsuccessful because, as operations managers pointed out, it is almost impossible to rule out the possibility of unpleasant surprises in an organization as complex as an hotel.

Sheraton has introduced the concept of 'empowerment' in its advertising, which tacitly accepts that things can go wrong (not necessarily in the hotel), but encourages the staff at all levels to use their own initiative in solving problems.

Similar problems of horizontal communication may occur in the sales function. In order to close a sale, unrealistic promises may be made about the size and capacity of conference rooms, for instance, which the client cannot readily check until the event actually takes place and the problems arise.

Another problem that arises with hospitality-type service organizations is associated with growth and expansion. An individual unit of any size under the control of a particular manager or owner/manager may be imbued with good practice in service delivery. However, success that leads to expansion, either at a given unit or by adding additional units, increases the problem of control. Ultimately, customers may become frustrated when service quality is not consistent throughout the different units of a company. This problem has tested various organizations as they have expanded from small, owner-managed units to larger, multinational companies.

Propensity to overpromise

Another factor that can influence the size of a gap between service delivery and external communications is the extent to which an organization feels pressured to acquire new business and to meet or beat the competition in their promotional claims.

As hospitality markets have become more saturated worldwide and demand in many countries has diminished, hospitality companies have increased their expenditure on above- and below-the-line promotion. Perhaps in these circumstances there is a greater likelihood that companies will feel tempted to make unsubstantiated claims for their products, either to hold on to existing market share or to improve the situation, relying to some extent upon the customer's difficulty in articulating his or her precise requirements. Similarly, if a principal competitor is making exaggerated claims for its product, it may be difficult to resist the temptation to follow suit.

COMMUNICATION AND THE CONSUMER

Consumers do not represent a homogeneous group. In addition to the various differences represented across market segments, there are also subcategories which can reflect the communication process. For instance, various studies have shown that certain roles are adopted by family members. These may be classified as follows:

- *Initiator* – the person who first suggests, or has the idea of purchasing, a product. This person may also have the greatest expertise in acquiring the evaluating information from different sources.
- *Influencer* – the person who explicitly or implicitly carries some influence either in determining the criteria for the decision-making process or in making the final decision.
- *Decider* – the person who ultimately determines any part, or the whole, of the buying decision.
- *Purchaser* – the person who physically makes the transaction and may have some discretion as to where the purchase is made.
- *User* – the person who eventually consumes the product. This may be an individual or the whole family.

Each family unit is characterized by differences of approach to decision making, but buying patterns for most product groups are consistent at given points in time. Changes in demographics, usage patterns, education and level of affluence influence these general patterns in the long term. These changes emphasize the need for continuous monitoring and research (as with any user group) in order to develop an appropriate combination of images and copy in advertising and below-the-line promotions.

Webster and Wind[4] identify five similar roles for organizational buyers, but the interaction between these roles and the nature of organizational buying differentiate it from consumer purchasing and present a different set of issues for the hospitality provider.

- Users – organizational members who initiate the buying process.
- Influencers – those who indirectly or directly influence the buying decision.
- Buyers – those who have formal authority for selecting the supplier and arranging the terms of purchase.
- Deciders – those who influence the final selection of suppliers.
- Gatekeepers – those who control the information flow to decision-makers.

Communication may need to be formulated and directed according to the nature of the organization. For instance, selling hotel rooms to a major airline may require approaches to the personnel director, the financial director and the operations director, all of whom may have different but probably complementary criteria for choosing a particular hotel company for its crew.

Reference has been made to the fact that organizational buying behaviour may be more rational and objective than individual buying behaviour, and therefore not as susceptible to persuasive communication. This proposition was made as long ago as 1924 when Paul Converse[5] suggested that industrial buyers tend to be experts and buy on the basis of objective tests. Later studies indicated that this thoroughly rational approach to buying does not necessarily prevail. Wilson[6] found that only 30 per cent of managers conformed to a rational decision style where monetary value is maximized in the purchase. Some 70 per cent of the sample of Canadian industrial purchasers did not maximize value, primarily because of the greater risk associated with the purchase. This issue is of considerable importance to the hospitality operator. There is a highly perceived risk associated with most services due to the complexity and variability of the product, causing an even greater dependence on subjective factors, such as reputation and image, that are open to modification by effective communication.

Despite some similarities between organizational buyer behaviour and consumer behaviour, there are considerable differences in relation to the communication process. These may be summarized as follows:

- A group decision process often characterizes organizational buying. In deciding the venue for a conference, for example, the finance director, the operational managers and the personnel department may be involved. This decision-making group is termed the 'buying centre' by Webster and Wind.[7] In organizational buying behaviour, the group is the most frequently used unit of analysis.
- Technical complexity is frequently an issue in organizational buying. The sale of rooms for air crews involves the consideration of scheduling, stay-overs and the logistics of having crews on standby in various parts of the world. It is rare that the individual consumer has to deal with this level of complexity.
- Interdependence between buyer and seller will probably be greater in organizational buying. This interdependence emphasizes the role of personal selling.
- The post-purchase process is likely to be of greater importance because of the need to ensure the continuation of an existing contract and the possibility of further sales, either of the same product, such as rooms, or of additional products, such as food and beverages.
- The organizational buyer is very closely involved in the design of the service product. For instance, special menu requirements are required for air crews for reasons of safety, nationality, religion and cost.

These two target markets, families and organizations, demonstrate some of the problems of determining appropriate communication policy for hospitality operations. There are many other target groups each characterized by a number of segmentation variables, including usage, frequency of purchase, size and quantity of purchase, and socioeconomic, lifestyle and behavioural factors.

COMMUNICATION THEORY

Schiffman and Kanuk[8] refer to two types of consumer communication: interpersonal communications and impersonal or mass communications.

Interpersonal communication

Interpersonal communication occurs on a personal level between two or more people and forms an essential component of the consumer's experience of the hospitality product – on both a formal and an informal level. The customer of any service organization participates in the manufacture of the final 'product'. Thus, a guest arriving at a hotel may explain a preference for a room with a view, away from the kitchens, on a floor below the fifth floor and so on. The receptionist is therefore charged with the task of 'customizing' the hotel's basic components to suit the needs of the consumer.

This type of communication is relatively formal and allows the receptionist, in this case, to charge for 'value-added' items (for instance, 'the only room available with a view is a business person's suite'). However, it also leaves this member of staff considerable scope in terms of how he or she communicates, if at all. One of the principal problems of large unit management is how you motivate operational staff to utilize the selling opportunity provided by interpersonal communication.

The situation is more problematic with informal communications. A hotel guest asking a member of staff for directions can influence the guest's perception of the entire company. This dependence on interpersonal communications makes the hospitality industry unique because, by definition hospitality tends to be about personal interaction rather than corporate persuasion. The nature of this relationship provides specific opportunities. If staff can be trained, motivated and provided with sufficient incentives, they can certainly justify such investment many times over through improved volume and average spend.

Other types of interpersonal, informal communication are equally important for hospitality operations. Word-of-mouth communication between individuals is often cited as one of the most important forms of communication because it is impartial, unsponsored and often used to justify low-involvement purchases. The relatively high personal risk involved in the purchase of a hospitality product, its relative intangibility and the absence of pre-trial means that the consumer is likely to investigate the views of 'respected others' or opinion leaders before they patronize or continue to patronize an operation. If, for example, a potential restaurant customer has not visited a particular operation for some weeks, he or she may seek reassurance that it is still maintaining the same standards. Word of mouth can, of course, be influenced by skilful public relations and other below-the-line methods of communications which are discussed in later sections.

Formal interpersonal communications are of the type that takes place between a company salesperson and a customer, but they can include direct mail and telephone selling too. This type of formal communication enables the company to make a comprehensive proposition to a prospective customer and to receive feedback which provides valuable intelligence for future communications and developing marketing strategy.

Impersonal communication

Communication directed at target markets, using such methods as advertising, is referred to as impersonal communication. A company's marketing communications are intended to induce purchase, create a positive attitude towards the product and imbue the product with meaning. The use of impersonal techniques such as advertising, public relations, design, sales promotion, merchandising, and of interpersonal methods such as personal selling, requires a co-ordinated strategy to achieve the maximum effect on the market. Each of these components of the communication mix is discussed below, but it is important to note at this stage that the hospitality industry has particular requirements of impersonal communication.

The issues of intangibility, pre-trial and high risk were discussed previously, and impersonal communications play an important role in resolving some of the problems caused by these factors. Advertising and promotion can provide tangible evidence of the unseen hospitality operation, including the physical dimensions, location and image.

The hospitality industry is fortunate in being able to obtain effective feedback from the marketplace on the value of impersonal communications. The customer is usually amenable to answering questions or even attending small-group interviews regarding the effectiveness of different promotional campaigns. More difficult, perhaps, are those members of the target market who do not become customers, but whose opinion is invaluable for developing future strategy.

Barriers to communication

These can occur at any stage in the communication process.

Sender

Exceptional care must be taken at souce to ensure that the sender has a clear idea of the intention of the message, in turn linked to objective appraisal of strategy and short-term objectives. The message generated by the sender or the appointed agent should identify quite clearly with a particular aspect of the operation. Many promotional messages fail because they try to convey too much information to the target group, including detailed specifications of the unit's room sizes, number of rooms, etc., until the message is lost in what may appear like estate agents' details of the property.

Message

The sender decides what to communicate and arranges a suitable combination of words, images, and perhaps personalities and music, using either symbolism or 'fact' to reinforce the point. The translation of a product concept into a form that can be delivered to a target audience is known as 'encoding'. This must be done carefully to avoid sending the wrong message. The notorious 'Strand' advertisement in the 1960s makes the point quite dramatically. The main character in a television advertisement for this particular brand of cigarettes was portrayed on a dark and rainy night under a street lamp taking solace from the brand. The message was 'You're never alone with a Strand'. The target market negatively associated the brand with loneliness and the advertisement had to be withdrawn.

Medium

The medium used can influence the interpretation of the message by the receiver. Some newspapers may give a sense of *gravitas* to the advertising that they contain. A reader may be more prone to accept the claims made in advertising for hotel business facilities when they are conveyed in the 'quality' press as opposed to the tabloids.

Receiver

Individuals are bombarded with a considerable amount of information every day, and, in order to cope, they have to be selective about the issues that they remember and evaluate. Balance theory postulates that individuals seek information that is consistent with their needs, interests and attitudes, and avoid information that is not.[9] The matter is complicated by the fact that consumers are not always aware of their motivations for buying.

Psychological 'noise' will also impair the target market's reception of the message. Consumers may not remember the sponsor of a particular advertisement and may buy a competitive product instead. Consumer attitudes or the attitudes of group members may also influence interpretation.

Some authors[10] have made a distinction between cognitive and passive learning and their role in interpreting communications. Cognitive learning is usually linked to high-involvement goods and a purposeful multistage decision-making process that draws on a range of information sources, including advertising and sales literature. The information derived from these sources will be augmented by existing knowledge and other information sources that assist the consumer in the decision-making process.

For low-involvement goods the information search is generally less purposeful, and communications will be effective only if they attract attention. Even then the message may not be retained or remembered for sufficient time to have an impact. Bettman[11] calls this 'incidental learning'.

The incidental learning effect was noted in research carried out to assess the impact of promotions on the target audience for a regional arts centre.[12] Various target groups were examined – theatre-goers, pop and rock concert-goers, cinema-goers and others – to assess the impact of different forms of promotion. It was evident that an 'incremental' effect was part of the process where potential customers would read newspaper advertisements and would hold the information in short-term memory. They would perhaps see a poster or read a review, and then when the opportunity arose for a night out, although they were unable to remember the detail, they could recall 'something interesting showing that week'. This often led to a prompt from a

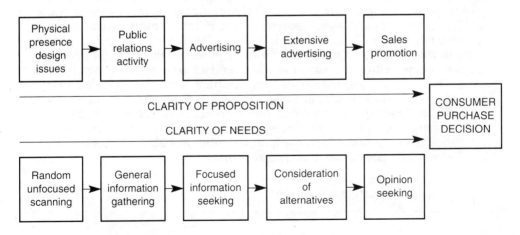

Figure 14.2 Incremental communication process and formation of consumer needs

friend or colleague who could provide support detail, thereby clarifying information discarded from short-term memory. It was apparent from quantitative methods used that, when respondents' were asked questions such as 'Where did you hear of this performance?', they generally cited 'word of mouth' as the key informer source. Depth interviews reveal the full extent of the information-gathering process, and provide evidence of passive or 'incidental' learning in support of the decision process.

DEVELOPING A COMMUNICATION PLAN

There are essentially five steps in developing a comprehensive communication plan:

1. Identify the target market and audience.
2. Determine the communication objectives in line with the overall marketing strategy.
3. Decide the appropriate media channels and budgets.
4. Decide on the promotional mix.
5. Evaluate and audit the communication plan.

Corporate communication of Hilton International

For international hotel companies the single most important barrier is language. Hilton tracks fifty nationality groups in its hotels worldwide. Nationalities are then identified which have English as a second language or business language. The type of communication has to be planned very carefully: 60 per cent of the German business market speak English, but if the company communicates only in English this may be perceived negatively by the market. However, communicating in the national language is not straightforward either. When the 'Take me to the Hilton' campaign was translated into Canadian French, it read, 'Lead me to the Hilton', a more prosaic style than that used in France: 'Now is the time for Hilton'.

In the majority of markets credibility is not an issue. Most people are familiar with advertising messages and interpret them successfully. It depends upon the level of involvement and the attitudes that individuals have already established towards the brand. It is extremely difficult, bearing in mind the in-built sophistication of most markets, to change opinions with advertising alone, and the cost of a concerted communication campaign would probably be prohibitive. There is a perception in most markets that:

- Hilton is prestigious and efficient;
- Hyatt is stylish and luxurious.

Identifying the target market and audience

The target market and audience is defined as part of a thorough analysis of the company's present position in the marketplace. A marketing audit is used to identify the issues in the internal and external environment, and the relative strengths and weaknesses of the company with regard to dealing with these issues. The purpose of the audit is to establish a set of marketing objectives which are compatible with the overall corporate objectives and strategies that direct the subsequent development of a communication plan.

Communication objectives

McDonald[13] simplifies the types of corporate objective and strategy as follows.

Corporate objectives

- Desired level of profitability?

Corporate strategies

- Which products and which markets?
- What kind of facilities (production and distribution)?
- Size and character of the staff/labour force (personnel)?
- Funding (finance)?
- Other corporate strategies, such as social responsibility, corporate image, stock market image, and employee image.

Objectives in each of these and other areas of corporate affairs will provide the basis of the communication plan, which will be supported by data from the marketing information system.

Most UK hotel companies in the 1980s represented a good equity investment because of the healthy demand for their core products and the dramatic rise in property prices. The more austere trading environment of the 1990s has reduced confidence in the hotel sector as demand for rooms and property prices have dropped. To a certain extent, advertising objectives are limited to maintaining market share, and a greater investment is necessary in public relations to reinforce flagging investors who are tempted to invest in more lucrative sectors, and nervous bankers who are prone to calling in loans from ailing companies. Only a careful analysis of the trading environment and a sensitive regard for the environmental factors influencing the firm can ensure an appropriate basis for framing communication strategy.

Target markets at Hilton International

For large, branded international hotel companies, there are four broad target markets that determine the approach to developing a communication policy. These are shown in the diagram.

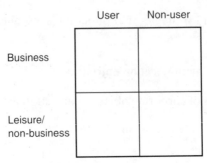

	User	Non-user
Business		
Leisure/ non-business		

Broad consumer segments for a branded international chain hotel company

In order to assess the use of conventional broad-based media like the press, hotel companies can obtain syndicated readership surveys that include a great deal of information on buyer behaviour, e.g.:

- travel habits;
- hotel usage;
- extent of usage;
- individual brand usage.

Pan European Study 5 (PES 5) represents the type of syndicated research used by hotel companies like Hilton International. PES 5 is commissioned by a syndicate of major international publications, such as *Time* and *Newsweek*, which have an audience that is predominantly business oriented. PES 5 can be used to select media for defined target groups and determine the cost and coverage of those media. This type of syndicated research can be supplemented with omnibus and random survey data.

It is possible to correlate significant variables, such as the number of trips against readership profiles, in order to focus specific promotions more precisely. It is now possible to get this type of information for most world markets: Europe, the United Kingdom, the Americas and the Far East. Advertising agencies can also provide data and research regarding the media habits of the target market.

Existing customers

The best media lie within the hotel itself: the service efficiency of hotel staff, the presentation of the hotel, and its visual and affective impact. The success of the brand makes it difficult to separate the impact of promotions and the impact of the service arrangements. For most of the large hotel operators, the largest source of business is going to be the company's own past users.

Defined groups of non-users

There is very little syndicated research that deals with completely novel markets like Hyatt's, Club Hyatt and Rock Hyatt, which are aimed at teenagers and young adults. Information must be interpreted from research published either by government agencies or by private research organizations.

Deciding appropriate media channels and budgets

The steps described here for developing the communication plan are not sequential. It may be that the objectives suggest a particular promotional mix, as in the previous example, which emphasizes below-the-line expenditure almost to the exclusion of media-based advertising. Certainly for smaller hospitality organizations, media planning is not a key issue, although as part of a consortium or as a unit it may be necessary for a small organization to co-ordinate promotional activities. Larger

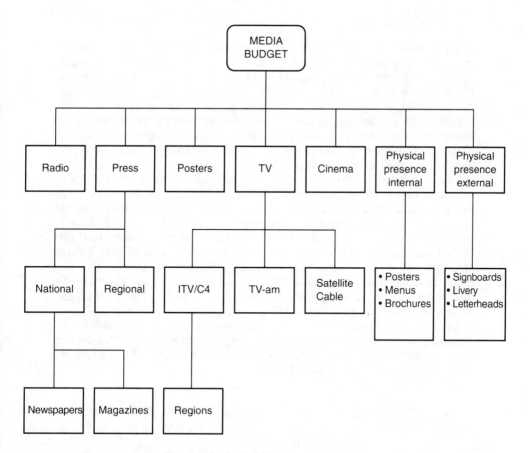

Figure 14.3   Budget allocation alternatives

organizations certainly have to plan their use of media channels to ensure that any promotions they execute are co-ordinated with other aspects of marketing and communication policy, and to take account of traditional seasonal fluctuations in demand as well as some of the long lead times for buying media space.

If a need exists to develop a media strategy, this may be directed in the first instance by the identified target market. For instance, large international hotels are competing in a virtually static business sector worldwide, and so planners might use appropriate media which provide access to particular subgroups of the business market. There may be creative reasons for using a particular medium, such as the need for urgency. Dynamism may be conveyed by using television in an effective way. The use of colour is particularly effective, but it is often prohibitively expensive except in long-running promotions like hotel brochures. Competitive promotions will also influence communication decisions. The role of distributors, such as travel agents, will be important. Effective advertising in certain media may persuade them to sell a given hotel company or travel package before others if they believe it will stimulate consumer demand.

Marketing communication budgeting at Hilton International

Communications are funded from rooms division revenues. There is a partial correlation between the number of hotel rooms that a hotel company offers and its expenditure on forms of communication. Expenditure tends to be based upon ability to pay rather than on market share, objectives or an attempt to match competing promotions. This type of approach is in contrast to other product groups that depend on high promotional costs to support the brand and high margins. The hotel business rarely enjoys high margins and yet it has to manage relatively high fixed costs.

For instance, Hilton International has eight hotels in Germany, whereas its principal competitor has forty hotels and five times the level of promotional expenditure. In most markets, the national population represents the biggest market for hotel accommodation, so in Germany, despite a relatively small communication budget, Hilton achieves its target occupancies. Some of this is due to the strength of the brand, but in most product groups there are established brands that have been in existence for at least twenty years; some of them are forty years old. It is difficult to assess the influence of communication (or lack of it) in these circumstances.

Some campaigns, like the 'Take me to the Hilton' campaign, are costed and budgets set accordingly. These campaigns, with specific target markets and specific offers, are usually successful. However, budgets for general awareness are rarely well spent.

Deciding the promotional mix

The components of the promotional mix for hospitality operations – advertising, public relations, design, merchandising, sales promotion, direct mail and personal selling – are determined by tactical and strategic issues relating to the marketplace and the product. The optimum combination will also be constrained by available resources, either staff or revenue. Within the hospitality industry, promotional budgets vary considerably and companies are constantly seeking ways of developing most cost-effective programmes. For instance, developing a comprehensive database will enable companies to target clients more precisely with a specific offer, reducing dependence on more general, above-the-line methods.

The various promotional tools should not be viewed in isolation from one another. They provide the components of what should be a unified approach to the market, complementing each other with a slightly different set of communication objectives, as indicated in Figure 14.4. In addition to these elements, there are long-term aids for the sales team, and similarly an event in a hotel unit that provides an opportunity for publicity must be handled in the short term by the public relations department or press office. Advertising can make a direct appeal, providing immediate advantages.

The state of the market will influence the application of these promotional tools. During the 1980s demand for hotel accommodation was buoyant in and advertising could be used to communicate directly with specific market segments. Advertising can

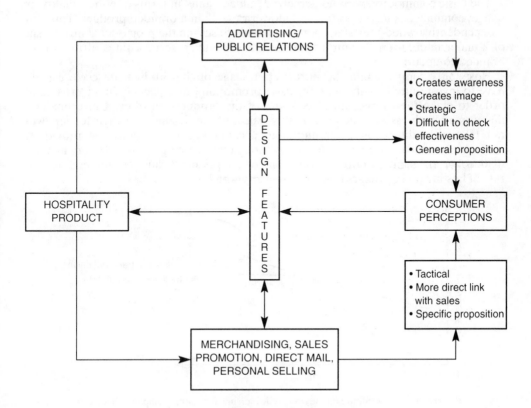

Figure 14.4 Hospitality communication mix

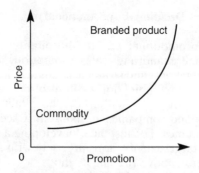

Figure 14.5   Relationship between promotion and price in product branding

still be used for this purpose in the 1990s, but the reluctance of the market means that its principal role is more likely to be to create or maintain awareness, in order that more specific sales promotion and merchandising techniques can be used – for instance, to emphasize value for money.

The nature of the product and its position in the product life cycle will also influence the use and combination of promotional tools. Figure 14.5 illustrates the relationship that exists between price, a highly branded product and a commodity product.

The basic commodity, with no perceived 'added value' in terms of either quality or image, commands a disproportionately lower price than a branded product. Thus, an independently owned four-star operation unable to sustain the promotional investment of a major international chain may not achieve the average rack rates of its heavily branded competitor.

Hospitality companies in the introduction stage of the product life cycle usually have to invest quite heavily in all forms of promotion but especially in advertising in order to make their target markets aware of the products on offer. Unfortunately, many small businesses economize on this aspect of the business, or their lenders will not take expenditure on promotion into account because it does not provide a realizable asset like land and buildings. Although there are other contributory factors, inadequate investment in promotion is one of the principal causes of the high failure rate of hospitality businesses in the early years of trading.

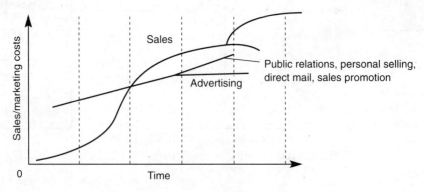

Figurre 14.6   Expenditure on the communication mix for mature companies in mature markets

More mature companies, having established themselves in the marketplace and in the purchasing schedule of the customer, may be able to reduce their investment on advertising. This will depend upon the nature of competitive activity in their markets and the level of investment in other forms of promotion. Investment in public relations and personal selling may be more appropriate for mature products because they can be targeted on narrower market segments. Figure 14.6 shows expenditure on the communication mix for mature companies in mature markets.

Each of the components of the marketing mix has its own unique characteristics which should be considered when developing the overall strategy.

The promotional mix at Hilton International

There is no fixed policy on how the communication budget is divided between below- and above-the-line promotion. Some elements of the communication mix like public relations will always be a fixed proportion of the budget for paid media.

The hospitality industry is, on the whole, not committed to consistent levels of marketing expenditure. The nature of the business tends to make expenditure episodic and dependent upon the particular project involved. Generally, across the industry over the past few years there have been significant increases in expenditure on paid media among major hotel companies. A lot of this increase in communication activity has been due to changes of ownership (Hilton, Holiday Inn) or corporate relaunches (Hyatt, Sheraton).

The nature of the promotional mix is determined in part by the existing attitudes of markets and target markets worldwide. In most developed countries, the proportion of the population that have experience of star-rated hotels for business purposes is approximately 3–4 per cent; in the United States, possibly as much as 6 per cent. A much higher proportion have experience through leisure use. Given the small penetration of the market worldwide, broad-based media such as television advertising are not appropriate.

Franchised hotel operations and those hotel companies with a high geographical concentration, such as Forte, can use broad-based media effectively. The physical presence of these hotels means that some reinforcement will take place through their signage and promotion – their units are their shop window.

If Forte were to open another twenty hotels in the United Kingdom, the company would not have to increase its promotional spend significantly. However, if Hilton opened a further twenty hotels worldwide, there would have to be a disproportionate increase in expenditure. The pattern of development and spread of the units is therefore important in determining the mix.

Sales promotion and merchandising tend to operate within a smaller region or country, and are geared to a local market. For instance, the 'Frequent Flyer' programme has several thousand members in Europe – a small number perhaps, but it makes sense to target this group with specific promotional campaigns because it represents a more precise target market.

Chain hotel brands have a disproportionate level of awareness that does not relate to a given population's experience of the products. Everybody knows of Hilton, but there is a very weak correlation between awareness and usage. It is therefore pointless developing campaigns to *increase* awareness; it is more important to make specific offers to specific target markets, and advertising can be used to do that.

An independent luxury hotel like the Lanesborough in London's West End depends entirely upon its ability to communicate with the marketplace alone or through agents. Every customer who stays in that hotel will have received information from Lanesborough's representatives.

Evaluating and auditing the communication plan

The evaluation of communication strategy is often under-resourced owing to the difficulty of establishing a direct link between many of the long-term promotional techniques, such as advertising and public relations, and strategic changes, such as increased market share or altered consumer buying patterns. Even an apparent improvement in sales following a promotional campaign may be due to other factors such as competitive activity. One of the reasons for companies employing direct mail or targeted sales promotion is the relative ease with which a correlation can be made between expenditure in these areas and market changes.

The implementation of continuous research programmes is essential in monitoring the success of communication plans. Communication research is broadly represented by communication/effect and sales/effect research. The former seeks to determine whether a particular communication is effective: for instance, whether it commands attention and can be recalled by the target audience. Sales/effect research attempts to isolate the likely effect on sales of particular communications, using a range of techniques that involve historical data[14] or experimental design[15].

ADVERTISING

Advertising has various applications, including the long-term promotion of corporate image, brand advertising and classified advertising, which predominantly involves communicating information about a product or service.

The management of advertising varies between organizations, but one of the first decisions involves the extent to which outside agencies should be used for the development of advertising. There are several options available to the hospitality operator, which may use a full-service advertising agency, a design workshop for the artwork or a good printing company with the artwork developed in-house.

A full-service agency will normally have the following departments that can assist the company's marketing departments:

- client accounts;

- media planning and research;
- creative copywriting and artwork;
- marketing consulting and research;
- production, artwork and media production.

The cost of a full service agency tends to put this sort of advertising beyond the budgets of smaller businesses.

A design workshop will usually deal with the creative aspects of the advertisement, such as artwork, message development and layout. But unlike an advertising agency, which earns most of its revenue from commission derived from the media, designers charge a fee for work completed and do not usually have an arrangement with the media. Professional designers, often employed by large printing companies, can provide an invaluable service to small operators with limited budgets which do not require the services of the larger agencies, but which need to make an impact through the press or other means.

Advertising objectives

As we have seen, advertising is just one component of the promotional mix, and advertising objectives should therefore be developed as part of the overall communication and marketing plan. This should take into account the strategic aims of the business, target markets, competitive activity, budgets and other issues.

The achievements of advertising and the manner in which advertising works also influence advertising objectives. Generally, advertising creates awareness in the long term which can be used to develop consumer purchasing behaviour. However, there have been various attempts to explain how this process actually works and the likely outcomes.

Earlier models suggest a 'hierarchy of effect'[16] which implies that consumers proceed through a series of psychological steps following exposure to advertising:

Awareness – Comprehension – Conviction – Action

Several theorists[17] and advertising practitioners have criticized these models because they cannot be tested empirically and the process is therefore questionable. Assael[18] suggests four hierarchies, which typify current attempts to explain the effects of advertising:

Complex buying behaviour – Learn – Feel – Do
Dissonance-reducing buying behaviour – Do – Learn – Feel
Variety-seeking behaviour – Learn – Do – Feel
Inertia – Learn – Do

Complex buying behaviour involves a considered and purposeful approach to the purchasing process, whereas dissonance-reducing behaviour is a means by which the consumer reduces the stress during the purchase of a product. Where experience of a hotel is not matched by expectation, for instance, dissonance will be reduced by re-interpreting beliefs or perhaps seeking reassurance from other guests about the experience. Both complex buying behaviour and dissonance-reducing behaviour may be regarded as high-involvement purchasing behaviour where information is actively sought by the consumer. Highly involved consumers will consider carefully all available sources of information and be attentive and retentive regarding advertisements. They will also tend to process information in order to make it 'fit' existing patterns of beliefs and avoid cognitive dissonance. Hence, effective advertising material makes an affective appeal rather than providing factual material which is open to wider interpretation.

Variety-seeking behaviour tends to apply to low-cost, low-risk items where the consumer can afford to experiment among a wide range of alternatives. This type of behaviour may apply to the purchase of fast-food items, but even these probably have a higher perceived risk and greater consumer involvement than most products that would be traditionally regarded in this category: for instance, items of confectionery, snacks and similar low-cost goods. Inertia may occur where the consumer perceives few differences between brands and has an extremely low involvement with the product. In fact both of these categories will be typified by low-involvement decision making, where the consumer tends to be a passive information-gatherer, often retaining 'unprocessed' information even though it is not compatible with beliefs. The low-involvement consumer needs to be exposed to frequently repeated advertising messages in order to establish levels of awareness in the medium to long term. The nature of low-involvement decision making has implications for advertising, some of which are described below:

- Frequently repeated key words or images should be used rather than detailed, infrequent information.
- High-involvement media like the press should be avoided; low-involvement media such as television are more appropriate.
- Actual product benefits may not be notably different from those on offer from other competitors, but advertising can emphasize intangibles such as fashion or image which may differentiate the product.
- The principal objective in advertising low-involvement goods is to encourage the consumer to include the product in his or her psychological schedule of possible brand purchases.

The formulation of advertising objectives is therefore dependent upon the complexity of the product and the extent to which the consumer might engage in a cognitive, decision-making process. Advertising objectives are usually stated in fairly simple terms that alow for some degree of measurement.

Exposure objectives relate to the reach (the total number of the target audience exposed to the advertisement and frequency (the average number of times a member of a target audience is exposed to the advertisement).

Awareness objectives are measured by the consumer's ability to recall advertising content in either structured interviews or random surveys.

Comprehension objectives are measured by the consumer's ability to translate the advertising content into everyday language.

Various guidelines have been established for advertising, due to its particular characteristics. George and Berry[19] recommend the following guidelines.

1. **Use clear, unambiguous messages**. Many advertisements for hospitality operations, especially press advertisements, contain too much information. These reflect the owner/manager's understandable interest in the specifications of the property rather than customer attitudes.

The complex nature of most hospitality operations means that advertisers must be selective in preparing the copy. A simple message dealing with one or two aspects of the operation (speedy check-in/check-out, or room service) supported by photographs or pictures will be more effective than an advertisement overcrowded with information. One of the most effective recent press advertisements for a large international hotel chain consisted of a red rose on a black background. The only text on a full-page advertisement was the name of the company in small type with a contact telephone number. This advertisement resulted in a record number of enquiries, and yet its appeal was entirely due to the message implied by the symbolism of the rose, rather than to any formal appeal or representation of the hotel to the target market.

2. **Emphasise benefits not technical details of service.** The rose in the previous example symbolized romance, and perhaps a degree of opulence, with no indication of how these might be reflected in the product portfolio of the company. Yet the target market appeared willing to accept the message.

Potential customers choosing a resort hotel for a short break are interested in comfort and relaxation and/or excitement; they are not especially interested in the number of items on the menu or even the number of bedrooms.

3. **Only promise what can be delivered.** Because of the high perceived risk associated with any service, discrepancies between the advertisement and experience will not be rationalized by the consumer as easily as a similar situation arising with a tangible consumer product. For instance, if there is a problem with a washing machine, the owner can rationalize the experience (though not reduce the frustration) with a fuller understanding of the technical reasons for failure, which may not affect that person's propensity to purchase another machine or the same make. The reasons for double booking, impolite staff and poor restaurant service may not be quite so well understood or rationalized.

A negative and discordant experience with a service product will also be more damaging because of the importance of recommendations among potential customers as a source of business. The advice often given to hospitality and other services is to advertise an aspect of the business that can be delivered consistently well, and around which a reputation can be built.

4. **Advertise to employees.** A customer's entire perception of a hospitality operation may be based on his or her interaction with the staff, and the inseparability of service-provider and service product can have important implications. Staff motivation and the provision of incentives are essential aspects of hospitality management, and advertising to personnel can help in this respect. During the 1970s a study in labour turnover within a large UK hotel company coincided with that company's first major television advertising campaign. There was a noticeable drop in turnover during the first few weeks of the campaign. Unfortunately, further analysis of this phenomenon was not within the brief of the study, but the hypothesis that the advertising campaign caused staff to identify more closely with the company, and perhaps gave them a sense of direction, is a tantalizing possibility.

5. **Obtain and maintain customer co-operation in the service production process.** The customers of any hospitality organization are also a composite part of the product and can provide an essential ingredient in the 'atmosphere' of the operation. Advertising can provide clues to the customer regarding his or her role in the production process – whether it is chic sophistication, or energetic participation. The images and message conveyed in the advertisement are an essential guide to the required behaviour of the guest.

6. **Build on word-of-mouth promotion.** Word-of-mouth promotion is an important feature of hospitality operations because of the lack of opportunity for pre-trial and the 'fuzzy' image that is often received by customers. Advertising can assist the

process through close association with public relations features, drawing upon press articles for material and supporting popular (positive) perceptions of the product. Some companies have even used negative material. One of the car rental agencies was judged to be second to the market leader and used the fact to emphasize to customers that they were guaranteed better service because as the second-best car agency it had to try harder.

7. **Provide tangible clues to give the intangible product a concrete dimension.** Notable aspects of the operation can be described or displayed to provide the consumer with clues as to likely outcomes or buying the product. Research is required, however, to establish customer priorities in choosing a particular operation as these may differ from the priorities perceived by management.

8. **Develop continuity in advertising.** Due to the long-term nature of a great deal of advertising and the infrequent purchase of many hospitality products, advertising should be developed in themes to run over a long period of time.

9. **Remove post-purchase anxiety.** Problems relating to inconsistent quality standards (or dissonance) are a particular problem for hospitality operations. Advertising can reduce post-purchase anxiety by stressing positive aspects of the product which consumers can use to rationalize and mitigate their experience.

Media planning

In determining an advertising strategy, the cost and suitability of the various media types should also be considered. The media fall into the following categories:

- Print media: local newspapers, national newspapers, consumer publications, directories/guides, business and professional publications.
- Broadcast media: regional television, national television, independent radio.
- Other media: transport, posters, cinema.

In judging the suitability of the media to achieve the identified objectives, an advertiser will have to consider:

- the market to be reached;
- the nature of the message to be conveyed.

The market to be reached will have a media profile which can be researched from the sources listed above, against which the objectives and the intended message can be measured within the context of the overall campaign. Each medium also has a qualitative dimension which will influence the receiver in his or her interpretation of the advertisement. Crozier[20] categorized the qualitative characteristics of the media under four headings:

- Usage scope – a newspaper is deliberately read, whereas a poster is seen incidentally.
- Creative scope – the extent to which the advertiser can use detailed messages, colour and so on.
- Vehicle effect – some newspapers may lend importance to advertising contained within their pages; others may be more frivolous.
- User friendliness – newspapers are relatively easy for advertisers to use, whereas television requires careful planning and pre-booking well in advance.

Once appropriate plans have been made, it may be necessary to brief an agency regarding the objectives and other criteria for the successful conduct of the advertising campaign. Without an effective working brief the advertising agency may interpret the objectives of the plan too broadly and allow its own creative mission to drive the campaign away from its original purpose. An advertising brief may include the following elements:

- measurable objectives;
- budget;
- profile of the operation(s), including location, specifications and principal markets;
- corporate mission;
- market analysis, including attitudinal data;
- details of future developments for the product portfolio;
- tariff structure and details of agencies used;
- yardsticks for the measurement of success.

The promotional brief invariably becomes the agenda for a dialogue between the agency and its client. However, at least the parameters have been set and these provide an important guide for the client in the discussions that follow.

Assessing campaign effectiveness

Assessing the effectiveness of a campaign is far from straightforward and depends extensively upon how well the objectives of the campaign were stated and in what terms. An objective expressed thus, 'to ensure that Blogg's hotels are considered to be the best hotels in Great Britain', is not helpful either in determining a means of achieving the aim or in measuring its ultimate success. Where objectives are measurable – for instance, 'to improve occupancy by 10 per cent during the shoulder months', – then the process of campaign assessment is simplified, but care should still be taken in the interpretation of the results. For example, if occupancy does increase by 10 per cent, it may be caused not by the company's promotions, but by an unprompted increase in demand due to other factors, or competing promotions creating displaced demand.

A great deal of measurement involves *ad hoc* research, surveying the target market's cognitive response, analysing its media habits and its ability to recall particular advertisements, and discovering its attitudes towards the product in question. Responses can then be correlated with other factors, such as sales and reports from the sales force and distributors to produce a more complete picture. Such tests still use the much criticized 'hierarchy of effects' model discussed earlier, which assumes a sequential progression from awareness to action. Assumptions are made on the basis that, because a target group has been exposed to the media, is aware of the product and is positively disposed towards it (they may even have purchased the product), then the advertising has been effective. From previous discussions regarding the relationship between attitudes and behaviour, it will be apparent that this relationship is difficult to prove, and that many factors have to be isolated and tested in order to assess the impact of advertising and other factors, including peer groups, on the motivation to buy.

In the absence of more reliable testing methods, the approaches outlined here continue to be the principal measures of advertising effectiveness. Companies wishing to assess their investment in this expensive and important promotional tool are urged to develop advertising objectives that lend themselves to various forms of measurement.

Most media offer some form of immediate testing. The international press media offer business reply cards which assist in identifying the perceived level of interest in a given product. Reading and noting studies conducted by research agencies helps to assess whether the target audience has remembered the advertisement. These studies may include a direct response element in the advertisement.

PUBLIC RELATIONS

The use of public relations (PR) has become considerably more important during the past decade; PR has changed from being a euphemism for press relations in a fairly reactive sense to being an important strategic tool in the communication and corporate plan. In some companies, PR has challenged the role of advertising as the lead communication process in recent years.

The composition of promotional budgets for individual companies is difficult to assess. This is because of the sensitivity of the information and because many companies do not know the total promotional spend for different units, departments and divisions of the organization. Whereas advertising obviously has an identified sponsor and advertising expenditure can be analysed and measured from company to company, PR expenditure is difficult to establish from outside the business except on an industry basis.

The slightly obscure role of PR in the portfolio of corporate activity is often a deliberate policy. For instance, a successful celebrity chef having a justifiable reputation for technical excellence would probably wish his high media profile to be attributed to technical excellence rather than to a PR company using its contacts to ensure optimum coverage. The impact of good PR on customers of hospitality and service products cannot be underestimated. Whereas a potential customer can discount or mitigate the influence of advertising simply because its sponsorship is known, PR has an almost subliminal quality where a name may be mentioned in another context. For instance, a restaurant mentioned or the nameboard seen during

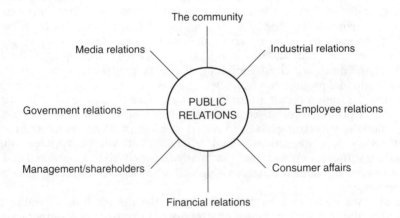

Figure 14.7 Significant groups for public relations activity

a television programme can cause or reinforce prior interest and encourage patronage.

The increasing influence of PR as a function is undoubted, as is reflected by the number of PR specialists taking very senior positions within major companies and institutions in the public sector. Overall, public relations expenditure in the hotel sector declined from £3,465,000 in 1991/92 to £3,154,000 in 1992/93, but it increased as a proportion of sales.

The Public Relations Association defines public relations as a management function 'responsible for effectively communicating a controlled message to an agreed audience to achieve a planned response'. Lord Mancroft has suggested a more frivolous definition of PR as 'the art of arranging the truth so that people like you', which implies the pro-active nature of PR to achieve stated ends. The presentation of the company and its policies can be crucial to its success. During the recent recession, several companies have failed because their weakened market condition led to a crisis of confidence among banks and investors. Even though their level of business was not critical, the financial community was sufficiently alarmed to withdraw its support.

It is possible that effective PR can prevent this type of situation, or at least delay it sufficiently for companies to rally their resources. The various groups represented in Figure 14.7 will all require information or messages for different purposes. Employees may wish to know about company policy on pay awards. The local community may be concerned about planned building works among many other issues. The content of the communication and its mode of delivery may be vital for the success of the company's plans in any of the areas mentioned. For instance, an unpopular building extension may be represented to as local community in terms of the jobs it will create in building it and in the enlarged and completed operation, as well as the amenities that may be available to the public.

The role of public relations

In addition to the specific communications necessary for each of the groups identified above, there are a number of strategic PR issues that a hospitality company should address.[21]

PR programme planning

This process is an essential adjunct to the planning procedure, where the decision to target particular markets and modify the product range may have implications for various groups connected with the organization. For instance, the decision to raise the profile of food provision in public houses generated several issues for a regional brewer:

- There was some uncertainty among staff about job security because the new proposals would require some radically different skills.
- The proposals needed a significant amount of finance, and shareholders and bankers needed to be reassured of the projects' feasibility.
- Many of the properties were listed buildings which would require significant redevelopment. Therefore planning authorities and the local community would need to be convinced that the proposals were sound.
- A new corporate identity was planned for the food service operations which required a new livery and logo.

All of the above needed the input of a PR specialist to represent the company's plans in such a way that they would receive minimum adverse reaction and if possible engender positive support. This example represents a major change of direction for the company concerned, but a public relations department should as a matter of routine be analysing and advising management regarding the problems and opportunities represented by company policy, defining PR goals and assessing results.

Creating corporate identity

This is of particular importance to hospitality companies, which provide little tangible evidence to the consumer prior to purchase. Corporate identity has to be managed very carefully because customers and industry analysts will assess every nuance of the business as it is revealed in the media and at other points of contact, such as company stationery and logos. Prior to contact with company representatives, it is therefore essential that these tangible clues contain the right message. The PR objectives should include presenting the name and building the company's reputation across a range of audiences and target groups, thereby establishing a 'corporate personality'.

Writing and editing

The first impression of a hospitality operation is often obtained from a written or oral piece in the form of a report, speech, film, house magazine or news release. All of these publications and the visual material that accompanies them must be managed very carefully in order to achieve the desired effect. A great deal of the written material issued by the public relations department will fall under the general heading of publicity, which normally takes the form of newsworthy stories presented to the media. Publicity is valuable to hospitality marketers for the following reasons:

- Credibility – good publicity is seen as editorial matter not advertising.
- Objectivity – publicity appears to be free of the sponsor's influence, and therefore the reader tends to be more receptive.
- Low cost relative to advertising – this means that publicity can be used effectively by small operators, but to have the right impact it is advisable to use copywriters who can write for an audience rather than a product.
- Topicality – the information is likely to deal with current issues and is therefore of greater interest to the readers.

Meeting and event organization

Whether internal, such as staff meetings or sales force briefings, or external, such as shareholders' meetings or community discussions, meetings are an important feature of any organization and must be arranged in order to ensure maximum positive effect. The role of professional communicators in this capacity is very important in achieving the right balance of spontaneity and structure in any delivery by a member of the company of organization. Politicians have realized the importance of effective delivery for some years, and employ the services of professional agencies to manage this function.

Events also provide an opportunity for the organization to enhance its image or standing with particular groups, either through direct action or more likely via sponsorship to appropriate events that will give exposure to 'publics' important to the firm. Sporting events have historically provided the main area of investment, but in recent years there has been increased interest and activity in other areas such as the arts, which have widened the scope and nature of sponsorship.

Media relations

The media provide an important focus for a great deal of public relations activity, either managing adverse reports or trying to get publicity for issues that enhance the reputation of the company. Most organizations maintain an archive in which all reports are kept, and which can be used to track issues and opinion affecting the organization.

Crisis management

The public relations department is typically under intense scrutiny during times of crisis for the organization. Interested parties, especially the press, will analyse every aspect of communication issuing from the spokespersons representing the company. Hospitality organizations are quite susceptible to high-profile, newsworthy issues because of the wide cross-section of the population drawn to their operations. A large, city-centre hotel can accommodate several thousand people in meeting rooms, bedrooms, restaurants and bars, and unfortunately there is a reasonably high probability that occasional interactions between customers, between customers and staff, and between customers and the surrounding environment will result in adverse publicity. The issues can be, and usually are, quite unexpected.

Most hotels are reasonably well prepared in the event of fire, with well-established procedures for the types of fire likely to be encountered. However, one large, international hotel group had a major crisis when a welder set fire to the insulation material between the walls. The resulting fumes and explosions could not be contained by the local fire department and advice had to be obtained from overseas. The fire did not cause a lot of damage to the fabric of the building, but because it was out of control for five days, maximum publicity occurred in the local and international press, requiring an enormous investment in public relations effort (as well as revised safety precautions) to overcome the bad publicity.

Crisis management can arise in several circumstances:

- The trading operation is interrupted.
- The financial performance is threatened.
- The public reputation of the company is or has been damaged.

It invariably requires a team effort to assimilate the facts, release and control the communications, liaise with third parties and communicate effectively with staff members who come into contact with the public.

DESIGN

Design is an important feature of the communication mix for hospitality operations. The importance of providing tangible clues to a highly intangible product was discussed earlier. The visual impact of company logos, livery, architecture, signage, reports and many other apparently peripheral items and issues gives the audience a first impression which influences its attitude towards the company. The aesthetic design of a building or stationery can deliver powerful messages to the receiver, as can the functional layout. For instance, the ease with which a guest can check into a hotel without having to negotiate stairs or corridors influences his or her impression of the operation. Whereas functional design is relatively easy to plan and anticipate, the impact of form, colour and line is more difficult to understand and often needs the advice of a professional designer who has experience of design in different commercial contexts.

There are a number of factors contributing to the growth of investment in design for the hospitality industry. These include the increasing sophistication of consumers, the increased investment in other forms of promotion and the branding strategies adopted by hospitality operations. Consequently, factors such as the appearance and physical layout of hospitality operations have become more important to the creation of an effective competitive advantage which can, in some circumstances, be protected by international copyright laws.

Design for hospitality operations has three core areas:[22] corporate identity; core product design and development; and exterior design, interior design and signage.

Corporate design

Corporate design has become an important feature of communications strategy in the service sector. A significant number of banks, building societies, tour operators, hotel groups, and other companies have conducted design audits and subsequently commissioned an overhaul of the visual elements of their organization, including

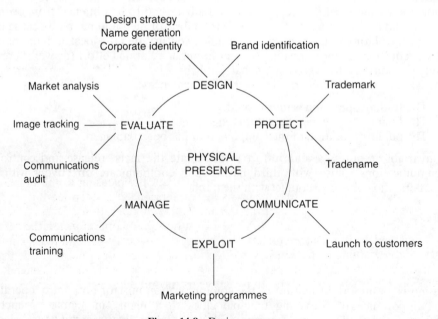

Figure 14.8 Design process

fundamental components such as products, staff dress and approaches to building design, as well as formal communications such as print and advertising. Because of the considerable expense involved in this process, image tracking and consumer attitude surveys have also become important. The problem arises, however, of how to isolate the contribution of design from the impact of other elements of the marketing mix. Short-term evaluation tends to rely on tracking studies which monitor the reaction of target groups, correlated with measures of customer satisfaction with the overall product and sales.

Core product design and development

The design of core products in hospitality operations such as rooms and food and beverage outlets is thematically derived from the strategic overview of corporate design. A hotel company wishing to imply a more informal and relaxed atmosphere in its operations may seek to reflect this aim in the range, price, theme and presentation of the food and beverages served in its restaurants. A recent survey indicated that the majority of restaurant customers resented the traditional presentation of menus in French and the formal ostentation that is often associated with a 'good meal'. It seems that foodservice operations are sending the wrong messages to their customers and perhaps contributing to the rapid growth of popularity of 'pub meals'.

Design should be an important feature of the product development process from the outset. Peters[22] has pointed out that many companies now employ a multi-disciplinary approach, with designers involved alongside marketing personnel from the start, rather than at the end when the key decisions have been taken. This new trend is partly an attempt to mirror successful Japanese practices, but it also recognizes the benefits of integrating all the disciplines into one cohesive team, namely:

- a common vision and commitment between marketing, design and production personnel;
- faster time scales because activities can be pursued in parallel, not in sequence;
- the opportunity to research a realistic, rather than a theoretical concept early on;
- feedback from potential users to the design process.

Exterior design, interior design and signage

Concerns about the environment and increased confidence about what constitutes 'good design', an issue that is much discussed in the press and media, have engendered a number of expectations ranging from the aesthetically pleasing to the functionally efficient. Most hospitality organizations have experienced a steep learning curve in the management of the physical appearance of their operations. During the early years of hotel expansion in the 1960s and 1970s, most hotel operators left the design of buildings and facilities to architects and interior designers with minimal input from operations personnel. The result was often unsatisfactory either because the physical layout impeded the efficient operation of the unit or because the facilities did not have the desired effect on customers. In recent years, hospitality operators have been able to contribute at an early stage of the project development, contributing their experience of successful design – often derived from a wider international context.

There appear to be three contributions that operators can make to the development of good exterior and interior design:

- a well-developed understanding of the business and its target markets;
- a practised sense of what represents good aesthetic and functional design in other operations;
- early involvement with the design process and design team.

SALES PROMOTION

In 1989 a survey of the United Kingdom's top fifty sales promotion agencies showed a 37 per cent growth in turnover between 1987 and 1988, from £135 million to £185 million.[23] Estimates indicate that expenditure on sales promotion may actually exceed advertising and is growing in popularity.

The growth of sales promotion as a marketing tool may be due to the fact that it is relatively easy to assess the impact of sales promotion on sales, which during a period of restricted promotional budgets is an important consideration. A definition of sales promotion is difficult because it includes so many different techniques. However the Institute of Sales Promotion provides a definition which gives a broad indication of the area: 'Sales promotion comprises a range of tactical marketing techniques designed with a strategic marketing framework to add value to a product or service in order to achieve specific sales and marketing objectives.'

Sales promotion objectives are determined within the framework of long-term marketing and communication objectives, although as the previous definition implies, they communicate short-term benefits to consumers, sales personnel and agents acting on behalf of the hospitality operation. Sales promotion objectives would probably include:

- encouraging the trial of new or existing products;
- providing incentives for sales staff;
- providing incentives for agents;
- generating repeat business;
- increasing the frequency of purchase or the size of unit purchased;
- encouraging display;
- reducing seasonal imbalance;
- undermining competing promotions

Most hospitality organizations organize and manage their own sales promotion campaigns, but the area is becoming more complex with a great deal of legislation to consider as well as the commercial pitfalls. The now notorious Hoover 'free flights' offer has cost the company approximately £20 million to date and several senior executives their jobs. The massive over-redemption on the offer and the reported tactics employed by Hoover to mitigate its worst effects led to court action and a major crisis of confidence in the company.

Pepsi, the soft drinks manufacturer, provides another example of the problems that can arise with sales promotion. A competition organized by the company in the Philippines gave a significant prize to the winner who received a 'lucky number' printed inside the bottle cap. Unfortunately 800,000 caps were printed with the winning number and 400,000 people have claimed the first prize. Arrest warrants have been issued for ten Pepsi executives, and the company has so far paid $10 million in prize money.[23]

Some of the common problems with sales promotion are:

- legal or code of practice transgressions;
- over-redemption of discount coupons;
- traders refusing to co-operate with the scheme;
- problems with sales promotion that include overseas travel or products;
- printing and typographical errors;
- inadequate levels of response to the sales promotion campaign.

Some companies prefer to use sales promotion agencies or incentive travel houses to manage the campaigns on their behalf, and take out insurance to cover errors of judgement in the calculation of audience response. However, the majority of hospitality companies still conduct their own campaigns. The techniques that are generally used include the following.

Consumer sales promotions

- competitions;
- free premiums (money or gift) with purchase;
- money off;
- discount vouchers;
- free samples;
- package deals;
- celebrity promotions.

Trade promotions

- competitions (sales, new business);
- free gifts;
- coupons;
- incentives (either special payments for sales effort or other forms of remuneration, such as holidays and seminars).

Sales force promotions

- commission rates;
- special bonuses;
- sales contests;
- points schemes.

Certain sales promotion techniques have been notably popular and attract a considerable proportion of the communication budget.[24] These are described below.

Free mail-in

This is a popular type of sales promotion featuring free rooms (usually only offered by larger chains for the group as a whole), food or beverages, or use of leisure facilities for a given target audience upon aplication. It can be targeted at specific groups, such as business travellers or couples, and more widely for limited periods of time when business is otherwise slow. Disadvantages include the high costs of administration, and the difficulty of predicting the extent of take-up.

Reduced price

This important technique is widespread, but a legally complex subject as it is subject to the Trade Descriptions Act 1968 and Price Marketing (Bargain Offers) Order 1979, which stipulate the criteria defining a discounted offer. Hotel companies and other hospitality operators can use this technique to good effect by discounting at different rates to various segments and thereby operating a differential pricing strategy. Similar disadvantages apply to this technique, and it is important to monitor carefully the redemption rates among different groups and to collate information about average spend levels and achieved rack rates.

Competitions

The chance involved in most competitions provides an element of excitement that participants find attractive, especially as they do not involve a personal financial investment. The technique is regulated by the Lotteries and Amusement acts 1976, and offers relating to competitions should be assessed professionally to ensure that they conform to the requirements of the Act. Prizes can be offered from the hospitality company's own portfolio of products with the possibility of add-ons such as car hire or entertainment. As the prizes are finite, there is little danger of over-redemption, and the narrow targeting also increases the odds of a win, making it even more attractive for participants.

Coupons

In 1988 approximately 4 billion coupons were issued, and nearly 300 million of them, worth more than £50 million, were redeemed. Hospitality marketers use coupons because they are easy to implement and manage. Coupons can be targeted carefully, can be tailor-made and provide predictable and measurable results. Hooper[25] cites several uses of couponing, which include:

- encouraging trial and retrial;
- reducing competing gap;
- emphasizing a saving at the point of sale;
- encouraging distributors (e.g. travel agents),
- providing a fast response to competitive pricing.

Disadvantages include misredemption by consumers and lack of support from participating units: for instance, individual hotel units may not recognize the coupons.

Trade and business incentives

Many hotel companies have identified the intermediaries acting on their behalf and referrals from other complementary services, such as booking agencies, travel agencies, car rental firms and airlines, as an important target for sales promotion. This is primarily to encourage sales, but also to reinforce communications from the company which could be reinterpreted by these third parties. A further use of these tailor-made promotions is to target the decision-makers in potential business clients in order to influence the decision-making process. This requires a longer-term approach than is traditionally found in planning sales promotions.

MERCHANDISING

Merchandising is one of the areas of hospitality marketing that has not so far been developed to its full potential. Hospitality operations are unusual in that opportunities exist to increase the average spend of customers who patronize them. Every time a customer books into a hotel or orders a meal, there are opportunities to increase the value of the order through a variety of media, including displays, tent cards, information packs and posters. This effort can be tied in to sales promotion via competitions on drink mats, free drinks with particular dishes and so on. Merchandising has been defined as 'any form of behaviour triggering stimulus or pattern of stimuli, other than personal selling, which takes place at retail or point of sale'.[26]

Buttle[26] suggests that successful merchandising employs three tactics to generate sales:

- accessibility;
- sensory domination;
- appeal.

Implicit in these three aspects is the need for merchandising to have an impact on the customer. Displays of goods, such as hotel-made chocolates or wines served in the restaurant, should be designed to encourage interest and trial. Faded and tired posters advertising the hotel restaurant may act as a serious disincentive to patronage, whereas a plate of hors-d'oeuvre in the guest bedroom or on the reception desk with other promotional material may achieve the desired result. Hospitality operations can provide high-quality merchandising material relatively easily from their routine operations by preparing food and beverages in an innovative, attractive way.

Many of the purchases made by hotel guests are low-involvement decisions, such as the purchase of a newspaper, a writing pad or postcards, meaning that merchandising stimuli are generally sufficient to evoke a purchase. There is some evidence to suggest that when consumers have time to spare and access to shops and services, they are likely to spend money on items in a random and unplanned manner. This type of impulse buying can be encouraged by effective merchandising.

PERSONAL SELLING

Personal selling can be one of the most effective marketing tools used by a hospitality operation, where selling objectives have been identified in a number of areas:

- Direct selling by staff in restaurants, bars and reception, which is short-term and opportunistic.
- Indirect selling by staff with no specific requirement to sell and with only incidental contact with customers.
- Selling by unit management or departmental heads, which can be long- or short-term.
- Selling by a specialized sales team with long-term sales objectives and a more sophisticated means of assessing their relative success in achieving sales targets.

The nature of personal selling makes it particularly applicable to the service sector, especially hospitality services. While the communications discussed previously will in varying degrees help to overcome the high perceived risk and intangibility associated with services, only personal selling can convey the *meaning* of hospitality through interaction between the customer or potential customer and the representative of the hospitality operation. Each of the selling situations noted above provides an opportunity for the hospitality operation to present and sell its unique aspects, leaving the customer with a positive impression and with the additional benefit of increasing the overall average spend.

Direct selling by staff

Operational staff in restaurants, bars, reception and other locations within a hospitality operation have the most frequent contact with guests, and incrementally they have the greatest impact on short-term sales. However, actually persuading staff in these positions to take their selling role seriously is difficult. Various means have been used by hospitality companies to encourage staff to regard their job with a broader view:

- sales training – this can be effective in the short term.
- Incentive bonus schemes – these are probably the most effective means of encouraging staff to sell, and can range from a percentage of sales to scales rewards that may include holidays or shares.
- Sales promotions – including competitions, voucher schemes and similar opportunities that can be used as short-term methods for encouraging sales during off-peak periods.

Many hospitality companies have used these methods to good effect. For example, 'The Hard Rock Café', Whitbread's, TGI Friday and 'My Kinda Town' have used the incentive bonus scheme successfully to raise the overall level of average spend.

Indirect selling by staff

Encouraging staff in hospitality operations who do not have regular contact with customers to sell when the opportunity arises is even more difficult to achieve. Many companies take the view that the investment in time and resources required to achieve a minimum impact on sales is simply not worth the effort.

The Disney Corporation extends its theatrical culture throughout the organization so that *all* staff working in the Disney World operators are actors, including the maintenance crews and cleaners. This corporate view means that all staff are trained in customer–staff relations to ensure that customers will be given appropriate information, which may provide the opportunity to sell, whoever they contact and for whatever purpose. The results are impressive not purely in the achievement of higher sales, but also in the creation of a customer-friendly and hospitable environment.

Selling by unit or departmental managers

Unit or departmental managers have the opportunity to engage in longer-term sales propositions, either through their routine activities within the operation or in other business meetings that may include sales calls. Operations lacking the resources to support a specialist sales team may include the sales function within the job descriptions of these managers. In this case, it is important to monitor this aspect of their work, perhaps providing some of the incentives mentioned previously for staff positions. Conflict can arise in operations where there is a specialist sales department. Departmental managers often take a proprietorial view and give priority to their own sales arrangements.

For example, where a sales department has an allocation of rooms to sell (possibly as part of a function package) it may find that the front office has sold some of the rooms, thus compromising its own arrangements. This type of problem is of course avoidable, especially with the range of technology available. Departments can check room availability very easily as long as they have access to the appropriate technology.

The specialist sales department

Selling is at the heart of enterprise and has a historic and international provenance. This well-documented area has a wealth of literature, often authored by 'gurus' who have been particularly successful in the field. To many customers the salesperson *is* the hospitality organization, at least in the initial stages of a transaction. Unlike previous examples of selling, which are likely to be more opportunistic, the sales team will have objectives derived from the company or unit's marketing plan. Monitoring the success of selling is easier than other forms of communication because the relationship between expenditure on the sales team, which may include salaries, company cars and bonus and incentive schemes, can be scrutinized on a routine basis.

There are several types of sales force organization. The most appropriate arrangement depends upon the size of the company, the diversity of its products and markets, and its marketing objectives. Regardless of how the sales team is organized, it will perform one or more of the following functions.[27]

Prospecting

The extent to which a salesperson brings in new business is an important measure of his or her success, and yet is often the activity that salespeople find the most difficult.

Communicating

This involves presenting the company and its products to potential customers at trade shows, seminars and other similar venues. It complements other forms of promotion and provides an introduction to the company that can be tracked in relation to enquiries received after the presentation.

Selling

This core activity requires careful training to develop 'sales technique', although most salespeople evolve their own personal approach. The characteristics of a good salesperson are the subject of much debate. Empathy, interest, in the product and dynamism have often been cited as important factors in the salesperson's character.

Servicing

Customers of hospitality services are particularly prone to post-purchase dissonance because the anticipated product, despite careful preparation, may not be an unqualified success. The role of the salesperson in these circumstances is vital, since he or she should be able to demonstrate the appropriate level of concern and even make arrangements that mitigate the worst effects of a crisis.

Information gathering

The salesperson is an important element in the market research system, collecting information on competitors, customer requirements and trends, and reporting at regular intervals (usually monthly).

Allocating

This is a particularly contentious issue because individual departments also have a sales role. Although the potential problems of double booking can be easily avoided, the political will is often lacking.

DIRECT MARKETING

The hospitality industry is particularly well placed to take advantage of direct marketing, either through the traditional media of mail and telephone or through the new, emerging technologies of direct response, radio and television. These diverse communications have one objective in common: that is, a formal offer to an individual or group. Many customers of hospitality operations have to identify themselves in some way – for instance, through a restaurant or hotel booking – providing valuable data that can be stored and used for research and promotional purposes. Even if customers do not give their personal details, they can be approached and asked to provide them as part of a routine survey. This is an important part of a marketing information system.

Direct mail has grown in popularity in recent years as companies have attempted to retain customers in a diminishing market. In 1981/82, £105 million was spent on direct mail postage; by 1987/88, this figure has increased to £180 million. The success of direct marketing in other sectors, such as retailing, has encouraged many hospitality operators to use their bookings diaries, reservation systems, sales department records and so on to create a database.

The development and affordability of computer technology has facilitated much of this growth even for small and medium-sized operators. However, the amount of information stored must be carefully analysed to ensure that the organization does not end up with a lot of superfluous data. A number of companies have failed to take advantage of the full potential of their database because the software used does not allow the user to compile reports and lists using relevant data variables. Specialist software is improving, however, enabling the management of large amounts of information. Alternatively, specialist agencies (including the Royal Mail) can advise on the creation of an appropriate database.

Marriott hotels have been developing their database for nearly a decade, and it currently holds records relating to over five million customers. Consequently, the database and direct marketing are now as important as advertising.[28] The chairman, Bill Marriott, explains that the use of the database for the Honoured Guest programme helps to encourage brand loyalty and is more useful than advertising in this respect. Research carried out by Marriott indicates that customers cannot differentiate adequately between the leading business deluxe hotels. The Honoured Guest programme was initiated to overcome this and to build competitive edge and customer loyalty.

Marriott's database is used to target business customers, who collect points per dollar charged to the guest room. These can be for 'free' stays in hotels and resorts around the world. The database programme also tracks customers' responses to additional incentives and the results are used to build a constantly evolving predictive model.

The use of a database gives hospitality organizations the opportunity to identify variations in consumer response, to tailor specific product packages, to develop better-targeted communication plans and, perhaps the most important advantage for a service organization, to offer a more personalized approach. The biggest drawback noted by hospitality operators is the intrusive nature of direct marketing and its 'junk mail' image. This can damage a company's reputation and image if it is not managed effectively.

REFERENCES

1. Parasuraman, A., Berry, L. L., and Zeithaml, V. A., 'Service firms need marketing skills', *Business Horizons*, 26 November 1983.
2. Zeithaml, V. A., Berry, L. L., and Parasuraman, A., 'Communication and control processes in the delivery of service quality', *Journal of Marketing*, vol. 52 (April), 1988, pp. 35–48.
3. Daft, R., and Steers, R., *Organizations: A Micro/Macro Approach*, Scott, Foresman & Co., Glenview, IL, 1984.
4. Webster, F. E., and Wind, Y., *Organizational Buyer Behavior* (Foundations of Marketing Series), Prentice-Hall, Englewood Cliffs, NJ, 1972.

5. Converse, Paul, *Marketing Methods and Policies*, Prentice-Hall, New York, 1924.
6. Wilson, D. T., 'Industrial buyers' decision making styles,' *Journal of Marketing Research*, November 1971, pp. 433–6.
7. Webster, F. E., and Wind, Y., 'A general model for understanding buying behaviour', *Journal of Marketing*, vol. 36 (April), 1972, pp. 31–3.
8. Schiffman, L. G., and Kanuk, L. L., *Consumer Behaviour*, 4th edn, Prentice-Hall, Hemel Hempstead, 1991.
9. Soley, L. C., and Kurzbard, G., 'Selective exposure reexamined', in Glover, D. R. (ed.), *Proccedings of the 1984 Convention of the American Academy of Advertising*, American Academy of Advertising, Nebraska, 1984.
10. Buttle, F., *Hotel and Food Service Marketing: A Managerial Approach*, Holt, Rinehart & Winston, New York, 1986, pp. 303–4.
11. Bettman, J. R., *An Information Processing Theory of Consumer Choice*, Addison-Wesley, Reading, MA, 1979.
12. Calver, S., *Poole Arts Centre: An Evaluation of the Impact of Media Promotions on the Target Audience*, Bournemouth Polytechnic report, 1985.
13. McDonald, M., 'Planning the marketing function', in Baker, M. (ed.), *The Marketing Book*, 2nd edn, Butterworth-Heinemann, Oxford, 1991, p. 83.
14. Palda, K. S., *The Measurement of Cumulative Advertising Effect*, Prentice-Hall, Englewood Cliffs, NJ, 1964, p. 87.
15. Buzzell, R. D., 'E. I. Du Pont de Nemours & Co.: measurement of effects of advertising', in *Mathematical Models and Marketing Management*, Boston Division of Research, Graduate School of Business Administration, Harvard University, MA, 1964, p. 157–79.
16. For instance, Colley, R. H., *Defining Advertising Goals for Measured Advertising Results*, Association of National Advertisers of New York, New York, 1961.
17. For instance, Joyce, T., *What Do We Know About How Advertising Works?*, J. Walter Thompson, London, 1967.
18. Assael, H., *Consumer Behaviour and Marketing Action*, 3rd edn, PWS, Kent, 1987.
19. George, W. R., and Berry, L. L., 'Guidelines for the advertising of services', *Business Horizons*, vol. 24 (July–August), 1981, pp. 52–6.
20. Crozier, K., 'Promotion', in Baker, M. (ed.), *The Marketing Book*, Butterworth-Heinemann, Oxford, 1991, pp. 13–15.
21. 'Public relations', in *The Marketing Guides 1·2*, Shandwick Ltd, 1989.
22. Peters, M., 'Design' in *The Marketing Guides 1–2*, Shandwick Ltd, 1989.
23. MacIntyre, B., 'Pepsi pays for jackpot chaos', *The Times*, 28 July 1993.
24. Survey on top fifty sales promotion agencies, *Marketing*, 18 May 1989.
25. Hooper, J., 'Promotion' in *Marketing Guide 12*, Shandwick Ltd, 1989.
26. Buttle, F., 'How merchandising works', *International Journal of Advertising*, vol. 3, 1984, pp. 15–19.
27. Kotler, P., *Marketing Management, Analysis, Planning Implementation and Control*, 7th edn, Prentice-Hall, Hemel Hempstead, 1991, p. 652.
28. 'The world's biggest hotel database', *Marketing*, 4 March 1993, p. 19.

FIFTEEN

Formulating marketing strategy for the hospitality industry

INTRODUCTION

In Chapter 14, communication was discussed as a vital strategic element for hospitality organizations, and importance was given to integrating the various promotional tools to achieve an effective focus. The main influence for communications and other management functions must be directed by long-term aims and objectives developed as part of a comprehensive strategy.

The use of the word 'strategy' is now so widespread within the lexicon of business language that it has become almost meaningless. It is often used as a type of mantra which, if repeated in the right circumstances, gives the impression of action but actually provides little direction for the organization. The use of the term as a description of longer-term planning is helpful, but unless it provides the right guideposts it is equally ineffective. The strategic plan should provide a blueprint for action which can be interpreted at any level of the organization.

The nature of strategy is further obscured by its specialist applications, in strategic marketing, strategic business planning, corporate strategy and so on. The context in which the term is used is not that important as long as clear guidelines for long-term action are included. Marketing strategy must therefore provide clear indications of which markets are to be targeted and the means by which they will targeted in the long term. The following description of what marketing strategy *does* emphasizes the dynamic aspect of the process and the importance of strategy as an action-based discipline: 'Marketing strategy is the process by which the organization translates its business objective and business strategy into market activity'.[1]

The acceptance of this explanation of marketing strategy has significant implications for the organization. In recent years, many hospitality organizations, especially in the United Kingdom and the rest of Europe, have grasped the terminology and professed their conversion to the cause of marketing. As a demonstration of their commitment they point to their enhanced sales force and their expenditure on advertising and on social skills training programmes. Marketing strategy is, however, based on a careful analysis of the marketplace and depends upon the use of appropriate marketing information. This necessitates a marketing information system which should provide management with continuous and timely information. The use of detailed market analysis enables the company to be pro-active and dynamic compared to those hospitality companies that traditionally depend upon their financial management and accounting systems, and which as a result tend to be reactive.

While strategic planning in the hospitality industry has evolved considerably in recent years, there is still a tendency for the process to be the preserve of senior management. Implementation at intermediate levels of the organization is often restricted, with middle managers unsure about the longer-term objectives of the organization or the means of achieving them. This approach needs to change as hospitality organizations become more pro-active at the unit and departmental level, in order to maintain their market position in the face of greater competitive and economic pressure.

MARKETING PLANNING AND MARKETING STRATEGY

The two terms 'marketing planning' and 'marketing strategy' are often used interchangeably, and the distinction between them is obscure and probably of little significance to the practitioner. Marketing plans should be prepared for the long term (three to four years) with clear guidelines for action. They should also be prepared within the context of the company's overall mission and corporate strategy. If there is a difference between marketing planning and marketing strategy, it is in the scale of the proposition. The marketing plan contains the tactical details for implementation, dealing with specific marketing activity, promotions, distribution, selling and so on. Marketing strategy provides the overall analysis of the organization and its environment with a means of achieving its overall objectives. The strategic plan may therefore be regarded as a substantial preface to the marketing plan.

The strategic planning process

The flow chart in Figure 15.1 indicates the approximate relationships between the various stages of developing marketing strategy.

Hospitality organizations face diverse markets and competitive pressures, and it is therefore impossible to develop a prescriptive approach to the process. Strategy in the hospitality industry is concerned with two substantial indicators in the economy: the level of business activity, and the amount of disposable income for leisure purposes. The larger organizations are concerned with these issues in an international context, either as direct traders in overseas markets or as the recipients of tourist expenditure in their own country. Multi-unit international organizations are confronted with a more difficult task in the development of an overall, long-term strategy. Individual units or units in a particular region may have to deal with local issues that impact upon overall company strategy. For instance, an international hotel company wishing to develop its short-stay business market as a feature of company policy may be seriously affected by a down-turn in business due to political and social instability in one region

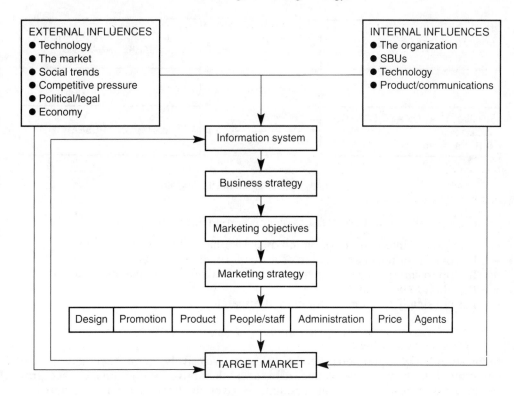

Figure 15.1 Strategic process

of the world. If the area is allowed too much autonomy to respond to local conditions, the overall image of the company may be adversely affected worldwide. But if central control is not relaxed, individual units may find that aspects of the standardized product are not appropriate to their locality.

The standardization of service to an agreed level is also a major problem for hospitality operators attempting to develop a company marketing strategy. The interaction between customer and staff member is such an important feature of the hospitality product that it must be part of the planning process and yet implementing and controlling this important aspect of the business represents one of the greatest challenges to hospitality managers.

The marketing information system

Central to the development of marketing strategy is the continuous flow of information from the marketplace, specialist agencies (e.g. advertising agencies), internal administration and management departments. In large organizations this would take the form of regular, usually monthly returns from the unit to regional head office, where the data are analysed and used in the decision-making process. Figure 15.2 describes the components of a marketing information system and the inter-relationships between them.

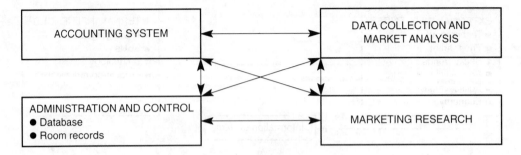

Figure 15.2 Marketing information system

Piercy[2] describes the characteristics of a marketing information system thus:

- It stores and integrates information on marketing issues from many sources.
- It provides for the dissemination of such information to users.
- It supports marketing management decision making in both planning and control.
- It is likely to be computerized.
- It is not simply a new name for market research.

Accounting system

Many hospitality operations depend almost exclusively upon their accounting department to provide marketing data as a derivative of the financial control mechanisms. This approach is understandable given the large investment in staff and equipment, plus the legal penalties for not keeping adequate records. Developing specific marketing reports is often seen as an additional expense, usually without an immediate payback. The nature of hospitality operations, however, means that they are in unique position to derive rapid feedback regarding key internal indicators. For instance, average spend per user group, marginal marketing costs per user group, and many other ratios which can be included in a trend analysis (amount last year, previous year and so on) provide vital data for the strategic planner.

Administration and control

The records kept on customers and staff can provide the basis of an extensive guest database. Guest histories can be evolved into an effective means of market segmentation by combining the data obtained from other internal and external sources. For instance, key information such as name, address, length of stay, company details and frequency of visit can be supplemented with information on the breakdown of expenditure, costs of services provided, services used and attitudinal data from surveys. Over a longer period of time, indices can be established for responsiveness to advertising and other promotional effort, and market groups correlated with other criteria such as exposure to certain media or consumption of other products. The development and management of such a system is expensive, but it can provide an important competitive lead in an increasingly saturated marketplace.

The main sources of information are:

- food and beverage reports;
- registration forms;
- company correspondence;
- staff reports;
- rooms reports;
- guest surveys.

Data collection and market analysis

A significant number of objective bulletins are prepared by academic bodies, consultancy firms or specialist research agencies, providing regular statistics on the hospitality industry. Such bodies include Mintel, Euromonitor and the Henley Centre for Forecasting. These various agencies can provide

- comparative data against which operation and company performance can be measured;
- subscription research, where the participating company gets regular reports of often comparative data, to which the company may contribute its own statistics;
- market research data on a continuous or *ad hoc* basis.

Each organization requires different types of information, and, as with internally generated data, particular ratios will have special significance.

Marketing research

While the previous components of the marketing information system are likely to be found in most hospitality organizations, albeit in embryonic form, the establishment of a functional specialism dealing with marketing research requires a considerable investment. Most organizations subcontract this activity to outside specialist agencies. Many of the criticisms of marketing research centre around the irrelevance of the data produced,[3] but this is often because management believe it to be a specialized area outside of their normal competence. This view is unfortunate because researchers are left to interpret the likely research objectives of the organization, and only realize the actual objectives on submission of the final report.

The need to identify precise objectives for marketing research is imperative if the findings are to be of any use to the commissioning company. Most research projects need to be continuous in order to provide comparative data which can also be consolidated with information derived from other parts of the marketing information system in the future.

Many companies use the marketing information system to construct models for planning and control. The use of these models is quite controversial: their ability to reflect the real world and predict trends is questionable, although continued advances in technique and technology will make their application an essential feature of the decision-making process.

The role of the marketing information system within the organization and in the strategic planning process represents a challenge to businesses as trading in a crowded marketplace becomes more difficult and the traditional use of experience and intuition becomes associated with greater risk. Overdependence on scientific method to the exclusion of intuition is perhaps a leitmotif of our age, but scientific method does have a role and it must be carefully integrated into the planning process.

Kotler[4] suggested that the integration of the marketing information system requires:

- the system to be recognized by the company as a valid long-term investment rather than a short-term imperative;
- organizational adjustments to be made to accommodate the system in a central role;
- new technology to be used to reduce the problem to something manageable.

The introduction of computer systems to handle comprehensively the information requirements of some organizations has met with extensive criticism as the technology has failed to live up to expectations. The situation will only improve when managements identify their own information requirements and have the confidence to state them.

THE INFLUENCE OF THE ORGANIZATION ON MARKETING STRATEGY

Discussions of the process of marketing strategy development often ignore the significant impact of the context in which it takes place. Hospitality organizations, like any other, contain a large number of interest groups anxious to maintain their own status quo to the detriment of policy implementation. Most planning processes involve change, and most interest groups will resist it. This management problem influences the achievement of strategic plans and therefore must be considered when delegating responsibility for implementation.

The organization

The implementation of strategy, according to traditional theorists, requires an instrumental approach to the process. This accepts that, having chosen its strategic route, the organization's structure will eventually follow, thus enabling implementation.[5] However, this explanation fails to take account of the many changes that are forced upon a company as it modifies its strategy over time. Many hospitality companies with an extensive asset portfolio and highly a developed set of specialisms may be unable to adapt very quickly to address new strategic objectives.

Hospitality companies are becoming more skilled at dealing with strategic change, including large-scale issues such as divestment and diversification. The use of various management–ownership arrangements, such as management contracts and franchising, also enables the industry to be more flexible in its approach to strategy implementation. However, the redirection of staff within the industry is more problematic, and since staff constitute most of the hospitality product, this is a major concern. Spillard[6] suggests that, because of this type of inflexibility, there is a case for suggesting that strategy sometimes follows structure. The resolution of this issue, producing a company flexible enough to respond to strategic change and yet consistent enough to develop its own strengths and provide a relatively secure environment for its staff, is essential for the hospitality company developing its strategy for the 1990s.

The successful implementation of marketing strategy must resolve another tension within the organization: the creative dynamism of marketing action and the territorial

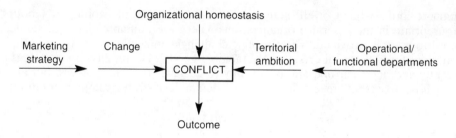

Figure 15.3 Organizational influences on marketing strategy

ambitions of specialist and functional departments. Figure 15.3 reflects this process, the outcome of which may not be strategically desirable.

The influence of the marketing department must be sufficient to effect change within an organization. Having undergone a major review of the loss-making restaurants in its hotels, the marketing department of a major hotel company decided to convert some of them to more profitable use as guest accommodation, offices and franchised restaurants. This major change was overruled by a head office dominated by food and beverage specialists, and the refurbishment funds were spent on redeveloping the restaurants, which continued to make a loss.

Other issues that will influence the development and implementation of strategy within the organization include:

- technology;
- management styles;
- human resources;
- product portfolio.

Technology

Some hospitality operations dealing in budget markets are able to implement strategic plans with relative ease because they have been able to reduce the scope for staff–customer interaction. The introduction of operational methods that do not require such a large staff input – for instance, buffets, self-registration and so on – have assisted in this process. The use of technology has been slow in reducing the overall staff costs, but it is beginning to enable hospitality companies to control some of the customer–staff interactions.

A lead has been taken from the banking and financial sector, where technology has largely replaced staff involvement with some transactions, such as cash withdrawals and paying in. Even more complex transactions such as loan applications are dealt with according to set criteria and with a minimum of staff involvement. This process has been relatively successful, where supported by promotions that emphasize the consumer-led approach of the bank or building society. The financial sector has been the subject of much criticism, however, and it is extremely difficult at present to isolate customer satisfaction with this type of service.

Recent research suggests that some customer groups, such as short-stay business-people, actually prefer minimal contact with service staff and appreciate highly automated reception procedures – for guest registration, settling accounts on departure and so on. Cowell[7] maintains that substitution of capital for labour 'is inappropriate in those service organizations where the human element of service is central to what is provided. The strategic challenges in such situations are different from those faced by producers of more tangible goods'. Hospitality organizations are currently auditing their operations not only to achieve cost effectiveness, but also to assess those areas that are less flexible to the demands of strategic implementation.

Management styles

The influence of management styles on strategic decision making and the achievement of marketing objectives is of profound importance. Within an organization there are differing styles of management depending upon a number of factors, such as the product–process relationship. For example, the restaurant of a *haute cuisine* operation is likely to be more mechanistic than the kitchen. Despite these departmental variations, the prevailing culture and its responsiveness to innovation and change will determine the successful accomplishment of organizational goals.

Thus Virgin Airways and British Airways compete for the transatlantic air traveller with organizations and management styles that are very different. Virgin is a decentralized organization with a more democratic, consultative style of management, which is perhaps more responsive to change than to British Airways, which still retains a formal hierarchy with traces of its public-sector origins. The progress of the two companies will be watched with great interest as they compete in such a dynamic and high-risk marketplace.

The nature of the external environment influences management style considerably. Khandwalla[8] suggests that the more hostile and fast-changing the external environment, the more risk-taking and organic the style of top management needs to be, and the greater is the potential for interdepartmental conflict.

Human resources

We have seen that the personnel in a hospitality organization are an intrinsic part of the product or service offered. Davidson[9] has emphasized the point by suggesting that 'In a service industry the secret of success is recognition that customer contact personnel are the key people in the organization'. Comment has already been made about the possible role of technology in service interactions, which may assist in standardizing and improving the efficiency of some aspects of the business. However, the critical impact of any hospitality product on the target market will be heavily influenced by the personnel involved. Motivation of service personnel is a key issue in the achievement of a hospitality organization's goals, to which conventional training and staff development will make a significant contribution. Some companies have found that direct financial incentives in the form of bonus schemes have an important influence on key service personnel.

Product portfolio

The range, quality and level of service product provided determines the extent to which the organization can implement strategic decisions, and the ease with which it can do so. Major fast-food chains, targeting new markets with new additions to their menu or new methods of service delivery, will have to develop technology and systems that can provide the standardized service which is the hallmark of their operations.

Extensive training and staff development will also have to be undertaken in order to ensure the successful achievement of these goals.

Strategic business units

Most hospitality companies, even small independent units, operate several businesses. A bed and breakfast operation will provide accommodation, a meal, and perhaps a bar or licensed area for recreation. The larger the hospitality business, the more difficult it is to define the precise nature of the business.

Levitt[10] suggests that product-led definitions of a business such as 'hotel and catering' are not helpful and may distract the strategic policy-makers in the formulation of effective long-term action plans. He maintains that the definition of the business should be in terms of its *customer-satisfying ability*, in which the hotel and catering operation may be described as serviced accommodation for short-stay travellers. In this example, emphasis is placed on the rooms; the provision of food and beverages is subordinate to this main aim and may even be provided on a concession arrangement by another company. Levitt proposes that companies shifting their corporate perspective in this way can achieve better clarity of purpose, and are in a stronger position to identify the appropriate marketing strategy. This approach to the strategic planning process also enables the company to identify its strategic business units more clearly.

In the above example, strategic direction is focused on the rooms as the essential proposition, on the assumption that this is what a short-stay business traveller actually wants, and on ensuring that the standard of the other facilities meets the needs of this particular market. The implications of trading on a product-led basis, implied by the definition of hotel and catering as a resource-intensive service, are that companies will attempt to optimize every aspect of their business, rather than concentrating on those that are significant to their target market. During the past ten years, many hotel companies traded on the asset value of their properties and regarded traditional activities – the sale of rooms and food and beverages – as a means of generating liquid assets. The drastic deflation of property prices has forced hotel companies to reappraise their businesses and to identify trading propositions for the long term.

Abell[11] defines businesses according to three dimensions:

- customer groups;
- customer needs;
- technology.

This type of definition is useful because the business can incrementally develop along these dimensions without losing sight of its core business. Hospitality operations need an additional service dimension which can be combined with technology to provide strategic direction. Figure 15.4 indicates the possible relationship between the dimension.

This type of approach enables companies to identify the nature of their business activity relative to the marketplace. It also assists in measuring competitive activity in key areas. Moreover, consideration of markets, products, competitors and service delivery facilitates the identification of the strategic business units which should direct the company's marketing and control functions.

- a semi-autonomous management structure, probably answerable to senior management, with executive or general management responsibility;

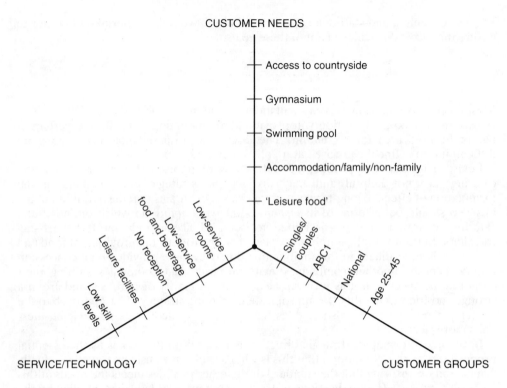

Figure 15.4   Definition of a leisure-based hotel business portfolio

- separate business plans and strategies which are prepared within the overall corporate strategy;
- direct competition in the area of the SBU's core business which will significantly shape marketing strategy;
- costs and revenue which are directly attributable to the SBU, and which can generally be monitored and controlled by effective systems;
- identifiable market segments for the SBU's products which are capable of being researched and analysed through the marketing information system.

The identification of SBUs with identifiable management structures can assist in the successful formulation and implementation of strategy. However, it can also lead to the formalization of interest groups within the organization, which might militate against radical but necessary corporate change. Figure 15.5 represents a hospitality organization based on SBUs.

Provided there is a strong executive with the power of veto, this type of structure can bring a dual advantage: managers have a good working knowledge of overall corporate goals, through their interaction with company strategists at a senior level, while also having control over their area of activity.

The purpose of identifying SBUs in this way is to develop marketing strategy, budgets and control mechanisms that are approved by the appropriate level of management in the organization, with a power of veto if these plans do not conform to the corporate mission or strategy. Senior management is in a position to analyse the

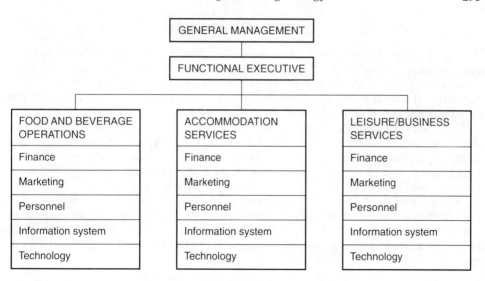

Figure 15.5   An SBU hospitality organization

submission made by the SBUs in order to develop an overall strategy and portfolio of business.

In recent years, various portfolio evaluation models have been evolved in order to analyse the relative potential of SBUs. The Boston Consulting Group, a leading American consulting firm, developed one such model, which has become extremely well known.[12] This approach uses a growth–share matrix to compare different businesses within a company, plotting market growth rate against market share.

While these models help managers to understand the relative commercial positions of businesses within the organization, like any model they ignore many factors in order to clarify a proposition. High growth and improved market share may not be the only criteria, and pursuing these as objectives may lead the company away from its core businesses. While these core products may experience slow growth, they may also be capable of careful extension. Several hotel companies were disadvantaged by their pursuit of cash-rich but volatile businesses during the 1980s, and have sought to consolidate in their core products in recent years.

ENVIRONMENTAL INFLUENCES ON STRATEGY FORMULATION

In recent years, new structures have begun to take shape, and the contemporary hospitality organization is typically leaner, more decentralized and more reactive to international development opportunities than its predecessor. This is partly in response to the competitive forces of the early 1990s, which led to corporate 'downsizing' and reductions in corporate marketing and other functional specialisms.

The need to adapt and match organizational capability to changing international markets and competition has been identified by Olsen.[13] His analysis, which is summarized below, illustrates the importance of sensitivity to environmental influences during strategy formulation.

Structural influences

A key feature of structural change is the growing worldwide dominance of multinational chains. Expansion is often facilitated by strategic alliances between component parts of the industry, thereby creating travel, lodging and foodservice networks. The alliances also benefit from rapid technological advances in tele-communications and computerized reservation systems.

The buyers of hospitality services have contributed to restructuring by consolidating their purchasing power so as to control the transaction more fully. For instance, corporate travel managers typically use fewer travel intermediaries and are using their purchasing power to obtain better prices for airlines, car rental firms and hotels, and to exert greater influence over how the supply inventory is utilized. To respond, operations and marketing functions must work closely in order to maintain high operating standards and an effective customer service interface. At the same time, they must analyse the events which are changing their business environment so that appropriate product extensions and refinements can be identified.

Investment capital influences

During the 1980s, the hospitality industry experienced an investment boom as property development worldwide attracted investment capital from banks and institutional investors. This led to higher expectations of financial performance as hotel firms, in particular, were required to achieve higher returns to satisfy shareholders. This resulted in the need for fresh thinking about how to market hotels, as return on assets became as important as percentage return on profits. The re-alignment which occurred will continue to influence marketing strategy, especially as high interest rates have forced many hotel operators to sell property and take back management contracts on firmer assets. A number of implications arise from this, notably the need to ensure that product consistency is maintained by hotel owners so that the brand image and reputation of the hotel operator are not adversely affected.

Technological influences

Multinational hospitality firms are beginning to harness technology in ways that are, in themselves, shaping organizational change and marketing strategy. The focus of activity is directed towards ensuring the fullest possible utilization of capacity. In this respect, global reservation systems are having a significant impact on where customers stay and how they get there. To stay ahead in global communications, hospitality firms will have to be able to adapt and apply changing technology to the reservations field. In addition to sales support, technology is influencing improvements in hotel security systems, transportation systems, decision making and corporate communications. As international firms need effective systems for communicating about customers, performance and environmental events, continuous updating on aspects of information transfer is needed to improve marketing effectiveness.

Pricing influences

Recession, high interest rates and the increasing influence of buyers, among other factors, have been influencing the pricing structure and, in turn, the product development strategies of the hospitality industry. Pricing has been influenced by the application of more sophisticated decision support and yield management methods. Keener pricing has also driven developments in the economy lodging sector, leading to the rapid diffusion of low-price and limited-service hotel properties. This has put pressure on all levels of the industry to achieve lower costs and to compete with lower prices so that economy concepts can be effectively positioned in the international marketplace.

Political and ecological influences

The laws affecting development, repatriation of profits, the employment mix of nationals versus foreign labour, the logistics of supply, and taxation represent some of the many ways in which the political environment is influencing international development. As hospitality firms expand, it is therefore important to study the local, national and international political and trading frameworks in which they have to operate. Increasingly, hospitality firms are also facing constraints relating to the ecological impact of development, and the industry will have to address concerns about waste water and solid waste disposal among other issues.

The complex and often unpredictable nature of environmental influence on strategy formulation means that hospitality firms which are seeking to expand across country and cultural boundaries must seek to identify the wider organizational implications. According to James:[14]

> Unless companies proactively develop mechanisms which address environmental risk at the strategy formulation, structural and operating systems level and devise effective managerial responses to contain the effects of environmental pressures, the viability of many global strategies based on multi country supply networks is questionable . . .

A fundamental question relating to the appraisal of environmental risk concerns the degree of fit between the product and the market. In order to consider this issue fully, it is necessary to establish a development policy which reflects the character and perceived strengths of the product.

COMPETITIVE INFLUENCES

Competitors within an industry will pursue quite different goals and objectives consistent with their resources and markets plus their own interpretation of how to engage other competitive activity. Michael Porter[15] conducted a rigorous analysis of the competitive forces that influence all businesses and their approach to developing marketing strategy. Porter postulates that there are five fundamental competitive forces acting on the business:

- threat of entry;
- threat of substitutes;
- power of buyers;
- power of suppliers;
- level of rivalry among current competitors.

The combined strength of these forces determines the profit potential of an industry and its approach to marketing strategy. The relative influence of the forces will vary from industry to industry depending substantially upon the service/technology–customer need – market segment matrix discussed earlier.

Threat of entry

Competition is one of the benchmarks of a free-market economy. The effect of a new company entering an industry is to make it more competitive as the new entrant attempts to secure market share. Obviously, existing companies in the marketplace will seek to deter new entrants through the erecting or reinforcing of barriers to entry. Porter lists seven main barriers to entry:

- economies of scale;
- product differentiation;
- capital requirements;
- switching costs;
- access to distribution channels;
- cost disadvantages independent of scale;
- government policy.

Barriers to entry in the service sector have traditionally been regarded as low, and the hospitality industry is no exception to this general rule. Even in hospitality businesses where there are high capital requirements, there are various options such as contract management, licensing or franchising which enable medium-risk entry into the industry. There are several instances of individuals and companies – Bob Payton's My Kinda Town is just one – entering the industry with mature product concepts, such as pizza, and achieving exceptional levels of turnover within a relatively short period. Individuals and companies can still bring their own interpretation of a product into an apparently saturated marketplace and achieve notable success.

However, there are examples of oligopoly within the hospitality industry. The brewing industry had erected effective barriers to entry by controlling access to the main distribution channels, through the public houses and other retail outlets. The recommendations of the Monopolies and Mergers Commission have loosened this control and allowed smaller brewers to gain better market access through their own outlets and through public houses owned by other breweries.

Threat of substitutes

The consumer of leisure industry products is unlikely to demonstrate loyalty to any one of them. Most consumers choose from an itinerary of activities which may, for example, involve going to one of the several pubs or restaurants. However, this narrow view of rivalry between restaurants or public houses fails to acknowledge the fact that consumers may choose to spend their leisure time and money in some other, completely different way: for instance, on a trip to a garden centre or a stately home, or on a picnic in a country park. There is also a trend of people using their spare time in more purposeful activities like learning languages or taking correspondence courses – activities which can reduce their leisure time and act as a substitute.

The growing internationalization of commerce at all levels also represents a threat to traditional hospitality providers trading in the business sector. Companies with substantial interests overseas may find it more viable to have overseas agents or offices, which may reduce the need for company representatives to travel and use hotel accommodation. The rapid development of new communication technologies may also reduce the need for foreign or domestic travel.

Porter suggests that the substitutes that should be monitored are:

- products that provide a better performance/price standard than the industry standard;
- products in industries earning high profits.

Power of buyers

The consumer is the ultimate influence on marketing strategy, but the collective power of buyers will vary depending on the industry and product. The ability of most hospitality operators to differentiate their products makes it more difficult for buyers to exert absolute power over the hospitality provider. For instance, hotel operator providing for the predominantly mid-market business sector will have several sources of business and will be able to offer tailored products – combinations of room, food and beverages, leisure facilities, office facilities, conference facilities, transport arrangements and so on – within a discretionary price range. In this situation it would be difficult for one buyer to influence the price to the disadvantage of the seller. This contrasts with some other industries like retailing, where large food retail companies are in a position to force the price of some agricultural products below the costs of production and insist on quality standards that further increase those costs. Porter identifies the following conditions that strengthen the power of the buyer group:

- The buyer group is concentrated, or purchases large volumes relative to seller sales.
- The products that it purchases represent a significant fraction of its costs or purchases.
- The products that it purchases are standard or undifferentiated.
- The buyer group faces few switching costs.
- It earns low profits.
- Buyers pose a credible threat of backward integration.
- The industry's product is unimportant to the quality of the buyer's products or services.
- The buyer group has full information.

Power of suppliers

Powerful suppliers can increase costs and thus have the opposite effect of buyers in an industry. Perhaps the most important components in the provision of hospitality service are the staff involved, who also represent the highest proportion of costs to the organization. They are not suppliers in the true sense of the word, but the sensitivity of hospitality operators to union activity in the industry demonstrates the importance of the payroll in determining overall profitability. Other suppliers of goods and services to the hospitality industry are not usually in a position to exert exceptional influence over the buyer. According to Porter, the following conditions strengthen the power of the supplier group:

- The industry is dominated by a few companies and is more concentrated than the industry to which it sells.
- The supplier group is not obliged to contend with other substitute products for sale to the industry.
- The industry is not an important customer of the supplier group.
- The supplier group's product is an important input to the buyer's business.
- Its products are differentiated, or it has built up switching costs.
- Suppliers pose a credible threat of forward integration.

Rivalry among current competitors

Levels of competition within the hospitality industry vary within it's component product sectors. For instance, large international groups competing in high-price business markets will approach competition at a different level to hotel companies competing for the economy markets. The large international hotels tend to avoid direct competition on quoted tariff prices although they will discount and offer varied product packages to different markets. Neither will they compete directly on productivity costs: for instance, pay levels will be kept at accepted rates. These may be actually fixed in localized areas, such as the West End of London.

Competition often focuses on the communication of product benefits or unique service offerings, in an attempt to build customer loyalty and differentiate the company and its products from similar products and companies in the marketplace. Hotel companies competing for economy markets are more likely to compete directly on price and service costs.

Even within sectors, the nature of competition varies according to geographical location. In some locations, a particular hotel company may have no competition, or the demand is so great that control becomes the priority, achieving increased productivity and reduced costs.

Porter suggests that rivalry is intensified by the following factors:

- numerous or equally balanced competitors;
- slow industry growth;
- high fixed or storage costs;
- lack of differentiation or switching costs;
- capacity augmented in large increments;
- diverse competitors;
- high strategic stakes;
- high exit barriers.

Companies can map their position relative to other competitors according to criteria derived from market research. For instance, if rapid check-out facilities and secretarial services are important to the business market, provision in these areas can

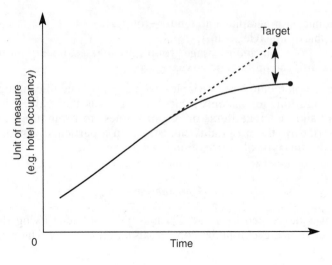

Figure 15.6   Strategic gap

be measured through guest surveys against the competition and mapped accordingly. A review of opportunities and threats offered by the resulting analysis provides direction for strategic decision making.

THE MARKET

The market ultimately influence the organization's approach to developing marketing strategy. There are currently several market-related issues that confront the hospitality operator, and these may be summarized as follows:

- market segmentation;
- gap analysis;
- level of market involvement;
- market–product positioning.
- international markets.

Market segmentation

Many commentators regard market segmentation as the most important influence on the development of marketing strategy, and it is an issue dealt with substantially elesewhere in this book. Effective segmentation must be established upon a good understanding of consumer behaviour: the needs, wants and motivations of the organization's target markets. This type of understanding is derived from careful research and experience of the marketplace, which will enable the definition of markets in terms that are strategically meaningful to the business. The principal market segmentation variables may be described as follows:

- area, country or region of market origin, including nationality;

- socioeconomic, demographic and tenure groups;
- psychographic or lifestyle groups;
- behavioural groups, including usage groups, usage rates, loyalty status and attitude towards the product or service.

These can be supplemented by variables which are of significant interest to the individual organization: for instance, business segments that have a high spend on profitable food and beverage items or responsiveness to promotions and so on. As mentioned previously, the hospitality industry is in a particularly strong position to collect and record this type of information from its records.

Gap analysis

Gap analysis was developed by Argenti[16] as a means of identifying the changes in strategy required to achieve organizational goals and objectives. The process involves the following steps:

1. Set goals or targets.
2. Extrapolate current performance using market and accounting data.
3. Measure the forecast gap. Once the forecast has been made, the difference between it and the goal or target can be measured.
4. Develop strategies to close the gap.

The strategy required to close the gap probably has some implications for the future development of markets. For instance, hotel companies traditionally trading in business-related markets may have to adopt strategies to make up the gap that exists between forecast levels of business and targets, either by developing the existing market with some value-added offer or by diversifying into new or complementary markets.

Market involvevment

This is an important concept for hospitality operations which have the ability to trade in several markets and maintain a high level of differentiation. The extent to which a hotel develops its leisure markets as opposed to business markets, and the strategy to be adopted within each of those broad sectors, depends upon:

- the organization's business strategy, cost leadership, differentiation and focus;
- the nature of the markets under consideration and their relative attractiveness;
- the available resources.

Market–product positioning

Analysis of the trading environment will lead the company to position its service products relative to identified market segments. Ansoff[17] proposed a series of alternatives for considering growth opportunities, which included the following (see also Figure 15.7):

Current products   New products

	MARKET PENETRATION	PRODUCT DEVELOPMENT
Current markets	MARKET PENETRATION	PRODUCT DEVELOPMENT
New markets	MARKET DEVELOPMENT	DIVERSIFICATION

Figure 15.7   Growth strategies

Source: Adapted from Ansoff, H. I., 'Strategies for diversification', *Harvard Business Review*, September/October 1957, p. 114.

- Market penetration – which will increase market share from existing products in existing markets.
- Market development – new markets for existing products.
- Product development – new products for new markets.
- Integration – forwards, backwards or horizontally. This involves developing the business into traditional areas of consumer demand or supply, or expanding the existing business as a form of market penetration.
- Diversification – new products for new markets.

These strategies are in order of increasing risk to the business, so that a company would primarily try to identify a means of expanding the business using existing products and markets, and then sequentially investigate the other possibilities for growth. The uncertainty created by the recession has discouraged many hospitality companies from pursuing diversifaction strategies because of the levels of risk involved.

International markets

The international dimension of market segmentation is an important feature of hospitality marketing, and will become increasingly important in the future. There are some opportunities even for small hospitality businesses in overseas markets through management agreements, franchising or direct management. The industry is quite unique in its experience or direct management. The industry is quite unique in its experience of overseas markets, either servicing overseas tourists in the home market or providing hospitality services overseas. The product can often be exported with very little modification: in fact, its appeal overseas may be that it represents a novel product, such as British pubs in America, or American burger restaurants in Europe.

There are a number of implications arising from market–product policy decisions which relate to market positioning and the adoption of an appropriate development strategy. Crawford-Welch[18] draws on Miles and Snow's typology[19] to identify the characteristics of three generic options for international development.

Option 1

- Market position: *Defender*.
- Product policy: Standardization.
- Role: Maintaining competitive advantage/innovative market development.
- Implementation: Best suited to hospitality firms which are competitive on price; good at controlling costs; able to achieve uniform levels of operating standards and efficiency via standardization; and able clearly to identify and define target markets and segments which are seeking these benefits.

Option 2

- Market position: *Analyser*.
- Product policy: Standardization, some market-led customization.
- Role: Minimizing risk/maximizing opportunities for profit improvement.
- Implementation: Best suited to hospitality firms which, by way of product specification, are able to encourage a degree of flexibility in service provision and/or 'do it yourself' customization by involving guests in service production so as to reduce costs. This approach assumes that guests can be made aware of the option to customize, that they know how to pursue this option and that there is sufficient interest in the customization benefits.

Option 3

- Market position: *Prospector*.
- Product policy: Customization.
- Role: Maintaining competitive advantage/innovative market development.
- Implementation: Best suited to hospitality firms which are able to increase the value added per employee via service enhancement. This requires an organizational commitment to service improvement, consumer research and environmental scanning, so that changing expectations are linked almost automatically to the process of service enhancement.

PRODUCT POLICY INFLUENCES ON STRATEGY FORMULATION

The previous section emphasized the essential relationship between markets and products in the development of marketing strategy. The pattern of demand for a product over time has certain implications that influence strategy development. The hospitality industry is renowned for its seasonal fluctuations in some markets, which sometimes cause severe problems for planning budgets and cash flow. There are also less predictable causes of fluctuation, such as the weather, exchange rate variations and social and political upheaval, which require tactical manoeuvres by the hospitality organization.

Research has attempted to identify longer-term trends for products around which generic strategies can be developed. The product life cycle is one such attempt, which has proved useful as an agenda for considering marketing and strategic action. This concept proposes that a product will go through a series of stages during its commercial life. These are generally acknowledged to be as follows:

1. Introduction stage – when a new product is introduced to the market.
2. Growth stage – when the product has been accepted by the market and there is a rapid growth in market size.
3. Maturity stage – when sales are increasing but at a slower rate, and prices and profits are declining. Mergers, takeover, diversification and integration may occur.
4. Decline stage – when saturation of the market has occurred and absolute sales of the product decline. Productivity becomes the main concern of the business.

At each stage there are implications for the financial well-being of the company, its marketing, production, pricing and staff. Obviously if this model were universally true, the process of strategic planning would be much simplified. However, its simple formula must be qualified by the considerable criticisms that have been directed at it.[20] These criticisms may be summarized as follows.

The curve of the product life cycle

Empirical studies have shown that many products simply do not pass through the four stages.[21] For instance, many products including hospitality services have been in existence for centuries, though arguably in different forms, and show no signs of going into the decline stage. The Savoy Hotel today would probably be recognized by the first patrons of the hotel when it was opened in the latter part of the nineteenth century. Even though the technology and the markets have changed, the nature of the service and the style and structure of the building are little changed. In support of the life cycle, most of The Savoy's competitors have long since been replaced by international chain hotels. Hotels like The Savoy serve a tiny percentage of the market who appreciate and can afford what is essentially an Edwardian-style hotel.

Level of aggregation

There is some dispute about the level at which the product life cycle applies. Porter takes the view that the concept applies at an industry level and would apply, for instance, to the decline of the steel and shipbuilding industries in the United Kingdom. Other research[22] shows that, while the concept has some validity at the product class level (e.g. fast-food restaurants), it has almost no validity at the brand level (e.g. Burger King and McDonald's do not follow life cycles). The hospitality industry provides little support for the idea of an industry progressing through the various stages described, even when considering the proposition at a sector level. It is also difficult to find product classes that have followed the pattern: fast-food restaurants may be seen as the modern equivalents of the pie and ale shops that abounded in Victorian England. However, some brands have not withstood the rigours of competition: for instance, the Lyons Corner House and the Aberdeen Steak House, among others, have disappeared or been modified by other companies.

The product life cycle as predictive tool

The predictive power of the technique is also in question. The fact that the hospitality industry is prone to seasonal and other fluctuations makes it difficult to establish precisely at what point a company lies on the life cycle curve. Most companies and products are probably in the mature stage of the life cycle, which would suggest a commonality of approach albeit within broad guidelines. In fact there is quite a variation in approaches, several of which contradict the generic strategy indicated by the life cycle theory. For instance, hospitality companies generally have high pre-opening expenses and high initial costs because the operation generally has to be fully staffed and stocked from the outset. The extent of gearing determines the amount of scope that the operation has for strategic manoeuvre, unless as part of a larger company it is able to absorb some of the costs. During the mature stage, when, according to the theory, promotional costs are supposed to fall because the market is aware of the product, hospitality businesses may have to invest *more* in below-the-line expenditure in order to sustain differential marketing strategies.

Company influence on the life cycle

Companies can change the course of the life cycle through a pro-active marketing strategy. Guinness has transformed its market appeal by creative and dynamic promotions which have changed its image from that of a stout to fortify the middle-aged and expectant mothers, to a fashionable, 'cult' drink aimed at no particular age group. The maturity stage can, it seems, be extended almost indefinitely until the product becomes redundant or is the victim of other factors, such as poor management or planning.

Product life cycle conclusions

Despite the criticisms of the product life cycle, it is a useful framework for understanding the forces that act upon a product and the possible responses by the

---

INTRODUCTION STAGE
- A rapid skimming strategy – launching the new product at a high price and a high promotion level.
- A slow skimming strategy – launching the product at a high price and a low promotion level.
- A rapid penetration strategy – launching the product at a low price and a high level of promotion.
- A slow penetration strategy – launching the product at a low price and a low level of promotion.

GROWTH STAGE
- The product is modified following a review of the initial launch.
- New, complementary products may be added, e.g. new menu items.
- An appeal is made to new market segments.
- The distribution network is extended.
- The promotional emphasis shifts from creating awareness to creating loyalty.
- Differential pricing is introduced.

MATURITY STAGE
- Market modification – expanding the market for the brand.
- Product modification – changing various aspects of the product.
- Marketing-mix modification – determined by market and product considerations.

DECLINE STAGE
- Identify weak products.
- Develop appropriate strategies and assess exit barriers.
- Assess the investment implications of competitive activity.
- Consider withdrawing the product.

Figure 15.8   Summary of possible product life-cycle stategies

functional departments within an organization. These various departments should be aware of the resource implications and the necessary performance criteria at each stage of the life cycle, and should consider them with regard to their own circumstances. It is apparent that there is no universal, prescriptive business response to any of these stages. However, there is an agenda for discussion which can provide the basis for making decisions about the product portfolio. A summary of possible product life-cycle strategies is given in Figure 15.8.

Product differentiation and branding

During the past decade, hospitality operations have been implementing product differentation and branding strategies in response to their own maturation. As hospitality markets have become saturated and the growth in demand has slowed in most sectors, hospitality companies have sought to distinguish their products from the competition, and to appeal to identified market segments rather than to the general consumer. There are problems associated with differentiation and branding, which include increased promotional budgets to communicate brand and product features, and the problem of ensuring consistent service delivery as an essential component of the branding process. Often the key to successful differentiation lies not in modifying the hospitality product for different market segments, but in careful promotion in order to modify the perception by the consumer of the product and their experience of it. Marketing strategy should be directed at identifying 'perceptual gaps' in the marketplace and moulding consumers' perception of the service accordingly.

The development of branding strategies by major hospitality companies such as Forte has also provided an important lead in the development of marketing strategy. Brands, however, need constant attention and high levels if investment to sustain competitive advantage in the long term. The value of established brand names such as Hilton and Holiday Inn is closely related to the perceptions of quality and consistency that they represent in the international marketplace. Yet an examination of current strategy indicates something of a divergence in product policy relating to international development. The debate centres around the role of standardization and customization in international development, and the extent to which product policy should reflect one or both of these in order to achieve desirable market positioning.

CASE STUDY: PRODUCT STANDARDIZATION AT HOLIDAY INN WORLDWIDE

In a study of firms operating in America and European markets during the mid-1970s, managers identified a number of factors which were considered to be critical to success.[23] Above all, it was important to have a standardized product which could be packaged, branded and distributed as effectively in export markets as at home. This development approach is being used by Holiday Inn Worldwide, which is commited to a major international expansion programme.[24]

The original Holiday Inn hotel concept or 'core brand' gained international recognition for setting and achieving consistently high standards in product design and service. Early innovations poineered by Holiday Inn were remote-controlled television and direct-dial telephones. In the 1990s. a uniquely sophisticated satellite communication network provides instantaneous information transfer between North America and Europe. The expansion programme is based on a brand extension strategy which will enable Holiday Inn Worldwide to operate hotels in three distinctive mid-market categories ranging from economy to de-luxe.

The basic parameters of the Holiday Inn product provide a standardized framework, although a degree of sensitivity to the market is necessary to ensure that customers are able to recognize the Holiday Inn style and standards in geographically and culturally diverse locations. Central to this is the reputation for quality and consistency associated with the Holiday Inn trademark. To safeguard these attributes, which provide a universally marketable brand, two procedures are used to scrutinize operating standards. First of all, standards are clearly and precisely defined in relation to specifications for hotel design and construction as well as for operations and service. The design specifications include detailed reference to every facet of the operation, ranging from the size of the guest room to the adequacy of fire safety systems.

As much of the network is franchised, it is the company's policy to restrict contract and licence agreements to those who understand the precise requirements for constructing and operating hotels to Holiday Inn standards. This necessitates a comprehensive quality audit system, and every hotel participates by undergoing an independent quality audit inspection twice a year as a minimum requirement. If problems are reported, the hotel fails the inspection and typically undergoes scrutiny three times over the ensuing six-month period. At the same time, a programme to correct the deficiency is drawn up in consultation with the owner and a timetable for implementation agreed. If the work is not carried out to the satisfaction of the quality audit team by the agreed date, the hotel faces exclusion from the Holiday Inn system. The quality audit programme is continually refined so as to improve the effectiveness of the assessment process.

CASE STUDY: PRODUCT CUSTOMIZATION AT HILTON INTERNATIONAL

Greater European harmonization during the 1990s involves rationalizing the legislative framework relating to business, while at the same time allowing European Community members to preserve their distinctive and culturally diverse heritage. In this context, it can be advantageous to customize hospitality services so that they reflect the customs, traditions and preferences of the marketplace, and it has been argued that clusters of countries or customer segments could be offered a branded variation of the core product, as defined by the benefits sought by the different country/segment groups.[25,26] This approach has been adopted by Hilton International, which has developed a Japanese service brand that reflects subtle forms of product customization.[27]

The number of Japanese visitors to Hilton International hotels worldwide has been growing rapidly, doubling since 1988 to reach a figure close to 21 per cent of the company's total visitor volume, and equalling the number of American guests. The total Japanese outbound market is projected to double again by 1995, but the Japanese are much less used to international travel than most other nationalities, as they have very different cultural expectations. This led to a decision to develop a service brand which would meet the culturally unique needs of Japanese business and leisure travellers.

Initially, efforts were concentrated on identifying 'best practice' within the organization, finding out how the hotels with an established Japanese clientele were responding to guest requirements. Those which, because of their location, should have been receiving a higher proportion of Japanese guests were also examined, and a relationship was identified between increasing Japanese business share and the implementation of customized service features that Japanese guests has requested. On completion of the audit-based comparision, a consumer research programme began in Japan, using hotel database information in order to find out what Japanese customers who travel internationally wanted Hilton hotels to provide.

The culmination of the research was the development of the Hilton Japanese service brand 'Wa No Kutsurogi', meaning 'comfort and service, the Japanese way'. it consists of distinctive service features and special amenities appealing to both Japanese business and leisure travellers. These include having Japanese-speaking staff at the participating hotels, providing safe deposit boxes, producing hotel information, menus, wine lists and safety instructions in Japanese, providing an Oriental food selection, often with authentic Japanese cuisine, and making available Japanese green tea and items such as slippers, bathrobes and Japanese newspapers. The brand is symbolized by a Japanese crane, the Tsuru, which is the national emblem of Japan, and signifies 'freedom, good luck, long life and happiness'. The aim is simply to attract more Japanese business to more Hilton hotels. The underlying assumption is that, if the majority of visitors feel comfortable with the hotel service environment they experience, the development will have been fully justified in terms of the additional guest satisfaction and new business generated.

For validation purposes, inspections are carried out by Japanese companies situated in the locality of the hotels. A succcesful inspection represents an indication of the local company's confidence in the hotel's ability to deliver authentic Japanese service. The idea emerged from the consumer research, and it offers an effective form of competitive advantage by allowing a selling approach to develop directly from the product itself. Fifteen successful inspections are needed for a hotel to take part, and these are repeated annually. Japanese manufacturers are used to working co-operatively with suppliers, so the idea of building a relationship by asking for their co-operation in defining and designing a product was widely accepted.

This approach was particularly helpful during discussions about the possibility of recruiting Japanese-speaking hotel staff from expatriate Japanese communities. The responses indicated that it would be less acceptable to recruit an expatriate than a new member of staff direct from Japan, because it was felt that expatriates who had been living away from Japan for five years or more would be less sympathetic to the principles of providing authentic Japanese service. This indicates the subtle nuances of cultural interpretation separating authentic styles that Japanese firms are willing to endorse from Western interpretations of Japanese service that are less acceptable and therefore less likely to succeed.

REFERENCES

1. Fifield, P., *Marketing Strategy*, Butterworth-Heinemann, Oxford, 1992, p. 13.
2. Piercy, N., 'Developing marketing information systems', in Baker; m., *The Marketing Book*, 2nd edn, Butterworth-Heinemann, Oxford, 1991, p. 251.
3. For instance, Leech, M., 'Research's future imperative', *Marketing*, 16 July 1980, pp. 33 – 4.
4. Kotler, P., *Marketing Decision Making: A Model Building Approach*, Holt, Rinehart and Winston, New York, 1971.
5. Chandler, A. D., *Strategy and Structure*, MIT Press, Cambridge, MA, 1962.
6. Spillard, P., *Organisation and Marketing*, Croom Helm, London, 1985.
7. Cowell, D.; *The Marketing of Services*, Butterworth-Heinemann, Oxford, 1991, p. 62.
8. Khandwalla, P. M., *The Design of Organizations*, Harcourt Brace, New York, 1977.
9. Davidson, D. S., 'How to succeed in a service industry: turn the organisation chart upside down', *Management Review*, April 1978, pp. 13 – 16.
10. Levitt, T., 'Marketing myopia', *Havard Business Review*, July–August 1960, pp. 45 – 60.
11. Abell, D., *Defining the Business: The Starting Point of Strategic Planning*, Prentice-Hall, Englewood Cliffs, NJ, 1980, ch. 3.
12. See, for instance, Kerin, R. A., Mahajan, V., and Varadarajan, P. R., *Contemporary Perspectives on Strategic Planning*, Allyn & Bacon, Boston, MA, 1990.

13. Olsen, M. D., 'Structural firm and industry changes in the international hospitality industry', *International Journal of Contemporary Hospitality Management*, vol. 3, no. 4, 1991; Olsen, M. D., 'Expectations of the future given events in the past', in Teare, R., and Olsen, M. D. (eds), *International Hospitality Management: Corporate Strategy in Practice*, Pitman, London, and John Wiley, New York, 1992.

14. James, N. 'Reducing the risks of globalization', *Long Range Planning*, vol. 23, no. 1, 1990, pp. 80 – 8.

15. Porter, M. E., *Competitive Strategy: Techniques for Analysing Industries and Competitors*, Macmillan, London, 1980.

16. Argenti, J., *Corporate Planning: A Practical Guide*, George Allen & Unwin, London, 1968.

17. Ansoff, H. I., *Implementing Strategic Management*, Prentice-Hall, Englewood Cliffs, 1984.

18. Crawford-Welch, S., 'Competitive marketing strategies in the international hospitality industry', in Teare, R., and Olsen, M. D. (eds), *International Hospitality Management: Corporate Strategy in Practice*, Pitman, London, and John Wiley, New York, 1992.

19. Miles, R. E., and Snow, C. C., *Organizational Strategy, Structure and Process*, McGraw-Hill, New York, 1978.

20. See, for instance, Wasson, C. R., *Dynamic Competitive Strategy and Product Life Cycles*, Challenge Books, St Charles, IL, 1974.

21. See, for instance, Rink, D. R., and Swan, J., 'Product life cycle research: a literature review', *Journal of Business Research*, September 1979, pp. 219 – 42.

22. Dhalla, N. D., and Yuspeth, S., 'Forget the product life cycle concept', *Harvard Business Review*, January–February 1976, pp. 102 – 12.

23. Sorenson, J., and Weichmann, S., 'How multinationals view marketing standardization', *Harvard Business Review*, July–August 1975, pp. 38 – 54.

24. Parker, A. J., and Teare, R., ' A brand extension strategy for Holiday Inn Worldwide Development', in Teare, R., and Olsen, M. D. (eds), *International Hospitality Management: Corporate Strategy in Practice*, Pitman, London, and John Wiley, New York, 1992.

25. Douglas, S. P., and Wind, Y., 'The myth of globalization', *Columbia Journal of World Business*, Vol. 22, no. 2, 1987, pp. 10 – 20.

26. Kale, S. H., and Sudharshan, D., 'A strategic approach to international segmentation', *International Marketing Review*, vol. 4, no. 2, 1987, pp. 80 – 90.

27. Bould, A., Breeze, G., and Teare, R., 'Culture, customization and innovation: a Hilton International service brand for the Japanese market', in Teare, R., and Olsen, M. D. (eds), *International Hospitality Management: Corporate Strategy in Practice*, Pitman, London, and John Wiley, New York, 1992.

INDEX